Rocking the Boat

Advance Praise for *Rocking the Boat*

"Celebrates the triumphs of ordinary women doing the extraordinary. I celebrate this moving collection of the stories of union women who changed the face of American labor."

—John Sweeney, President, AFL-CIO

"Gives long-awaited recognition to eleven courageous women in the labor movement who made tremendous sacrifices to improve employment opportunities for all women and men in the U.S. This uniquely human account of their trials and triumphs is inspiration to all in the continuing fight for equal employment opportunity, fair pay, and a safe workplace."

—Congresswoman Patsy T. Mink

"The strength. commitment, and continued resolve of these women in the face of what seemed insurmountable forces is inspiring and instructive for those of us involved in social change. Our debt to these outstanding women can best be paid by carrying on their work."

—Morton Bahr, President, Communications
Workers of America

"Brings back many memories of the founding days of the National Organization for Women (NOW) . . . provides a timely lesson in coalition building and the importance of women and men working together on economic, political, and social issues so vital to our future."

—Betty Friedan, founding president, NOW, and
author of *The Feminine Mystique*

"You could say that it's too bad that Dorothy Haener and the other women in this book had to 'rock the boat' to get the union movement to accept and acknowledge their talent. But thank goodness they had the guts and foresight to do what they did. And thank goodness there's this book to tell the story of how they made our whole movement better."

—Stephen P. Yokich, President, UAW

To the union women of the future, in sisterhood and solidarity

Contents

Preface

We have been thinking about this book for twenty years. In 1975, Joyce Kornbluh, with a small seed grant from the Rockefeller Foundation to the Institute of Labor and Industrial Relations (ILIR) at the University of Michigan, initiated and directed the oral history project "The Twentieth Century Trade Union Woman: Vehicle for Social Change." The project's requests to organizations, newspapers, and journals generated the names of over four hundred women active in the U.S. labor movement between 1900 and 1970. Eventually responding to a detailed interview guide that was designed collectively by an advisory committee for the project, eighty-seven women discussed their work, union, and family lives with volunteer interviewers.

Brigid O'Farrell, then with the Women's Research Center at Wellesley College, was one of the volunteer interviewers in Massachusetts. With tape recorder and interview guide in hand, she met Anna Sullivan, who entered the Chicopee textile mills when she was fourteen, joined the Textile Workers Union of America, and at age seventy-two worked for the Springfield AFL-CIO Labor Council. Florence Luscomb, a graduate of MIT in 1910, marched for women's suffrage, organized clerical workers in the 1930s, and campaigned for peace and civil rights for most of this century. She lived in a commune as she neared her ninetieth birthday. Rose Norwood, in her apartment in Boston, recounted her years as an activist with the Women's Trade Union League and her organizing at the telephone company in the early 1900s.

Over the next three years, union women graciously shared the stories of their lives. In all, fifty-four interviews were legally released after being transcribed and edited by many younger women undergraduate and graduate students who worked with Joyce on the project. Over seven thousand pages of transcripts were deposited in several university archives. An oral history primer, *Workingwomen's Roots,* was published by the project and used in many high school and college classrooms and in union locals across the country. The Anna Sullivan interview, edited by Lydia Kleiner and Brigid O'Farrell, appeared in the journal *Frontiers* in 1977. But there was no book celebrating all of these women and we moved on to other activities.

During the 1980s, Brigid worked with a group of interdisciplinary scholars at the Wellesley Center. Her writing focused on women in blue-collar jobs, equal employment laws, and unions, and she taught in the Northeast Summer School for Union Women. Later she moved to the National Research Council in

Washington, D.C., where she turned her attention to issues of pay equity, work and family, and child care. Joyce wrote about women's labor education programs and the Workers' Service Program in the New Deal, taught at the University of Michigan, directed the ILIR's Program on Women and Work, and initiated the Michigan Summer School for Women Workers, inspired by the residential schools for working women in the 1920s and 1930s. Periodically we discussed the possibility of sharing the interviews with a wider audience.

In 1991 we revisited our old plans to work together and develop a book that would be accessible to a broad range of readers. Our most difficult task was to narrow down the number of stories to be included. We read over the transcripts, selecting from interviews with union women from Alaska to Puerto Rico, from Boston to Hawaii, from unions of garment makers, steelworkers, and autoworkers to teachers, telephone operators, secretaries, and waitresses. Many of the women had died, but others were still active.

The tug was always to include more of the women who had been interviewed. How could we not include Frieda Schwenkmeyer, an organizer for the Amalgamated Clothing Workers of America, as she described a scene in the South: "We received a call that the house of a union man was being watched, that out on the road (in front of his house) fifty cars were stationed and that when the union visitors left the house, they were going to lynch them. Would we send out reinforcements, men and guns? I was in charge and I had to make that decision . . . and oh, the argument was heavy. But there wasn't time and I said, 'Who wants to go?' and every single organizer put up *her* hand."

Or Anna Sullivan, who talked so lovingly about her father and the secret union organizing meetings he would attend. "But in order for him to get into a meeting, he had to have five union labels on his clothing, and that was looked at, the shoes, the hat, the suit, the underwear, and the shirt. And this was one of our jobs. The children had to be sure that he didn't leave without those labels."

Or Geraldine Roberts, who organized domestic workers in Ohio because, "When the lady hired me, she told me to open my mouth and she looked at my teeth. She said any girl that brushes her teeth, with a mouth this clean, was a pretty clean gal. 'I don't like dirty help in the house,' she says. So I would tell workers, 'Why don't we organize and get us a union? Why should we let them treat us like this?' "

In the end we decided to focus on a small number of these activists and use their stories to illustrate a larger narrative of women, unions, and social change across a sixty-year period of American labor and women's history. We chose stories that were both compelling and diverse with regard to union, geographic region, family status, and racial and ethnic background. In both their personal experiences and their reflections on the historical events they participated in, the eleven women in this volume speak for many others.

Along the way, we have been greatly encouraged by the interest expressed in publishing this collection. Esther Peterson's interview was first published in *Labor's Heritage,* and the Feminist Press requested our chapter on Maida Springer-Kemp for the *Women's Studies Quarterly's* special issue on working-class women. The interviews in the original oral history project have also been receiving continuing attention from historians. For example, Nancy Gabin's book on auto workers, *Feminism and the Labor Movement,* and Dorothy Sue Cobble's book on waitresses, *Dishing It Out,* and her essay in *Not June Cleaver* draw in part on interviews from this collection. Stephen Norwood refers to his grandmother Rose Norwood's interview in his book on the telephone workers, *Labor's Flaming Youth.*

Texts of the original interviews, as well as the forty-three additional interviews in the collection, are available at the Bentley Historical Library at the University of Michigan; the Schlesinger Library at Radcliffe College; the Bancroft Library at the University of California, Berkeley; the Reuther Archives of Urban and Labor Affairs at Wayne State University; and the Library of Congress.

Acknowledgments

*R*ocking the Boat, like the oral history project from which it grew, has been a collaborative effort. First we want to thank Jessie De La Cruz, Dorothy Haener, Ah Quon McElrath, Esther Peterson, and Maida Springer-Kemp not only for so generously taking the time to be interviewed in the 1970s, but for talking with us again in the 1990s. Each woman also carefully read through a draft of the chapter on her life, searched for photographs and articles, and introduced us to other researchers and activists who have been most helpful.

We also thank the families, friends, and colleagues of Mary Callahan, Catherine Conroy, Lillian Herstein, Carmen Lucia, Fannie Allen Neal, and Alice Peurala for their encouragement, support, and assistance in making this book possible. Carmen's daughter, Marge Whipple, and Fannie's daughter, Alonzetta "Sweet Pea" Ford, talked with us, provided articles, and found photographs of their mothers. Lillian Herstein and Catherine Conroy had no surviving family members whom we could identify, and we could not locate Alice Peurala's daughter or Mary Callahan's sons. Articles, photographs, and memories, however, were provided by others: Paul Anderson, Ann Crump, Colleen Davis, and Yvette Herrera, Communications Workers of America; Gloria Johnson and staff at District 1, International Union of Electrical Workers; Russ Bargmann and Mel Chang, International Longshoremen's and Warehousemen's Union; Marsha Zakowsky, United Steelworkers of America; Mary Ann Forbes, African-American Labor Center; and Keir Jorgensen, Union of Needletrades, Industrial and Textile Employees.

For background information on individual women and their unions, we would like to thank Sister Austin Doherty, Alverno College; Rita Heller, County College of Morris, N.J.: Mary Allen Jolly, University of Alabama; Joyce Najita, University of Hawaii; and Margaret Rose, California State University at Bakersfield. Yevette Richards, University of Pittsburgh, shared her doctoral dissertation on Maida Springer-Kemp with us and generously commented on a draft of that chapter. Her work on African-American trade unions in New York and the complicated political issues in Africa were particularly helpful. Janet Zandy, Rochester Institute of Technology, also read Maida's chapter and reaffirmed for us the importance of having union women tell their stories.

As always, the archivists have been extremely helpful and patient. Francis Blouin, director of the Bentley Historical Library, University of Michigan, where the original interviews and tapes are housed, was on the advisory committee for the 1975 oral history project. He and his staff have been especially encouraging and supportive. Stuart Kaufmann, director, and the staff of the George Meany Memo- rial Archives in Silver Spring, Maryland, provided access to the microfiche copies of the interviews as well as to the AFL-CIO library and photo archives. Special thanks go to Lynda DeLoach, photo archivist at the Meany Center, and Robert Reynolds, managing editor of *Labor's Heritage,* for their assistance with the ear- lier Esther Peterson article. We also acknowledge with appreciation the staffs at the Schlesinger Library, Radcliffe College; the School of Industrial and Labor Re- lations Archives, Cornell University; Special Collections, Georgia State University; the Reuther Archives of Urban and Labor Affairs, Wayne State University; and the Bethune Museum Archives in Washington, D.C.

We owe a great deal to a good friend and colleague, Suzanne Moore, who provided early interest and enthusiasm for this project. She read through the tran- scripts, participated in interviews with Esther Peterson, helped us decide on some of the interviews to include, and produced the first edited draft of the Jessie De La Cruz and Ah Quon McElrath interviews. Ruth Shinn and Morris Weisz provided assistance with the Esther Peterson chapter, and Caitlin O'Farrell supplied much- needed clerical support. We also thank Lucile DiGirolamo for her hard work, unfailing common sense, and good humor.

This book would not have been possible without the people who contrib- uted to the original oral history project. For many, it was a labor of love under- taken in addition to other assignments in hectic work, student, and community lives. Eve Berton, Deborah Duke, Lyn Goldfarb, Eileen Haggerty, Marta Hernandez, Lydia Kleiner, Brady Mikusko, and Christine Miller administered and coordinated staff at different times during the four years of the project. The effort and skills of those volunteers who conducted the original interviews were crucial: Elizabeth Balanoff, Karen Budd, Betty Craig, Lyn Goldfarb, Alice Hoffman, Lydia Kleiner, Anne Loftis, Christine Miller, Marlene Rikard, Marion Roffman, Martha Ross, and Seth Wigderson. Elizabeth Balanoff, Alice Hoffman, and Marlene Rikard provided additional assistance and advice on locating people and sources for the women they interviewed. We appreciate the work of many typists, transcribers, indexers, and proof readers on whom the project relied. Seed money for the project was provided by the Rockefeller Foundation, with the assistance of Joel Colton, Lydia Bronte, and Jane Allen.

We are grateful to Alice Hoffman, former president of the Oral History Asso- ciation, whose continued advice and many other contributions added immeasur- ably to the project and this book, and to Barbara Wertheimer, who directed the Institute for Education and Research on Women, New York State School of In- dustrial and Labor Relations, Cornell University, and was part of the original plan- ning committee. She was a labor educator, scholar, and dear friend.

We are greatly indebted over the years to friends and colleagues with whom we have discussed issues related to labor union women in general and this book in particular. The contributions of many are reflected in the references used in this work. For a long time Mary Frederickson, history professor at Miami University, has provided intellectual stimulation and nurturing care. Most recently she graciously made time in a busy schedule to review the manuscript for us. The Center for Women Policy Studies in Washington, D.C., has provided a much-appreciated home for writing and thinking.

We also want to express our thanks to Leslie Breed, our helpful and always cheerful agent, Leslie Mitchner, the very supportive editor in chief of the Rutgers University Press, and Elizabeth Gretz, our meticulous copyeditor.

Finally, we are most grateful for the support, warmth, and technical assistance of our family and friends, especially Hy Kornbluh, Kathe Kornbluh, David Frassrand, T.J. Glauthier, and Jeff, Paul, Tad, and Pat Glauthier.

We have developed a collaborative and supportive working partnership, much in the working tradition of the women in this volume. We have done our best to maintain both the accuracy and the spirit of the original interviews, but accept full responsibility for any errors of fact or interpretation that may have occurred in the editing process. This has been a challenging effort for us both, one that has been moving, exciting, and fun. We are eager to share these stories.

Rocking the Boat

Chapter 1

An Overview:
And Not Falling Out

> Periodically, during that era, the tailors, including my father and all of my relatives, would go out on strike. I used to hear stories about the picket lines. . . . I would say to my father, "Why can't you take me to the picket line?" One morning he was summoned to the picket line and I went with him. The pickets were jammed against the door, trying to get into the plant, and the employer went up to the second floor. He shot into the crowd and killed a young woman, not far from where I was: Ida Braverman. When I saw the blood and heard the hysteria and anger of the people, I was just furious. I would have just as soon got even with the employer if I had a gun—shot him, and got even! But that made up my mind, and I said to my father, "I know now what you mean, and when I grow up I'm going to be an organizer."

The child kept her promise. Carmen Lucia left her large Italian family in Rochester, New York, and for fifty years crisscrossed the country organizing for several unions. She confronted the hostile worlds of management, police, and the Ku Klux Klan; raised her daughter alone; and experienced the sacrifices and satisfactions of life as a union organizer. For her entire career she sought equal pay for equal work and recognition on the job for working women, including herself, and continually challenged unions to develop more women leaders.

Carmen Lucia was one of many women in the U.S. labor movement whose powerful stories need to be available to contemporary readers. Through her words, and those of ten other women in *Rocking the Boat,* we experience the turmoil, hardships, and accomplishments of thousands of union women over half a century of profound workplace and social changes and major historic movements and events: through two world wars, the Great Depression, the New Deal, the McCarthy era, and the evolution of the civil rights movement and the women's movement. *Rocking the Boat* is a celebration of strong, committed union activists whose stories inform our understanding not only of their personal lives and choices but of working women's collective contributions to our history.

The women in this book were dubious about why people wanted to hear

1

their stories. They were committed to the concepts of collective action, equality, and unity, not individual action and recognition. They felt they had done what they had to do and were careful to recognize others who were involved in their success. They channeled their frustrations and anger into "chipping away" at various forms of exploitation in workplaces and social institutions. They focused on "getting things done," not on getting credit. They dealt with reality and did "the very best they could within that reality."

Most of the women in this collection did receive recognition in their unions and communities, and some were elected or appointed to influential positions. But these women, and the many other women whose lives, issues and contributions they reflect, have been largely ignored in the recorded history of the labor movement and the women's movement in the twentieth century. We present their stories, gathered through an oral history process, not as examples of leaders to be set apart and honored but as representatives of many other working and union women, as co-workers, and as workplace feminists whose lives offer us support and inspiration in the ongoing struggles for economic and social justice.

The Process

In *Writing a Woman's Life,* the author Carolyn Heilbrun says that "women must turn to one another for stories; they must share the stories of their lives and their hopes and their unacceptable fantasies. . . . New stories will find their way into texts if they begin in oral exchanges among women in groups hearing and talking to one another." Oral history enables us to part from the content and forms of traditional historical and bibliographic writing by focusing on the lives of ordinary people, using their own words.

Oral histories facilitate this process for many women who are not writers. The collaboration between interviewer and the woman interviewed affects the storyteller and the listener, shaping the resulting story by the questions asked and answered as well as by the questions that are not asked and the answers that are not given. Memories transform, highlight, and fail, and in the end are one person's recollections, filtered through the interviewing, transcribing, and editing process. An individual story alone is not a finished quilt, but one of many patchwork squares. *Rocking the Boat* is a collection of squares that have long been missing the quilt of their collective history.

The eleven women in *Rocking the Boat* were chosen because they have compelling stories, and they tell them very well. To make the lengthy interviews more readable, the question-and-answer format was eliminated and sections were arranged in chronological order. With great care to keep the women's distinctive voices, words were added where necessary to clarify points for readers not familiar with the issues or organizations being discussed. Paragraphs introducing each section put the women's words in the context of the times they are describing.

Rocking the Boat is not a comprehensive historical study and analysis of working women or the labor movement in this century. Many other scholars have undertaken that research and documentation, and the notes include selected references to other works with more detailed material about the historical contexts, specific unions, and crucial issues that were part of the daily lives and union work of the women in this collection. This book, however, adds names and faces, triumphs and tragedies, to the growing body of research about working women's history in this century. We hope these stories will encourage readers to talk about these issues with other older women workers and activists, grandmothers, aunts, and neighbors; to conduct oral history interviews with those individuals who have stories to pass on; and to utilize the other interviews in "The Twentieth Century Trade Union Woman" oral history project.

Individual Differences

In many ways, these eleven women are each very different. Some dropped out of school at the elementary level; others finished college. They include women who were married, divorced, single, with and without children. Some worked in jobs traditionally held by women in garment factories, telephone companies, schools, and on farms. Others took on "men's jobs" in auto plants and steel mills. Some were in unions with a majority female membership and others were in unions with few women members. Some were also involved in the civil rights movement; others helped shape the contemporary women's movement. Their politics reflect a range of ideologies common, but often contentious, within the labor movement and the Democratic Party. They did not always agree on the best policies and programs to accomplish their goals and agendas. What then unites the stories of these eleven individuals into a common narrative of women, unions, and change over the past eight decades?

Connecting Themes

The women in *Rocking the Boat* are connected by the themes that emerge from their individual lives to form this narrative and also by the collective methods that they chose to accomplish their goals. Their stories highlight the continuous involvement of union women in issues affecting their lives, and the lives of their co-workers, since the early 1900s. These women participated in the women's suffrage movement and lobbied for state laws to protect women and children. They campaigned for political candidates who supported their efforts and reaped the benefits of federal legislation such as minimum wage laws, labor laws guaranteeing workers the right to organize into unions, and civil rights laws prohibiting discrimination in employment and wages. All of these women engaged in the debate about the benefits of protective legislation for women and the controversy over an equal rights amendment. Their attitudes and positions evolved and changed over time. Their commitment to the labor movement and to the importance of maintaining coalitions with people from different economic, social, and cultural perspectives, however, remained central to effecting social reform.

Four major themes emerge from their personal stories. Each woman shares a passionate concern for workers, respecting their dignity and self-worth, with a strong commitment to improving wages, working conditions, and the quality of life on the job. They express anger over workers who are bullied, overworked, and injured. Mary Callahan, for example, remembers vividly that her first strike had little to do with wages, but concerned dignity and a degree of control over the workplace.

Each woman sees labor unions, with all of their "bumps and warts," as Maida Springer-Kemp puts it, as the best force available for improving the lives of workers. Although they experienced hurtful racism and sexism within the labor movement, both Maida and Fannie Allen Neal report that unions are better than most other institutions and organizations, and especially better than employers, in dealing with issues of diversity and equity.

All of the women experienced some form of discrimination when union men did not live up to their ideals of equality and fairness, but they acknowledge that opportunities for this kind of challenging and rewarding work on behalf of economic and social justice were not available to them elsewhere in society. "The kind of fulfillment you get from what you accomplish in the union more than offsets all the kind of pain and trouble you had as you went through the problem times," recalls Dorothy Haener. After fifty years in the labor movement in Hawaii, Ah Quon McElrath concludes: "Trade unions are still, in our kind of society, the only social organization that can lift women immediately out of poverty and give them some measure of control over their lives."

Each woman takes enormous pride in her union work and the accomplishments of other union women. Each talks about the power of women on picket lines, the rewards of signing the first union contract, the empowering process of talking with the "boss" and resolving workers' problems. Each woman has found her own voice and has helped others to articulate and assert their own workplace issues. Thus, while acknowledging the frustrations, disappointments, and difficulties of working—sometimes as the first and only woman—with male union officials and co-workers, they take great satisfaction from their accomplishments

as organizers, labor educators, political activists, shop stewards, elected officers, union staff, and, always, as advocates for women workers. Jessie De La Cruz
says that she always talks about the union, because "that's the best thing that
ever happened to the farm workers. It gives me great pride to know that I had
something to do with it—that I was involved, that I was organizing people."

Collective Lessons

In their daily work with the labor movement, the women's movement, and community organizations, these women continued to chip away at overarching exploitation and discrimination in the workplace and in other institutions, using
methods they felt were effective for themselves and for other women. As they
approached the end of their union careers, they were clear about the importance
of working together, step by step, to achieve full economic and social equality.
They pragmatically learned to balance the "means" of reaching their "ends." Esther
Peterson recalls that as a lobbyist on Capitol Hill, she needed to "count the votes"
to know how far she could go without losing the votes she needed to win on
certain issues. Lillian Herstein was supported by members of her union when she
ran for national president of the American Federation of Teachers because they
viewed her as an experienced organizational "realist," someone who knew the
potentials as well as the constraints of "working within the system."

Five areas of collective action emerge from the experiences described in this
book. First is the importance of organizing women into unions. Each of these
women successfully helped to organize other women workers in traditionally female jobs into unions. Some also helped to "open the door" for women to enter
higher-paying nontraditional jobs and union membership. From organizing hat factory workers in the South, clerical workers in midwestern auto plants, teachers in
New England and Chicago, farm and cannery workers in California and Hawaii,
they talk about strategies in organizing campaigns. They tested modes of organizing all workers, and especially women workers: on-the-job committees; house
visits; leaflets and education programs; community-wide publicity; cultural activities; community coalitions; lobbying for legislative support; testifying in public hearings; demonstrations, strikes, and picket lines; family involvement, soup kitchens,
and consumer boycotts; and always developing workplace leaders to share in
the decision making and day-to-day union responsibilities during and after the
union organizing campaign.

Second, they recognize the need for shared leadership and the need to have
women in leadership positions within unions. They encouraged other women to
run for office and helped develop women's committees and educational programs
to enhance participatory skills and workplace and union knowledge. The women

in *Rocking the Boat* identify their role models and mentors, both male and female, who encouraged them to run for office and helped them gain positions of influence within their unions. They highlight the need to work together with union men. Although several of these women became vice presidents of their unions, they acknowledge that there was little support for a woman to become an international union president at the time when they were active. Indeed, there was frequently little encouragement for and often opposition to expanding women's union roles and focusing on the importance of women's issues.

Several of the women speak of their need for "tough skins" to run for office and to confront management, union officials, and union members about discrimination against women. Catherine Conroy fought stereotypes within her predominantly female union to win support and votes in her union election campaigns and support for staff assignments. Although all recognize the importance of the Coalition of Labor Union Women (CLUW) and the growing number of women's committees within unions in developing women's leadership in the unions, they cite this issue as a continuing problem in the contemporary labor movement.

Third is the importance of building bridges to other organizations to establish effective coalitions that raise issues faced by women and minority workers and work together toward solutions. The Women's Trade Union League, the National Consumers' League, the Young Women's Christian Association (YWCA), and the Jewish Labor Committee are just a few of the many community-based organizations these women worked with in the past. In more recent years, several of the women in this collection took part in President Kennedy's Commission on the Status of Women, directed by Esther Peterson and the Women's Bureau of the U.S. Department of Labor. According to Dorothy Haener and Mary Callahan, the commission very usefully brought together women from different economic and political backgrounds.

In the Wisconsin State Commission on the Status of Women, Catherine Conroy developed lasting friendships with feminists in her state. Eventually, it was at a meeting of the state commissions that several of the women in this collection helped form the National Organization for Women (NOW). These women also worked with civil rights organizations such as the NAACP, the Congress on Racial Equality, and the A. Philip Randolph Institute to strengthen the labor movement and to bring its strength to the civil rights movement. They were active in local community groups and civil rights commissions, and some of them were active internationally. For Maida Springer-Kemp, with her many years of experience working in Africa, International Women's Year was "a very constructive way of reaching across the world to women."

For each of these women, however, at certain times goals differed and alliances with other organizations were strained. For the majority of union women, keeping the protective labor laws that they had fought so hard to win took precedence over an equal rights amendment (ERA). Even those women who saw the damage the protective laws could do and who supported an ERA would not take a public position until their unions also publicly supported such a measure. In the 1970s affirmative action programs clashed with union-supported seniority principles and practices, causing differences between labor, civil rights, and women's groups. The women included here supported the hard-won principle of seniority, which they believed benefited women and minorities in the long run.

Fourth, throughout these decades the women in this collection were actively involved in workers' education programs. They worked with women's organizations in programs such as the training school for union organizers established in 1914 by the Women's Trade Union League, the Bryn Mawr Summer School for Women Workers, and government-sponsored programs established in the mid-1930s under the New Deal. They also participated in labor education programs sponsored by their own unions to teach basic skills and knowledge of trade unionism. Many of the women started as participants in these programs and in their later years became teachers and resources for other union women, helping to mentor them and to share information, skills, support, and inspiration for their participation in their own workplaces, unions, and communities.

Fifth, all of these women reflect on the importance of government and the need to be actively involved in the legislative and political arenas. They talk movingly about how federal laws improved their lives. The 1935 National Labor Relations Act gave them the right to join a union. The 1938 Fair Labor Standards Act, which stipulated a minimum wage, gave them a floor from which to negotiate for higher wages for the workers they represented. Fair employment practice laws, the 1964 Civil Rights Act, and the Voting Rights Act all made a difference in their lives.

Fannie Allen Neal talks about the importance of the public accommodations section of the Civil Rights Act, which for the first time enabled her as an African-American to eat and sleep in some peace and comfort as she traveled around the country registering people to vote. Alice Peurala details how she used Title VII to expose sex discrimination in the steel industry. Jessie De La Cruz and Ah Quon McElrath fought for state laws in California and Hawaii to protect farm workers who were excluded from protection by national labor laws. All of these women were involved in lobbying for legislation, supporting political candidates, conducting voter registration campaigns in unions and communities, and sometimes running for political office themselves.

These women also chronicle the negative impact policies and politicians can have on working women. In the 1950s they felt the beginning of a wave of anti-union labor laws. They attempted to defeat the Taft-Hartley bill that again made it more difficult to organize workers into unions because of technicalities, long delays, and imposed legal proceedings. Under the Taft-Hartley Act some of the women in this collection had to sign affidavits stating that they were not members of the Communist Party, and they also had friends and family members called before the House Un-American Affairs Committee and Senator Joseph McCarthy.

Despite their proactive involvements, these women were also affected by large shifts in the economy and society that were beyond their control. They felt the devastation of the Depression in the 1930s and the industrial decline of the 1970s. Alice Peurala's steel mill was eventually shut down owing to a combination of company mismanagement, imports in the steel industry, and a general shift away from industrial production in the United States. Carmen Lucia's union merged with the Amalgamated Clothing Workers of America after a losing battle with imports, technological change, and a change in fashion that sent the market for hats plummeting. Mary Callahan was one of the first union leaders in the electronics industry to warn about the threat of imports and automation, but eventually her plant, along with most of the domestic electronics industry, went out of business.

Dorothy Sue Cobble, in her insightful article "Recapturing Working-Class Feminism," argues persuasively for expanding the definition of feminism, which has been dominated by white, middle-class women, to include "union feminists." She defines union feminists during the period after World War II in part as those who "sought advancement as a group, not merely as individuals. They argued that economic justice and fair treatment for the majority of women can be provided only through employee representation and collective power, not through individual upward mobility."

These stories expand the definition even further to include women active in the decades before World War II and those who supported protective policies for women workers as well as those who fought for sex-blind policies. Changing attitudes toward protective legislation highlight the consistencies, developments, and complexities in the ongoing narrative of women, work, and change that is continuing as we approach the twenty-first century. From Lillian Herstein, who worked hard for protective legislation in the second decade of this century, to Alice Peurala, who saw in 1967 how protective legislation was used against women to bar them from higher-paying jobs traditionally held by men, these dynamic responses are a continuing theme in these women's lives as well as in their economic and social contexts. While the contemporary women's movement helped influence union women to support equal rights, as "protection" came to be seen as discriminatory, union women helped influence the women's movement to address other important issues in working women's lives, such as pay equity, a higher minimum wage, child care, and health and safety on the job, that came from the realities of their day-to-day experiences.

How have these themes continued in the 1990s? Similar consistencies and changes can be seen today in organizing, leadership development, education, coalition building, and public policy strategies. Unions remain a practical and central force for union women as they modify and adapt their issues and use new means to achieve their goals. Union women have higher wages and better benefits than their nonunion sisters, yet only 13 percent of women workers are union members. As union membership continues to decline from its peak in the 1950s, organizing women, who make up almost half of today's work force, has never been more important for women or for the labor movement. New strategies are being developed to organize women, particularly those in part-time and contingent work, within the existing labor laws.

Increasing the numbers of women in union leadership positions is an important goal of the Coalition of Labor Union Women and the increasing number of women's committees, departments, conferences, and workshops in individual unions. Labor education programs for women, which reemerged in the 1970s, offer a range of projects, from university-based labor studies courses to the network of residential summer schools involving the collaboration of union and university staffs with rank-and-file women union members to develop their skills and encourage their participation in leadership positions.

Coalition building and political action remain central strategies, with all of their strengths and strains. Unions joined with women's organizations in a broad coalition in the 1970s to secure passage of the 1978 Pregnancy Discrimination Act, and in the 1980s for the Civil Rights Act and the Family and Medical Leave Act, finally passed in the 1990s. Today this coalition seeks changes in existing labor laws to once again make it simpler for workers to join unions. In addition to labor law reform, other immediate items on the coalition's agenda include an increase in the minimum wage, support for affirmative action, an end to hiring permanent replacements for striking workers, passage of pay equity legislation, and national programs of health care and child care. This agenda, however, faces considerable political opposition. The continuous commitment and unending work undertaken by the women represented in this book offer a guide and model for political action in our own era.

The women in *Rocking the Boat* are all practical and pragmatic, balancing competing and sometimes conflicting demands as workers, trade unionists, members of minority groups, and family members. The importance of fighting for justice and equality while also putting food on the table sometimes resulted in choices and compromises not always understood or appreciated by many of their sisters in the women's movement and their brothers in the labor movement. The process of change is complicated and difficult, but the eleven stories that follow have much to teach us. These women all learned how to rock the boat and not fall out.

Chapter 2

Equal Is Equal, Brothers

Lillian Herstein, American Federation of Teachers (1886–1983)

"The most important woman in the American labor movement." That's how *Life* magazine described Lillian Herstein in 1937. Teacher, union organizer, labor educator, and political candidate, Lillian was a delegate from the Chicago teacher unions to the Chicago Federation of Labor (CFL) and for twenty-five years was the only woman on its executive board. With a degree in Latin from Northwestern University, she joined the Federation of Women High School Teachers in 1916, teaching in Chicago high schools and junior colleges for thirty-six years while also organizing and leading other union, political, and community groups.

An early workers' educator, Lillian was a leader in the Chicago Women's Trade Union League, taught at the Bryn Mawr Summer School for Women Workers, and headed the Chicago WPA workers' education program during the Depression. In the 1920s she helped form the Farmer Labor Party and made an unsuccessful bid for the U.S. Congress. An effective speaker, she worked with mine workers and steelworkers and helped organize the Brotherhood of Sleeping Car Porters, the first major union for African-American workers. At a time when women had to quit teaching if they married, she remained single.

During World War II, Lillian joined the U.S. War Production Board as its Woman Consultant on the West Coast, helping women workers in the war industries. In 1951, at age sixty-five, she retired from the Chicago school system, but continued her work by involvement with the CFL and the Jewish Labor Committee, by writing and teaching for unions, and by working on political campaigns in the 1950s and 1960s.

Throughout her life Lillian fought to secure human rights and equality for women and minorities, believing that "one cannot tell where genius lies by race, color, creed, religion or sex . . . but we must fight for each individual's right for fulfillment, not just for society's sake, but for the individual." She died at age ninety-seven in 1983.[1]

After the Civil War

Lillian Herstein was born in Chicago in 1886 to a Russian Jewish family that had emigrated to the United States in the 1860s. The youngest of six children, she was influenced by the intellectual atmosphere in the Hebrew bookstore owned by her father, who also earned additional money working as a sexton in a neighborhood synagogue. Family political discussions were frequent because her father was a lifelong Republican, while her mother was an active Democrat. Lillian learned the importance of participating in community and civic activities, but there was little union consciousness in her childhood home.

I am the child of immigrant parents who came from Lithuania near the German border. My father had read about how Abraham Lincoln freed the slaves. Abraham Lincoln was a Republican, and then and there, before he set foot on American soil, my father became a Republican. By the time he came to America, he and my mother had a son, the only one born in the old country. My father came first, as so many immigrants did, and then sent for my mother and the boy. My father became a sexton of a synagogue in Chicago. Then he opened a bookstore of Hebrew books. He was like a great many Jewish men of that era, very much interested in scholarship and not in those manual occupations that were in demand in America, and would have brought more lucrative rewards. We lived behind the store and had some rooms upstairs. My sister Augusta was the first child born in America.

We were socially minded and my parents felt that this was a wonderful country. About that time (1891) women in Illinois were given limited suffrage, the right to vote for university trustees. My mother was the only woman in the precinct who went to vote. She took me by the hand; I was about five years old. The clerk, when he was registering her, said to me, "What about you, little girl?" "Oh, I'm going to vote, I'm going to be president some day." We had that consciousness. We would never miss an election to vote.

My father was all for that. He wanted her to vote. But he didn't see the labor movement. He didn't see the economics that made unions necessary. He would think unions were terrible. "Why these poor immigrants come to this wonderful country and we have to go and have unions!" If I thought anything about unions, I thought they were a lot of nuts that ought to appreciate this great country.

I was only twelve years old when my father dropped dead of a heart attack. My oldest brother died at twenty-three, and my mother was left with five children and this precarious bookstore business. She had $500 insurance, that's all. Providing for the family became a real problem. Orthodox Jewish people were reluctant to deal with a woman in these religious activities. All the children in the family went to work except me. I went to high school, the only member of the family that went to high school.

Northwestern University

Lillian said that school meant everything to her, "Just everything!" She finished high school and with financial aid from an uncle, some help from her brothers, and a job at Sears, Roebuck for $6 a week attended Northwestern University in

Lillian Herstein at the blackboard in 1926, while teaching on the faculty of the Trade Union College in Chicago. New York Times, September 26, 1926.

Chicago. There she majored in Latin and Greek and also studied German. Two professors strongly influenced her life, making her aware of politics and religious discrimination. She graduated in 1907 and, after five years of working in high schools in surrounding Illinois and Indiana communities, finally found a job in a Chicago public high school. After a few years she was promoted to Crane Junior College, a public school where she worked for the rest of her teaching career.

John Adams Scott was my professor of Greek, a most remarkable man. We would meet and we would read—translate—two hundred lines of the *Iliad* in every class session. Then he'd tell us about things going on in the world. Of all things, John Adams Scott was a delegate to the Republican state convention in Springfield, Illinois. Now, can you imagine this great scholar? He goes to the convention. He came back and we'd do our translating in class, never shunting the classwork, and then he'd tell us about the convention. Wasn't that remarkable for that man? He was a very great influence in my life.

Another great influence in my life was Arthur Wild, who was professor of ancient history, a typical Bostonian with the typical fairness of the Puritan. Once at a reception he took me aside. There were three Jewish students on the campus at Northwestern. He said I was one of his good students and asked, "Now Miss Herstein, I'm wondering, do you feel any discrimination here because you are Jewish?" I said, "No, I don't." And I didn't. The discrimination at Northwestern University was not on the basis of religion or race—although there weren't too many Jews or Catholics—but on the basis of money.

As we got to the senior year, we were all applying for jobs to teach. I joined the Fisk Teacher's Agency. One day I got a letter from George Palmer, who was a former Northwestern University man and head of the Fisk Teacher's Agency. He said, "You know, Miss Herstein, I've been baffled by how you haven't gotten a job and now I know why. I think you're big enough for me to tell you the truth." He said, "I have sent your papers when they said they wanted somebody like you who could teach six subjects and everything, just the person they wanted. They didn't take you because in one of the letters, Professor John Adams Scott, in recommending you, called you "a brilliant Jewess." When Scott heard that, he was furious. But he wouldn't change the letter. As a result, I couldn't get a teaching job in Chicago. I learned the geography of Illinois by the places that wouldn't hire me.

High School Teachers' Club

Teacher unionism in the United States started in Chicago in 1897, with a group of teachers who lobbied local and state governments for higher salaries and pensions, more funds for public schools, and an end to political corruption. They lacked collective bargaining procedures, however, to negotiate with their employers. By the early twentieth century teaching was a feminized profession offering high status and low pay, and women elementary school teachers formed the core of early teacher activists. In 1916 Chicago teachers initiated a move for a national teachers' organization, the American Federation of Teachers (AFT), affiliated with the American Federation of Labor (AFL).[2] In 1915 Lillian joined the newly organized Federation of Women High School Teachers. She became a delegate to the Chicago Federation of Labor, a citywide organization with official representatives from many different unions, and began her "second career" as a union activist.

I thought being a teacher was the most wonderful thing in the world. After several years of working in other places, I decided to come into Chicago and try for the exams. I took the exam and I passed. At first I substituted and was called up to go to the Wendell Phillips High School, a marvelous high school. They had a very good faculty and they were always pioneers. They were the first high school where teachers had only five classes. The normal teaching load was six classes. I was given an algebra class, a German class, a class they called business English, and physiology. To make my program equal five classes I worked for two hours in the office, which was a very good experience. Finally I got a job just teaching English, and I enjoyed the experience very much.

At that time there were three Chicago educational organizations: the Principals' Club, the High School Teachers' Club, and Margaret Haley's famous organization, the Chicago Teachers' Federation, the first one in the world affiliated with labor. The Chicago Teachers' Federation was for elementary school teachers. The president of the High School Teachers' Club was a bright little woman who taught chemistry at Wendell Phillips. She was a real person, and she came and asked me to join. Part of my training was that you always participate. My father used to say that when people carry the flag so far, you must pick it up, like a relay race. True to my training to share responsibility, without any hesitation, I joined the High School Teachers' Club.

Lillian Herstein

Candidate for

CONGRESS

Second Congressional District

Farmer-Labor Party

 561

A political card from Lillian Herstein's congressional race in 1932. She lost to the Republican candidate, P. J. Moynihan. *Chicago Historical Society.*

One day one of the men teachers came to me and said, "We're getting another organization more effective than this, that's affiliated with labor." Only men were members. They had to have separate men's and women's groups, but they were also organizing a union for women called the Federation of Women High School Teachers. I was having lunch, and we were three young, very stylish teachers, so I told them about it and I said, "I wonder what it's about. I'll tell you, girls, it's only three dollars a year. I'll join and I'll tell you about it." I entered the labor movement as casually as that! Separate unions for the men and women was just custom. In fact, some men teachers in Boston left the American Federation of Teachers because it stood for equal pay for men and women. That was the way.

I became the delegate from the Federation of Women High School Teachers to the Chicago Federation of Labor during that period. Then I was elected to the executive board of the Chicago Federation of Labor. I was the only woman on it for twenty-five years. The person before me was Mrs. Raymond Robins of the National Women's Trade Union League and before that, I think, Mary O'Riley of the Chicago Teachers' Federation, the union for elementary school teachers.

The Women's Trade Union League

At this same time, Lillian became active in the Chicago local of the Women's Trade Union League (WTUL), an organization formed in 1903, which worked closely with the teacher unions to establish early workers' education programs. Women teachers, like Lillian, were the backbone of the WTUL, identifying with other poorly paid workers and participating in many union organizing campaigns and educational programs. She also marched with the league in 1920 for the right of women to vote, and lobbied for protective legislation and shorter hours for women workers and against child labor. In the 1950s, as Chicago WTUL's last president, she continued to urge the unions, "Take advantage of women's ability. Give them good positions and responsibilities in your unions."[3]

My oldest sister, Augusta, the first one born in America, worked in Mandel Brothers as a saleswoman and then in Marshall Field's department store. In those days they worked twelve hours a day. They had no stools to sit on. When they worked overtime, they got fifty cents for supper. Gusta was very fond of me, and there developed between us a very close relationship. By that time she was the oldest and I was the youngest. Gusta—if she'd had a chance! She just didn't have the opportunity. She worked at Field's and about that time Mary Dreier Robins had organized the Women's Trade Union League of America with the idea of doing something for working women.

At this time, the failure of the American Federation of Labor to organize women into unions and to include Negroes in their unions created a pool of scab labor for employers. On visits that the social worker Jane Addams and Mary Dreier Robins and others made to London, they were impressed with the Women's Trade Union League that was organized in England, and they worked to establish a similar organization with headquarters in Chicago. Their purpose was to encourage women to join unions and to work for protective legislation for working women and children.

The women that were admitted to membership in the league's national and local groups were socially minded, influential women. They were designated as "allies." They served the cause but insisted that the power reside in the women trade union members of WTUL, who were the only representatives on the board of the league. These women "allies" not only contributed funds generously, but they were influential in getting a hearing in many a labor dispute. They had status and prestige in the community.

There were several times when we had to deal with intransigent employers who would not confer with labor people, but some of the prominent allies in the WTUL could get us an entrée. The league helped many a men's union, too. Sometimes a hard-pressed union of men appealed to the league, and our influential allies were able to get them a hearing.

Somehow or other, my sister Gusta got in touch with the league. They would meet on Sunday afternoons, and Mrs. Robins would speak and that proved a great inspiration to my sister. That was her first contact, really, with the labor movement. In those days, saleswomen didn't belong to unions. So I joined the Women's Trade Union League of Chicago, which was conducting classes for workers in labor history, parliamentary law, and English.

A Labor Spokesperson

John Fitzpatrick, from the International Union of Journeymen Horseshoers, who was president of the Chicago Federation of Labor, supported the organization of women workers and helped them affiliate with AFL unions. Lillian called him "the most militant, honest labor leader in America," and they had a long, mutually admiring relationship. He encouraged Lillian to become a labor spokesperson. Described by others as an "attractive little girl, with rosy cheeks and black hair," she began to speak nightly and on weekends on street corners or in union halls during the 1918 miners' strike and the 1919 steelworkers' strike, as well as in a number of other union organizing and union strike situations.[4]

Agnes Nestor, president of the Chicago WTUL, asked me to go over to the Chicago Federation of Labor, which was also meeting on Sunday afternoons, to announce our league classes and urge the union delegates to come and enroll. I took the leaflets and went over to 175 West Washington Street. The meeting room was blue with smoke. The delegates were mostly men, because there were very few women organized in unions. I timidly approached the president, John Fitzpatrick, who was very gallant. They were having a hot debate before a city political election and I waited to be called on. I heard Ed Nichols, the CFL secretary, say to Fitzpatrick, "Hey, what's that damn skirt here for?" I faced the large group of men with fear and trembling. I thought they wouldn't listen to me when I began to talk.

After my speech, they all applauded and up walked several men, and they said, "You're the person we're looking for. We have women working in industry and we can't get them to join a union. You're what we want. If we can get you to a meeting and if you can tell those girls that you're a high school teacher, a college graduate who belongs to a union, that will really turn the trick." That really was my real push into the labor movement. I became in demand to speak all the time—this union, that union. That started my second career, one of great activity in the labor movement.

I met Tom Tippitt in 1918. He was a coal miner in Peoria, Illinois, and he came to Chicago and spoke to John Fitzpatrick. He wanted a good woman speaker. That day I had lunch with Tom and Ida Glick, a member of the WTUL, and he was telling both of us about the steel strike and about how angry the miners were. He said, "Will you go?" It was Saturday afternoon. I went over to Marshall Fields and I bought a nightgown, toothpaste, and a toothbrush and called my family—and went with him to Peoria.

When we got there, there was a great big meeting and there was a great deal of talk about violence. The miners know how to use dynamite because they have to use it to loosen coal. I knew all about all of this. The meeting was lousy with Secret Service men. There was a picture of me on a poster announcing the meeting. I remember I had on a tri-cornered hat. The Secret Service men would take the posters off the wall and put them in their pockets. So I had to make a speech for peaceful picketing without letting on I knew there was danger of violence.

I said, "The men who are coming in here to take your jobs don't know that you're on strike. They are just poor devils out of jobs, and these de-tective agencies have hired them and have not told them there is a strike situation here. I'm sure that if you go up to the top of the mine at 5 A.M. when the miners go to work and go with your children and when these men approach the mine, say to them, 'Do you want to go in there and take the bread out of my children's mouths?'" Oh, somebody said at the time that I was a cross between the Virgin Mary and Joan of Arc. I always tell that I got the youngest picket on the picket line. She was six months old, and her mother and father joined the group at 5 A.M. with the baby in their arms and as these scabs came in—and it was true, they didn't know there was a strike—they said, "Now, you're going to take the food out of my baby's mouth."

From then on I was very active, always at the command of any union that wanted me. For ten successive years on Labor Day I spoke in the coal fields of southern Illinois and every October 12 for years found me speaking at the memorial services for the victims of the Virdin mine strike who are buried in Chicago's Mt. Olive Cemetery. There was a steelworkers' union in Joliet, Illinois, and John Fitzpatrick had been appointed by the AFL president Samuel Gompers to organize the steel workers. I became deeply involved in organizing steelworkers, too.

The men used to have me come out during the 1919 steel workers' strike to talk to their people. The strike was spectacular and attracted worldwide attention. The strike went on for several weeks, and we lost. But I always said to the CIO, the Congress of Industrial Organization, when they finally organized the steel industry in 1936, that we'd paved the way for them because we dramatized for America the issue of the twelve-hour day and the other terrible conditions in the steel industry.

Workers' Education

By 1920 Lillian represented the Federation of Women High School Teachers in the Chicago WTUL, forging a link with the Chicago Federation of Labor and teaching WTUL evening classes for workers. She wrote many articles during these years about the importance of workers' education, and for several summers in the 1920s was an instructor in residential workers' education programs at the Bryn Mawr Summer School for Women Workers, the University of Wisconsin, and the University of Chicago. During this time many cities prohibited married women from holding teaching jobs, and Lillian felt that women had to choose between marriage and a career. She chose a teaching career. She shared a four-room apartment with her sister, who was a widow, and her sister's little girl. They had "a bedroom, a sun parlor where one of us slept, and an in-a-door bed."

At this time, there were several activities arranged to give workers opportunities to study. Many of them had gone to work in their early teens; many
were immigrants. There were night school classes conducted by the public
schools, taught by public school teachers who needed the money to eke
out their inadequate salaries. There was always a group of workers that
was eager for education, probably more men than women. A lot of these
people would go to night school. The union people interested in education
for their members insisted on the distinction between what was usually
called adult education and workers' education, which should concentrate
on the needs of workers in our highly industrialized society. But who were
the adult education teachers? They were tired public school teachers teaching tired workers in evening classes. They never corrected their papers.

The national WTUL, which was then situated in Chicago, inaugurated
in a modest way in 1914 the first resident school for workers. They would
recruit four working women and bring them to Chicago for a year at first,
then for six months, for very carefully planned courses. Some of the classes
were regular college courses in labor problems or trade unionism. But we
had a tutor to help the women students. Our wealthy allies were very generous in providing the necessary funds. When I was teaching at Crane Junior College, I asked, "Why couldn't they take English in my classes; then I
could give them the extra help. The burden would be on me and it would
be easier on them." That was probably against the Illinois tax law to take
non-Chicago citizens and put them in a public school, but I never learned
that until many years later. One of our trainees was Fannia Cohn, who subsequently became for many years the education director of the International
Ladies' Garment Workers' Union.

In addition to the resident schools that the national WTUL did for several years, local leagues had their own classes, as we did in Chicago. We
were the center for any trade union groups that wanted an educational meeting, and we were available for any educational services that a union needed.
We had a committee with representatives from the WTUL and the Chicago
Federation of Labor. This was handy because the CFL paid the expenses of
printing, and we could announce the classes at CFL meetings. The courses
that were popular were English, parliamentary law, public speaking, and
trade unionism. For many years I taught the English and public speaking
classes.

Bryn Mawr Summer School for Women Workers in Industry

The WTUL programs served as models for workers' education programs that proliferated in the 1920s and 1930s. Lillian helped organize several of these projects, including the Bryn Mawr Summer School for Women Workers in Industry, a residential program established in 1921 by M. Carey Thomas, president of Bryn Mawr College, with the help of the philanthropist John D. Rockefeller, Jr. The school aimed to teach thousands of women factory workers to understand American society, its democratic process, and their place in it. Lillian was one of the first union teachers to join the faculty. The school was recently celebrated in a documentary film, *The Women of Summer.*[5]

I'll never forget our first meeting at Hull House in Chicago. The Bryn Mawr Summer School was the brainchild of Bryn Mawr College's president, M. Carey Thomas. She wrote to us at the Chicago WTUL to gather a group of working women. They were all trade unionists. In the question period, Hilda Shapiro, a member of the Amalgamated Clothing Workers of America, said to Miss Thomas, "Do you think that we working women would fall for a fake like you're talking about? We know all about the welfare plans of employers. The game is to break up unions. I'm on to your game." Well, Miss Thomas took the attack with dignity and understanding. She said, "I don't blame you for being suspicious. My class certainly has not been fair to you working people and has tried many schemes to subvert trade unionism. All I can give you is my own word that this is a sincere effort as I have described it."

Hilda Shapiro was in the first class. I came to Bryn Mawr in the third summer of this program, one of only two women teachers from the labor movement. We both taught English. I subsequently also became a member of the Bryn Mawr Summer School's national administrative committee as a labor representative. There were a hundred women enrolled in the school from the whole country, all working women, and they had to be women who worked with the tools of their trade; nobody in a supervisory capacity was admitted. Of course, the Philadelphia newspapers (Bryn Mawr is near Philadelphia) saw the school as a Communist revolution. We had a time! We would be written up in the newspapers and some of the Bryn Mawr College alumni were alarmed. We had some very hard times with bad publicity.

It was the best teaching I ever did. I realized what it means if you can give individual attention. I suppose I had about forty-five pupils. In my work in Chicago high schools I had 150: five classes, thirty in each class. At the summer schools for women workers I taught the way I never have been able to teach since. I had the "language handicaps"—the immigrants. I had an interview with every girl. I'd get her talking, and I'd say, "Now, that's something you should write about"—their first days at Ellis Island, or the first accident on the job the girls witnessed. At the end of the summer when we were selecting material for our magazine, "The Script," most of the material came from the language handicaps because they wrote so well. It was a great experience in their lives.

One year the big argument was about admitting waitresses. Many of the working girls felt that waitresses were immoral; they made dates with the men they waited on and so on and so on. We finally discussed it on the administrative board. One of the working girls from New York said, "If they are immoral, it's because of the conditions under which they work. If they got wages instead of tips and didn't have to smile at every man they waited on, they wouldn't be tempted. We should not keep them out of the school. What we should do is change their conditions of work." That was a very good argument. So the school took them in.

But the hot fight was the admission of Negroes. I remember when we had the discussion at the school by the whole student body. One lovely redhead from the South said that she herself had no prejudice, but when it was announced in her small town that two of their girls were going up to Bryn Mawr College to study in a workers' school, they prayed in their churches for them. But if they learned that the school admitted Negroes, no other girl from the community would be sent. She had a point.

The students voted to admit Negroes. When they came, everybody held their breath as to what would happen. Well, the strange thing that happened was this. The students were always having buzz sessions in their rooms. These Negro girls would go to one buzz session after another. They'd go to the white girls from the South and they said, "Look, you must realize the background of these Jewish girls, the things they've suffered in Europe." Then they would go to the radical bunch and say to them, "Now, you've got to picture a southern town where the center of the town is the church, where even the YMCA is controlled by the employers, where there are company schools." (I'll never forget when I first heard of company schools, I thought I'd die.) The Negro girls interpreted each group to the other. Amy Hewes, who taught that year, was a professor of economics at Mt. Holyoke College. She said, "We may not have learned much that year, but by God, we learned about the world and those working girls established a democratic working procedure."

The significant thing about these residential schools was that for the first time workers were able to give their whole attention to study. They didn't come after working hours, tired and taught by tired teachers. The resident schools gave them the leisure to study the way other people do. This movement of workers' education spread from these humble beginnings to where the unions have taken over these programs and have done them very well. If you have a liberal president of a union, he favors it. If not, he lets it go.

The Brotherhood of Sleeping Car Porters

During the post–World War I period, Lillian became active in organizing industrial workers. As a delegate from the Chicago Federation of Labor to the 1922 Illinois Federation of Labor convention, she gave the keynote speech urging labor people to amalgamate all craft unions into industrial unions that would unite workers regardless of their trades. Lillian became an early champion of A. Philip Randolph's organizing campaigns to form a Brotherhood of Sleeping Car Porters (BSCP), which was founded in 1925 to represent African-American workers on the railroads. She maintained a commitment to civil rights throughout her life.[6]

A long time ago, in my early days, the Brotherhood of Sleeping Car Porters had a hard time organizing. Every time they had a meeting, there were spies in the meeting, and the next day workers would get fired. But they held out. Philip Randolph held out for a union, not to be an auxiliary to any other union, in a nonvoting capacity.

There was to be an election. I got a call to come speak at a big meeting on Canal and Harrison. I was told that the Chicago and Northwestern Railroad, the company, had some stooges going around urging people not to join the union. I go out there, surrounded by a whole group of Negroes. The only two speakers were Frank McCulloch and me, both white. The white men passing by made all kinds of remarks about me—miscegenation—so I said to the Negroes, "Don't pay any attention to that. I don't care anything about that."

Then for some reason we had to go see the president of the Chicago and Northwestern Railroad. We went to his office and when he saw Frank and me, he could have killed us. His whole idea was that these Negroes are nice and law-abiding; they don't want unions. It's just these white agitators. He got so insulting that one of the Negro delegates standing next to

me was getting mad. I said, "Don't get mad. Let's go where they are count-
ing the votes. Let's look at that and not pay any attention to him." The Sleep-
ing Car Porters won. It was the first Negro union directly affiliated with the
AFL. Many meetings were held celebrating the event. At the one held in
Chicago, the porters asked their three best white friends to sit on the plat-
form and be honored: Mary McDowell, who was head of the University of
Chicago Settlement House; University of Chicago economics professor Paul
Douglas; and me.

The New Politics

Starting in the 1920s, Lillian immersed herself in political as well as union activi-
ties. Teachers in the public schools were very directly affected by local politics
through school boards and city budgets. In 1932 she ran for Congress in the
Illinois second congressional district on the Farmer Labor Party ticket. There was
much talk at this time among the unions about a third party, particularly by the
Amalgamated Clothing Workers of America and the International Ladies' Garment
Workers' Union (ILGWU, or ILG). But by 1936, the labor movement was behind
Roosevelt. Lillian was in full support of Franklin Roosevelt's reelection campaign,
although earlier she had questioned "this charming squire's courage and wisdom
to do what was needed in this bleak year."[7]

Many of us were engaged in organizing a really big Farmer Labor Party.
It was going to be a very effective party, and the unions were asked to send
delegates. I spoke to various meetings asking them to send delegates, and
John Fitzpatrick and I were national committeemen of this newly organized
party. I was teaching for a living all this time. I was doing everything gratis
and I would rush to meetings.

Personally, I was very interested in political activity. In the 1930s I came
under the influence of Professor Paul Douglas, who later became Senator
from Illinois, and Morse Lovett, who was a distinguished liberal. Douglas
influenced me to run for Congress from the second congressional district
on the newly formed Farmer Labor Party. Mr. James Mullenback, who was
the arbitrator of the Amalgamated Clothing Workers' union and a distinguished member of the Chicago Board of Education, endorsed me. Most of
the labor movement was still voting according to the Gompers formula to
elect their friends and defeat their enemies in the Republican and Democratic parties. John Fitzpatrick, president of the Chicago Federation of La-

bor, and Soderstrom, president of the state Federation of Labor, however, all wrote letters recommending my election. In 1932, I did not support Roosevelt. I supported the Socialist Party candidate, Norman Thomas, for President and he supported me for Congress.

My mouth had always watered to be in politics, but apparently my timing was wrong. In 1932, I was not elected. Some of my students went to polling places to be watchers and they were in one precinct where the Republicans and Democrats were watching each other and counting the votes very carefully, and finally they came upon ten or twelve that were not easily classified. They were arguing about their allocation and finally one of them said, "Oh, all right, let's give those to the skirt."

The agreement was that no matter how the campaign went, after the election we would meet in Chicago and form a third party. After the election, the delegates did meet in Chicago, as had been agreed to before, but the enthusiasm of the labor people for a third party had evaporated. When Roosevelt went into office, he introduced a great deal of his welfare program and all the third party people were converted to Roosevelt, even Paul Douglas. For the 1936 campaign, we opened an office on Dearborn Street. I was asked to be director of the speaker's bureau for Labor's Non-Partisan League. At that time I was director of lectures at the junior college so that I had no classroom responsibilities. I came to the office after school hours every day. Our office was a beehive of activity.

One time we organized a march because Roosevelt was to come to Chicago to speak at the stadium on West Madison Street. We actually marched from Michigan and Congress streets all the way down Michigan to Madison, all the way to the stadium. John Fitzpatrick led the parade. Roosevelt was to speak and everybody tried to get into the stadium. We got in, we sat on the platform. That was the first time I had ever seen Roosevelt. There was this thunderous applause. Never once in that evening did he sit down or rise, so the only picture that the audience had was this tall, handsome, strong-looking man, and never were they reminded of his infirmity. Well, that was 1936, and that was part of my labor political activity.

Eleanor Roosevelt

Eleanor Roosevelt was active in the Women's Trade Union League of New York and subsequently in the National Women's Trade Union League. When the Roosevelt administration came into Washington "with all its promise," support for labor education and for the WTUL was expanded because of her interest. Lillian organized a meeting with Eleanor Roosevelt and midwestern leaders of the AFL

and the CIO in her apartment in Chicago. As a result, Lillian directed a WPA workers' education project at the University of Chicago in the early 1930s. The WTUL
decided to reestablish the annual convention, which had ceased meeting during
the early years of the Depression, and Eleanor Roosevelt played a key role in these
plans. The WTUL's headquarters had been moved to Washington, D.C., and its
secretary was Elisabeth Christman of the Glove Workers' Union.[8]

During the Depression, hardly any union conventions were held, because
there was no money, but the WTUL decided to have a convention. At the
board meeting of the WTUL, Eleanor Roosevelt said, "My, I wish you would
bring some of those textile workers from the South." Elisabeth Christman
said, "Oh, we'll try to bring some of them, but their unions have no money.
Those unions, they couldn't send anybody."

Plans for the convention were being made and one day, Elisabeth ran
into Mrs. Roosevelt on a street in Washington. Mrs. Roosevelt said, "Oh,
Miss Christman, how are you getting along with the convention?" And
Elisabeth said, "I have everything for the southern girls. I've got the money
for their transportation. Now, I'm working on their hospitality, where they
stay." Mrs. Roosevelt said, "Just wait a minute." And she went to the telephone and came back and said, "Miss Christman, you know that big top
floor of the White House where there are those big beds? How would the
girls like to stay there?" I thought Elisabeth would die. She said, "Oh, Mrs.
Roosevelt, that's too much." Mrs. Roosevelt said, "That's all right. I've got
the place and enough beds for the southern girls, and I want Rose
Schneiderman and Molly Friedman, who was in the ILGWU, to stay at the
White House too." Mrs. Roosevelt knew them personally.

It was a marvelous WTUL convention, the first one in a long time. One
of President Roosevelt's secretaries got hold of Elisabeth and he said, "Miss
Christman, I'm talking for the President. He wants to meet his guests tomorrow at tea." Elisabeth said, "Oh, that's too much. We don't expect it
and you don't have to do that." He said, "Listen, Miss Christman, you can't
tell the President who his guests are to be."

At three o'clock they gathered in the Blue Room in the White House as
they usually do for teas. Soon President Roosevelt was ushered in, in his
wheelchair. Elisabeth said he couldn't have been more gracious if he were
entertaining the most important ambassador of an important country. They
had a wonderful tea which was written up in *Time* magazine. That was a
never to be forgotten event for these working girls. During their stay at the

White House, Mrs. Roosevelt put little mementos in their rooms that they would take home and cherish all their lives.[9]

National Leadership

In 1936 the three different teacher unions in Chicago decided to strengthen their position by forming one union, the Chicago Teachers Union of the American Federation of Teachers. The national AFT then voted to leave the AFL and join the Congress of Industrial Organization, a new organization representing the mass-production industrial workers led by the United Auto Worker and the United Mine Worker unions. Lillian supported continued affiliation with the AFL because in Illinois there was a large network of AFL unions and councils that supported AFT lobbying in the state legislature. Recognizing Lillian as a well-seasoned unionist who combined a passion for social justice with a realistic view of social change, Chicago teacher unionists mounted a campaign supporting her as a candidate for president of the national American Federation of Teachers. She didn't hesitate to take minority positions, but whether she won or lost, she was always willing to continue working within the structures of the labor movement.[10]

At the 1936 convention of the American Federation of Teachers in Tampa, Florida, I was a candidate for president of the union and was defeated largely through the efforts of the communists. That was an interesting story. Several workshops had been arranged and they had their "lieutenants" in the workshops, and whatever the discussion was, when I took part in it, they sensed that I wouldn't be anybody that they could manipulate. The candidate that was running for reelection was Jerome Davis of the Divinity School of Yale University, who was a very fine man and was not a communist. But they thought they could use him, so they favored him. The vote was relatively close and he was reelected.

Everybody thought how game I was because I got up and said, "We've had an election in the very best tradition of the American Federation of Teachers, very democratic, and everybody had a chance to vote and now we have the results. The thing we should do is unite our efforts in the interests of teachers." It was the hour after I had been defeated. I suggested that we should not sharpen our spikes, but work together in the interests of the organization.

Shortly after the AFT convention I went to the AFL convention as an observer. Jerome Davis, who was the recently reelected president of the AFT and had never attended an AFL convention, came over to me and he said, "Lillian, I'll need your help. I have never attended an AF of L convention and you know all these people." I said, "Well, Jerome, I certainly will help you as much as I can."

At the next AFT convention I was on the resolutions committee and presiding was Davis, the man who defeated me. We had a very long and hot debate on the CIO. I presented a minority report against making any gestures toward going into the CIO, and I had very good reasons. One of the most important considerations was that education in America was still largely a local matter, and the teachers' union got its support from the local federation of labor as we did in Illinois, not the national. We had the unqualified support of the Illinois State Federation of Labor. In fact, there was no local CIO in Chicago. If you don't have a state CIO, how can they lobby in the state legislature for you? We lost. The majority voted for the AF of T to join the CIO.

At the next convention of the American Federation of Labor I was a delegate from the Chicago Federation of Labor, but not from the AFT, which was now in the CIO. According to the constitution of the AFL the central bodies were called "one lungers," because they could have only one delegate. Of course, it was an assignment much sought. I had been nominated several times before to be a delegate, but always there would be some older man who, if he didn't go that year, would never get to go; so I would withdraw for him. This time delegates came to me and said, "We don't want you to withdraw; now you go." I was the delegate to the AF of L.

International Work

In 1937, President Roosevelt appointed Lillian to the delegation of government, business, and labor representatives from the United States to the annual meeting of the International Labor Organization (ILO) in Geneva, Switzerland. The ILO was established after World War I and is now affiliated with the United Nations. With over 120 member states, the organization tries to improve labor standards and working conditions through the ratification of recommendations and conventions, technical assistance, and education. On that same trip, as a representative of the AFT, Lillian attended the International Congress of Teachers and addressed the Conference of the International Federation of Teacher Organizations in Paris.

It was a very interesting convention. There were twenty-two people in the American delegation. The ILO was built on a tripartite principle with the government of each country having two representatives, so the weight of power is in the government. The leading employer organization, which at that time I think was the Chamber of Commerce, had one delegate, and the labor movement had one. That's four voting delegates. The worker delegate was Bob Watt of the painters' union of Massachusetts. For each item on the agenda each delegate is permitted two "technical advisors." Obviously, it's the technical advisors that really do the work, because they're the experts in their particular field. There were seven items on the agenda. I was the technical advisor to Bob Watt on child labor legislation.

Our meetings were in a big hall in Geneva. The items on the agenda were several. The two very important ones were the forty-hour week in the textile industry, and raising the age when children could go to work from fourteen to fifteen. The whole conference meets in plenary session a few times, but the technical advisors meet in their own group. We met every single day thrashing out what we wanted and what we were supposed to do. Very hard work! We had mimeographed copies of the child labor laws and conditions in every country. The Secretariat, the group of experts who were in Geneva all the time, about four hundred people, did a very fine job.

We had this hot debate about child labor in our committee. The delegate from India got up and said, "Our children are working at the age of eight." He said that children in a hot climate like that mature early. We American delegates reminded him that was the argument given to us in America when we tried to get child labor laws in the southern states. Grace Abbott from the U.S. Children's Bureau was marvelous. She said, "We're going to stick to our resolution."

When the voting came in the plenary session for the child labor resolutions, Bob Watt came over to me and said, "I want you to cast the vote for the United States." He gave me that honor, and I got up and said "Aye." We won in favor of raising the age from fourteen to fifteen when children could go to work. The forty-hour week and also the child labor resolutions carried.

The conference was over after three weeks, and I decided that as long as my transportation was paid back and forth it was economical to spend some time in Europe on my own. I went to the Scandinavian countries and then came to Paris and attended the International Congress of Teachers and addressed that convention. We concentrated on educational problems. I went to Ireland, but I had promised I was going to come back in time for the AFT convention in Madison. I came back in August.

Mayor Kelly

Lillian used her position with the teachers' union and the Chicago Federation of Labor to advocate for many public school reforms, including higher tax assessments for public education, and better conditions for schoolchildren and teachers. This sometimes brought her into conflict with local politicians. In the 1940s she confronted Chicago's powerful Mayor Kelly over a political slush fund that pressured teachers to contribute. In 1942, when the junior college department of lectures that she headed was abolished, she attributed this move to Mayor Kelly's animosity toward her. She was protected, however, from losing her teaching job by Illinois's Otis Law providing for teacher tenure.[11]

I remember when Kelly was mayor of Chicago and it was a hard time for the schools. There really was an oversupply of teachers, and they could do what they wanted with us. Mayor Kelly conceived to outwit us and he got his man, McKay, as head of the school board. It was the time of the Depression and he was going to get us out of a financial jam. We were paid in tax anticipation warrants. They carried a 6 percent interest, but who could keep them? Teachers were selling them for $75, which meant they lost $25. Oh, my. It was very bad. There were all kinds of proposals—what to do? Abolish the teachers' college? The junior colleges? Or what? The junior college had been in operation by that time for twenty-two years, but there was no law that created it. So we introduced a junior college bill and I lobbied it through successfully.

Then Mayor Kelly began wrecking the schools. It was terrible. He had the bright idea of having a fund. The big football game of the year was between the champions of the public high schools and the parochial schools. It was a marvelous game. Whatever team won in each league was a pretty fine team. Kelly's proposal was that all the teachers buy tickets and from that fund, he would send baskets of provisions to poor families, delivered by his precinct captains. Don't you think that's cute?

Well, we opposed that. There had always been a fund for years to which teachers contributed. We used to pass the hat around. The children contributed too. Then, through an authorized social agency, the money was distributed to poor families on Thanksgiving and Christmas. We did it every year. But now, in regard to Kelly's project, teachers would say, "But my principal came up with tears in his eyes; he had been given fifty tickets and if he didn't sell them to us, he'd have to buy them." So we said, "Let him buy them." I said there's no point in our contributing to the political slush fund of Mayor Kelly.

That got to Mayor Kelly. He told John Fitzpatrick that after all he did for labor to have a member of their executive board to say that. Well, Fitzpatrick said, "I don't know about what you've done for labor, but I'm sure that if Lillian said that, she probably knew what she was talking about." Several of us never contributed to that slush fund. Finally the North Central Association of Colleges and Universities came out with the statement that they would take the Chicago high schools off the accredited list if these practices continued, and that's when Kelly had to step out and we got Kennelly as the reform man.

A Woman Consultant in World War II

After the bombing of Pearl Harbor and the United States' formal entrance into World War II, more labor people were drawn into service in war production activities. The U.S. War Production Board was made up of seven members, one from the AFL, one from the CIO, and the others from industry. Lillian was increasingly unhappy with the Chicago Federation of Teachers, disagreeing with the local union's president over many issues. Feeling he didn't consult with the union members, she eventually resigned from the local union executive board, although she remained a committed AFT member. Soon, however, she was hired by the War Production Board as a woman consultant, supervising the entire West Coast region on the problems of women workers in war industries.[12]

Joseph Keenan, who was on leave as secretary of the Chicago Federation of Labor, was a labor vice president of the War Production Board. He appointed me a woman consultant for the War Production Board with a very fancy title that I can't even remember. My job was to gear community facilities to the needs of women working in war industries so that they could stick to the job. He sent me to the West Coast, first to California.

There were the problems of housing, child care, getting to and from the plants. Another problem was in-plant feeding. When I first started this work, the churches had come to the rescue, and they used the basements of churches for child-care facilities. They were awful. We reported that these nurseries were dark, damp, and dreary.

My territory was the whole West Coast. It was very hard. It was only toward the end of the war that I was given an assistant. Child-care centers had to be built as the mothers worked eight hours a day. I think those mothers at the Kaiser Shipyards child-care center paid seventy-five cents an hour. In other places, I got the fee reduced to fifty cents.

Another problem was that by the time the women workers arrived after work from the plant into town, all the food in the markets was gone. So in this lovely nursery that was established by the Maritime Commission under the Kaiser Shipyards, the nursery school teachers said, "We'll prepare a dinner for you and a dessert—a whole complete dinner." The mother would come early in the morning and deposit her child. She would order a dinner and when she picked up her child in the evening, she picked up the dinner. It was a great convenience and a real help to the war effort. The teachers were devoted to service. There wasn't a thing that a mother would need that they didn't do. They would say, "Bring your darning; we'll do that for you." They were very resourceful.

Just before the war came to an end, right after the Japanese surrender, I was in Seattle. I was on a train going to Portland when we heard that General Fleming, head of the WPA in Washington, had the bright idea that we should close all the child-care facilities. Well, their fathers were still overseas, and what were we going to say to all the mothers? "Can't have any child care," when the fathers were still over there? I talked to Joe Keenan long distance and suggested to him that I make a trip around my West Coast territory and find out how many working mothers still had husbands in the war and would need child care. I went all over and found a great many.

Helen Gahagan Douglas was congresswoman from California at that time. I came back to Washington, D.C., and got a hold of her, and she just hit that issue in the head. She got a resolution in Congress that child-care facilities should not be closed. I furnished her with the numbers of working women from my district whose husbands were still overseas. They kept the child-care facilities open for quite a while. It took a long time for the soldiers to get back, and some of them were injured and their wives still had to work.

Retirement

In 1951, when she was sixty-five, Chicago school board regulations required Lillian Herstein to retire from the Chicago school system. She immediately went to work for the Jewish Labor Committee, which had been organized in the 1930s to rescue European labor leaders who were Nazi targets and then, after the war, focused on improving race relations in this country.[13] Lillian also represented the

WTUL on the Chicago Federation of Labor. Lillian continued her community activities with the Chicago Human Rights Commission and the American Civil Liberties Union on many human rights and labor-related issues. She also taught classes on American government for the Ladies Auxiliary of the Brotherhood of Sleeping Car Porters and continued writing for union publications. In the mid-fifties, she wrote a series of columns for the national "AFL-CIO News," advocating smaller public school class size, higher salaries for teachers, and federal aid for education. She worked actively for Adlai Stevenson's campaigns for President in the 1950s. An interview with Lillian at age eighty-five appeared in the *Chicago Tribune* in September 1971. Carol Kleiman wrote: "Diminutive in size and boundless in brilliance, Miss Herstein still knows what's going on in Labor, and cares. She remembers every detail and date. . . . Chicago labor history, the ups and downs, had worldwide significance because so many battles were fought here in organizing the meat packing, railroad, and steel industries, and the teachers. And on the scene in each one of them was Miss Herstein."[14] Lillian Herstein died in Chicago at age ninety-seven in April 1983.

All the reasons that operated for discrimination against women in universities and professions operated among unions. Union men used to say, "Well, they're only temporary in industry." They often didn't even try to organize an industry that was predominantly women. We used to say in those days that the two weak points in the American Federation of Labor movement were the two pools of labor that they left untouched, which was organizing women and organizing Negroes.

Equal pay is something women must work toward, although we've come a long way toward it. How industry resists equal pay! The very idea horrifies them. I used to discuss it with union leaders and say, "Equal is equal, brothers." But it hasn't happened yet.

Women who choose to do housework and raise children must be respected, too. I don't agree with any put-downs of housewives. If all work is equal, the education system will adjust itself and will not be based on perpetuating myths of racial, sexual, or economic superiority. There's got to be respect, respect for every kind of work. All work ranks the same with God, but, unfortunately, not with man.

Chapter 3

First a Troublemaker, Then a Troubleshooter

*Carmen Lucia, United Hatters,
Cap and Millinery Workers
International Union (1902–1985)*

Carmen Lucia was first and foremost a union organizer. In 1916, when she was fourteen, she began work in a garment factory in Rochester, New York. Over the next fifteen years she became active in the Amalgamated Clothing Workers of America (ACWA), the Neckwear Workers' Union, the YWCA, and the Bryn Mawr Summer School for Women Workers. Always strong-willed and idealistic, her early union experiences were difficult, but she soon found satisfaction as an organizer for the United Hatters, Cap and Millinery Workers International Union (UHCMW), a job that kept her traveling throughout the country for forty years.

In the 1930s she was beaten and jailed while organizing in California, Texas, and Illinois. As a single mother, arrangements for her daughter were difficult during the many months she was away from home. Based in Atlanta from 1944 to 1960, she became a vice president of the union and member of the general executive board. She chaired the UHCMW's southern organizing drive and the organizing committee of the Georgia State Federation of Labor, and was a member of the AFL Southern Policy Committee. She reached out to African-American workers and faced the Ku Klux Klan. She was described in the *Atlanta Journal* as the "ranking woman union official in the South."

In the 1960s, despite the decline of the hatwear industry and her own health problems, Carmen continued to organize. Still a "troublemaker," at the last union convention she attended she gave an "Equal Rights Amendment speech they'll never forget," urging union women to demand equality and recognition from their unions. She retired in 1974, and was remembered by union leaders for never flinching from dangerous missions and for her special skills as an organizer. Living with her daughter and four grandchildren, she continued to write poetry and keep up with current events. In 1980 she returned to Rochester, where most of her thirteen brothers and sisters still lived. She died in February 1985.[1]

Rochester, New York, 1900–1920

In the early part of the twentieth century, Rochester, New York, was a fast-growing city with a population that went from 36,000 in 1850 to over 162,000 in 1900. Immigrants from eastern and southern Europe flooded the city seeking jobs in the booming garment industry. Among them was the Lucia family, from Italy. Carmen's father, Raefaelio, was a cabinetmaker by trade, but joined other relatives working in the clothing factories, while her mother, Angela Rizzo, cared at home for their fourteen children. Eventually they owned their own house, with what Carmen described as the "inevitable grape arbor" in the backyard.

I was born in Italy, April the third, 1902, in Calabria, the south. I was two years old when we came here in 1904. We landed in Rochester, New York, and I'm glad of it. We were fortunate enough not to have landed in New York City, with fourteen children. Rochester had individual homes, and we all went to live in the neighborhoods at first where the people spoke our tongue. That helped a great deal.

The first place we lived in was flush with the railroad tracks. Trains would stop and change and make a raucous noise—to us that was a fairyland. I always remember the trains going by and stopping, waving at the motormen and the people in the train, wishing I could be in there and wondering where they were going. I was very young, but what I loved most was the end of the train. There was always, I don't know what they call it in English, but we used to call it "alogia" in Italian. It was always shining. It was gold to me, it was brilliant gold; but it was brass. And always a black man polishing it, and so it was a mirage. I thought, someday I'm going to be in one of these trains and I'm going to go, and sit there and see how it feels. I had a feeling of always wanting to go, and hearing that eerie sound at night drew me to all kinds of places. I think that had a terrific influence on my wanderings.

The union was in the process of being organized, but there was terrific opposition in the city. Periodically, during that era, the tailors, including my father and all of my relatives, would go out on strike. I used to hear stories about the picket line. I was younger than twelve then, and I would say to my father, "Why can't you take me to the picket line?" One morning he was summoned to the picket line and I went with him.

The pickets were jammed against the door, trying to get into the plant, and the employer went up on the second floor. He shot into the crowd and

Carmen Lucia (*front row, third from right*) organizing workers at the Stetson Hat Company, Norwalk, Connecticut, 1943. *Courtesy Marge Whipple.*

killed a young woman, not far from where I was: Ida Braverman. When I saw the blood and heard the hysteria and anger of the people, I was just furious. I would have just as soon got even with the employer if I had a gun—shot him, and got even! But that made up my mind, and I said to my father, "I know what you mean, and when I grow up I'm going to be an organizer."

From School to Work

Carmen was independent and stubborn even as a child. These were traits that would be both a weakness and a strength in her union work and family life. A union article in her later life pointed out that she was first a troublemaker, then a troubleshooter. She was the third child in a large Italian Catholic family and the one who stayed home from school to help each time her mother had a baby, and to turn the wringer for the washer woman who came every Wednesday. She quit school at age twelve because she "didn't like the teacher," and went to work at the Steinbloch garment factory when she was fourteen.

I went to a Catholic school for poor Italian children on the grounds of the Sacred Heart Academy. You can imagine the difference between the wealthy children in the academy and the poor children in the old gymnasium. The nun who taught us was crazy about my sister, because Matty would ask no questions. The Sister treated me shamefully every time I asked a question about the Bible, or I asked about God. She couldn't stand me and made my life miserable.

I was a good speller because I read well. I used to go to the library and borrow books and read. We had a spelling bee one day. I finally got to the head of my class, and there was a boy at the head of his class. Sister was determined I wasn't going to win, and I was determined I *was* going to win. She gave me the hardest words to spell. She couldn't seem to discourage me. She finally said, "Carmen Lucia, stop making eyes at Sam." Sure I was making eyes at Sam, but not amorously. I was hoping he dropped dead. She shamed me and that embarrassed me. At lunchtime, I took my tribe of brothers and sisters, all younger than me, and I took them home in the middle of the day. My first strike!

Dad said, "If you're not going back to Sacred Heart School, you're not going to school at all." I said, "Suits me. I don't care." So I stayed home for two years. I couldn't go to work until I was fourteen. On my fourteenth birthday, April 3, 1916, I went to work. They put me on a sewing machine and put my foot on the pedal. I had never seen an electric machine in my life. There were two needles, one going this way and one that way, and both of them stuck in my finger. To this day I'll never forget the horror of it, and the pain.

They paid me two dollars a week. I didn't like the fact that there was such a pay differential between men and women. That was the first thing I noticed, although that was one of the first shops the Amalgamated Clothing Workers' union had organized. I realized, of course, that the union can't work miracles overnight. It takes time to settle. But I said, "Why can't we work piecework? I'm faster than anybody in this department. I want to earn as much money as I can."

I went on piecework, and the first week I made about eighteen or twenty dollars. I was delighted to bring it home to my parents. We gave our entire pay to my father, and he gave us money for car fare and little incidentals. He wasn't stingy, but you know, I had hand-me-downs all my life. I got my first dress that was my very own when I was about sixteen years old. My mother made it for about three dollars. It was white and black plaid dimity tied with a sash in the back. But one thing I learned was that unless people work together and band together and share everything together, they can never be happy and they can never overcome poverty.

The YWCA and Union Work

In 1914 a group of immigrant workers representing locals in the men's and children's clothing industry broke away from the more conservative, craft-oriented United Garment Workers and formed the Amalgamated Clothing Workers of America. Sidney Hillman was elected president, and membership grew from about 40,000 to 177,000 by 1920.[2] In these years, the national YWCA established "industrial departments" to offer recreation, education, and support for young women workers. The Y classes for working-class women included subjects such as economics, as well as leadership and public speaking, and encouraged women to become active in their unions. Rochester had a very active YWCA Industrial Department, and Carmen began to take workers' education classes in the evenings.[3]

Then along comes my activity in the YWCA. They had an Industrial Department and they had a woman, Elizabeth Hiss, who headed it and she was very, very liberal. She imbued us. We belonged to the union, but we didn't know why. It was sort of a casual thing, although I loved it. I loved the first strike I had been part of, and I loved the picket lines and the excitement of coming and going and everything. Elizabeth Hiss knew I had a block somewhere I had to get out of. I wasn't a pretty child. I had always a kind of competition in the family. They were all good looking except me. I began to feel that I was stupid. But she worked miracles. She made me believe in me. She finally believed in me so much that I became very active in the YWCA Industrial Department.

I became active in the Amalgamated Clothing Workers' union and became chairlady for the union in the Steinbloch Company, for about two hundred people. I took care of the complaints. It was a large shop. I was considered a rebel then. The managers said I had a negative point of view. I really didn't. I used to ask a lot of questions. I wasn't satisfied with answers I'd get, and I'd be very aggressive and insist I wanted to understand more about it.

We had all kinds of union locals. There were seven clothing workers' local unions in Rochester vying for power. They used to have locals for every language-speaking group: a Polish local, a Lithuanian local, a Jewish local, an Italian local. We had a women's local—talk about segregation. I

Carmen Lucia (*right*) is presented with a union-made hat by an organizer of the Designers Local at the International Convention of the United Hatters, Cap and Millinery Workers International Union, ca. 1959. *Courtesy Marge Whipple.*

was in the women's local. Women were all in one local regardless of where we worked or our language. There were no blacks. And there were political differences. How could you weld all of this into a melting pot where there would be no differences of opinion on policy?

Well, it was voting time for the new union officers. I attended the meeting at the women's local. The women were backward; they were scared. Men ran those locals. There was no such thing as women's activities in those days. So I attended this meeting and the quarrel was, where are we going to hold the election? How are we going to hold it so that there will be no stuffing of ballot boxes? Someone kept saying, "Let's have it in each plant." I didn't like that idea, because there'd be control on the people that worked in that particular shop and there were about twenty thousand tailors in one plant. So I spoke up and I said, "Why have it in different plants? We've got a big office here, a huge hall. You could have a committee to watch the ballots, one from each local if you don't trust each other, and we could control it that way much better." Other people happened to feel the same way I did about it. I just happened to bring it up.

Abraham Chapman was the new manager of the Amalgamated union joint board in Rochester in 1925. He asked who was that girl he heard that spoke at the women's local about having the election in the union hall, and he said, "Well, I'd like to meet her." His secretary was leaving at the time, and they were having an awful lot of Italians coming into the union, see, and they couldn't speak English. Not that my Italian was so perfect, but it would do. He liked me, and he said, "I'd like to put you on as my secretary." They sent me for a couple of weeks, half-days, to learn typing. After that, I went at night to learn shorthand—at my expense. I used to go in and argue with him. I'd always be fighting with somebody! It was quite an opportunity for me, because I wanted to get out of working in the clothing factory. I felt that I could do better, and, well, going into the union office is something I'll always cherish. It was very, very interesting. So I was there from about 1925 until 1930.

A Bryn Mawr Summer School Student

By the late 1920s the YWCA was a major recruiting source for programs like the Bryn Mawr Summer School for Working Women. Through the YWCA in Rochester, Carmen and three other young women attended the school in 1927. Hilda Smith, director of the summer school, encouraged her; Carmen began to develop her speaking skills, and her poetry was published in the school magazine. Helping others, a need she shared with her oldest brother, was reinforced by her Bryn Mawr experiences. A group from the summer school went to Philadelphia that summer for a rally supporting Sacco and Vanzetti, the Italian anarchists charged with murder in a payroll robbery. Several months later, when the two were executed, she described her reaction, "We went out, my brother and I, and we sat on the curb of the street and we both cried. Our friends are gone. We must do something to save others from getting the same treatment."[4]

I had a brother, the oldest of the children, who helped a radical union called the Industrial Workers of the World. He was an idealist if ever there was one. He was about fourteen years older than me and I loved him dearly. I loved him for his sincerity and I loved him for his courage, because it took a lot of courage to stand up for causes. So, of course, I tagged along with him. It got into my blood. Now, there was a restlessness in the air. There was an awakening on the part of people. Wages were very poor. People wanted to be recognized as individuals and treated as such. I felt that there was a stirring in the air, and a need for workers' education. I never had an opportunity to get into these things, because my father was very strict about what we could do. But when the opportunity came for me to go to Bryn Mawr Summer School, the family agreed, and I went as a student for eight weeks in 1927.

Hilda Worthington Smith. We called her Jane. Those that loved her the most called her Jane. She was the dean of undergraduate students at Bryn Mawr College. She directed the summer school and she took a liking to me. She encouraged me. They were the most delightful weeks. If ever I learned about the world and its problems, I learned it there, because I was so ignorant of a good many things that were going on all over the world. They started with the English class, the grammar and all. We even looked at the sky, and learned something about the sky, and we learned about science and about animals and they'd tie it all up with dramatics. We'd have the nations all represented, especially because we students did come from all over. You could feel the vibration, the response to this wonderful opportunity that had been offered to us. It was a wonderful system.

In that short period of time you can imagine how much we had to absorb. Then we went to visit industries, too. We went to coal mines, and we actually saw people in various mining operations. During that period the Sacco and Vanzetti case was exploding in the air and in the conscience of the American people. I was very active in that because my brothers were carrying the torch for them in Rochester. Several people from Bryn Mawr got arrested in Philadelphia when we went to one of the rallies for them. My world kept getting bigger and bigger, and I was getting more and more excited. I was having skates on my feet and wings on my body. I wanted to fly where I heard of anything that was worthwhile.

Breaking Away

Carmen completed high school at the Rochester Business Institute. After her second session at the Bryn Mawr summer school in 1930, however, she decided not to go back to Rochester. Her family was too strict, and she was having disagreements at work. Feeling that the Italian workers were not being fairly treated by the union, she confronted union officers about this issue. The manager of the Rochester ACWA joint board disagreed with her position, and eventually, she said, "I just up and quit." Through a friend in the summer classes she met Louis Fuchs, president of the New York Neckwear Workers' Union, who was hiring organizers to unionize factories that were moving from New York City to small towns in other states where there were fewer union members. The unions would follow the factories to the new town. Carmen was hired by Fuchs and sent to Connecticut to organize a "runaway shop," a necktie factory from New York City that was hiring all Italian girls in New Haven.[5]

In 1930 I decided I had had enough of parental guidance. I loved mine—they were wonderful, but I felt Dad was a little bit too strict. I felt, oh, if I go back to Rochester from Bryn Mawr, I'll never be free, because an Italian girl leaving home was like becoming a prostitute in the eyes of the Italian community. I was to be married to Leo Kowski. He had been with the Amalgamated Clothing Workers as financial secretary, and he had quit and gone to New York. He happened to be a divorced man and my people were Catholics, which was one reason why I didn't want to go back home. I didn't like that kind of scandal.

I wrote my sister that I loved so much and said, "I'm sorry to leave you with this burden, but you have to break the fact to the family that I'm not returning. I'm going out to work on my own. And I'll try to send money home as often as I can." In those days they paid for union organizing work, but you could hardly call it money. In fact, while I was organizing for the Neckwear Workers' Union, I made less than I did sewing in the garment factory. But that want of change, that train, was still calling me; that eerie sound of the train was still in my ears. I was twenty-eight.

Then, there it was, a runaway shop. Fly-by-night shops they were called. People would wake up in some town and they'd find that there was a little factory that had moved in from New York or New Jersey, and that workers were needed in these factories. The union had an outside organizer by the name of Rose Sullivan, a beautiful Irish girl from Boston. She was from

the telephone workers' union, an officer from the AF of L organizing committee. She and I worked together. I said, "You know, I have an idea. You
let me go in and work, bore from within, so to speak. I'd be of much more
use to you on the inside so I can get acquainted with people and give you
names and addresses: give you all the information going on, and at the same
time build a cadre of people who would be really and truly interested in
building the union."[6]

For about a week, I kept going with my lunch in my hand and my scis-
sors and everything. I worked on the sewing machine. I learned how to make
ties. I was living with an Italian family who knew that I was a union organizer but never told it. I pretended I was an orphan. They used to call me
Little Orphan Annie. Here I had thirteen brothers and sisters and I was a
Little Orphan Annie. I could put on a very pathetic story. The girls all felt
sorry for me. I didn't have a mother, I didn't have a father, I didn't have
anybody. Nobody loved me. I'd shed a few tears sometimes. I think I should
have been an actress. I became very popular.

We got the majority of workers signed up for the union in no time. Then
finally they asked for union recognition. When the strike was called, I was
the one delegated to pull the power. In those days that was the way they
used to call a strike. They'd shut the electric power off and say, "Everybody out!" I'll never forget the day of the strike. It was in winter. Those days
in New Haven were bitterly cold! Right away we organized a soup kitchen.
The strike was very bitter and long, from the twelfth of February, Lincoln's
birthday, 1930, till the day before Thanksgiving.

We had arrests of all kinds. I was arrested, oh, any number of times
because I used to get the cops' goat. I learned later on to handle them differently. But then we used to berate them, "Brass buttons, blue coat, can't
catch a nanny goat." I was young, and you can imagine, the cops would
get so irritated, they could skin me! I was pretty quick on the trigger on
everything. I was arrested about ten times in one day alone, because as
soon as I was released, I'd go back on the picket line and I'd start all over.
"Can't keep me in, you know! The union will get me out!" Which was ridiculous, because it cost the union money. But I enjoyed it.

We had Yale University students who would come and help us in the
morning. We also established contact with the Divinity School in Yale. Rose
was wonderful for that sort of thing. She was the type of person that could
ingratiate herself with the rich women. I'd get the material for her, get the
little girls that should be interviewed. She would enlist the sympathy of the
wealthy women to the extent it would help. We had a little Italian girl who
looked like she had never had a square meal in her life. We used to use
her as our Exhibit A. She told her story so pathetically. All week making

ties and maybe earning five dollars. Those prominent women, some of the women, were really crying.

Then I was in charge of giving out the union strike benefits, seven dollars a week, five dollars a week. The money was running out. The shop got full of scabs, workers the boss hired to replace the strikers. With 350 workers out on strike, we had to give up. We didn't even have a break in the ranks of the people. I had the dirty job of telling the people that there's just no more strike benefits—sorry. We couldn't get the people who were on strike hired back. This was my first campaign where I was almost totally responsible. It broke my heart.

The Depression

During the Depression, the unemployment rate reached 25 percent and there were very few jobs. Carmen married Leo, but he became very ill. Like many other women during that time, Carmen had to look to the government, family, and friends for financial help. With the Roosevelt administration, however, came the National Recovery Act, and unions began to organize with some protection from the government. In 1932, the Neckwear Workers' Union needed Carmen to organize first in Philadelphia and then in Chicago.

I went back to New York. Oh, in the meantime, I was married. I was supposed to have been married any weekend. I'd say to him, "As soon as the strike is over, I'll come to New York and marry you." So the pickets got tired of hearing me say, "Well next weekend, I'm going to get married." One Friday afternoon they picked me up bodily and put me on a train! They decided that I ought to get married, that's all there was to it.

This was during the Depression and my husband got very, very ill, and was in the hospital. He had a tubercular kidney. I became pregnant and we didn't have a cent to our name. We had to register for some government relief money. I knew it would break my people's heart. The Italians were very proud in those days, and getting relief was the last thing. My family was wonderful. They kept coming to New York City from Rochester even though they didn't like the idea that I married Leo, because he was a divorced man. They'd leave some money in a drawer or something like that. They didn't want to embarrass me by giving me money.

By that time the bread lines were notoriously long. Oh, it was awful. Now this was already 1931. Our baby, Margie, was born in 1932. I had to stand in line, pregnant, big as I was, from eight o'clock in the morning until five o'clock at night to register for relief. I didn't make it the first day, so the next day I went a little bit earlier, and finally got registered. Hilda Smith heard that I still didn't have a way of taking care of myself, so she made arrangements through the hospital to have me taken care of free of charge, to have my baby.

I had to continue working, even though I had my baby, because my husband was very, very ill. He couldn't work, so he took care of the baby while I was gone. We had a general strike of the neckwear workers in Philadelphia in 1934. There was quite a number of them, and I was assigned to take care of the picket lines, going from one place to another where neckwear workers were striking. One morning there was a picket line of about two or three hundred people, and we were arrested because we had formed a daisy chain around the plant. Holding hands so they wouldn't let anybody in. They hurled us into patrol wagons and they filled up the jail with screaming girls and top-quality union sons. We were in there almost all day. They got so tired of us singing, flushing the toilets, rattling all kinds of things against the bars. We made it very, very tough for them.

I wanted to dramatize things and make it like theater, but also present the facts. For some strike activities we would always choose the prettiest girls, the most slender girls, because it was just like an advertisement. I'd hurriedly make dresses and have the girls in white dresses with red sashes. They always looked so striking. Now when I was at City Hall in Philadelphia, there's a curving stairway that goes up to another floor. As I watched at the bottom while the girls went up I thought what a beautiful picture that was, to see those young girls imbued with the spirit of doing something, really catching the spirit of democracy in action. We had moments like that on picket lines that I treasure so much.

From Philadelphia I was sent to Chicago. I had to go wherever the union sent me in spite of the fact that I had this little child. In Chicago, when I went on the picket line, the pickets were standing in a corner with their signs, but not picketing. I went over there and asked, "What's the matter? Why aren't you picketing?" They said, "That cop over there, he's a mean bastard." "Oh, come on," I said. "You have a legal right to picket, as long as you picket and you don't bother anybody, he can't do anything to hurt you." They said, "That's what you think." "All right," I said, "give me the sign and I'll go."

I thought, if I take the picket sign and chant union slogans they'll follow me. They didn't. They knew better than I did. When the scabs came out, now what could one woman do with a sign? There were police all over. They had formed a cordon for the scabs to come through. I thought, they're not going to keep me from going through there. I said, "Excuse me. I've got to picket." So I did that. I was foolish then. I put my hand on a woman and I said, "Listen, honey, I want to talk to you." I would never have attacked her.

As soon as my hand touched her shoulder, I don't know what happened. A ton of bricks fell on me. I was severely beaten by the cop. Taken into an alley. If I hadn't had a big fur collar on my coat, he'd have bashed my brains out. He was that mean, and he got mad when I defied him. What I found out was that the other union organizer had forgotten to pay the cops that day. In those days, you had to grease their palms in order for them to leave you alone. Especially in Chicago. So they really beat me. When I got to the police station, it was the first time that I really began to feel the pain. The cop had pulled my arm out of my socket. I was bleeding from several places. I was too angry to feel pain at the time, but when I cooled off a little bit, I found that I was hurt.

Finally the union found what police station I was in, and they came and got me to the hospital. The doctor yanked the arm to put it back in the socket. I've never forgotten that pain as long as I've lived. The girl whose arm I had laid the hand on felt very badly. She saw the beating I got. I understood that she went the next day and got the girls to go and join the union. She said, "Anybody that could be beaten up like that for the sake of trying to help us should be rewarded." The beating was worthwhile. We got the shop in the union.

Then I had an accident in Chicago. A Greyhound bus hit me. That was my fault. I didn't have a penny to come back to New York. The union dropped me and didn't pay me anything, but part of the Jewish labor movement, called the Workman's Circle, had heard about my accident. They'd always been my friends. They raised the money to pay my expenses back home. I began to think that I'd never go back to organizing again. I vowed to my father and my husband that I'd never have anything to do with the labor movement again.

Finding a Union Home

Jane Smith, from Bryn Mawr, found Carmen a job in a government workers' education program, but she left that job because the manager made passes at her. A vice president from ACWA asked her to help on an organizing drive in Troy, New York, but once again Carmen challenged the ACWA leadership because she thought they were not negotiating a satisfactory agreement for the women workers, and she was fired from that union staff job. Then a friend from the Cloth Hat and Cap Makers of North America suggested she meet their international president, Max Zaritsky, who was looking for organizers on the West Coast. Zaritsky liked the rebellious young woman and became her mentor and friend. For her daughter, he became Uncle Max. Carmen later said, "Bless his heart, I loved that man, he was a wonderful soul." When Carmen started, in 1934, the union merged with the United Hatters of North America and became the United Hatters, Cap and Millinery Workers International Union.[7]

This was 1934, because Margie was born in 1932. I didn't lose any time, because I had to work. When I heard California, it was far away but good, because that's what the doctor had ordered for my husband: sunshine, lots of sunshine. I thought this was a blessing. My husband was taking care of the baby. He was a very good person, a very fine person. So we talked it over, and he thought it was a good idea. I didn't know at the time that the union was supposed to move my family. They didn't. They never considered me the head of the family; never, even with a child. So I left New York on March 15, 1935. By the first of May, my husband and my baby arrived first in Los Angeles and then San Francisco.

A few months after we settled a strike in Los Angeles, I was sent to San Francisco. I couldn't do no wrong in that city. It's an old union town. No matter what I touched, it turned to gold. I had more luck. I was told to concentrate on millinery people. The people were of a different type and variety. They had a general strike in San Francisco in 1934, and they knew about unions. The milliners, I organized them. Ironically, I organized the men first. I couldn't get the girls at first. There were about eighteen millinery plants. It's very hard when they're small plants and you have to go from one place to another. It isn't like one large plant where one circular would do the trick, or one speech would do the trick. You've got to work that much harder. I was the only organizer from our union in San Francisco and in a short period of time, in six months, I had organized the four or five hundred milliners.

Then came the capmakers, and then came the men's hat industry. There was a consolidation of the two unions in 1934; the United Hatters and the Cap Makers' Union. In about six months, I was able to notify the union office in New York, that I had a majority in all of the shops. I could pull out the blockers who were the main workers in the shop. Key people. I could pull out the men, and then the girls couldn't work anyway without the men. I had enough girls. I had them all organized, so then I had time on my hands.

The Million Dollar Babies

In 1934, after two workers were killed by police on the San Francisco docks, a massive general strike paralyzed the city for four days. This well-publicized incident, followed by the Wagner Act and the rise of the CIO in the 1930s, led to successful union organizing campaigns in San Francisco. Before leaving the Bay Area, Carmen assisted in organizing eight cap manufacturing plants, brought two thousand members into the Department Store Workers Union, and organized thirty-seven stores for the Retail Clerks Association.[8] There were jurisdictional fights between the unions, but Carmen was more interested in organizing workers than in building any one union. She did not hesitate to take on powerful leaders like Harry Bridges, president of the International Longshoremen's and Warehousemen's Union, who, she said, "had it in for me because he wanted to have control of the Retail Clerks and I wouldn't let him; I put every obstacle in his path." By this time Carmen's husband was frustrated with his inability to work and her long hours spent in union organizing. He became dissatisfied with their marriage, and they soon divorced.

One day a young girl, Miriam Fromm, came to see me. She was with the five-and-ten-cent store girls. The warehousemen's union had been on strike and she wanted to respect the picket line, so she didn't go into work. She and several other girls were fired when the warehousemen settled their strike, which I thought was pretty bad. She said, "Well, you've been so successful, maybe you can help us. If you've got the time." Time is what I had. I said, "Sure, let's get a leaflet out and use the millinery workers' headquarters." I used to love to get leaflets out, and we did have a pretty nice hall in San Francisco. We called a meeting, and we had about fifty people the first time.

Let's get the big stores. Not only the five-and-tens, but let's go up to the big shots. We went after all of them: variety stores, and the big stores— the City of Paris, the I. Magnin, all these beautiful stores, even Gump's. We had 250, 300 people who signed up with the union out of all the stores. Lo and behold, the numbers kept mushrooming, mushrooming, mushrooming. Every time we'd call a meeting we'd double and double the number of people interested in joining a union. By September we were sufficiently strong to ask for union recognition. We settled without a strike with all the major department stores in the city.

Then Gump of the famous Gump's Department Store called me. He wanted to meet the young lady who had organized his clerks. It was like a command performance. To tell you the truth, when I went into that store I was aghast at the wealth. I was so chagrined when I looked at the chair where I was sitting down. It was sixteen thousand dollars! I'd never sat on such a plush place in all my life. Gump said, "Stand up, young lady, I want to see what you look like," just as though he was the king. I did. He started to tell me what type of people work in his place. They have to be educated. They have to know all the history of every antique that is there. They've got to know about the jade collection that is internationally known. They've got to be manicured and they've got to be this and they've got to be that.

Then he asked me the question, "How did you get my people?" "You just gave me the answer," I told him. "You want them to have all those facts, all that knowledge, and you don't pay for it. You pay the same as Sears Roebuck pays. Same wages. So why shouldn't they respond to the possibility of bettering their conditions?" And we got them into the union. We licked the employers real good.

But the variety stores, the five-and-ten-cent stores, were left out. The next day we started to work to organize workers in the five-and-tens. In a short period of time we were able to get workers in Chinatown to join the union. We had Chinese posters. Then I decided I would take the bull by the horns. There were only about four or five hundred workers in the five-and-tens. We were going to try to get a union shop there if we could. The open shop is always very difficult. You can't keep your members; the management replaces them, there's no way you can keep them in the union.

I got the warehousemen to respect the picket line. The girls voted for the strike and we called it and in four days we had them licked. The press called the young salesgirls the "million dollar babies from the five-and-ten-cent stores." I had the young women dressed up in white bathing suits with red ribbons around them. They'd bring their babies on their shoulders and everything. The leaflet said, "Take Our Mothers Off the Street. Little Children Like to Eat." We won. The next Wednesday, we had a meeting of Local 1100 of the Retail Clerks Union, which embraced all of the five-and-tens and the other stores.

While I was in San Francisco, I was having marital trouble. We didn't get along. Granted I was too busy making love to the union. He hadn't found a job yet. I had to continue to work. I thought by that time he'd get me out of the movement. But I always asked and he always came when the union moved me around the country. I included him in everything. There had been signs. He fell in love with a girl about twenty-five years his junior, a beautiful girl, and so I gave in. Once I thought, well, I can't blame him. In a way, he's broken-hearted about his life. He's been out of work for seven years and the illness and then the Depression; it was not his fault.

Texas over Twenty-eight Years

Texas was a different story from Carmen's experience organizing workers in San Francisco. Texas was extremely hostile to unions in the 1930s. Union activists and organizers faced opposition from the Chambers of Commerce, the Open Shop Associations, the police, and the Texas Rangers. Workers who wanted to organize unions had to meet secretly. Union organizers, including the United Auto Workers organizers at the Dallas-Ford plant, were severely beaten. For three decades Texas was Carmen's greatest challenge as an organizer, from 1937, when she led her first Texas strike, to 1965, when she signed her last Texas contract. Throughout these years, the issues were low wages, seasonal layoffs, and speed-ups. Carmen described the similarities and differences between anti-union activities in Texas in the 1930s and the 1960s: "We find very little change. Instead of blackjacks, they now use Taft-Hartley. Instead of brass knuckles, we now have the Landrum-Griffen bill. Instead of tar and feathers, they have given us the right-to-work laws."[9]

Zaritsky called me up, timely, right opportune. He said, "Our organizer was beaten up in Dallas, Texas." It was in 1936–37. "We need to get us a strike there and we need you very badly." I had never been in the South. At the Dallas-Ford plant company goon squads were beating up all the CIO people from the automobile workers' union who were trying to organize. The company brought in ex-convicts to beat up all the union people. They beat up the lawyers—they tarred and feathered them. So I went. What happened at our plants was that a good many of the men, they'd picket during the day and go scab at night. We didn't know that. Of course it killed the strike. There was wholesale blacklisting. The strikers couldn't get another job. All we could do was file complaints and charges with the labor board.

In 1939 there was the Resistol strike in Garland, Texas. Somebody came from the Resistol Hat Company and said that they wanted to be organized, and they notified the international union about it. Mr. Rolnick was the company owner. We got the sanction from the international union for a strike, but the workers were ill prepared for it. You see, in organization work, it's very important while you're doing the organizing work to prepare the workers for the eventuality of a strike and what it would mean. Point out all the hazards and the risks that they take, and then they're prepared for it. Well, of course, I didn't have time to do that. The union had sent me to organize in Illinois and then called me back to Texas to help organize workers at Resistol. I arrived there the day before the strike.

On the picket line I never lose my temper. I could be the sweetest person to someone because I always feel that someday I'm going to have to talk to that person, even the scabs. I hate scabs like poison and it was an effort to be nice to them, but I made it a point to be nice. But we lost the strike. There were labor board cases. We got some people reinstated, but the town was against us.

Twenty-five years later we organized this company. In 1958 I came back to Texas to organize these workers. The same Mr. Rolnick was moving another of his plants from the East to Texas. One day I was traveling through Texas for my work and I stopped in this little town because there was an antique shop and I was crazy about antiques. While I was there, I saw the local paper. It said "Baer Rolnick to Locate Here," as if this article were written especially for me. About six months later the Rolnick shop in Longview, Texas, was full of workers, and we started a little organizing. And we had luck; we had luck.

Our method of campaigning, home-to-home visits, takes a long time, but I think it's worthwhile getting a nucleus of union supporters inside the shop that is so convinced that they want to help. Home-to-home visiting is very tiresome, but we used to see two, three, or four people in a night, depending on how much we had to work to get them to sign a union card. I always used to go out and do organization work in the evening. I'd go to cities where there were all kinds of beautiful things to see, and I never saw them. I never took time to go and see them. What free time!

We also found out that signing union cards was not enough. The real test is when the union election is held. Because the moment the election is announced by the labor board is when the employer really begins to turn the heat on, makes speeches and what have you, switches people around, makes a good many of the foremen and floor ladies regular workers so that they could vote against the union.

We had perfected the use of the union label to be able to use it against the employers without breaking the law. In other words, we were picketing not the stores themselves but the product, which was permissible at the time. I don't think that ACWA or the ILG unions have been able to perfect this kind of campaign to the extent that we did in the hatters' union. They tried it at a number of places, and they didn't succeed, but that's how we finally got Texas. The union label did it. That's how we kept the union issue alive.

Well, we won that Resistol election by a substantial majority. The company went to the labor board and challenged the election. The board ruled them out. This takes years, you know. I'm saying it in two minutes, but it takes years. Finally they ruled. In the meantime, while we were waiting for the decision from the labor board, we went back to the original Resistol shop and got his workers in Garland, Texas. The first strike was over, and the other two elections we won through the labor board, leafleting and continuing to visit workers in their homes. So, of course, we got a pretty good union contract.

Atlanta and the South

By 1944, 70 percent of the men's hat workers, 80 percent of millinery workers, and 90 percent of the cap workers in the United States were organized. In 1946 the CIO and the AFL began to focus on organizing the South. Zaritsky moved Carmen from Texas to organizing campaigns in Illinois, Georgia, Connecticut, and finally gave her a home base in Atlanta, Georgia, to supervise the union's southern organizing drive. She chaired the organizing committee of the Georgia Federation of Labor and was appointed to the AFL Southern Policy Committee. Although Carmen continued to face danger and violence on the picket line and continued to travel all across the South, in Atlanta home life for her daughter was more stable.[10]

In 1940, I was in Chicago when I got a call from Zaritsky that I was needed in Atlanta, Georgia. It'd be a question of a few weeks, he said. Well, nobody else from the union organizers wanted to go south. I was the only damn fool that wanted to go. All of them had a base of operation. I didn't have a base of operation. I never had a local with strength, with members behind me. I'd go from one place to another.

My little girl was not quite seven when I left San Francisco. It was a problem because every time that I was moved, the child rebelled. She had an awful childhood. The union officers never would let me go home. They said that I didn't have a husband. I had a child, but the child didn't count. I wanted to be in one place so that at least I could call home, even if I wasn't there. My daughter was being moved all the time, the poor child. Finally, from 1944 to 1960, I was operating out of the Atlanta office, going to all these other places. I kept going back and forth to Greenville, Alabama, to Corsicana, Texas, to Richmond, Virginia, to Winchester, Tennessee, but always back to the Atlanta office.

I lived in Atlanta a little more lavishly, but it was not from the pay I got from the union. It's because I befriended a woman who was a very lonely person and when she died, she left me her property. That was the first time I began to breathe easier, with some degree of giving my daughter Margie more than she had before. I wanted to send her to a school where I wouldn't have to worry about her, a boarding school. She went to high school for four years in Atlanta, years which helped a whole lot. Then she went to college.

When I went to Atlanta I was shocked. I had never had any dealings with black people. They were a mystery to me. Actually, they didn't even exist for me. That's the trouble. We didn't take pains to find out what was happening to them. I began to change. What do you expect of people who for two hundred years had been treated like slaves? I began to change and try to understand. I began to work with them and found that they were just fighting for their rights.

I became a chairman of the organizing committee in Atlanta for the labor council. When I brought the workers into the labor temple building, the Negro women told me that they couldn't use the ladies' room. I said to the central labor body, "If you want me to do organization work in this city, you better furnish me with another labor temple if you don't want these Negro people in this labor temple. Otherwise, they're going to use the fountains and they're going to use the restrooms."

In 1963, at the M & B plant of about four hundred workers, 90 percent of them were black. We went to see the NAACP. Scabs were going in, and our boys started being a little rough. We got an injunction served on us. Luckily we had a judge who was very sympathetic. When their lawyer was trying to tell him that I was very radical and that I had been to the NAACP, he says, "Well what's wrong with her going to anybody to appeal for help? After all, she's representing black people." But we couldn't get to first base with this company.

In a small town where workers and employers have to live together, there's all kinds of fears. But the fear of being fired, the worst I saw was in Greenville, Alabama. Because the man who ran the factory for the Hat Corporation of America owned the whole town. He was head of the bank; the department store was his; the judge in the courthouse was his cousin. They were all related. So they held the town in the palm of their hands. The workers were all white; no blacks allowed.

The southern girls were the backbone of almost every strike. I mean almost every campaign I conducted it was always the women that responded more readily than the men. Mostly in the South, because I think that first of all, a woman is forced to think in terms of expenses and taking care of the house and everything else. So many of these women—their husbands were nowhere to be seen. They really had the responsibility. In Texas it was even worse. They didn't even know where their husbands were half the time. But they were lovely people, very warm-hearted people, even the scabs.

They were very poor people. I never saw such abject poverty as I saw in the South. Some of their houses were on stilts, or on a block of wood or cement maybe. It does get cold, in spite of what people say. In those days, they used to have pot-bellied stoves in one room. If you'd sit near the stove in order to keep warm, you'd burn up; if you'd go away from it, you'd freeze. They didn't even have curtains on their windows. They didn't have any rugs. You could see the dirt through the cracks in the wood. They'd stuff the windows with paper to keep the drafts from coming in. When it came to unemployment insurance, the employer put obstacles to getting their benefits in their path. Two hat workers, Willie and his wife—she was a wonderful person—they didn't even have spoons and forks to eat with.

And oh, the children. The teachers were so mean and cruel that they would punish the children of the parents who belonged to the union. They would hold them back. They would keep them after school. They would scorn the children.

Once on the way into Greenville, Alabama, I saw a truck stopped on the highway. As I slowed down, two men got out with guns and they said, "If you're going to Greenville, Alabama, we have to tell you we'll give you twenty-four hours to get out of town." I got in the car and continued right on to Greenville. Willie hurriedly called a meeting of the people in his home. He said, "We got to get Miss Lucia out of town. Her life is in danger." In the middle of the night they escorted me out of town. That's the last we saw of the company, because it closed its doors. They overexpanded during the war. It had nothing to do with the union, but we got blamed for it.

Women in Unions

Carmen continued her strong commitment to labor education, particularly for women workers. She served as a vice president of the National YWCA, as a member of the League of Women Voters, and on the boards of the Affiliated Schools for Workers and the Bryn Mawr Summer School for Women Workers. Although she initially opposed the Equal Rights Amendment in 1944 as anti-union, she later changed her position to support, and ERA was endorsed by the hatters' union convention in 1960.[11] In 1950 she traveled to France as part of a labor delegation, the first union woman to be included in these teams from the Department of State's Economic Cooperation Administration under the Marshall Plan.[12]

In the *Atlanta Journal* in 1947, however, Carmen said, "The time has now arrived when there must be more effort and emphasis placed on the development of woman leadership. Their talents must be given greater recognition."[13] Carmen demonstrated a lifelong loyalty to the labor movement and had many opportunities for development in her union, but she was also aware of differences between women and men. She "resented the way the [labor] movement treated women. I would train men who didn't even know what was going on and they would make twice as much. I would raise Cain about equal pay for equal work, which didn't endear me to the union leadership."[14]

In the late fifties I was in Holyoke, Massachusetts. The day I was to leave, Alex Rose, who was now the president of the union, called me up and said, "I want you to take the plane this afternoon and go to Milwaukee." I said, "I'm not going to go to Milwaukee. I haven't been home in seven months. The boys go home every weekend." They all lived around there: Boston and so forth. "I've been stuck here for seven months with this strike, working seven days a week. I'm not going!" "Well, I've decided that you're going." "You may have decided, but you can't make me go."

He says, "Well, what are you vice president of this union for?" I said, "It doesn't mean a damn thing to me. You don't pay me a vice president's wages. If it's the vice president that has to do the work, get your New York vice presidents to get off their fannies and get them to do some work!" I was so mad I hung up on him. I went home to Atlanta. It was July and I didn't hear from them until September. I was worried. I was getting paid, I don't know why I was worried, but I wasn't enjoying it. He finally called me to say I was wanted.

By 1965 there had been a change in our office here in the international union. They didn't have much money and they had to cut the union staff, but they didn't want to lose me. I was going to retire in 1965. Al Smoke, the secretary-treasurer of the union, respected my work and appreciated me a lot. He was very nice. He said, "We can't afford to lose you entirely. Couldn't you work part-time?" I said, "Well, if you don't want to lose me, pay me what you pay the men, and I'll stay on a few more years." "No, we're not." Then I said I'd work for nothing, which was stupid. I was so proud, that if I couldn't get a man's wage I'd work for nothing. I worked from 1967 to 1974 for a hundred and forty dollars a month. I look back and I think, "I'm just a damn fool."

But I gave 'em hell at my last union convention. I gave them an ERA speech they'll never forget. I got the biggest round of applause. I said to the union girls who were at the convention, "Look, I'm on my way out. I'm trying to do this for your sake, not mine. Not for your sake, but for all the women in the industry. For heaven sakes, follow it up. Don't let go of it."

The Hat Lady

Max Zaritsky retired as union president in 1950. Alex Rose, the new president, continued to develop more cooperative arrangements to help shore up the declining hat industry. The union initiated advertising campaigns to promote wearing hats, made loans to manufacturers, and in some cases purchased companies about to go bankrupt. But the UHCMW membership declined from a high of forty thousand in 1944 to fifteen thousand by 1974. Machines replaced workers, foreign imports increased dramatically, and fashions changed. To be well dressed, Carmen recalled, a woman no longer needed fourteen hats, "seven for the cold season and seven for the warm."[15]

Carmen remained a valued organizer, but the constant travel, her increasingly poor health, and new approaches to labor relations in a steadily declining industry all took their toll. In 1974, at age seventy-two, she resigned. Although Carmen had many disagreements with Alex Rose, at her retirement dinner he recounted her numerous organizing campaigns and union victories: "She never flinched from the most dangerous mission, but pressed forward, sought out the oppressed and disadvantaged workers, and brought them encouragement and hope for a better day." Secretary-Treasurer Alfred Smoke related her special skills as an organizer and "her talent for inculcating warmth and trust for the union among insecure workers." He reported that her latest campaign, the NLRB election in the M & B plant in Richmond, Virginia, resulted in a victory for the union of almost 3 to 1.[16]

After her retirement, Carmen lived with her daughter and four grandchildren in Connecticut. Her daughter had married in 1951, and in Carmen's words, "She's grown into a magnificent mother, a wonderful wife, and quite intelligent and interested in worthwhile causes. I'm very proud of the fact that what little help I gave her must have been of some help or other." Carmen continued to write poetry and kept up with current events. In 1980, with her health failing, she returned to Rochester, New York, where several of her thirteen brothers and sisters were still living. In 1984 she attended a reunion of the Bryn Mawr Summer School and participated in the filming of *The Women of Summer.*[17] The film is shown every year at St. Anne's Nursing Home, where Carmen lived until her death in 1985 and where several of her sisters still live.

Carmen was known to many as the "Hat Lady," because she always wore a hat in public to promote the industry and the union and because she loved hats.

She helped the mayor of Atlanta organize a "Hat Day" to help boost the industry. She was a fiery speaker who also wrote poetry and articles for her union's newspaper. She got local unions involved in humanitarian activities and labor education. Indeed, she wore many hats, "as a mother, a labor organizer, a rebel, a union official, a humanitarian, and a poet."[18] At the time she retired, Carmen was frustrated with the union bureaucracy and the leadership, as she had been for much of her union career. She retained great faith in the workers, however, and the importance of organizing unions to improve people's lives. In her 1976 interview she reflected on her life.

I did have a reputation. The employers were afraid of me. I don't know why, but my name used to strike terror. I didn't mean it that way, but that's what used to actually happen. People that don't have a definite point of view go with the wind. They change so quickly. That doesn't mean that you can't sometimes change for the better. But some people changed from one day to another depending on who was speaking or who was leading or whatever was a more favorable position to take. I have never been that way. The union knew who to call when they wanted the job done.

Years ago, Harry Bridges thought I wanted to take over the Retail Clerks Union, but I had no such aspiration. I never wanted that kind of top job, and I'll tell you why: I was afraid I'd lose my contact with the people and I'd become greedy. I'd become totally unaware of the workers' problems. I saw too much of that going on when they got jobs that went to their heads. They weren't the same people, and I didn't want to become one of them.

I was called upon by a lot of universities to speak. I remember one time I was introduced and the chairman said, "We have three speakers: a lady, a gentleman, and a woman organizer." I turned that into a joke and I had everybody laughing. Yes, I'm still an organizer!

Chapter 4

You Can't Giddyup by Saying Whoa

Esther Peterson, Amalgamated Clothing Workers of America (1906–)

In 1993 President Bill Clinton named Esther Peterson as a delegate to the United Nations General Assembly. Internationally known for her advocacy on behalf of women, working people, consumers, and the elderly, she has also served in the administrations of John F. Kennedy, Lyndon Johnson, and Jimmy Carter. In 1981 she received the Presidential Medal of Freedom, the United States' highest civilian award.

Esther's accomplishments over the last thirty years have built on her earlier experiences in the labor movement. With support from her husband and while raising four children, she worked for thirty years as a union organizer, labor educator, and lobbyist. Born in 1906 and raised in a Mormon household in Utah, she received degrees from Brigham Young and Columbia universities. In 1930 she became a teacher in Boston; volunteered her time with several unions, the YWCA, and the Bryn Mawr Summer School for Women Workers; and then became an organizer for the American Federation of Teachers.

In 1939 Esther joined the education department of the Amalgamated Clothing Workers of America and was the union's first legislative representative in Washington, D.C. She became the first woman labor lobbyist for the AFL-CIO in 1958. An early supporter of President Kennedy, she was appointed by him as assistant secretary of labor and director of the U.S. Women's Bureau in 1961. She served as executive vice chairman of the President's Commission on the Status of Women and was a driving force behind passage of the 1963 Equal Pay Act.

In the Johnson administration, Esther began a new career as an advocate for consumers and the elderly that led to work with private industry and advocacy organizations both at home and abroad. She maintained ties to organized labor, however, and remains at heart "a long-time union member and one who will always have the interest of the workers at heart."[1]

Growing Up in Utah

Born in Provo, Utah, in 1906, the descendant of Danish pioneer immigrants, Esther Eggertsen was the fifth of six children raised in a Mormon household. Her father was superintendent of schools for Utah and ran the family farm while her mother raised the children and helped support the family by taking in boarders. Esther recalls working alongside her parents on their farm as she grew up, picking fruit to help earn money for college. Some of her fondest memories are of her family sitting around the dining room table, putting up fruit or making rugs, while their father read aloud from the classics: Balzac, Thoreau, the Greek philosophers. Her parents instilled in her the importance of thinking and speaking one's mind. Esther received her bachelor's degree from Brigham Young University in 1927, majoring in physical education, and then taught recreation for several years at Branch Agricultural College in Cedar City.

My first trade union experience was when I was in the eighth grade or so, in 1918, during the big railroad strike in Utah. Representatives of the railroad company came to Brigham Young University, right next to our house, and recruited strikebreakers. They recruited some of the students who boarded at our house. We were one of the few families then to have a little car, a Dodge touring car, and we were asked to drive these students, the strikebreakers, up to the strike. I remember going along for the ride.

I shall never forget seeing all the confusion, and all the people milling around, and horses, and their opening the way for us to get the car through the picket line. The car had to stop a minute and I saw a woman, standing there with two little children clinging to her. She looked at me and said, "Why are you doing this to us?" It has haunted me to this day. If I were an artist, I could still draw it. It reminded me later of some of the Käthe Kollwitz drawings of strong faces.[2] And it hurt me. I can remember feeling something was wrong; I knew something was wrong. I wouldn't go back to the strike; I just wouldn't cross that picket line again.

During my college education at Brigham Young University in Utah, these issues never concerned me. We never studied about labor, and I had no idea what was going on in our Utah coal mines and copper mines and that the immigrants who were brought in to work there were treated rather badly during that period. I didn't know about that until I came back to Utah after I got my master's degree from Columbia University and began to talk to some of the people and found out what the situation was during those days.

But I do think that early 1918 strike experience had a lot to do with what directions I later took.

Moving East

Esther received her master's degree in 1930, from Teachers' College, Columbia University, in New York City. There she met her future husband, Oliver Peterson, then a graduate student, at a Sunday afternoon discussion group. Oliver went on to get his M.A. at Harvard, teach at a school for workers in Chicopee, Massachusetts, and work for the Federal Emergency Relief Administration (FERA), part of the New Deal effort to provide help for the unemployed during the Depression.[3]

Oliver is the one who really changed my life tremendously. He took me to hear Sidney Hillman down at Cooper Union in New York City. He took me around to the slums. He took me to the factories. Oliver was studying sociology at Columbia University and working at the YMCA in Brooklyn.

He came from a Norwegian background and had had a rough, tough life. His father died from tuberculosis when Oliver was little and left his mother with five young children on a farm in North Dakota. Oliver helped run the farm and worked nights pressing pants. He was active in the Farmer Labor Party and had joined the Socialist Party in the early years. I learned from him what farming was like. "Were you ever hungry?" I asked him. "Oh, we skipped a few meals." I'll never forget that phrase, "We skipped a few meals."

He opened up a whole new direction for me. My family was very liberal as far as religion. We always had to defend our positions. I was on the debating team and active in many causes when I was in school. So I had a little seed. But it took someone like Oliver to really turn me to the labor movement.

The Heartbreaker Strike

After receiving her master's, Esther held a job in Boston for six years as a physical education teacher for the private Winsor School for Girls. At Oliver's suggestion she volunteered to teach night classes at the Boston YWCA industrial department, a program similar to those in Chicago and Rochester described by Lillian Herstein and Carmen Lucia in Chapters 2 and 3. The students were young women

Esther Peterson (*first on right*) at the Utah Hotel, Salt Lake City, where the Mode O'Day clothing company signed a contract with the International Ladies' Garment Workers' Union, August 12, 1941. Joining the celebration was Rose Pesotta (front row, second from left), an ILGWU vice president who recruited Esther to work on the organizing campaign. *Rose Pesotta Papers, Manuscript Division, New York Public Library.*

who worked as domestics in private homes and as factory workers in the garment industry. Esther learned from them about strikes and industrial homework, a system in which entire families worked at night in crowded tenements to make ends meet.[4] In 1932 she married Oliver; their first child, Karen, was born in 1938, followed by Eric in 1939. During this period she juggled teaching and union assignments.

When I went to teach at Winsor, I also got deeply involved in the labor movement. In our family we were raised to do something in addition to our usual activities—to always give of yourself. Oliver said, "Do something new, Esther. Branch out a little." I volunteered at the YWCA in Boston and was assigned to the Industrial Department. Those were the days when the Y was extremely liberal. They had programs to help "poor working girls." That was the first time I had first-hand experience with industrial workers.

The girls didn't come to class one Thursday night because they said they were on strike. I remember Oliver said, "Go find out why," and I did. It was the first time that I had seen the tenements of Cambridge. That was the first time that I had ever seen industrial homework. I'll never forget as long as I live seeing all these people working around a table in their apartments, making hang tags for Filene's Department Store. Oh! This whole family could make a living only if everybody worked, including the very young children.

The girls in the family who were also factory workers had gone on strike, and the family was upset because that meant they wouldn't be bringing in their money to contribute to the family. I got acquainted with quite a few of these working families. I loved these strong families. They were so much stronger than the families of the privileged girls who I met during the day. The contrast to me was really startling.

The girls told me that they went on strike because they were making Hoover dresses. They were getting $1.32 for making a dozen dresses. Their pay envelopes, which I remember so well, held from $4.50 to $5.00; the highest I ever saw was $7.00 for a week's work. This was during the 1930s Depression, before the National Industrial Recovery Act or the Fair Labor Standards Act. Every dollar meant something. The girls said the strike was spontaneous because the factory owners had changed the pattern of the dress—changed the pocket from a square to a heart. The heart—the sewers couldn't make as many in an hour, because they had to sew around the curves of the pocket. So we helped, and we named it the Heartbreaker Strike.

I wanted to help them. I was just furious at what those kids were going through. I went out and picketed with them in the mornings. I went down one morning and saw policemen drive their horses up against these women. Just the same memory of the experience I had earlier in Utah. I went to Miss Lord, the director of the school where I taught. She said, "We hired you to teach, and you're a good teacher. What you do in your private life is your own business, as long as it doesn't interfere with your teaching." She supported me. I helped organize a citizens' committee. We made speeches to women's groups in that whole area. I learned how to activate people and we won. We organized a union. We helped get that first union started there in Boston in the garment industry.

Teaching at the Bryn Mawr Summer School

In 1932 Esther met Hilda "Jane" Smith, who had come to Boston to talk about and raise money for the Bryn Mawr Summer School for Women Workers in Industry where Lillian Herstein had taught and Carmen Lucia had been a student. In addition to programs like the YWCA Industrial Department and the National Consumers' League, many unions such as the Amalgamated Clothing Workers of America, the International Ladies' Garment Workers' Union, and the Textile Workers Union of America helped recruit women workers for these residential summer programs. Esther served as recreation director, developing plays, pageants, choral groups and field trips. She also sat in on classes taught by other instructors, who came from union staffs as well as from the faculties of the nearby colleges. Through the school and her union work she met Fannia Cohn of the ILGWU and Rose Schneiderman from the WTUL. She became active in FDR's reelection campaign and met Eleanor Roosevelt.[5]

Hilda Smith had come to the Winsor School to talk about the Bryn Mawr Summer School for Women Workers in Industry. She was there to raise money. That was another big change in my life. I saw this woman and I thought, that's the way I want to be. I remember I had my gym suit on, because I was a gym teacher, and I went up to her after she spoke and asked to talk with her. She offered me a job as recreation director at the Bryn Mawr Summer School for Women Workers. Oliver was to be librarian. I worked there summers from 1932 to 1937.

These summer schools for women workers gave the women techniques of speaking and organizing. It gave them an understanding of the labor movement. This was a training ground for these women to develop leadership. We had mock meetings, for example. They said that they would never dare to stand up at union meetings in front of all the men. But we helped them and taught them how. We put on plays. We now call it role playing. They'd take parts. They took the parts of the boss, the workers, the citizens. The whole point was to be practical . . . where you are now, not some theoretical event down the pike.

It was interesting to me, this tremendously strong democratic process that Hilda Smith insisted on: the faculty having a say and the students having a say. You really have to begin to have faith and trust in people. It was a great experience for the young women to think they had a say in shaping the school's policies. I think it was rough, but it worked. The Bryn

Esther Peterson (*holding poster*) helped register union women to vote in the 1944 election. Sidney Hillman sent her to her home state of Utah to help reelect President Franklin D. Roosevelt and U.S. Senator Elbert Thomas, a strong supporter of organized labor. *Schlesinger Library, Radcliffe College.*

Mawr Summer School had a very great impact because we were really experimental in method. I'll never forget sitting down with Jane and having her explain that what we needed to do was to have the students see the whole world and where they fit into it. We didn't have textbooks. It was the girls' experiences that were our textbooks. We'd just ask, "What was it like when the boss said those things?" We acted out whole events. The program was built out of their lives, and it began with who they were and where they were.

I think that is a lesson I learned that helped me all through my life. If I am studying unemployment, I go to the unemployment office and talk to the people. You must have a user concept. You don't start way up at the top and come down. I learned that at the Bryn Mawr Summer School for Women Workers.

I didn't think of the Bryn Mawr Summer School for Working Women as "feminist." We didn't think in those terms in those days. I didn't, anyway. But I remember the woman's focus. I just thought of them as strong women. I know you've heard this song; I think it's one of the first working girls' liberation songs. I helped write the music, and I'm told that Fannia Cohn of the ILGWU wrote the words. I worked so hard on it:

In the black of winter in 1909,
When we fought and bled on the picket line;
We showed the world that women could fight,
And we rose and won with women's might.
Hail the Waistmakers of 1909,
Taking a stand on the picket line,
Breaking the power of those who reign,
Pointing the way, smashing the chain,
And we gave new courage to the men
Who carried on in 1910
And shoulder to shoulder,
We will win through the ILGWU.

I first met Mrs. Roosevelt on one of the campaigns with Rose Schneiderman from the Women's Trade Union League. In those days, we had radio, but we didn't have television, and we had street corner meetings. One of my jobs was to go and get a group going at a street corner and sing and harangue, and then we would all crowd around and the others would come in for the union like Bessie Hillman and Frances Perkins and Eleanor Roosevelt. We were all women who were working for the Roosevelt election. I did a lot of leading singing in those days.

At that time the women from the Hudson Shore Labor School, formerly at Bryn Mawr, were going over to Val Kil, Mrs. Roosevelt's summer cottage, for a Sunday picnic. The night before, Mrs. Roosevelt was in Chicago giving the acceptance speech for FDR. We were sitting around the room and the girls started crying, and they said, "She won't be there tomorrow. We won't get to see her." I said, "You know Mrs. Roosevelt. If she said she'll be here, she will." But they couldn't believe it.

Well, they were all worried about what they were going to wear. They very busily ironed and borrowed white blouses from each other and ironed their best dresses, their Sunday best, and they go over to Val Kil. And there is Eleanor. She greeted us in a wet bathing suit. She said, "I thought I invited you to a picnic." She found bathing suits for everybody and she served hot dogs.

Personally, along with other experiences of the period, teaching and being at the Bryn Mawr Summer School changed my life completely. It gave me a whole new direction. I left my old profession completely and wanted to throw my lot with the labor movement. Here I was out of college, graduated with honors, and I didn't know a thing about the labor movement. I just didn't understand the world. I became converted to the labor movement at that time as the avenue for accomplishing the things I believed in.

Organizing

Bitter labor struggles, triggered in the 1920s by the textile mills and garment factories moving south in search of cheap nonunion labor, continued during the Depression. "In 1925, there were more spindles in the Southern mills than in New England."[6] Union membership thrived, increasing from 17 percent of the labor force in 1929 to 34 percent by 1934. During the 1930s in Boston, Esther increasingly took part in organizing activities. She volunteered her time with the ILGWU and the Textile Workers Organizing Committee. In 1938, she took a union job in the area she knew best—teaching. She became an organizer for the American Federation of Teachers in New England.

I often helped out the ILGWU before we moved to New York City. I did some teaching for them in New England in their workers' education programs. I also helped with the Textile Workers Organizing Committee, especially with the organizing and the sit-down strikes of textile workers. I used to stand outside the factories and lead singing during the textile sit-down strikes. It was marvelous standing there with the people hanging out of the factory windows, singing along. I always worked through the central labor unions. Bob Watt, who was secretary-treasurer of the Massachusetts State Federation of Labor, was very helpful to me. He took me around to all the factories and to the strikes. I did a lot of organizing in those days, and it was a very exciting time for me.

I really got excited about the labor movement and felt that I should put my lot with it. Since I was a teacher, and I had joined Local 189, the workers' education local that was organized in the mid-1920s, I thought I should organize teachers. So I started to work for the American Federation of Teachers in the New England area. I was paid by some Harvard professors who were the radicals of those days: Ray Walsh, Alan Sweezy, and Bob Lamb and these great names of people who were kicked out of Harvard later on. They pooled money that they got for tutoring students and paid me. I worked under their direction. I did a good job and I had some tough experiences.

First I went to Lawrence, the textile town. The taxi driver, taking me from the bus station to the hotel, told me about a big meeting of teachers that night, who were really "up in arms" about pay cuts. I went to the meeting and got a feel for what their grievances were. After the meeting, I went right to the Central Labor Council and told them who I was and why I was there. They telephoned some of the teachers who were at the meeting, who came right over. I got the Central Labor Council to cooperate with them. That was the first teachers' local union I organized.

I also organized in Springfield, Massachusetts, and in Bennington, Vermont. In Springfield, there was a nasty article about me on the front page of the daily newspaper. The day after the article, I went right to the top, to the superintendent of schools, and said, "I'm here to organize your teachers. I'm not going in the back door. My father was superintendent of schools in Provo, Utah, and he's been superintendent of schools for the state of Utah." The Springfield superintendent was flabbergasted. "What the hell are you doing here?"

"I'm a former teacher at the Winsor School in Boston, and I believe in this deeply," I said. I decided I'd do it all in the open, absolutely open, after that article in the newspaper. The resentment was really terrible in Springfield, but we got a teachers' local union started there, and then in Bennington, where it wasn't as hard. I really organized three teachers' union locals. I thought it was terrible not to do more, but looking back, it was really good.

Union Staff

In 1939 the Petersons moved to New York. Oliver was working for the U.S. Office of Price Administration, "on sugar rationing and things like that," and Esther became the assistant director of the Department of Cultural Activities (later renamed the Department of Education) of the Amalgamated Clothing Workers of America–CIO. The ACWA membership was growing and J.B.S. Hardman, longtime educational director, was developing the education department to train these new workers in the basics of trade unionism.[7] Esther was teaching classes, administering cultural conferences, starting a union chorus, and running field trips. Some of these activities, she recalls, were similar to the summer programs at Bryn Mawr, and she often used the techniques developed during those years.

I met Jacob Potofsky, who was then vice president of the Amalgamated Clothing Workers, through his daughter Delia, who was an undergraduate student at Bryn Mawr College during the years I worked as recreation director for the working women's summer school. She said, "Look, Pop, the union needs Esther." That's how I came to work for the ACWA when we moved to New York City. I was the assistant director for the ACWA's national education department, working with J.B.S. Hardman, who was a great influence on my life.

I did a lot of education work, teaching classes, running conferences, bringing the union contract and reading it to the workers to let them know their rights. We did a lot of cultural conferences in those days, because Hardman believed that education was a part of culture. I organized a chorus. We took the members to museums. We put on a play, "America, You Called Us to Your Shores," where we analyzed why members' families had come to the United States from different countries, for jobs, for religious reasons. It was very good, very effective. Hardman loved it. I also did a lot of organizing for the ACWA and the ILGWU.

I went over as education director in New Jersey when there was a runaway shop. I had a little difficulty then because some of the Italians that were in the Amalgamated were dealing a little too cozily with some of the racketeers. I got scolded for telling people to stand up to them. I brought their union contract and read them their rights. Which is what I would do again. But Hillman defended me. I went to Louis Hollander, the union vice president, and he sat there behind his newspaper. He knew he had to see me. I just sat down. "Well, what do you want?" I said, "I want to talk to you, not to your newspaper. I won't talk until you look me in the eye and I know you're listening to me. If you can't do it today, I'll come back sometime." "Okay. I'll hear you." I said, "Louis, now listen to me. Just come on. I want to know: do you want this program or not—you told me you wanted the program. Here's what it means."

After that he admired me. He said, "Well, this gal's got guts. I like that." I decided you just must not shrink from tough encounters. That toughened me. I had the security of a husband and a family and that's always given me a little bit more courage to stand up. But that toughened me. It's hard sometimes, trying to stand up for the things you believe in. It's been extremely good for me, helped me no end, to learn to deal with tough labor leaders.

There were other women on the staff. Eldon Lamar was assistant editor of the paper and Gladys Dickerson was director of research and then Bessie Hillman was on the executive board. They were wonderful. There were a lot of good women. I was concerned that there were all these men on the executive board except for Bessie. I remember raising that issue a great deal. It was ridiculous, because women were the largest part of the union. They were the backbone of the union and did all of the work. But all the unions were dominated by men. That's not only the story of the unions, it's the story of society. It was a man's world.

I was not as aware of all these issues back then. I lived a rather narrow life of my own. We did talk about women on the union executive board, but not a great deal. Edith Christianson was one of our very good organizers and we tried to organize ourselves, the staff. Hillman didn't like it. We said to Hillman, "Aren't we workers?" and he said, "No, we are working for the workers." Our staff union was squashed. You couldn't change Hillman's mind on things. He was so ego-strong. He was not easy to work with.

Back Home In Utah

In 1941, the ILGWU organizer and vice president Rose Pesotta suggested to the ILGWU president, David Dubinsky, that Esther Peterson be hired to help organize the Mode O'Day clothing factory in Salt Lake City, Utah. Pesotta, who had met Esther at the Bryn Mawr Summer School for Women Workers, was organizing the Mode O'Day plant in Los Angeles. The plant made low-priced cotton dresses for three hundred retail outlets in twenty states and in Hawaii. It was crucial to organize the nonunion Salt Lake City plant to prevent the firm from diverting orders from Los Angeles to Salt Lake City in case of a strike.[8] Esther spent the summer of 1941 in Salt Lake City, working closely with Rose Pesotta, who flew in periodically from California. The successful campaign culminated in the signing of a union contract with the ILGWU on August 23. Esther and her children stayed with her mother in Provo, and she commuted the forty miles to Salt Lake City. She returned to New York and the Amalgamated in the fall.

After we moved to New York City, the ILGWU president, David Dubinsky, called me. "Ess-tair, Ess-tair, I need a Mormon." There'd been some runaway shops from Los Angeles to Utah, and that is my home state. Part of it was that I was non-Jewish and had no accent. In unions like the ILGWU and the ACWA, it was important to have someone like me. I'm sure that it was also because I had an education. But I never exploited any of that. I would never take out a union card in either the ILGWU or the ACWA because I felt that it's not right for me, when I haven't worked in a factory. I always felt that I was staff and I was working for the union members. It's been a principle that I've felt was very important in my life.

Organizing in Salt Lake City wasn't easy. I had to do it cold. I stayed outside the factory door and talked to some of the women. It was an old building. There was one big room with lots of machines. They were making housedresses. Everything was piece rate in those days. I started with one woman and I'd get one address; and then I'd get another one, and then another one. Then what I did was start going to their homes and talking to them about conditions in the plant. We had little 3×5 cards, we got them from the NLRB, the National Labor Relations Board, and it said something about letting the ILGWU represent them in collective bargaining. I had them sign it and I guarded them with my life—they were like gold to me. After I got one to sign, I'd ask who do you think I might ask next. There was a great reticence on their part to be involved, because in a way it was an antichurch activity.

I tried to buy radio time to tell the union's story. I went into the KSL, which is a Mormon Church–owned radio station headed by a man who was a friend of my brothers. "Esther, what are YOU doing here, disturbing the peace?" The gossip around was that I had turned communist, and everything was just awful. It was hard on my family, but they were wonderful. They were tolerant. My father had died by then, and Mother was a little upset, but there was this tolerance from my family, which I've always appreciated a great deal.

The church ward teachers would follow me from door to door when I did house visits. "Tell the girls in the factory to have nothing to do with this person who has fallen from the ways of the church." But in six weeks, we had organized a good local. I hired the fanciest ballroom in Utah, at the Utah Hotel in Salt Lake City. We signed our first union contract there and installed the new local union executive board. It was a wonderful party. The women came all dressed up. There were workers, management, and some leaders from Utah's government. I was very proud of the local.

World War II Activities

During World War II, Sidney Hillman, president of the Amalgamated Clothing Workers of America–CIO from 1914 to 1946, was appointed by Roosevelt to head the Labor Division of the U.S. War Production Board. He asked Esther to co-direct the ACWA Committee on War Activities with his wife, Bessie Abromowitz Hillman. In addition to her cultural/educational activities, Esther organized workers in six plants of the nonunion Greif Company, which had received a government contract to make military uniforms. She also worked with Bessie Hillman to integrate ACWA-organized garment shops with newly hired African-American women workers and to integrate blood banks for the American Red Cross.[9]

One of the exciting parts of my life in those years was helping organize some locals for the ACWA in Staunton, Virginia, and in Pennsylvania. Companies couldn't get government contracts to make military uniforms unless they were union. So, finally, although these companies had been fighting the ACWA for years, they had to accept the union. I was the one that was sent into these shops to help convince the workers about the union. It was tough. They had been really geared against the union for so long. In the years before, the company had thrown out every union organizer who ever came to town. But now the difference was that they couldn't throw me out. There was an agreement that the company would treat me civilly. I was allowed to have union meetings in their cafeteria.

Sometimes I took Karen with me, who was four years old. I think it was the best thing I ever did. Karen used to stand right by me when I spoke, right by my side with her little red pigtails. I'd usually lead singing and talk to the workers. During the days, I'd leave her in the workers' homes while I was working for the union. One family she was staying with lived right by the railroad track. When I came to get her, she was black with dirt and beaming with happiness. Every day the family would go and pick up coal that had dropped off the trains, and she'd been picking up coal for them. It was quite something. These experiences stay deep inside you, when you see such things and experience them yourself. People were always so beautiful and generous and lovely to me and Karen.

I also did some work with Bessie Hillman. She helped me no end. She knew what she was talking about, and the women in the shops loved her. One of the assignments I had for the union during World War II was to help integrate the shops. The employers needed more machine operators; they wanted to hire blacks, but at that time, it was a new experience for our white union members to sit next to women from different racial backgrounds. Bessie helped me accomplish this. We went into the shops and interviewed some of the women workers, and paved the way for every new minority hire. Bessie was wonderful at that. She had her feet on the ground. I just loved that woman. We integrated, but it wasn't easy.

We also worked together, and with the American Red Cross, on integrating blood banks. When we went into the Red Cross and saw the "gray ladies" cutting and rolling bandages by hand, we got some of the union cutters who, after working all day in the garment shops, then went to the Red Cross at night and cut bandages with their electric knives.

I also worked hard in the South, in Virginia, where I did a lot of work for the ACWA on issues of discrimination. I remember the first days down there, the segregation. Blacks would be sitting together over in a far corner of the room. They had to use a side door. It was beautiful for me to go back to these local unions a few years later and see black workers sitting throughout the audience when we had a meeting. I'm very proud of that.

Lobbying For the Minimum Wage

In 1944 the Petersons, then with three children—Iver was born in 1942—moved to Washington, D.C., because Oliver was transferred. Esther's experience as a labor organizer and educator proved valuable in lobbying on Capitol Hill and campaigning for pro-labor Democrats. Led by Sidney Hillman, the Amalgamated Clothing Workers' union and the Congress of Industrial Organizations were developing an increasingly active role in Democratic politics and policymaking. Under Hillman's direction, Esther Peterson became the union's first legislative representative. She lobbied with other unions, working with people like John Edelman from the Textile Workers Union, and continued to teach workshops and report in the union newspaper on a range of legislative issues. A major focus was increasing the minimum wage, established under the Fair Labor Standards Act of 1938.[10]

My husband was transferred to Washington and I resigned from the ACWA. I had three children and no one to help me. I just visualized, "Well, Esther, this is something that you give up." But then Hillman called me, "Esther, we need you." I found another person to help me at home. Then I began working as legislative representative for the Amalgamated, representing Sidney Hillman on Capitol Hill. The union wanted to get an increase in the minimum wage, from 30 cents at that time, and asked if I would represent them on this and I did. That was a very fine and basic experience for me. I worked closely with Sidney Hillman then. I learned so much from him, training and teaching me. It's not book learning. It was just practical experience on how you handle various situations. He took me by the hand and introduced me to Robert Hannegan, Democratic Party chairman, who was the super fellow in the Democratic Party at the time. He introduced me to all these other officials. "This is my gal. I want you to listen to her. She can get me on the phone anytime if there is any question."

I worked with John Edelman who was another great man, the legislative representative for the Textile Workers Union of America. He taught me a lot of the red tape of lobbying. We established an office in the Warner Building. Hillman had been on the National War Labor Board for production workers and he set this up for me.

We worked up a whole plan of what was John's idea of the "victim witnesses." I did a lot of work bringing in the actual workers. That was very difficult because most of these people could lose their jobs. We had to see that the union brought them in and that they were protected. They were all the left-out ones, the least well organized ones.

I remember then working out a strategy, and that was when we were part of the CIO, and the AFL and the CIO weren't too friendly in those days. Thanks to Hillman, somehow, they accepted the strategy that I worked out and I took some pride in it. We had to get a unified AFL-CIO group because we could never get to first base with Congress with a divided labor movement on this minimum wage issue.

I went to L. B. Schwellenbach, who was the U.S. secretary of labor at that time. I talked to him about his setting up and calling us, so we could have a joint labor committee. I couldn't call it because that would be CIO; Walter Mason, the AFL lobbyist, couldn't call it, that was AFL; but a neutral government group could call it. So we established a Minimum Wage Committee, which was a joint committee of the AFL and the CIO, and that's how we got united on that. I was the chair of the committee on the CIO side. I represented Hillman and the CIO.

These things evolve, you know, you have a conversation. You have to be very subtle about it. Never take credit for the idea, it's terribly important. I had John Edelman help me, and I think I made it seem that it was Schwellenbach's idea. It's terribly important to bury that personal pronoun as much as possible. I think that's one of the prices we pay, but if it works— at least it's worked in my area.

We had some meetings in my home; we'd meet at the Willard Hotel, in neutral territory. We had auto, steel, electrical, clothing. The ILGWU was on the other side, they were AFL, and rubber. We had the major industry unions. Four or five people were really active. That's when I learned an awful lot about communist strategy, because they were the ones who were really active: the Electrical Workers and the Longshoremen, Harry Bridges's group. I think they wanted to defeat the minimum wage bill by going beyond what was feasibly possible. They wanted to extend coverage of the bill further than what we thought was practical. We just didn't have the votes, and they knew it. We would lose.

During the campaign we would meet two or three times a day maybe, depending on the strategy of what we were working on, on the Hill. We had to get ready for a hearing or we had to get witnesses. We had to make sure people could get off work to get there and there was an awful lot of maneuvering to get the proper witnesses.

We had education programs to educate the workers about the legislative process and how a bill could get through Congress and where to put on pressure. We got them to write letters or whatever. I telephoned information to Amalgamated to be in their newspaper. I did a great many speeches. We worked with the YWCA, and the joint congressional committee helped us. We didn't branch out really to the extent that they do today on coalitions. I did some, but it was pretty much working with unions. I spoke to a lot of union conventions.

But then I would speak on the whole political picture, not just on minimum wage. I used to speak on the whole labor program a great deal. We worked on housing, on education, on unemployment insurance, on social security. We were working on all of those issues, they were all part of labor. The positions were pretty clear. They had been determined by union conventions and resolutions. I would go to New York to give reports to the ACWA executive board.

I had a broad assignment, and that was to get that minimum wage through. I would call the union officers regularly on the telephone. We used the telephone a great deal. But the point is I think I was left pretty much to work out a strategy. It was never a nine-to-five job. Some days it would be double full-time and then again it wouldn't be. It was very uneven and, of course, it depends on the issue. The day a bill is on the floor you work like mad. You work like mad when you get it onto the floor, when you get it on the calendar. It's not the same every day.

We targeted congressmen and senators wherever we had members. We would go to them and say, "We have so many locals in your area and these are the names, and these are the people." Then we would try to bring those delegations in to talk to those congressmen. But we only did it where we had votes, that's what's important.

What I would always try to do is find the person who was key to that congressman, whether it was the secretary or his administrative assistant. I never tried to just say I have to see the congressman. I would try to see who was influencing him, and oh, that was one of the best strategies I ever had. If you had that person on your side, then the doors opened.

The whole opposition to a minimum wage increase was that it was too expensive, that people would lose their jobs if companies had to raise the minimum wage. But one of the strategies that I am very proud of was that we went into these little communities and talked to the merchants, to the little local business people on Main Street and they said, "Hooray," because then their customers would have more money to buy with. So the point was it had an economic advantage to say that they had to pay a minimum wage.

On the Campaign Trail

During this same period Esther began doing more campaign work for specific political candidates. Under Hillman's leadership, the CIO had established its Political Action Committee to support specific candidates, and Esther worked on presidential campaigns in her home state of Utah for Roosevelt and Truman, and on the Senate campaign of the Utah Democrat Elbert D. Thomas.

Elbert Thomas was very marvelous—from Utah, on the U.S. Congressional Labor Committee. I went out and worked in his political campaign. Hillman sent me out. The Political Action Committee wanted to get him elected. I worked for him and took my kids out that summer, and they stayed home again with Mother and my family. I worked closely with him, negotiated for him. He claimed that he would not have been elected if it hadn't been for me.

We initiated a lot of things then that are now just accepted. We had registration day, and then we set up a telephone bank of women, of wives of trade union people, in Carpenters' Hall. We got the telephone company to give us ten telephones and telephoned all the union members that we had and the districts that were heavily Democratic to get them to come out to vote. That helped no end. I was very pleased with that. I think that was one of the first telephone banks that was established, to tell the truth.

We had a sound truck go around city streets and stand at the corner, and then we had runners go around the block, and then we would say, "At this point at such and such a time certain candidates will be there." We were able to develop a crowd to come and listen and we did that in lots of parts of the Democratic areas where trade union people lived, which made a big difference.

Combining Work and Family

In 1946 the Peterson's fourth child, Lars, was born. Esther seemed to have few problems combining her work and family life. She was aware, however, that she was very fortunate; she had a supportive husband, good full-time household help, and respect from the men she worked for, and says, "That's why I'm sympathetic with women who have to work, but cannot have that type of help." She could afford to work part-time and employ a housekeeper. She was also given considerable flexibility in her schedule. She recognized that this was in part because, as someone who was not part of the traditional Jewish, immigrant base of the garment industry, she was valuable to the leadership of the ACWA and the ILGWU in reaching out to new union members and the general public.

I do know I have been fortunate, because I have had a supportive husband and I have had supportive help at home, which makes all the difference. Oliver felt that I had a contribution to make. My housekeeper was wonderful, and one of the first things that I was able to do when we moved to Washington was to get a cooperative nursery school going. I could never have had a nine-to-five job during that period; I just couldn't have done it, that's all. My requirements were—I'll do the work, but if my kids need me, they need me; that's all there is to it.

I was actually pregnant with Lars when Hillman told me to do this job and had introduced me to Hannegan. I remember saying to Hillman, "I'm pregnant, you know." He said, "Esther (they used to get angry with me when I would get pregnant), oh, you'll get the bill through." Well, I was getting bigger and bigger. I remember all the generosity, all the people who would say, "Come on, Esther, hurry back." They'd say, "We'll set up a maternity room up on the Hill, an obstetric room, set up in case the baby comes while you are up there." They used to say to me, "If it's a girl we'll name her Mini for minimum wage, and if it's a boy, Max for maximum hours." Hannegan sent me flowers and we talked by telephone. I was in good health; the babies were healthy. So it was kind of fun.

Labor Ties Overseas

In 1948 the Petersons moved again. Oliver was appointed labor attaché to the U.S. embassy in Sweden and later in Belgium. Esther again resigned from the ACWA, but was soon asked to come back to the States to help organized labor, this time by Philip Murray, president of the CIO, and Jacob Potofsky, who became president of the ACWA following Sidney Hillman's death in 1946. She returned to Washington to work on repeal of the Taft-Hartley Act and then again on a lobbying campaign to increase the minimum wage. She attended various international meetings and worked with many Scandinavian and European women trade union leaders. While in Europe, the Petersons also felt the chilling reach of Senator Joseph McCarthy and his "loyalty hearings." Hundreds of American citizens were called before the Senate Committee to defend themselves against charges of being communist, and Oliver Peterson was one of them.[11]

In 1948 we went abroad. President Truman appointed Oliver to the Foreign Service. During his administration, Truman said we should have labor attachés. Labor governments were beginning to pop up all over, and we had no experts. Oliver was one of the first labor attachés. I was working on the Truman campaign, and we left the next day after it was declared a victory. I won money on that; I knew he was going to win. I was very proud of that.

I had been in Sweden a short time when I got a call from Potofsky asking me if I could possibly come back because I was the only one that seemed to be able to get to Senator Thomas from Utah. That's when the unions were trying to get the Taft-Hartley law repealed. The law had been passed over President Truman's veto, and after he was elected again we were trying to get it repealed. They sent for me, and I went back with my baby. Julia, who had been my housekeeper before, took care of Lars. I worked in Washington, D.C., for almost two months on two things: one on the minimum wage and the other helping on the Taft-Hartley repeal. I seemed to have entrée to some of the congressmen and senators that others didn't have. So I helped.

While I was in Europe with Oliver, I did a lot of trade union work there, too. I kept up my contacts. Trade unionists visiting from the United States stayed with us. I did a study on household employment for the U.S. government. I went to the ILO, the International Labor Organization, a couple of times from Sweden for the U.S. government. I was a delegate to the first meeting of the ICFTU, the International Confederation of Free Trade Unions. Phil Murray called me and asked me—there was a seat that was vacant—and could I run in from Sweden and represent them? It was an exciting time for me to have Phil Murray call me and ask me if I'd go in and take this spot and help them, which I did.

Oliver was transferred to Belgium in 1952. We were in Belgium when the McCarthy hearings came up. My husband was investigated, and I was brought into it. He was a labor person and they didn't like labor. He had to hire a lawyer and return to the States for the hearings. It took a long time, and I couldn't talk to anybody about it. I was over there alone with four little children. I was banned from everything. I went through hell.

They used me. I was used against my husband definitely. There was an FBI investigation against me. They said that communists had been in

my home. A man from the retail workers' union came to my FBI investigation and testified against me as though I were one of the communists. He
had wanted his people covered in the minimum wage fight, but I just knew
we couldn't cover them—we didn't have the votes—and he had been furious. Also, we entertained blacks all the time at our house in Sweden. Paul
Robeson, the black actor and civil rights activist, stayed with us, and they
said he was a communist. Some people didn't like that. It was a lot of things.
But CIO President Phil Murray in his testimony said, "This is what's so good
about Oliver and Esther." We worked with everybody. We were very radical,
no doubt about it.

Oliver was completely vindicated. Phil Murray, everybody came to our
defense. We had no problem, but it was a bad period. It was one of the
hardest things. What McCarthy did to people was really terrible. Killed my
man. We paid a big price for what we believed in the labor movement. It
was emotional.

After that, I worked part-time and volunteered. I worked with the ICFTU
and helped organize the first International School for Working Women. It
was in LeBreviere near Paris. There were women from twenty-seven countries. There were problems with the languages and different styles of teaching, but we worked it all out. Later, I wrote a pamphlet against communism,
"Women, It's Your Fight Too."

Labor's Lady Lobbyist

The Petersons returned from Europe in 1958, after completing Oliver's assignment in Brussels. Ill with cancer by that time, Oliver retired from the Foreign Service and joined the faculty at the American University in Washington, D.C. Esther
had planned to return to the ACWA, but with Hillman gone and disagreements
between Potofsky and then secretary-treasurer Frank Rosenblum, she became a
lobbyist instead for the Industrial Union Department (IUD) of the AFL-CIO. She
recounts that in this period she experienced her first personal encounters with
discrimination because she was a woman. She also began to work again with
John Kennedy, whom she had first met when he was a congressman and who
was now senator from Massachusetts.

When I came back from Europe, I went to the Amalgamated. There was a
lot of tension. Oliver had been quite ill then; and it was the first time in my
life where I felt that I really had to work. I was real nervous about getting

the kids through college and everything. I thought I'd go back to the Amalgamated, but I had trouble with Frank Rosenblum. He didn't want me back. I was just furious. Hillman was gone and I had been in the Hillman-Potofsky faction, not the Rosenblum faction. Potofsky was president, but he was kind of weak. He didn't stand up and say, "Now look, we've invested a lot in this woman. She's done a great deal." I could feel that there was no warmth toward their taking me back on staff, which was a great disappointment.

But you have to stand up for yourself. I said, "I've got plenty of places that I can work." I always used to stand up for others, but it's terribly hard to stand up for yourself. It's very important, something we have to do. That's something I've learned. I made that mistake with LBJ a couple of times when I didn't stand up when I should have. So I learned my lesson a lot. I was tempted then just to take a job up on the Hill, which I'd been offered. But I didn't want to leave the labor movement. Deep down, I loved the labor movement.

I came to Washington and became legislative representative for the Industrial Union Department of the AFL-CIO. Jim Carey was the AFL-CIO treasurer, from the electrical workers' union, and he asked me to work and I did. I worked on minimum wage again, on the increase in the minimum from $1.00 in 1956 to $1.15 finally in 1961. I worked on unemployment compensation and a good deal on unemployment insurance. I did a lot on social security, quite a bit on housing—all the issues that the ACWA had worked with.

I was to take the place of somebody who'd been there before. Some of the women there talked to me: "Don't let them undercut you, Esther." I was getting about six thousand dollars and I was below the salary that the person had been getting that I was replacing. I asked Jim, "Well, shouldn't I get the same, at least the same?" It was the first time I'd ever asked anything money-wise in my life. He said, "You know, Esther, Oliver has a job. He's doing all right." I said, "Is that the way you bargain for people? Do you base your wage rates on the family income, on the husband's working?" The late fifties really stands out in my experience. It was the only time that I felt personal discrimination.

I worked with John Kennedy. I got to know him in the U.S. House of Representatives, when he was first elected. When I came to Washington I was assigned to work on the minimum wage. Here I was in this room with steel, auto, rubber, coal, the big unions. I came in and they stood up. I thought, "Oh my Lord." So I said, "Look, I'm not going to stand up for you, please don't stand up for me." Later on, Phil Murray told me that after that meeting they said, "What should we do with Esther?" The practice was to assign every union legislative representative a congressman and a senator to keep them informed about the unions' positions. Someone said, "Oh, give her to Kennedy. He won't amount to much." The best break that I ever had.

That's when Kennedy was in the House. I worked with him then and there I got really sold on him. The thing that I really loved about that man was he was not afraid to ask questions. I explained to him the minimum wage law, and he was so secure as a human being that he could ask questions. Oh, he was a joy to work with, just a joy. If he was given a one-page memorandum on an issue before a hearing, he would ask questions on that and he was just great. Then we went away to Europe, and when I came back to Washington one day in the halls of Congress I heard, "Esther, Esther, where have you been. I've missed you." He was a senator then.

I began working with Kennedy again when he was on the Senate Labor Committee. I got more acquainted with him and that's when I decided I wanted him to be President. I decided to support Kennedy very early, when he needed the help, and I think that meant a lot to him. We had lunch in his office and he wanted me to help him in Utah, which I did. I was there quite a bit. I would take the kids with me and Mother would help. I was assigned to the Democratic convention, covering Utah and that territory when Kennedy was nominated. I was at the convention.

I worked pretty much full-time for Kennedy. I was paid by the labor movement. I went over and handled the labor desk for Kennedy, handling labor things around the country. Labor people helped me no end, at every local meeting, every state convention, where I wanted a message from Kennedy to be read. That was a big assignment that I just took on. I felt it was very important. People on the AFL-CIO staff helped me write these messages, and someone there kept giving me the places the meetings were. We had a good operation, a very good operation.

I was there the night of the election. I had certain districts I was to report on very quickly so we could tell the way it was going. I remember later, after we won, I got a call from the White House, and they asked, "Esther, what do you want?" "What do I want?" I didn't work with Kennedy to get a job. At the time I said, "What about the Women's Bureau? Because I am concerned about working women." He said, "What about the United Nations?" I said, no, because Oliver was very ill then, and I couldn't possibly leave Washington. But it's interesting to me that I was asked about the UN at that time, in the early sixties. So for me it's kind of a continuing circle. I said, "It's the Women's Bureau, I think, where I would be able to do my best work." And that was right.[12]

The U.S. Women's Bureau

Esther Peterson was nominated to be assistant secretary of labor by John F. Kennedy on August 11, 1961, confirmed by the Senate four days later, and sworn in by Secretary of Labor Arthur J. Goldberg on August 17. In addition to directing the Women's Bureau, in 1962 her responsibilities expanded to include supervision of the U.S. Bureau of Labor Standards, the Bureau of Employees' Compensation, and the Employees' Compensation Appeals Board, and she became assistant secretary for labor standards. At age fifty-five, Esther Peterson began a new career in the public arena. She served as executive vice chairman of the President's Commission on the Status of Women under the chairmanship of Eleanor Roosevelt. Her assignment from President Kennedy was "to develop plans for advancing the full partnership of men and women in our national life."[13] She began her assignment with an issue close to the heart of America's working women, equal pay for equal work—not the Equal Rights Amendment, which she saw as hurting working women at the time.[14]

I became director of the Women's Bureau. We established the first Commission on the Status of Women. Kennedy was mad at Mrs. Roosevelt because she had supported Adlai Stevenson for president. But I said she was the best person for the job. She became chair of the commission. That was another great experience. We began with equal pay. In Sweden I had learned about equal pay and issues like that, because they had it in their union contracts. I strongly believed, as I later testified in the 1963 hearings on the Equal Pay Act, that the right to receive equal pay should be inscribed with our other measures to free workers from want and from injustice. Our democratic creed calls for it. This is the fullness of time to give it expression. I believe in this, as in other matters related to human equality, that we can never go astray if we follow the path of justice.[15]

"Equal pay for equal work" became the policy of the Women's Bureau, and, through its efforts, the law of the land. To help break down that notion that women workers were somehow different on the job from men, we abolished the practice in government of designating "job male—job female." We helped win the end of sex-segregated help-wanted ads, and fostered the widespread use of day-care centers in federal facilities. Predominantly women's jobs were also added to coverage under the Fair Labor Standards Act, even domestic workers.

Our efforts at that time were concentrated on extending the Fair Labor

Standards Act to cover more women workers, working for collective bargaining agreements in women-dominated industries, and seeking passage of the Equal Pay Act. We wanted equality for women, but we wanted bread for our low-income sisters first. Only after basic protection such as equal pay and federal wage and hours laws were in place, were we willing to consider the Equal Rights Amendment. I wanted to get consideration of women into the warp and woof of everything. Passage of the Equal Pay Act was an initiative the commission worked on. Mrs. Roosevelt and many commission members testified on behalf of the bill, and we were delighted to secure passage in 1963.

I might add that the issue of comparable worth, or "quality and quantity," was hard fought at that time, and the predominantly Republican women who supported the Equal Rights Amendment in 1960 were not with us. They had a part in our losing the comparable worth provisions. The commission position on the Equal Rights Amendment was a carefully worded compromise that strongly supported the principle of equality, but encouraged interest groups to seek a court case that would clarify the fourteenth amendment rather than seeking a new amendment.

The thing that got me on the Equal Rights Amendment was that the people who testified for it were the very ones who would not support equal pay, would not support increasing the minimum wage, would not increase coverage under the Fair Labor Standards Act, bringing in all the left-out people. I thought, baloney on you people. I cannot forget what I have seen and known and smelled and tasted and the way women were left out, and there's still a problem. The problems today are women in poverty, women with no homes, or any kind of support. We need to get into issues of housing and health care. We need to go out and talk to these poor women who have no access to houses and doctors.

I went down in history as opposing the inclusion of sex in Title VII of the Civil Rights Act of 1964, which prohibits discrimination in employment. It's true; I was opposed and I am very pleased that it turned out that I was wrong. But at that time, and in that climate, I was fearful that adding in women's rights would defeat the bill. I could not risk advancing women's rights on the backs of my black sisters. Black women were suffering far more than their white sisters, and I didn't want to do anything to jeopardize the Civil Rights Act. Of course, I was wrong. Thanks to the women who did a marvelous job of pushing it through, the act did pass, and the changes effected through the enforcement of Title VII paved the way for many of us to support the Equal Rights Amendment.

A New Career

After President Kennedy's death, President Johnson asked Esther to stay on at the U.S. Department of Labor, but also to become special assistant to the President for the newly created Office of Consumer Affairs, which she did from 1964 to 1967. When asked about this focus, she replied simply that she had been involved in consumer issues over the years and the President had asked her to take on this responsibility. She was at the forefront of those who worked to pass legislation for truth in lending, unit pricing, meat and poultry inspection, and occupational safety. After the Democratic presidential defeat in 1968, Esther went back briefly to the ACWA, but found little support for her growing interest and experience in consumer issues.

From 1970 to 1977, she served as vice president for consumer programs for Giant Food Corporation and also hosted a consumer radio talk show. President Jimmy Carter reappointed her to head the Office of Consumer Affairs from 1977 to 1980. Oliver died in 1979.

In the 1980s Esther represented the International Organization of Consumers Unions in the development of the United Nation's Guidelines for Consumer Protection, worked with the Older Women's League, and helped to organize the United Seniors Health Cooperative. In 1981, in recognition of her achievements, she was awarded the Presidential Medal of Freedom.

Over the years, Esther has given generously of time and talent on issues of importance to organized labor and working women's organizations. She was recently honored by the Coalition of Labor Union Women and the National Committee on Pay Equity, and was inducted into the National Women's Hall of Fame. In 1993, in an appointment by President Clinton, she served a term as a delegate to the United Nations General Assembly. She continues to live in Washington, D.C., close to several of her children and grandchildren, actively lobbying on current issues and supporting candidates for public office. When asked for advice, Esther Peterson said, "The whole point is to stick to what you believe and don't compromise too far. Compromise, but always compromise upward. That always meant so much to me because you must never just stay on a level. You've got to move. As the song went in that old ILGWU musical *Pins and Needles,* 'You can't giddyup by saying whoa.'"

Chapter 5

We Did Change
Some Attitudes

*Maida Springer-Kemp, International Ladies'
Garment Workers' Union (1910–   )*

In 1955, Maida Springer, a forty-five-year-old factory worker and union activist from the garment district of New York City, was one of the first African-American women to travel to Africa on behalf of the AFL-CIO. An international labor pioneer, she has worked for fifty years with trade union leaders from many African countries, including Kenya, Nigeria, Tanzania, Ghana, and South Africa, establishing education and training programs and acting as a critical link between labor leaders on both continents.

Interwoven with her work in Africa are activities in the International Ladies' Garment Workers' Union, which she describes as "one of the most exciting unions in the world." After joining the ILGWU during the Depression, she became active on several union committees. A few years later, she became a union shop steward, an ILGWU education director, and one of the first African-American business agents. In 1945 she was chosen by the AFL to represent them on a goodwill mission to England for the U.S. Office of War Information Exchange. That same year she was named one of the Women of the Year by the National Council of Negro Women.

In the 1960s Maida became an international representative for the AFL-CIO International Affairs Department and then worked with the affiliated African-American Labor Center and the Asian-American Free Labor Institute. She also worked as a general organizer for the ILGWU in the South and served as Midwest director of the A. Philip Randolph Institute and as vice president of the National Council of Negro Women. Increasingly she focused on the needs of women trade unionists in the United States, Africa, Indonesia, and Turkey.

While recognizing problems of racism and sexism within unions, Maida continues to see the labor movement as a major force for improving the lives of working women and men. Today she lives in Pittsburgh, near her son and his family.

She continues to travel to Africa, and her home remains a meeting place for visitors from around the world.[1]

School and Community

During the 1920s the flourishing African-American culture in New York City was expressed in the Harlem Renaissance, which included music and literature as well as intellectual and civil rights movements. Maida Stewart grew up in this atmosphere with her mother, Adina Stewart. Maida was born in the Republic of Panama in 1910. Her father had come from the West Indies to work on the Panama Canal; her mother was born in Panama. After her younger sister died at age three, the family emigrated to New York, arriving at Ellis Island in August 1917. They lived at first with relatives in Harlem, and then her parents separated. Maida says little about her father, but describes Adina as intelligent, vivacious, and "always young." Her mother worked first as a domestic and then as a cook and beautician, eventually opening her own beauty shop. Family and church played important roles in Maida's youth, but she was also strongly influenced by the African-American leaders of that time. Her mother was a follower of Marcus Garvey, founder of the Universal Negro Improvement Association. Maida attended high school at Bordentown Manual Training and Industrial School for Colored Youth, a private boarding school in New Jersey, where she heard speakers like W.E.B. Du Bois, a leading intellectual and one of the founders of the National Association for the Advancement of Colored People (NAACP), and Paul Robeson, a great actor and civil rights activist.

The first school I ever went to was in the United States. But I could read and write when I came here. The public schools in New York City, that was something else. I was enrolled in St. Mark's, the Catholic school near our home. Then I went to a black boarding school in New Jersey. This was a black industrial school for boys and girls. They had football and tennis and all of these things, but it was an industrial school. It wasn't a "hoyty-toyty" school. They attempted to set a standard. They gave you the best that they could offer.

The teachers were excellent men and women who had very superior educations. Miss Grant taught English literature. She spent the summer in Europe, and every September she came back and opened up a whole new world. Poetry had meaning. Medieval architecture had meaning. Rome, Switzerland, Africa—all had meaning. One of the professors there was

Maida Springer-Kemp (*far right*), International Ladies' Garment Workers' Union, AFL, was one of four women representing the American labor movement, through the U.S. Office of War Information Exchange, who spent eight weeks in England sharing wartime experiences in 1945. She was the first African-American woman to represent labor abroad. Other members of the delegation were (*from left to right*) Grace Blackett, United Auto Workers, CIO; Anne Murcovich, American Federation of Hosiery Workers, CIO; and Julia O'Conner Parker, International Brotherhood of Electrical Workers, AFL. *George Meany Memorial Archives.*

William H. Hastie, later Judge Hastie. He taught me science. My history professor was a Harvard graduate. His father had been a janitor at Harvard. And seeing him stand there and talk about the ex post facto law, these were great awakenings. To see Paul Robeson standing on the platform in our assembly at the school. He was then at Rutgers. He was great. These were the images I had. Dr. Du Bois talking over our heads because he was always the elegant aristocrat and giving you a worldview. These were the role models of men and women of intellect and men and women who talked about what a social system should be.

In terms of identity, the Garvey Movement was another great influence on my life. We came to the United States at the point that Garvey, the burly black Jamaican, was really at the top of the mark. My mother, of course, immediately joined the Universal Negro Improvement Association. I listened to men and women of the day passionately speaking a language that most black Americans were not speaking. These were passionate men and women of vision, Americans, West Indians, and a few Latins, and they were talking about a society in which men and women, regardless of color or race, should share. There should be a caring, and then the challenges began: don't buy where you can't work, develop your own industry, develop your own initiative in the community, own buildings. We were one of the early stockholders in the Terry Holding Association, which was a building society.

My mother marched as a Black Cross Nurse in the Garvey Movement, and she had this child by the hand. I went to the meetings because there were no baby-sitters. We were not sophisticated enough for that in those days—so wherever she went, I went. And so I listened to all of this. In our home, people from our part of the world, from the Caribbean Islands—many of them congregated in our house. My mother was a marvelous cook and a joyous woman, so there was always a coterie of people, and there was singing, and there was talking, and beyond that, a realization of a role we had to play in this society.

It didn't matter whether on Monday morning you were scrubbing floors or were a porter someplace, or whether you were doing the most menial job. This was all the society would permit to be open to you. Many doctors and lawyers in that early period were people who had worked at menial jobs and worked on the shifts in order to continue their studies. It was only a very small percentage of black Americans whose families could support a fine education.

Factory Work

Like the lives of most young women of her day, Maida's life was dramatically affected by the Depression. While in high school, she got a job in a garment factory, one of the few places hiring young black women. There she learned to use a pinking machine, "to cut the jagged edges on the garments." After graduation, in 1927, she worked as a receptionist until she married Owen Springer, a West Indian from Barbados. Their son, Eric, was born in 1929. Owen had a good job in a dental equipment firm and expected his wife to stay at home, but when the Depression hit, he had to take a large cut in salary. Maida went back to work in a garment factory.

In 1932 I went to work in a garment shop, first as a hand server and later as a power machine operator. In those days I had a lot of family in-laws. My sister-in-law lived on one floor and she had seven children. I lived on the top floor. I never had a baby-sitter, never needed one. When I moved away from 142nd Street, if Owen and I were going out someplace, one of the older girls came and spent the night. That was the family.

The industry was in a chaotic condition. The union was very weak. People came in very early in the morning, didn't have their lunch hour, and all sorts of things. If the manufacturer of the garment thought something was wrong with it, you fixed it for nothing. It's hard to describe.

I kept threatening that I was going to the union. The cutter and I became very friendly. It was unusual in those days to see a Negro man a cutter, but he was excellent, and since they paid him next to nothing, and it was nonunion, he was able to hold the job. Most shops were nonunion shops. But I knew something about unions. I had heard A. Philip Randolph speak in Harlem and had some positive views about unions. I joined the dressmakers' union, Local 22, of the International Ladies' Garment Workers' Union in May 1933. I went in and told them what was happening at work because it was just getting under my skin. The fee to join the union was $2.50 and dues were 35 cents a month.

Union Activism

The unions in New York's garment industry were largely dominated by European immigrants with strong ties to socialist and communist organizations. Communist influence started to decline in the ILGWU beginning in 1926, after a disastrous five-month strike led by the communist trade unionists. In 1933 the National Industrial Recovery Act first gave workers the right to organize unions. Under the leadership of David Dubinsky, elected president of the union in 1932, the ILGWU's New York Dress Joint Board called a general strike. On August 16, 1933, 60,000 workers, mostly women, marched to the strike halls in New York, New Jersey, and Connecticut. The strike was brief, but the union won increased wages and better working conditions. Union membership rose from 50,000 in 1933 to 200,000 in 1934. The number of black women dressmakers in ILGWU Local 22 increased from 600 to nearly 4,000. Maida began a lifelong career as a strong union activist, and the Springer family's way of life was forever changed.[2]

We were part of a social revolution. You see, the garment industry was built by European immigrants, most of whom were victims of oppression in their native lands. Their political opinions ranged from anarchism to Zionism, but communists made up the largest group. Charles "Sasha" Zimmerman, the manager of my own Local 22, had been an ardent communist. After the 1926 strike, which nearly destroyed the union, he turned against their ideology and became their most bitter foe and target. The worst of it was over by 1933, but you still had lots of problems after that. In the big local unions, you had challenge and conflict. I was involved in all of that because the communists constituted the opposition to the union leadership. The communists were not concerned with the domestic life of the

Maida Springer-Kemp's union work in both the United States and Africa was strongly influenced by A. Philip Randolph, president of the Brotherhood of Sleeping Car Porters and vice president of the AFL-CIO. She is shown here with (*left to right*) Ashley Totten, international secretary-treasurer, BSCP; Anselmi Karumba, general secretary of the National Union of Garment Workers in Kenya; and Randolph, ca. 1962. *Library of Congress.*

worker in America. They had a political ideology that was destructive to improving workers' conditions.

When the strike was settled, industrywide, then we had to begin to build the union. Just hundreds and thousands of workers were enrolled into the garment workers' union, and this was a great excitement. My own Local 22 was one of the bigger locals. Everyone who was not Italian belonged to Local 22, the dressmakers. We had 32 nationalities. We prided ourselves on this. We immediately began focusing on educational work, because we had all of these raw recruits. So they began all kinds of classes—English for the non-English-speaking, classes on parliamentary procedure, classes of all kinds to provide a very simple, basic understanding of the union agreement. It was really the first important agreement that we had. I began on that level as an activist.

You still had the Italian workers belonging to Local 89, which was the Italian-language local; they spoke Italian. You think of Luigi Antonini, with his flowing black tie, who looked like a great opera impresario. He brought to the garment workers a kind of cultural content, because any celebration meant going to the opera or bringing the greatest of the opera stars to the garment workers. When we had our celebration in Madison Square Garden after we won the general strike, everybody from the Met was there to sing for the workers. You had the great freedom song of the Italian workers, "Pan y Rosa," "Bread and Roses." That's why I say that, for me, the trade union movement was always a great love affair and a great excitement.[3]

I'm a member; I work in the shop. I go and work in the shop every day from 1933 until 1941 or 1942. But I'm active, very active—chairman of the education committee in my local during one period. I took all the courses that were required of me. Those early courses were for activists to be more intelligent and to be more informed. For those who were, I suppose, more aggressive than I, they looked forward to becoming an officer. But, on my life, this was not my concern. I could not be a member of the Committee on Prices in my local union if I did not know what I was talking about. I could not represent the shops. So I took the courses I did on the advice of my business agent so that I could be a better union member.

I was an executive board member of Local 22 and represented the union on all kinds of committees. A bread and butter committee, when I worked in the shop, was to settle prices. Our wages were based on the settlement of the piece-rate price: what a worker would be paid for each piece completed. I was on one of the first committees of the local, and I was to represent workers in structuring our base, how we settled the garment, what we were to be paid. I was elected by my shop to be their representative on the jobber's premises, the manufacturer's premises, to argue for what we would be paid for making the garment. It was complicated to learn. At first, it was most frightening, but you had the guidance of your union representative, you had training, and you and other workers who represented other shops, you met together. But the employer tried to intimidate you. This was a brand-new experience.

The union changed our way of life. I'd go off to training programs on weekends, and Owen would not go. I wanted him to understand what I was trying to do in this country. I would say, "Eric needs the best chance we can give him. We only have one child, and the union has made it possible for women to be involved, to expand my opportunity." I think he resented it, which made life difficult for all of us, but he was a wonderful human being, a wonderful father. By the time Eric was ten years old, he had all kinds of involvement in activities after school, and his father came straight home from work or my mother was always close.

The New Deal

The early 1930s ushered in the Roosevelt administration with a far-reaching labor and social legislative agenda. In 1935, the National Labor Relations Act ensured the right to organize and bargain collectively, and in 1938, the Fair Labor

Standards Act provided the first national minimum wage. The ILGWU was a very progressive union, proud of its early policies against segregated locals and pay differences based on race. Maida learned to lobby and work with people in the Roosevelt administration. In 1942 she ran unsuccessfully as a candidate for the American Labor Party for the New York State Assembly from the 21st District in Harlem.[4]

W̲e were fighting for legislation, for all of the things that went on in the Roosevelt administration in which labor was so closely identified. My first lobbying experience was on minimum wage. The minimum wage was 37 cents an hour. I think we were asking for something like 50 cents. Well, the way those senators and congressmen talked about it, you would have thought we all had tails. This was my first exposure to government. I was so incensed for years because here I am, a proud citizen, and these people are talking to us as though we're scum. One senator, he read a statement about mother love and how changing the wage structure would destroy mother love and the family. Now what mother love had to do with wages, I don't know. Women would still have to work.

The labor movement was just beginning to be recognized. There were friends of the labor movement working for legislation to strengthen unions, like a national labor relations act. After Roosevelt was elected, it became a reality. When I went to work in the garment industry it was chaotic; we did not have a strong union. In those early days, people did a lot of work at home, so that after a worker spent twelve hours in the factory, she then took work home, often to a Lower East Side apartment heated with a coal stove. It was a sweated industry indeed. But by 1935 we were considered the wild ones, because President Dubinsky demanded and negotiated and got a thirty-five hour work week. This was unheard of! Only the union printers had a thirty-five-hour work week. They said it would drive all the manufacturers out of business. It didn't, of course. Most of the manufacturers only got richer.

Innovative things were done by the trade unions in terms of health, in terms of leisure. Unity House, for example. Where could a worker go with a limited income and no money for a vacation? Unity House is a resort in the Pocono Mountains run by the ILGWU, where union membership made it possible for you to go away the way a wealthy person might go. The Amalgamated Clothing Workers' union pioneered in housing and banking, establishing cooperative housing projects and banks that were available to union members. You had men of great genius and innovation who saw that union leaders had to create the climate of change and fight for housing, health care, and recreation, in addition to wages.

I would be called out of the shop, for example, to go to a meeting at lunch to represent the union. On one occasion, it was a luncheon meeting at the Waldorf-Astoria. This was a great honor. I came to work that morning in my moccasins and working clothes, you know, a heavy coat. I was a size ten then. The whole shop got involved. I was loaned somebody's pocketbook; a dress was taken off of the dressform and fitted on me, and somebody else gave me a better-looking coat than the one I had on, and I marched off to the luncheon dressed to the nines. Three women who were there, Madame Chiang Kai-shek, Madame Litvinov, and Mrs. Roosevelt—and there I was, representing my local union, representing the ILGWU in solidarity.

I went back to the shop and stitched my dresses, and at six o'clock I went to the union board meeting in my moccasins and my old coat and my tam-o'-shanter. There was a great howl because a few hours earlier I had been so dolled up. This was the kind of political and social atmosphere of that whole period.

Education Director, Local 132

With World War II came a great change in the work force as young white men went off to war. In 1942 this change became a major challenge for Maida. To prepare her for going on the union staff, Sasha Zimmerman, general manager of the New York Dress Joint Board and a good friend and mentor, arranged for her to become education director of Local 132, a union of button and novelty workers. According to Maida, the membership was 70 percent male, 30 percent female, working in metals, plastics, and materials such as acetone. The union lost about 40 percent of its young male members to the war, and the new members, many more of them women, came from diverse ethnic and racial backgrounds. Maida saw education as a key to effective interracial unionism, based on her own experiences at programs like the Harlem Labor Center and the Hudson Shore Labor School.[5] During this time, Owen went into war work and commuted during the week to a shipyard in Baltimore. The men in the yard made good money, but shared very crowded living conditions.

I became, in 1942, the educational director of the Plastic Button and Novelty Workers Union, which was one of the accessory locals of the ILGWU. It included all kinds of nationalities: Poles, Germans, Swedes, and Italians.

While they hated one another sometimes, they jointly hated anything black. All these new people were coming in: the poor devils who had escaped the gas chambers of Hitler; the Negroes who had just come up from the South, who had never had a working experience in an industrial setting, in a factory; women who were strange to mass employment, housewives who were just coming to work—and a part of the training was to make all of these people understand something about the union.

So we had classes, which I initiated, two or three sessions. We had lecturers who came down and talked about the union and the contract and the union constitution and the rest of it. Well, the first thing you do is start out by indicating that they have one common bond. You didn't have to love one another, we would tell them, but you wanted decent wages, hours, conditions of work. You wanted those safety measures to affect everyone and you wanted every worker to have a sense of responsibility to the other workers—there were some highly dangerous materials that you worked on—the plastics and acetone and poisons and the rest of it, so that you had to be responsible for the other worker. You used some heavy machines. You could stamp off a man's hand or stamp off a woman's fingers. Also, the introduction had to include good trade unionism. For people coming from a racial community where they had never been exposed to anyone that did not look just like them, this required some doing.

For example, I would organize a weekend institute. We would have marshmallow roasting, frankfurters, and after you had pumped trade unionism and workers' education and the history of the labor movement over a weekend, each evening you tried to do some of the social things people did there—country dances and the rest of it. A couple of young women came to me and desperately wanted to go, but the brothers in the family said that if "niggers" were going to be there, particularly men, they could not go.

So how could I persuade their brothers? I started with the mothers. I developed some allies. Most of the mothers I won over. It had to do with a belief that I was one Negro that maybe they thought met their standards. Their standards were much lower than mine in most instances, but, again, these are the prejudices you had to deal with.

This was my first paid union responsibility. But it was a lasting experience since it was a small local union—five thousand members in contrast to Local 22, for example, which had twenty-five thousand members—and the staff was a small staff. As the educational director, I also went to the plant doors at four or five o'clock in the morning and issued leaflets when the shifts changed. The union staff did all sorts of things together. An interesting by-product of this, with the war on, was that we developed a labor newspaper. It brought families together. Brothers who were in the same army found one another when they got this little union magazine, "The Voice of Local 132." We were all very patriotic. (The Red Cross had a blood bank, but I refused to give blood for the reason that they segregated the blood, even though Dr. Charles Drew, a black doctor, perfected the plasma technique so useful during World War II.) It was a union staff of five or six people. We knew every shop steward. We knew every committee, and we did change some attitudes.

Civil Rights

In 1932, before becoming a union member, Maida went to hear a speech by A. Philip Randolph. Randolph "really turned my head around at that meeting," she reported, "talking about the rights of workers and the dilemma of black workers and white workers who could be easily misused and abused . . . that there must be a joining."[6] Randolph became a mentor and close family friend who would have a lasting influence on Maida's interconnected commitments to the labor movement and the civil rights movement in both the United States and Africa. Although she was committed to helping women, she believed "the first barrier is always race." In 1941, owing in large part to Randolph's efforts on behalf of African-American workers, President Roosevelt signed Executive Order 8802, prohibiting job discrimination on the basis of race, creed, color, or national origin in government and the defense industry. Mass rallies were held around the country to support establishing a permanent Fair Employment Practices Committee (FEPC) after the war ended. A major effort was a rally in Madison Square Garden in 1946, and Maida became executive secretary for the project.[7]

We were involved in staging a Madison Square Garden rally to establish a permanent FEPC. Mr. Randolph called Sasha Zimmerman and President Dubinsky, and said, "We would appreciate it if you would allow Maida to help us put this rally together." I was terrified at the idea. The only people who could fill the Garden in those days were the communists. In addition, I did not think I had the administrative qualifications and the fund-raising abilities to do it. You know, there were some things I was modest about.

So, to everyone he sent to me, I said, "No, I will not do it." Then Brother Randolph called and asked me to come see him. I walked in, and he said, "Now, Maida dear, the cause of social justice is at stake. We had, as you know, Executive Order 8802." Since I was prepared to march about that, I said, "Yes, sir," and he said, "Now, our colleagues in the Congress, and so and so, and Mrs. Roosevelt is going to lend her support and she will talk with Franklin." You know, I walked out of there with my head bowed and a check for a $3,000 down payment on Madison Square Garden. Billy Bowe, an officer of the Brotherhood, escorted me to the Garden to make the transaction official. The Garden in those days cost $6,000 empty.

You had to raise money and then on and on. We had good fortune. Helen Hayes, Orson Welles, and a host of others—they did the dramatic part of the program. But the building of such a program, I can't tell you. I was twenty pounds lighter and twenty years younger, and terrified. You knew you were going to get help, but how do you stage all this, and how do you keep the momentum going as you raise money and as you do the drudgery. There was strong support from groups like the NAACP, the Urban League, people in the arts, and the churches. Max Delson, a prominent socialist lawyer in New York, did a lot of work to limit our mistakes. You got the support of groups of trade unionists and young people from colleges. Then you were busy calling all over the country and you were busy with promoters. In terms of raising the money, I had to carry the stick for this project. Union leaders used to say to me, "Well, Springer, how much is this conversation with you going to cost?" But with a dedicated staff of people to work with, it got so that you learned in the doing.

We filled Madison Square Garden with twenty-five thousand people, and we had a five-hundred voice choir that no one believed was possible. I used to hang my head because they would say, "What do you mean, a five-hundred-voice choir, whoever heard of such a thing?" There was a woman who was trained, a gospel singer, choir leader. I heard about her, I hotfooted over to meet her. She liked me, and I liked her, and she said, "Yes," and we began to work. She did not have five hundred voices, but she began building and building around it. The Garden was the backdrop. These men and women, the women all in their dark skirts and white blouses, and the men with their black suits and white shirts, were a dramatic presence. A lot of these women worked as domestics. On the night of this rally, most of their employers were there to see them perform.

It was impressive. All of the people who came to contribute and share in that occasion were extraordinary, so it was quite an experience. If someone has faith in you, and asks you as Brother Randolph did, you try. If he had told me to walk the water, I would have tried. I tell you, I would have tried. Especially with my own union backing me up, and saying, "Yes, we want you to do this." They paid my salary for the period. The trade union movement was superb, and this was AF of L and CIO. They worked at making the rally a success. This was the meeting for the forward thrust on legislation for a permanent Fair Employment Practices Committee, the catalyst of these laws around the United States.

Business Agent, Local 22

The heart of the garment industry, and thus a major focus of the union, was the piecework system. How the work was assigned and the price paid for each piece determined wages and working conditions. Maida knew the system as a worker, a union activist, and a local union education director. The next step in learning the roles and responsibilities of local union leadership was mastering the complaint process from the staff side. In 1945 she returned to Local 22 to learn the internal mechanics of the complaint department, to settle complaints about wages and grievances about working conditions, and to deal with all of the regulations that had to do with contract negotiations. In 1947 she went on the staff as a business agent, the second African-American business agent for Local 22 and the first to be responsible for a district.[8]

Well, going from an activist in the shop, when you thought you knew what you were doing, to a business agent is quite a jump, because as an activist, you think you know the instruments of the union. You walk up to the window at the complaint department office and you tell them you want this, you want that. You get a lot of action. But as a business agent, you were then the responsible person and the person who had to resolve the complaints or they would complain about you.

As a business agent, I had fifty-eight shops. The shops were small. The section of the industry which I was given some responsibility for was called the Better Makers because you began with the wholesale price of $10.75, which was higher priced. You had a wide range to cover and you had to overcome the suspicion of the very talented and wise men and women who were the craftsmen in the industry. Now they had to respect you, to believe that you could resolve their grievances, and stand up to the employer and be able to defend them.

A business agent's responsibility is to see that the shop functions, that the worker is treated fairly by the employer, and that the union committees function properly. Because it's a piecework system, you had to see that the slow worker had an advantage as well as the fast worker, because the employer's tendency would be to give all of the big bundles to the fast workers and all of the rags and tags and single garments to the slower worker.

He would naturally lean to what would be more profitable to him. It's a horrible system. It dehumanizes you, but I don't know what the answer is. It's a system that we grew up with, and it's now expanded because the needle trade has become a multinational corporation.

Every garment shop was a small government. You had to be cognizant of the personalities that you were dealing with. After you got over the suspicion that you didn't know what you were doing and you were black and you were a woman, after you had overcome that, then you had to overcome the suspicion that you were probably selling the workers out to the employer. Now this had nothing to do with color or race. This just meant that you were authority and you were suspect.

You made sure that you did certain things when you walked into a shop. You greeted your unpaid elected union officers. The chairlady or chairman worked there every day and if there was a grievance, you got the chairlady and a union committee to work with you on solving it. Then you went in and sat down with the employer, but under no circumstances do you go into the employer's office in a hurry. In your anxiety to get the job done quickly, since you have a long list of shops to service, you may do that. When you walk out, the assumption might be that you have made some deal to the workers' disadvantage. You walk into a shop and sometimes by the time you're through, you've created a riot. You had to know the union contract. Your business is policing the union agreement. I did that for thirteen years. Your responsibility to the union members was every hour of your life.

You don't just start as a needle worker, a garment worker, without a good deal of discipline, and a good deal of disappointment, and a lot of inconvenience in your personal life. I've had discrimination, I've had a lot of discrimination. I've had a lot of problems. I have been rejected. There were racial hostilities in the union. I would be an awful liar if I said that there were not. We tried harder, but we suffered from all of the prejudices and disabilities of our society. Within the union there were sufficient men and women who were concerned, who tried. But there were officers of the union who really could never see the black worker or the Spanish worker, moving straight across the board. You had that to fight.

On the job there could be discrimination. It was a piece-rate system. The bulk of the workers, maybe operators in the dressmakers' union, got paid for what they made, but there were certain lines. With the cheaper line, you could get a job where you just work and work and work and kill yourself to make it. With the better line, you had to be more skilled and make the whole garment. A case could be made, and was made, that people were excluded. Black people or Spanish people were excluded from the better lines. There were jobs that the men just said to themselves, "These jobs are not for women." The employer and the workers agreed that we will not let women be the tailors. There were many subtle ways it could be done. Both race and sex discrimination existed.

When I was made a member of the union staff, the manufacturers' association said that their officers would not be seen with me. I was the first black business agent. Sometimes you get sick of being the first of this and the first of that and the first of the other. But my own union leader, Zimmerman, said, "All right, nobody will function. You don't want her—you won't see her—you won't see any of us. She's an officer of our union." We won and he never told me. I found out months later that the association had officially protested. This is what always creates my constant affection and love for what a workers' organization has done to raise the sights and the sense of respect for the working men and women in the United States—which industry on its own would not do.

Role Models

While Maida was profoundly influenced by several prominent men, such as Du Bois, Randolph, Dubinsky, and Zimmerman, she also attributes much of her commitment to the labor movement and women's rights to a number of strong women activists. Among them, Mary McLeod Bethune, founder of the National Council of Negro Women, offered guidance and support. Maida's close friendship with Pauli Murray—feminist, lawyer, minister—was reflected in Murray's autobiography, *Song in a Weary Throat,* which is dedicated to "Maida, incomparable companion, critic, and guide on the pilgrimage."[9] Maida worked closely with women in the Amalgamated Clothing Workers' union, such as Esther Peterson and Dolly Lowther Robinson, but perhaps most important to her development in the union were the role models from her own ILGWU, especially Pauline Newman and Fannia Cohn.[10]

I think part of the feeling I have had, my own constant passion about the labor movement with all of its bumps and warts, is because I came up at a time when there were so many role models. Pauline Newman, who was then directing one section of the health department of the ILG, this woman had been in the 1911 Triangle Shirtwaist Company fire. She was one of the giants, determined, articulate, volatile about workers' dignity and the pursuit of excellence, wherever you are. Rose Schneiderman, who headed the

Women's Trade Union League, brought the women of wealth and promi-
nence to understand the concerns, the problems of working women. Fannia
Cohn was at the ILG national headquarters in the education department. I
respected her.

Fannia Cohn, Pauline Newman, and a host of others were among the
rambunctious, tenacious women who made themselves heard. Talk about
the Uprising of the Twenty Thousand. When the men in the unions wanted
to settle for less, these women garment workers were prepared to stay on
strike and be hungry and to march in the winter. The men had families
and other responsibilities and felt that they ought to make the compromise,
but the women felt that they had reached the point of no return, and they
could do no worse. I think sometimes our madness is part of our survival.
All of these women touched my life and mind, and so I did come up at a
time of great transition.

In the garment workers' union, where the majority of the membership
are women, deep down below I imagine there are people with those prejudices that women do not stay in the union and therefore it's harder to get
them into leadership. But the majority of the members of the union, most
of them women like myself, were members for twenty-five and thirty years.
Even though a woman has been a member and attended meetings and done
all these things and brought up a family, there is the myth that she thinks
like a woman, that she's going to be away from the meetings, from serious
contract negotiation—which, in fact, is not so. It's a block one has to get
over, but the doors are more open now, out of pure necessity and some
intelligent leadership.

International Background

Part of the labor movement's involvement in World War II was an exchange of
workers to share experiences and ideas. Maida's first international experience began in 1945, when the AFL and the CIO were asked by the Office of War Information Exchange to send four women workers to represent the American labor
movement and share wartime experiences during several weeks in England. The
AFL nominated Maida and Julia O'Connor Parker from the International Brotherhood of Electrical Workers (IBEW). Maida's appointment, as the first African-
American woman to represent labor abroad, was a history-making event
documented in the *New York Times*.[11] While in England she also made her first
contact with a group of young African trade unionists. Through them she learned
more about the Pan-African movement, dedicated to ending colonialism and establishing independent African nations.

I remember standing up on a table in a huge factory in England and after saying whatever I was going to say, asking them to join me in a trade union song. The factory owner, you know, two thousand workers, everybody stopped, and people were waving their hands and singing. Some of their women were among the strong militants in their unions, as were women in the United States. But insofar as being in the top leadership of the trade union movement, the British Trades Union Congress was a male organization, just as the AF of L and CIO were male organizations.

An opportunity to meet the Queen of England was of course very exciting. We had some interesting moments because the ladies-in-waiting had to tell you how to behave, and we had to argue among ourselves the night before about who was going to curtsey and who would shake hands. We were very strong about the democratic way of doing things. But Queen Elizabeth was so utterly charming she just put us at ease.

My colleagues—they had problems. The CIO thought that it was the egalitarian organization of the world and that the AF of L was the reactionary organization of the world. The CIO was considered more progressive. Here you are with this black woman representing the AF of L. The CIO ladies were horrified that the CIO had been upstaged. My partner, Julia O'Connor Parker from the telephone division of the IBEW, had sat with Samuel Gompers in the discussions for the International Labor Organization after World War I. She was horrified at first at the idea of having to share responsibility with this Negro woman, but we developed mutual trust and respect. We were a good working team. We were the conservatives. I had never considered myself a conservative until that time.

But when doing any of our public discussions, the larger issue was the trade union movement as a social and economic force; what it represented to millions and millions of working people. This was the goal, and how do you get a government and the employers to see that the worker is not just a pair of hands, that the worker has a mind, the worker has a home, has a family, and needs to be treated with respect, to have wages commensurate with what he or she is doing, to have a decent standard of living. If this was our goal, we had no problems.

My unofficial introduction into the politics of black Britain began at a press conference in London. George Padmore, a reporter, asked to see me. He was both an author and one of the leaders of the Pan-African Congress that had just concluded a conference in Manchester which W.E.B. Du Bois had chaired. I met Jomo Kenyatta, later president of Kenya, who asked, "Young lady, what does the American working class know about the struggle against colonialism?" I accepted this as a challenge.

Oxford and Africa

In 1951 Maida received a scholarship from the American Scandinavian Foundation to study workers' education in Denmark and Sweden for three months. She then spent the academic year as an Urban League Fellow at Ruskin Labor College, Oxford University, England, where she forged strong and lasting ties to the labor leaders of Africa also studying there. She made her first trip to Africa, on loan to the AFL, as a delegate to the newly formed International Confederation of Free Trade Unions' (ICFTU) first seminar in Africa.[12] She worked closely with A. Philip Randolph and George Meany, who became president of the AFL-CIO. By this time Eric was at Oakwood, a Quaker boarding school in Poughkeepsie, New York. Owen had become one of the first black workers to secure a job in the New York transit system after the war. He was a member of the union, but was never active and never encouraged Maida in her union activities. They bought a house in Brooklyn, and Maida's mother lived with them. By that time, Maida said, Owen would not discuss her year-long trip with her. They divorced in 1955.

In London, at Ruskin College, I worked with African students, and some of these men were senior labor officers. They were down at Oxford and I was at Ruskin, but I attended some of the international lectures at Rhodes House because I was interested in international affairs. So I had contact with all of these men and women from Africa—mostly men, there being very few African women in the colleges in England at the time. Many of the men were part of the revolutionaries who, while they had a façade of accepting the status quo, were busily working at changing the status quo. We sat up nights discussing the future of Africa.

My first trip to Africa was as a representative of the American Federation of Labor. The international labor movement, the International Confederation of Free Trade Unions, of which the AF of L and CIO were members, invited the American unions to send as observers two delegates to the first ICFTU meeting in Africa. This seminar in Africa was for about three weeks, and included trade unionists from all over the continent who were able to come—many of them had been in jail. The emphasis was on an exchange of views, and they were talking about agriculture, mining, wages, hours, conditions of service, workers' education, the prospects of independence, and the role of labor in that world that was to come.

You must remember, this is early 1955. Ghana was the country that was preparing for independence, even though its leader, Dr. Nkrumah, had been jailed. It was very interesting that the man who jailed him, the governor general, was the man who was at the prison gates to welcome him out to form a government. These were very exciting times. There were two delegates from the United States, one prominent officer from the United Auto Workers and myself, and there was a delegate from Canada. I was the only woman. It was a time of very serious work.

After this conference, of course, there were resolutions and a program. I came back to the United States and made some recommendations; reported to the AF of L, reported to the ILG, because I was an officer of that union simply on loan to the AF of L. One of the problems that the AF of L–CIO had was that we felt some of the decisions taken were very good on paper, but they took so long to implement. A. Philip Randolph, as a vice president of the AF of L–CIO and president of the Brotherhood of Sleeping Car Porters, was one of the strong forces in the executive council of the AF of L-CIO. He championed actions which would more rapidly move programs to help the trade unionists be a social force for good, as we recognized and saw the transition in Africa toward independence. He made some of the most stirring addresses and worked within the AF of L–CIO council for change.

He was kind of the catalyst, a standard for the young Africans as they attended international seminars and saw him within the leadership of the AF of L-CIO in the international labor movement. He gave a sense of dignity, courage, and intellect. He was speaking on behalf of workers who had had the least, because the Brotherhood of Sleeping Car Porters had a long and bitter struggle. He was a great example, and I was fortunate to have been able to serve in some capacities as a result of Brother Randolph's help in saying that "this young woman, I believe, can share constructively."

One of the myths that I would like to lay to rest is: many Americans looked at President Meany as the conservative who only saw the status quo. He was concerned with what was good for workers and what was good for the citizen, and I don't think he's ever deviated from that. But he was an absolute optimist, and a challenger and a supporter when it came to working toward faster change in Africa. There is not a program with which I was associated subsequently, when I was on the staff of the AF of L–CIO in the Department of International Affairs, that President Meany did not actively support; he put his weight behind any proposition that he felt would give the worker a fairer chance on the continent of Africa.

I could tell you intimately about the differences between President Meany and President Randolph. They had very different approaches, and I do not pretend that Mr. Meany saw the need for the rapidity with which things had to change. They had a difference in method, and Mr. Meany had a fine Irish temper. But these two men had mutual respect, and other people were angry that Mr. Meany and Mr. Randolph were not angry with each other. They disagreed on method, and Mr. Randolph felt that unions should be aggressive in combating racial discrimination or thrown out of the AF of L–CIO and the rest of it. Mr. Meany was not going to go that round. But on Africa, they had no differences. Mr. Randolph's voice on colonialism was the voice that President Meany concurred with. We were being asked by the trade unions in Africa to help them.

AFL-CIO International Representative

In 1955 the AFL and the CIO merged into one federation, consolidating their international activities. After the merger, the international department intensified its work with unions in the rest of the world. This included developing labor education programs and job training centers in Africa.[13] While there were many political and ideological reasons for labor's involvement in Africa, Maida's main concern "was to develop a cadre of trained African trade unionists who would be prepared to participate in the development of their independent countries."[14] She developed lasting friendships with men such as Tom Mboya, who became general secretary of the Kenya Federation of Labor. She was influential in interpreting their goals to the American labor movement and focusing the AFL-CIO's attention on the problems in their countries.[15] During this time, Maida remained very involved with ILGWU Local 22. In 1960, however, she joined the international staff of the AFL-CIO, and devoted her energies full-time to Africa.[16]

One of my experimental projects was based on a discussion with some African leaders, one from Rhodesia and one from Nigeria. I developed a program for trade union leaders in the African needle trades or related industries. Some of us had been thinking for years that while you taught the rudiments of trade union representation and the functioning of an organization that has to function with officers and representation and writing letters properly and learning how to deal with management, there was a second phase, which I was particularly interested in. That was training workers in employment.

So, beginning in 1956, these trade unionists, these garment workers, talked to me and said, "You are our sister in the needle trades; you see the need. We need to upgrade and we need to teach ourselves. Could you help us?" Well, I tried for years and we were getting nowhere with it. I did a memorandum. This was roughly 1961–1962. President Meany said, "If you can put together the arrangement, this based on the request of the trade union movement in Africa, the AF of L–CIO will be supportive in the ways that we need to be. You just go and work it out with President Dubinsky."

I always knew that when President Dubinsky raved and stormed, if I kept quiet, I had won. He said, "Springer, you always come with your unilateral ideas," and I said, "No, this is not a unilateral idea, it's a recommendation. I've gone to President Meany with this, and he's approved it. You have the school, and I have come to ask you if we can use the school. There are workers in our industry in Africa who need to improve the standard of their representation as well as their knowledgeability of our standard of work." Finally, he said, "Go ahead and act," and so it came to pass. I have been singularly fortunate because the leadership of the American labor movement has always given me the kind of leeway for what was unorthodox. Well, the school is now fourteen years old. This was nation building; this was looking toward independence and looking toward a way that the trade union movement could work with the independence movement.

I worked at this with the commercial workers in Africa, worked with the motor drivers to set up a school in Nigeria. I saw the training of workers in industrial competence as a priority second to their knowledgeability on dealing with the employer and understanding the union contract and the legislation in their country.

Tom Mboya, general secretary of the Kenya Federation of Labor, on his first trip to the United States in the fifties, was here under the auspices of the American Committee on Africa. The organization had very little money, and I always offered help in my small way—a room. We had an old house in Brooklyn, a typewriter, a telephone, and food. We didn't have money, but these were the things we shared with dozens of young Africans who were in the United States for various purposes. He was twenty-three years old when I met him in 1955. He and my son were peers in age—I don't know who was a few years younger—and so I always thought that Tom was my second son. He was probably forty-six in terms of his sense of the fitness of things, his keen perception, his composure, and his rapid mind. He was a very rare human being. He never lost his sense of humor.

In the mid-fifties, preventive detention was still the way of life in Kenya under British rule, and Africans had to be off the street by nine o'clock at night unless you had a pass. Unless you had some reason—that you were working somewhere or you were doing something—you could be arrested summarily. I have been threatened with arrest because as I walked down the street it was assumed that I was an African woman being on the street without a permit or some reason for being on the street. I've attended many meetings of local trade unions in Kenya and was careful to protect the leadership from breaking curfews and other laws that put them in jail. When it got to be nearly nine o'clock, Tom had already organized the ways in which everyone could get back home, to ensure that they were not arrested.

So Tom and I worked on many projects. I suppose the one that stands as a memorial to our work is Solidarity House, the trade union center in Nairobi; the William Green Fund contributed the first $35,000 for the building. Vice President Randolph presented the check to the Kenya Federation of Labor. In the planning process, we had gone around to the then colonial government with a simple statement of fact. The idea was that the workers in Kenya would do something like buy a brick as their involvement and contribution to it. And so we tried to state this. We were suspect, of course, by the colonial government, but since we had nothing to hide, we gave the Kenya Federation of Labor rationale and its American counterpart supporting it, which subsequently became international support, through the International Confederation of Free Trade Unions. In July 1978 there was a seminar for women workers, and the opening ceremony was held at Solidarity House. The tradition, the history, of this workers' center continues.

The Women's Movement

Throughout her long career, Maida expanded opportunities for women workers and fought discrimination on the basis of sex as well as race within both the workplace and the labor movement. She fought for women garment workers across the United States. In 1959 she advocated for a vocational school for African women, and in the 1960s helped to establish the Institute for Tailoring and Cutting for women and men in the garment industry in Kenya. In 1970 she became vice president of the National Council of Negro Women. In 1980, as a consultant to the Asian American Free Labor Institute, she helped establish the women's bureau of the Turkish Federation of Labor. Her concerns with race, women workers, and international affairs came together at the World Conference of the United Nations' Decade for Women in Mexico City in 1975.[17] She also came to recognize the limits of her special status. While helping with organizing drives in the South, she noted in a letter to Dubinsky that "Negro workers are aware of their need of a strong trade union movement, but we need also to believe that the trade union movement has moved from the concept of a few chosen for their high visibility to an inclusiveness which makes unionism meaningful to all the workers in industry and at all levels."[18]

I am a supporter of the women's movement. In the same way that I think the labor movement is very often misunderstood, I think that the women's movement is misunderstood. The women's movement should be here to stay. It's simply another step in our development. I am a retired member of the Coalition of Labor Union Women. There was a need for such an organization. The National Organization for Women has settled down. Both NOW and CLUW are training grounds for building self-assurance and for participating in constructive ways.[19]

The IWY, International Women's Year, the meeting in Mexico City, was a turning point in the historical development of the role of women. The press emphasized the conflict because that's what sells newspapers. I was in Mexico City as a part of the program of the National Council of Negro Women. I was then a vice president of the National Council of Negro Women. We had within the conference our own program of meetings with women from Africa, the Caribbean, and Latin America. Dr. Dorothy Height, president of the National Council of Negro Women, then hosted twenty-seven of these women who traveled with us after Mexico City, because this was part of the International Memorial Year for Mary McLeod Bethune, the beloved African-American educator and civil rights reformer, and we were celebrating Mrs. Bethune's 100th birthday. These women went to Mississippi with us to look at rural development, at the kinds of programs that are very related to the kinds of programs there are in Africa, in the Caribbean, and in Latin America.

International Women's Year, as far as I'm concerned, was a very constructive way of reaching across the world to women. There was much that was substantive and what many people forget is that we are not talking about International Women's Year, and, thank you very much, it's finished. We are talking about International Women's Decade, which is a ten-year period. There are meetings going on all around the United States, regional meetings, and there are meetings going on in many countries. There are programs that are being structured as a result.

Anything that's underfinanced is vulnerable. A women's program is almost always taken tongue-in-cheek, and the assumption is "Let's get on with it and perhaps we can forget about it after." But the problem is that the women are not going to let anyone forget about it after, because every nation in the world subscribed to the document of International Women's Year and International Women's Decade. Now the fact that programmatically there has to be a great deal of effort made and funds provided for continuity, therein lies the tale. I don't think we will get 100 percent of our objective, but then nothing ever does. Oh, I'm enormously pleased and fortunate that I was one of the minor participants in the International Women's Year.

Work and Family

Long before commuter marriages, blended families, and caring for elderly parents were the subject of research, popular articles, and policy debates, Maida was living these issues. During her years working in Africa she remained based in the United States because she was the head of a household that included her son, her elderly grandmother, who moved from Panama when she was ninety-four, her mother, and her elderly stepfather. In 1965 Maida resigned from the International Affairs Department of the AFL-CIO and returned to the ILGWU for a combination of work and family reasons. She explained that there were increasing tensions between her trade union worlds in Africa and the United States, as many African leaders focused increasingly on nation building and absorbed the labor union, limiting the workers' freedom of association. That same year she married James Kemp, a lawyer, who was president of Local 189 of the Building Service Employees International Union from 1946 to 1983. He was an active leader in the Chicago Federation of Labor and the Chicago NAACP, sharing Maida's commitment to both labor and the black community, and he very much wanted Maida to return to work in the United States. Although she and Kemp separated several years later, they stayed in contact until his death in 1983. Maida reflects on the importance of family and work in her life.

My son grew up in a period when there were still very limited opportunities for the young black intellectual. The advice I gave him was "Pursue excellence, but be the best you know how to be. Then, whatever the context of your capabilities, always remember that you give a helping hand to someone who is striving, because there but for the grace of God, there you go. You are always one step removed from a mother who was a factory worker and from a grandmother who eventually owned a beauty parlor but before that worked as a domestic in this country. Never forget that."

I think the best contribution I have made is to have set an example for my son, who is a lawyer, but who has never forgotten that his responsibility is not only to himself and his family, but that he has a social responsibility to give back something to the society that helped to fashion his life. And to see his children now growing up with a sense of history. They have parents who are teaching them that they have a commitment—that's my best contribution.

The next is a privilege that in the labor movement, I have been able to learn and learn enough to make me humble, and always know I've got to pay back something. I'm an industrial worker and I have had some of the best training and best experience in the world. I come out of a factory. While I have attended a variety of schools, I always try to learn things. I've none of the snob labels, I've never taken myself seriously.

I haven't told you about my failures. You have a lot of those, too. You make bad judgments. I had learned early on, you have a disappointment, you get up, you wipe the blood away and go on to the next thing. Don't dwell on it. I've had my share of bloody experiences. I usually recover very quickly. As I look back on it, the bad spots were my being too highly motivated, too highly emotional about what I was doing. Very often I didn't see it from the outside, but I was so involved in what I was doing that I was blind to the motivations of others and my trust was misplaced. This happens to everybody. We wipe the blood off our noses and keep going.

In whatever field, pursue excellence, learn as much as you can about your field; do not wear your ability across your chest. If you have it, you do not need to flaunt it. Have a sense of history and do not believe that you created the wheel, because you will always learn that there were wheels there long before you came along, and that what you are doing is building. Have a sense of community identity. Give something back to society; give something back to your forebears. Never be so single-minded that you think there is only one way to live and only one choice. Learn not to be bitter about defeats and not to be arrogant about successes; each can limit you. Life is a combination of things: family, sharing, a personal relationship, which does not rob you of your self-respect and your own identity.

Always remember that the person who has done something against you—or the society, the people in that society—they are the lesser human beings than you are, or else they would not have to resort to denying you the right to opportunity. They are smaller people than you are, because in order for them to be superior they must teach you to be inferior. Never let anyone do that to you. Always remember, if bruised, you hurt; if bruised, they hurt. If cut, you bleed; if cut, they bleed. They have an Almighty that they go to in their end, as you do, and if one can get a perspective on all of this, even though you're temporarily humiliated, look at the source from which it comes, and never stop respecting yourself.

Sister Maida

In 1965 Dubinsky offered Maida a vice presidency in the ILGWU, but without a membership base in the union, she declined and instead became a general organizer in the South. As a troubleshooter, she was involved in organizing drives in North and South Carolina, Georgia, and Florida. In 1969 she focused her attention more on the Chicago area as Midwest director of the A. Philip Randolph Institute, an organization Randolph established to work on issues of race, workers, and unions. She continued to travel to Africa on behalf of unions, African-Americans, and women workers. In 1973 she returned to Africa, first joining the staff and then later acting as a consultant to the African-American Labor Center (AALC), an AFL-CIO affiliate. In 1985 she attended the World Conference on the United Nations' Decade for Women in Kenya. In 1991, at the age of eighty-one, she spent the winter traveling in East Africa with her family and also had an opportunity to visit old friends. Today she lives in Pittsburgh, near her son and his family. She continues to travel and welcome visitors to her home.[20]

Maida Springer-Kemp is a remarkable woman. Some years ago, Dr. Julius Nyerere, president of Tanzania, wrote to A. Philip Randolph, "In Tanganyika, she is 'Sister Maida' in more than a conventional sense. She is one of them. She is equally at home in Kenya. She has already worked a near miracle in Uganda where she helped to reunite a labour movement which was being fragmented."[21] Today, for many women and men on several continents, she remains "Sister Maida" in more than a conventional sense.

Chapter 6

Forty Years I'm Secretary-Treasurer of the Local

Mary Callahan, International Union of Electrical Workers (1914–1981)

For sixty-six years Mary Ries Callahan, electrical union activist, lived and worked in Philadelphia. During the Depression, as a young widow with a small child, she took a factory job in the rapidly growing electrical industry. She was a founding member of Local 105, United Electrical Workers–CIO (UE) and she became a union shop steward, trustee, and for forty years, her local union's secretary-treasurer. During World War II, she pioneered in negotiating benefits like maternity leave. After the war, the bitter political struggle between the communist and anticommunist factions in the UE increased, and Mary and her local helped form the new International Union of Electrical Workers (IUE).

Mary remarried and, with the support of her husband and two sons, became a national union leader. In 1959 she was elected chair of the Radio, TV, and Parts Conference Board, a national economic board that coordinated bargaining among employers and local unions in those sectors of the industry. She was one of only two women on the IUE's international executive board. In 1961 President Kennedy appointed her to his Commission on the Status of Women, the only woman representing labor since Esther Peterson was serving in a governmental role. Later, under an appointment by President Johnson, Mary also served on the Citizens' Advisory Committee on the Status of Women.

Mary was one of the first union leaders to voice concern about the effects of foreign imports on jobs in this county. The U.S. electrical industry declined, and her conference board was eliminated. She maintained a seat on the IUE executive board, however, as chair of the newly formed IUE Women's Council. Mary retired from the IUE in 1977, for health reasons, and in 1981 she died of cancer. Harry Block, the former District 1 IUE president who signed her up in the union, said that her greatest contribution was "to tell women they could make it in the labor movement."[1]

Fishtown

Mary Ries was born on Halloween, October 31, 1914, in the northeast part of Philadelphia known as Fishtown. Her father, from the German Catholic community, finished high school and worked for most of his life as an insurance salesman. Her mother, of Protestant German background, went to work in a hosiery mill when she was fourteen until she married at age twenty-three. She then stayed home and raised her family, Mary and her younger brother and sister. Like her mother, the young Mary saw marriage and family as her future.

I lived in the section called Fishtown. My mother said that in her day the shad used to come up the river, and there were big shad markets. Then, of course, the pollution of the Delaware River ended all the shad. It was a blue-collar neighborhood, definitely. It had built up around the factories down on the waterfront, around the old shipyard that's now out of existence. It was not an integrated neighborhood. There were no black children. There was an Irish church, the English-speaking church. There were four German churches around me. There were old houses, big, rambling houses. It was a community of families. Your aunts, your uncles, everybody lived close by. My father had a lot of brothers and sisters and my mother had a lot of sisters, and we were all within walking distance, so that we had cousins by the dozens, literally.

It was a regular mill neighborhood. Almost everybody walked to work. The sugar refinery took in one-third of the population. People worked in the "sugar house." Before the thirties they worked in paint manufacturing. The textile mills were a long, long, old line in Fishtown. Then 1925 to 1935, that's when electronics and radio opened up. The radio center of Pennsylvania was right up above our neighborhood. You had Attwater-Kent and Philco company factories. Philco was gigantic.

One of the first ways I made money was at World Series time. At the different textile mills, we'd stand outside and we'd chalk the results of the World Series game and they'd throw pennies at us. This was before portable radios, naturally. It was before night games. I remember this big hosiery mill where the fellows would holler, "What's the score? What's the score?" I used to be pretty good at printing the scores on the asphalt street. That's how the fellows in the mill would know what was going on.

I dropped out of school strictly because of finances. I went to two years of commercial high school. It was just the beginning of the Depression, and it was easier for me as a young girl to get a job in a candy factory for $2.50

a week than it was for the company to hire somebody at a livable wage. I married when I was sixteen. My parents didn't like it, but there just was no other future around. I felt I was getting somebody out of the ordinary because he had a job. A lot of people got married young. There just was nothing else. My parents with two girls and a boy, maybe they thought that's only two left that we have to worry about. I worked at the five-and-ten for a while, and then I became pregnant and quit.

Out to Work

By 1930 there were over 300,000 employees in major electronics factories like the General Electric works in Schenectady, New York, and the Westinghouse factories in South Philadelphia. Between 1933 and 1937, the employment of production workers in the electrical industry increased by 87 percent. In Philadelphia, Philco became a major U.S. manufacturer of radios. As early as 1910, 36 percent of the over 33,000 employees were women working in clearly designated women's jobs. By 1939, women represented 54 percent of the workers in the radio, radio tube, and phonograph divisions of the industry, and Mary was one of them.[2]

I didn't go back to work until my husband was killed in an automobile accident. I was nineteen when he was killed. I had the one boy, Michael. He was two years old. I didn't have any money to keep a home of my own. I went home to my parents and just made two extra mouths for my father to worry about feeding. There was no such thing as insurance or social security or anything. Nothing! It was just be glad you have parents. I probably could have gone to an aunt or uncle in Fishtown. Somebody would have taken us in.

I learned by that. It was something I could never have learned from a book. I've never had a bad time in my whole life, from the day I was born. There has never been anything in my life that frightened me or put me in despair. It just seemed to me that I was born under a lucky star. Everything I wanted to do just happened. Even when I was widowed, which I thought was the end of the world, that's when I went out to work. Up to that time I had never worked outside of those odd jobs like in the five-and-ten or the candy factory. I went to work when I was just twenty.

When I first tried to go to work at Philco, you stood outside and the personnel manager would come out and he'd say, "Who will work for 26

Mary Callahan at a meeting with James Carey (*right*), president of the International Union of Electrical Workers, and Al Hartnett (*left*), secretary-treasurer, 1960. *International Union of Electrical Workers.*

cents?" Some of the people would fall away, and he'd keep going until he got all the way down to 22 cents. Then when he'd see that everybody was going to back away, that was the bid and he'd take the people who were willing to work for that rate and take them into the plant.

I went to work at International Resistance Company, IRC, on the tenth of September in 1935. That's my seniority date. I'm still there. We made what were called "resistors," the volume controls that the kids of today wouldn't even recognize. It's the control that's in your television or radio, only magnified about fifteen times. Electric phonographs were just coming into being. We went from these gigantic things to miniature ones down through the years. I was an electrical tester, testing to make sure these things would not burn up in the set. Later I was an inspector on the assembly line.

The resistor at that time was glass covered with carbon and was about an inch-and-a-half long. The rate was to test 1,640 an hour. If you did this for 80 percent of the time, which would mean Monday to Thursday, you would get 38 cents an hour instead of 36 cents. You would do it all the way up to Thursday night. You never learned. The carrot was in front of you. Then on Friday they would give you such terrible work, some of these rejects to redo to see if you could get a few good ones out of it, which automatically pulled you down to about 1,500 or 1,200 an hour. Therefore you lost all those 2 cents that you made from Monday to Thursday, which was another reason for the union. You just didn't like people leading you around by the nose and making a fool out of you.

We were 85 percent women, the whole plant was predominantly women. There is the old myth that women are so dainty; they can handle these small assembly projects so much better than a man. But yet the real reason to hire women is because an employer can pay a lesser wage. When you go into anything that's delicate and expensive, like a diamond watch, the workers are all men. But when it comes to cheap jobs, the company says a man would be too clumsy, but what they really mean is, "For one-third of the price, we'll get you women."

I looked at it as a dead-end job, a place to get money to live because I didn't want to be on the welfare rolls. Times were so bad, I was glad to get the job. For the first eight weeks I was going to quit every night, but I couldn't afford to. They could have fired me and I think I would have felt better. My conscience wouldn't have bothered me.

Joining the Union

The Depression ended "welfare capitalism," a management system used in the electrical industry to provide workers with reasonable wages and additional benefits, such as life insurance, which helped keep union activity at a minimum in the 1920s. In the 1930s activists began to organize workers at both the local level and the national level, preparing to bargain with corporations as large as General Electric and Westinghouse. James Carey, a leader of a union local at Philco Radio Corporation in Philadelphia and an AFL organizer, was elected president of the United Electrical Workers at the union's founding convention in 1936. Women were actively recruited and Mary joined the UE with her family's support.[3]

About six months after I was hired, I became active in the union for reasons of dignity. Believe it or not, it had nothing to do with money. We had just come out of the Depression. I had no money and I was a widow, and I was glad to get a job at 36 cents an hour. But that wasn't the real reason I joined the union. The reason was that we were at the beck and call of the management. If you went in to work and they didn't have enough work, they'd send you home. Or, if you were late, even if it was by one minute, you had to sit in the office until the manager came in, which would be nine o'clock instead of seven. If he was in a good mood or if they had a lot of work, you went to work. If he was in a poor mood, he sent you home. If you had just gotten up and walked out anyway, you'd have lost your job— and jobs were still scarce in 1935.

We worked from 7 A.M. to 1 P.M. one week and from 1 P.M. to 7 P.M. the next week. They were short hours, six-hour days, no relief periods or anything like that. Most of the women I worked with were in their first jobs and came from homes where it wasn't a financial necessity for them. They had somebody to fall back on, but they didn't like being pushed around either. When we had the opportunity in December of 1935 to start a founding union committee, we all hopped on the bandwagon. We all joined one night; my union dues book number is 118 and I'm a charter member. I was 118th in the line and there were three hundred and some of us.

We were organized by the UE members of Philco. There were two locals, 101 and 102. One was in the radio-TV plant and the other was in the metal stampings plant. There was a formal organizer, Jim Carey, who had just been made president of this new union, the UE. But we were organized by rank-and-file UE members of Philco. These were not union staff organizers. They all worked in the plant. We had contacted them because some union organizing leaflets had been given out, and we said we were interested. We put out flyers in the plant that there was going to be a mass meeting close by the plant, eight o'clock at night.

Those rank-and-file UE members were young men and women workers who had joined that union themselves, and they had something we didn't have. They had freedom of movement, but most of all, they had the freedom to object. If something was unfair, or in their opinion was unfair, they could object and they had a union committee that would handle it. If we objected, we would have to go in to the personnel manager. If he was in a good mood that day, he might correct it; but if he wasn't, that was the end of you, and you had no recourse; it was the same as quitting. Members of the union recounted the different things that happened in their plant. The same things were happening to us; but at least they seemed to get their problems alleviated.

We were out of work on a one-month union recognition strike. The strike was very bad for me economically, because we weren't making that much money to begin with. Eleven dollars and ninety-six cents a week I was making, and I had one son. Of course, during the strike, my father and mother

Mary Callahan (*right*) meets with union delegates at the IUE international convention, 1966. *International Union of Electrical Workers.*

took care of milk bills and things, but I know I didn't even go to the victory dances, which only cost a quarter, because I didn't have lifts on my shoes. I'd have to wait until I got a paycheck to get them repaired, and I wasn't about to go to a dance with worn-down shoes.

We would walk to the picket line. I lived twenty-two blocks from the plant. That was forty-four blocks I would walk every day to picket. Our plant is in a big office building, the Terminal Commerce Building, and there's a railroad underneath, so that the pavement slopes. These pickets from Philco showed up one day, and every one of them was on skates. It's an enormous building, better than a full city block on each side and then down under the railroad. So everybody wound up then with skates. It was all right going down, but you'd have to take them off and walk back because there was no way of getting up those hills with those skates.

We won the union recognition strike, and we settled the first union contract without even getting a penny raise. But we were all so happy that we could go back to work and nobody could fire us without just cause, that money was secondary. We received a union shop, a union contract negotiating committee, a grievance committee, the right to have the washrooms unlocked, and a regular relief period. Before the union, you had to have special permission in those six working hours to use the ladies' room. We had a witch as a "forelady," and she wasn't born on Halloween. If she just felt she didn't want to be bothered turning the key, you couldn't go to that ladies' room; you just stayed at your workbench until you quit at one o'clock. Then they unlocked the ladies' room. This did more to organize than anything to do with the rates or working conditions of other kinds. Of course, the hours of work were important, the shifts were important. But that was the start, and from then on we got everything that people today take for granted.

Becoming an Officer

Local 105 was one of the first locals organized by the new UE. There were two locals in Philco and two locals at RCA in nearby Camden, New Jersey. The UE offered joint workers' education courses with local universities, the YMCA, and the Philadelphia Labor Education Association to train their new union members, and they encouraged women to be involved in union activities. Some locals had women's committees, and by 1944, eighteen women were local union presidents, one-third of the full-time UE organizers were women, and Ruth Young became the first woman on the UE executive board. Soon after Mary joined the UE, she ran for office.[4]

I became a shop steward immediately and a trustee in 1936. That means you have to audit all the books. Then from there to local union recording secretary in about 1942. I became the local's secretary-treasurer in 1946. For forty years I'm the secretary-treasurer of the local. I have to handle all the local union finances. We have a CPA who oversees me. I just asked people to vote for me because I thought I could do the job. I said, "After all, you vote every year; and if I don't do the job, you can get rid of me next year and put somebody else in." I didn't know what a union was anymore than anybody else did, but I figured I'd learn.

Another thing, I wasn't tied up too much with boyfriends and what not.

I lived at home. My boy was taken care of so that I had more free time to go out. A lot of the women were engaged to be married, setting up houses, and they were going to quit work. That was the thing you did at that time. You only worked a certain length of time, and then you left. I could see that I was going to be working for many years, and I figured I wanted to mold things to suit me! Yet these same women are still working with me. They never did quit, because the war came along and they stayed there. But in 1937 they had no intentions of staying. We have quite a few women with forty years' seniority in that plant.

For the second contract we were going after money, and I was on the negotiating committee. Everybody smoked in those days. The company representatives sat behind three big mahogany desks on one side of the room, and they had their ashtrays and their notebooks and all. They put a big wastepaper basket in the middle of the floor and lined the union committee up, standing along the wall, like statues. No tables or anything. They had it all set up, because that's the way they were. This was set up just to meet with us.

So I objected. Nobody said anything, but I objected to it, and I said, "I think we're here as peers; if you can't provide a table, then you three get into this Indian pow-wow and smoke your peace pipe over on this side around a wastebasket." The company vice president, he was very nasty, and he said, "People like you, we don't need. You're fired." So the committee said, "Well, you fired all of us," and we walked out of the room. We couldn't refuse to meet with them, but we said until things were better, we wouldn't meet. So we didn't meet anymore that day. The next day we came back, and there was a table and it was done the way it should be. That was just common decency.

I was shop steward about seven years. We had gone up to about 2,800 workers in two plants. In 1943, I took over the Logan plant in another part of the city. We had about 1,400 people there. My title was director of the Logan Union Office. Basically, I was the chief steward handling the dues money. Union members had to pay their dues every month. It was very unwieldy, and it was also something that had to be supervised, because you were handling their money; it wasn't yours.

The War Years

Increasingly during the war, men were being drafted out of the plant, and more women were coming into the plant, often in the higher-paying men's jobs. In 1945, women members of the electronics work force numbered 347,000, or 48 percent. Incentive work or piecework, a system in which workers are paid for each item they produce plus a bonus over a set production level, was a major problem. Because of the wage freeze during the war, Mary's local union was able to negotiate new nonwage benefits and family supports such as child care to help working mothers. Surveys at the time show that while a large percentage of women wanted to keep their new-found jobs after the war, many agreed to give them up to provide employment for the returning veterans. At that time, local union leaders like Mary did not question the practice.[5] In 1939 Mary had married Ed Callahan, an activist in the Bakery and Confectionery Workers Union, but he soon went off to war. Now other UE union activists, including District 1 president Harry Block and secretary-treasurer George Berry, provided support for her union involvement.

During the wartime period, when there was a War Labor Board and no increase in monies, our local negotiated things that were fantastic, that nobody ever heard of before. We had a Christmas bonus that's still in existence that other workers didn't have. All kinds of insurance, maternity leave, maternity benefits. When my son was born, I got seventeen dollars a week. This was a fantastic amount of money. Anything that was progressive, that wasn't cash, we had. Full seniority and time off and all that jazz had been negotiated about 1942. We had all kinds of bonuses for returning veterans. We negotiated four weeks' vacation for twenty years' employment service before any of our union members ever had twenty years of service. We got vacations paid at your average earned rate, not just the guaranteed base rate. We even had a SUB, supplemental unemployment benefits, before they ever had it in any other plant. We've had voluntary overtime since 1946. During the war we didn't use it. The words were there in our contract, but everybody worked whatever was required of them during the war. But after the war was over, we went right to the letter of the contract. We've had voluntary overtime ever since. Our local was very autonomous.

I would say the most important problem was protection of incentive workers. We became an incentive plant, and the people weren't getting their "just down time," as we call it. Through no fault of the workers, the machine would be down or there wouldn't be any parts and they'd sit there, losing 8 or 9 cents an hour. They would just be getting the base rate, which naturally was lower. The other problems were lateness and absence because of children, especially in the war years: the women not getting to work because they didn't have anyplace for their kids, or the kid came down with the measles that day and there was nobody to mind him.

That's why I thought child care was so essential and why the food program was needed. If you worked a ten-hour day, and we did in wartime, then went home to cook a meal, the kids would only get hot dogs or baked beans, or whatever was real fast to make. And there was food rationing and everything else. So in our plant, whatever they had in the plant cafeteria, you could order something to carry home at night. Just the same as you have in some of your prepared foods now in some of the stores. Now you buy frozen food too, but it was a little different in those days.

I served on a subdivision of the War Labor Board. It was called Woman Power—how we could help the women with child care, with home-cooked meals, because there was a war on. Everybody knocked themselves out to get the women to work on the assembly lines, to get the woman-behind-the-man-behind-the-gun bit. As soon as the war was over, they forgot all about these other kids that were born and needed child care, or that women still needed balanced meals to take home to their kids or to their husbands or to their old parents. For three years those programs operated like clockwork just because there was a war on. But in peacetime, forget it! Child care is gone. It's funny, if you go around shooting people, then they'll feed the kids so you can make the bullets.

In the plants, men were doing some of the better-paid molding jobs, and of course the skilled trades have always been male. Apprenticeship papers used to read "a male citizen of the United States under twenty-one years of age." Men were the fixers, which is a semi-skilled job, machine adjusters, meter mechanics, molders, or materials handlers. Everything that's supposed to be too heavy for the women to do.

Men's jobs had a differential rate; there was a general male rate and a general female rate and there was about an 8-cent difference. Everybody understood that there was a common labor grade for a female and common labor grade for a male, and nobody questioned it. Not the "girls," as they've always been called. Even today we have the habit of saying "girls" when somebody is retiring at age sixty-five. It was always the "girls" and the men, or the fellows, and we women had our place and they had their place and we didn't question it. I know I didn't. I didn't come on as a feminist by a long shot because I knew that I came from the test department and I'd always stay there. Being an incentive plant, the women, in the overall, have always made more money than the men, except in the skilled trades. That's just the way it was.

But then, in the war years, when the men went out of the plant, the women took over these jobs. We took over the drill press, the punch press, any job except skilled trades, because those did have to have special background and training. Even on these so-called semi-skilled jobs, the machine adjusters, we had women who did that. When the war was over and the fellows came back, the women voluntarily gave up those jobs. They were going to have babies; they were never going to work anymore. When the company filled the jobs, they automatically filled them with men. All the job postings on the bulletin board would say "female" or "male." We never questioned it; either as a union or I, as a person, never questioned it.

By the time my son was twelve years old, the war was still going on. I had remarried in the meantime, in 1939. My second husband was very active in the union. I met him at a union meeting. He was the shop chairman, business manager in the Bakery and Confectionery Workers Union for many years. But my husband was over in Europe during the war. My mother hadn't come to live with me yet. So I used to take my son up to the union office, and he'd sit up there and do his homework. I found out later that the reason he liked to go was because he did all his arithmetic on the adding machine. He was real happy to go up there where we had a radio and an adding machine.

For twenty-five years, Harry Block and George Berry were reelected our district officers. They were very close friends of mine and of my family's, even my children. During the war, I remember George taking my older son hunting. He needed somebody to start him off. He's forty-three now, and he's not only a hunter, but his three sons are hunters and my younger son too. Now me, I could never get interested. But this was the kind of relationship we had with other union officers.

The Riot Act

The end of the World War II brought new turmoil to the unions. As war production stopped, employment in UE-organized factories fell from 700,000 to 475,000 in 1945. Employers sought to return to prewar conditions. Unions, however, tried to make up for wages and benefits lost during the war because of no-strike pledges, while also accommodating demobilization efforts and returning veterans. In 1946 the UE succeeded in shutting down every GE and Westinghouse plant in the United States and Canada, a strike that Mary Callahan took part in. The UE was demanding increased wages, but the electrical companies began a concerted effort to reduce the union's influence. During this time Mary also gave birth to her second son, Edward Callahan, Jr.[6]

I walked the picket line at the General Electric strike in 1946. I was there the famous day when the Riot Act was read. I'll have to admit I didn't know what a riot act was. This was a term we used at home if you did something: "You just wait, your father's going to read the riot act to you." I just figured that was like a sort of chastisement, and I didn't know there was such a thing as a Riot Act that made your picket line immediately illegal. We all gathered in the square, on Elmwood Avenue. I was right in the front lines because one of our leaders in the UE, he says, "Women and veterans to the front!" We were there with the American flags, and they read the Riot Act. Nobody dispersed. The cops came with the horses and really disbanded us. Some of the pickets were beaten. It was very bad.

I'm running and I'm thinking, "Ye gods! I must be scared," because my stomach was fluttering and really shook. Cops on horses chasing me. Right up on the porches. I finally ran into a lady's house. She opened her door and let me in. None of her family worked at General Electric, but she just didn't approve of what was going on. She would let strikers run through her house and go out through the backyard because the horses weren't back there.

It was a very bad day. I remember it very well. I finally got home, and I still felt bad that night. My husband says to me, "Maybe you should go to see a doctor. You shouldn't be so upset like that. I told you to stay out of it. You didn't have to be with all the guys in the front." I went to the doctor's and found out I was three months pregnant and didn't know it. That's what all the fluttering was about. I just was not aware of it. What a way to find out. Cops chasing me on a horse.

For me it was hardest right after the war, between 1946 and 1950. I had another son born in 1946. I have two boys fourteen and a half years apart. After my father died, my mother lived with me for twenty-nine years. In fact, I would never have worked, and I guess all the things that happened in my adult life after I became active in the union would not have taken place, if my mother didn't live with me. I was off from work for three months' maternity leave. I was full-time with the union, but it was perfectly feasible, with all my activities, to just take the three-month period. It wasn't as strenuous as if I had been working on the assembly line. If I had been on the line, I probably would have taken six months just to get adjusted.

While you're supposed to be a union representative for twenty-four hours a day, let's face it, there's nobody working twenty-four hours a day. You have more time off during the week. So there may be a lull, say, on Tuesday and Thursday, but the majority of the work is on weekends. You can get more people out from the plants to attend weekend activities. There's a lot of weekends involved.

Sometimes I resented the fact that I wasn't home; I wanted to be. But at the same time, I worked not just because of my devotion to the union, but because I had to make a living, because we weren't affluent with one salary anymore than anybody else in this day and age. That part used to bother me because I would rather have stayed home some nights when I had to go out on union business. But if I hadn't gone out, then I wouldn't be where I am today, because you just can't be a fair-weather union official. It's just a matter of your choice, what you want to do. I wanted to work at what I was doing.

The UE-IUE Split

After the war, a factional struggle around issues of communism was played out in the UE as well as in many other unions. In 1941 Jim Carey's defeat as national president of the UE reflected increasing influence in the union by certain UE leaders who were alleged to be members of the Communist Party. Strong anticommunist leadership was centered in Mary's Philadelphia. In 1946 Harry Block, president of IUE District 1, established the UEMDA, the UE Members for Democratic Action, made up of local- and district-level officials, to fight the increasingly left-wing direction of the union. In 1947 the Taft-Hartley Act was passed by Congress. Under Title I, Section 9(h), it required every union official to swear an oath that he was not a member of the Communist Party.[7] In 1949 the CIO convention expelled the UE, along with the Longshoremen and eight other smaller, allegedly communist-run unions. Philip Murray, president of the CIO, then unveiled the charter for a new electrical union, called the International Union of Electrical Workers, to be headed by James Carey.[8]

We were in this big battle in the United Electrical Workers as to whether the international union officers were following the communist line or not. We were of the opinion that they were. Local 105 felt that we were affiliated with a leftist union. There were all kinds of ideologies, but I didn't pay that much attention to them. I was too interested in maintaining a job, getting the war won, getting my husband home. Between 1941 and 1946 they were just things on the side that you talked about, but they weren't the important things. It was afterward, in 1946, where all these ideologies broke out, where we took sides.

Yet even during the war, we, Local 105, were stepchildren. We weren't getting any service from the UE. We were just paying dues. I would be less than honest to say that it wasn't offered. I mean, the UE would have sent somebody in, but we didn't want them because we had no choice; we had to take who they sent. There was a motion on the books that nobody could come into the local without the express consent and approval of the membership. We didn't care for the UE staff appointments.

The play for power in our union took place from 1946 to 1950. There were just about two women in our local union who stayed around with me. We were very strong in the United Electrical Members for Democratic Action, what we call the UEMDA. We'd go to conventions and we'd fight and put up our candidates, and we never won. I belonged to the UEMDA and did most of their paperwork in Philadelphia, because that city was the headquarters for the people in the international union from the other electrical workers' locals who were heading this up.

The McCarthyism that went on in the fifties was very sad. But this was different. Ours was a purely philosophical argument that we weren't going to have our union dues money and our union dedicated to something that was contrary to what we thought was everybody's democratic rights. However, I objected to the Taft-Hartley noncommunist affidavit. I had no objection to filing anything about being noncommunist, but why only the union people? Companies never had to do that; they never had to sign it. The worst part of the Taft-Hartley was the trimmings. It had everybody waving an American flag while Congress did away with the union shop, and the anti-union right-to-work laws won out. This is where the powers that be in Congress at that time really got even with unions and took a lot of their strength away. The AFL and the CIO never adequately worked to repeal that 14(b) of Taft-Hartley, the right-to-work, when they had the muscle. They should have used it, and they didn't use it.

Then in 1949, the CIO expelled the United Electrical Workers. I was not at the CIO convention, but as soon as the telegram came that the UE had been expelled and that Phil Murray, CIO president, had granted a charter to a new union called the International Union of Electrical Workers, we met in Town Hall in Philadelphia. There was at that time 1,800 in our local, and I think the whole 1,800 was there. The vote was unanimous to switch to the IUE. We were the very first local. Looking back on it today, maybe it would have been better if everybody had stayed together and fought a little harder. When you start fragmenting yourself you're doing no good, but at the time, the factional political fights had been going on within our own union for quite a while.

National Leadership

During the 1950s Mary was involved in some community activities, like her son's boys' club, but increasingly her time was devoted to the new IUE. In addition to being secretary-treasurer of Local 105, she was chair of the AFL-CIO Community Relations Committee in Philadelphia, chaired the women's activities department of the AFL-CIO Committee on Political Education (COPE), and represented Local 105 as its member-at-large on the IUE district executive board. During this time the union formed seven conference boards to coordinate collective bargaining for different locals with different employers, but in the same sector of the industry. In 1955 Mary was elected secretary of the IUE Radio, TV, and Parts Conference Board. The board represented more than ninety thousand workers in eighty-nine collective bargaining units. This experience underscored Mary's observation that "automation poses one of the greatest challenges confronting locals in the industry."[9]

I was secretary of the Radio, TV, and Parts Conference Board, then I was chair of that board. There were only two women delegates besides me. The rest of the delegates were men, and I was reelected every year by them, and very friendly with them, and had no problems at all. That's how I came to get on the IUE executive board back in 1959. When I changed from being the secretary of the conference board and became the president, I went on the IUE international executive board. We had a conference board of about three hundred people at one time, and it went down as low as fifty people, down to twenty-five, because there just was not money to send delegates. That was the Radio, TV, and Parts Conference Board then, and later the Electronics Conference Board.

That job took a lot of research, telephoning, trips, and visiting people to try to get common goals in the radio-TV industry, trying to get all the same expiration dates of union contracts. It was the forerunner of what we know today as "coordinated bargaining." We didn't have the same employers, but the various companies seemed to sell all their radios and televisions at the same price. We figured there should be the same kind of wages for the workers. If the wages were low, it didn't make the product any cheaper; it was still just as expensive as the high-wage product. Those negotiations took up a lot of time, a lot of thought, a lot of energy.

When we went to union meetings, traveling with the men on the same trains, planes, and staying at the same hotel was never any problem, but

it was just being the odd one. I found it very lonely when I was in my forties and early fifties, because then you're at the time when you realize that
you want to go out at night and there's nobody around. Many a time I've
eaten my dinner in a hotel room rather than go down to the restaurant
alone. I wouldn't try to go with any men unless they asked me to go with
them; and if it wasn't my own union delegation, if they were strangers, nobody would even think of asking you to go to dinner, because they figured
if you wanted to go, you'd say, "Hey, how about if I go with you?" That's
the only thing I ever found wrong.

My colleague on the international executive board from Canada, Evelyn
McGarr, said to me, "You know, Mary, I was so glad when you came on
this executive board. You don't know how many nights I ate in the hotel
room alone. Now that you've come on here, we go out with men more often
because there's two of us and it doesn't look like you're just trying to get
somebody to take you out for a free meal." When I was with the local union
people, I had this kind of companionship. In the higher union echelons,
however, I notice it's less friendly. Maybe it's competition. I've often thought
of that.[10]

The President's Commission

President Kennedy's Commission on the Status of Women was chaired by
Eleanor Roosevelt and directed by Esther Peterson in her role as director of the
Women's Bureau. The twenty-six commission members were selected from a wide
range of organizations, including unions, corporations, universities, and women's
groups. In addition, there were four committees and four consultations involving
hundreds of people. There were two members on the commission representing
the labor movement, Mary Callahan and William Schnitzler, secretary-treasurer of
the AFL-CIO. The commission was specifically mandated to review the Equal
Rights Amendment issue. Mary opposed such an amendment. Like Esther
Peterson and most other union women at that time, she instead supported protective labor legislation and equal pay for equal work laws.[11]

On that very first commission we did a lot of work. We had hundreds of
people from all walks of life, not just the twenty-some members of the commission. We started out with schools, child care, social security, the ERA,
anything and everything that had to do with the status of a woman in the
United States, from the cradle to the grave. It was very interesting. There

were people with whom I had never expected to sit down at a roundtable. Like Mrs. Roosevelt, who in herself was just incomparable, all her knowledge. I mean, just as a person, she was great. Then, to sit with an editor from the *Ladies' Home Journal* and somebody from Radcliffe College and other people who had their Ph.D.'s in all kinds of things. Even some merchants and people from great big department stores.

In the beginning I thought, "I'm really outclassed here. There's nobody here that I even have a common interest with." I was very gratefully surprised, really surprised at these people, international businesswomen, professional women, university women. On these particular issues, we were all of the same frame of mind. Maybe we wanted to go different roads; we weren't unanimous. But at least our goals were the same. This country could not overlook its woman power. The country itself was losing out by not using the knowledge and talent and gifts of its own citizens, regardless of sex.

In no way was anybody anxious to push the woman out of the kitchen into the work force if it was a woman's desire to be a homemaker. Of course we had disagreements. We had some violent arguments. Those that were manufacturers or employers weren't exactly union conscious, and I wasn't exactly trusting of them either. But when you got to talk to them as persons, you could understand that, "to each his own."

I was on the protective labor legislation subcommittee. I was opposed to the ERA, because I thought it would remove the legal protections for women that took fifty years to get. The position that IUE and some of the women on the our committee took was that all this protective labor legislation should be reviewed. Those laws that were discriminatory and obsolete should be abolished. We should keep all those that were good and make them applicable to anybody that works, not just sex-wise. Then the ERA would be okay.

We were not opposed to ERA as such, but because of what it was going to do to the protective legislation that we wanted to have extended to men. Evidently, the men don't want the protections. I don't know why they don't; they're very foolish. Everybody should have a relief period on a job. Everybody should have a lunch period. Everybody should have a rest period and some chairs close by to sit on so they don't have to continually stand. These were things that only women had because of the protective legislation. We only had them because these were the little sops they gave us in lieu of a decent wage and equal opportunity. But, however we got them, we had them. Just get those laws changed so that the men can enjoy them, and then we'll go for the ERA. But if you go for the ERA now, that's going to be the end of the laws; and we are going to be back where we were fifty years ago. Then we would discuss it and discuss it.

Anyhow, the Civil Rights Act of 1964, Title VII, eliminated the protective laws. It had nothing to do with the ERA. It was judged that these laws were discriminatory because they were only for women and didn't apply to men.[12] It hasn't done too much damage to us to rescind those laws, but some of them should be reviewed. I don't think that anybody should work eight hours without a break or a lunch hour. We in the unions are protected. We did this for ourselves. But unions always stood for social justice, and some of the things that were rescinded seemed to me to be very, very unfair. These benefits should have just been extended to men. My concern is for all people.

We called for equal pay for equal work. That was the very first thing that was ever passed. Mrs. Roosevelt was still alive when we made that recommendation to the President of the United States, who was Kennedy at the time. The commission members unanimously were pushing for an equal pay for equal work law. The Equal Pay Act was passed in 1963. Nothing that I know of ever came out of those meetings unanimously, except equal pay for equal work. In fact, there were some minority reports because there were things in there about abortion, about marijuana, and things like that where there just couldn't be even a majority opinion.

Then every state had a commission on the status of women. There was national follow-up, the Citizens' Advisory Council. When Nixon succeeded President Johnson in office, of course, the courteous thing you always do is write and tender your resignation from any commission to the outgoing president. That part was all right. So I had a call from the U.S. Department of Labor right after Nixon had taken office and the woman told me she was calling for President Nixon about the Citizen's Advisory Committee on the Status of Women and he had two questions. I said, "What's that?"

First of all, he wanted to know my age, and secondly he wanted to know my party affiliation. So I said, "Well, you tell the President for me that my age is none of his business. It's not a secret, but my age doesn't mean a thing. And if he doesn't know that any reliable AFL-CIO member is Democrat, then he shouldn't have been President in the first place." I've never heard from him since!

An Industry Decline

Although the electrical industry continued to grow in the United States, many electrical products were manufactured overseas. By 1970 the IUE local unions coordinated by Mary's conference board had lost fifty-five thousand members, and there was no longer any viable U.S. radio-television industrial sector. Mary was one of the first board members to sound an alarm about the effect of imports on jobs covered by her union and in her own workplace. In 1970, she reported in the *IUE NEWS*: "We're not against balanced trade; it's healthy and necessary. But we cannot stand for the wholesale export of our jobs. American corporations must realize they have an obligation to the people they employ. Runaways must be stopped."[13]

At one time we were 2,800 Local 105 IUE members, but with runaway plants, diversification of the various products, and the company-opened plants in the South and Southwest, we're only 280 members now in our local in 1976. We followed the runaway plants and organized two of them. Then the foreign imports are just about the end of even those plants. They're down just as low as we are. We've been bought out by a conglomerate. This is just going to be the end of the independent American worker, and that's no joke. It's a fact.

This new company, TRW, that bought out the old International Resistance Company. is a diversified conglomerate that makes automobile parts as well as electronics. Right now we're having a problem. We're on our last legs, because the powers that be from the top of the corporate structure have given our company about two years to make good. They're in what they call a "crisis for survival." They have a plan for survival. I just hope their plan includes all the people who have had forty years of service like me, and the other 280 of us.

We always had good union meetings. We're one of the few locals who do. We meet right after work, across the street; we meet at the Hotel Philadelphia at five o'clock. We guarantee that the meeting will start on time and it will go no longer than an hour and a half, unless the membership votes it longer, but we will not prolong it. We had a meeting fine. If you missed your third meeting you were fined a dollar until you attended. We have excellent attendance. We have better than 50 percent attendance, and always have. Now we've changed our meetings to once every three months rather than every month, because there's not enough of us. We have a forty-eight-hour notice for calling a special meeting if it's necessary.

The Women's Council

In 1972 the Radio, TV, and Parts Conference Board was merged, but a new policy position was created on the IUE international executive board to represent the newly formed IUE Women's Council with a voice, but no vote. Under the direction of the social action committee, every local and district also established a women's council. The 1972 IUE convention also established the Title VII Compliance Program to educate staff and members and review contracts and practices for possible discrimination. Under this program, the IUE general counsel, Winn Newman, assumed an important role in litigating court cases to implement Title VII, including pregnancy and wage discrimination.[14] Mary worked on these issues through the women's council, "but always I was secretary-treasurer of the local in Philadelphia."

A chairperson of the Women's Council was to be elected by the delegates to that Women's Council. That person would sit on the IUE international executive board. Well, I was the one who was elected to that position, and I have been sitting on the executive board the same as ever since 1959, except now I don't have a vote anymore, just a voice to report and discuss.

It's my responsibility to make sure that everybody, women and men, are justly treated. Then, furthermore, to publicize this amongst our locals in our own women's councils and to disseminate information about new programs for women in other unions. There's been a lot of lip service to affirmative action. Well, our union says it has to work; and if affirmative action doesn't work, somebody's going to move in and make it work. I think that's why we're the union with the biggest number of cases in the court—the EEOC cases—because we do follow through, not just about discrimination because of race, color, or creed, but also about discrimination based on sex. The general counsel of our international union is really up to his neck in this thing.

There was an awful lot that had to be undone because we didn't realize at first what was discrimination. When I say "we," I'm talking about being a woman on the local level. As a leader I never thought much about discrimination. I figured who the heck wants a job over there; it's a male job. Probably if we had more so-called male jobs in our plant I would have realized it; but being 85 percent women in our plant, we were in a majority anyway. It didn't seem like there was any kind of discrimination. Actually there was, because jobs were posted that way, male-female. There was nothing in the collective bargaining contract that made the jobs male and female. It was the way of life. This is how you conduct a plant. Men just couldn't possibly do this intricate work and women couldn't possibly do heavy work. It was ridiculous! But that's been ironed out.

On the conference board that I chaired, I first started to hear from other plants about their very great problems. There were some plants where married women were laid off first, regardless of their seniority. Now we are dealing with other problems. For example, should maternity be treated the same as any other temporary disability for matters of insurance payment? When you are temporarily disabled because you're pregnant, should you receive the same insurance benefits as somebody that's temporarily disabled because they have a hernia or a broken leg or something else? The case is *Gilbert* v. *G.E.* and this has been argued before the U.S. Supreme Court, but they haven't rendered their decision yet.[15]

We don't have that problem here in Local 105, TRW. I argued it with the company, and I went to the Human Relations Commission down here in Philadelphia. We were successful in having the company set it up as a policy. Pregnancy is treated here as a temporary disability, the same as any other kind. We collected something like $5,400 in back pay for our people for the two years that we argued about it. We didn't have to go to court. We just seemed to be able to get it across to them that it was the right thing to do and the legal thing to do, and that was the end of it. We grieved it as a local union position.[16]

For a Woman to Be Active

During the 1970s the IUE, along with many other unions and the AFL-CIO federation, changed its position on the Equal Rights Amendment and began to support the ERA. Mary, too, supported the ERA once the protective laws were no longer an issue. She remained uneasy with many of the feminists, however, and turned to other union women through the Coalition of Labor Union Women, organized in 1974. Unlike the WTUL, CLUW did not have "allies" or wealthy women who helped the union women. Union women formed their own separate organization. Gloria Johnson, then director of education and women's activities within the Social Action Department and longtime staff person on the Radio, TV, and Parts Conference Board, helped found CLUW.[17]

Now, I think the ERA should pass. I don't know whether it will, but I'm certainly working toward it. For different reasons entirely. Some of the southern legislators who oppose the ERA say that because of chivalry their women cannot be put upon. Then you look at the southern states with the lowest wages, the worst working conditions. In these places where they're opposed to the ERA, the same people are opposed to anything else progressive. For that reason, we do have to pass the Equal Rights Amendment, just so we can do away with all forms of discrimination.

An ERA is not going to change the protective labor legislation, because protective legislation is already changed. Opponents of ERA say that our daughters will have to go to war, or both sexes will use the washroom, and there will be no more morality. Well, we've had the ERA here in Pennsylvania for three years, and it hasn't changed my way of life one bit. Up in that airplane, I went over states where they didn't have the ERA, and I still had to stand behind that man to get in that washroom!

But union women may be a little bit suspicious of women in other organizations that you would term "feminist." We don't see eye-to-eye yet on a lot of the ways to reach a goal. I think those women can't understand that a union contract is a benefit to a woman as well as to a man. They are of the opinion that you go in and you pick out certain things that are just for women and the men are something else. Union women don't see it that way. They see that a union is a union, that's what it is, unity of the sexes, of the races, what have you.

I think the feminist leaders are very snobbish. Sometimes they're suspect because I don't think they're for real. Some of them are looking at, "How can I become the manager." Not, "How can we all get along and improve our lot in life?" It's, "How do I get up there." This is the way businesses are run, unfortunately, not just with females, but with males, too.

We can't see where the janitor is any different than the toolmaker. The janitor is doing a job and the toolmaker is doing a job, and they're being paid in proportion to what they do. But their status is no different. It doesn't make you a higher level because you have a higher job. In the business and professional groups, and even with the university woman, the university is higher than the high school, and a doctor is higher than a clerk. It's a caste system, which union people don't have. It means nothing to me whatever job a woman does. As long as she's part of the union, she must be doing something or they wouldn't have hired her. Her "caste," whether she's the boss's secretary or not, is immaterial to me.

A long time ago, I guess it must have been about 1968, I attended a meeting at the home of Esther Peterson in Washington. It was after she had left her job as the deputy secretary of labor under President Johnson. A group of us met, and we thought it would be so nice if only we could get all the women in the unions together. There were women from all the industrial unions: women like clothing workers, the auto workers, laundry workers. I came out of Esther's house and I said, "Well, I guess it will be like everything else; we'll have to push it." But it seemed to die. I completely forgot about it, because we didn't get anywhere.

Then about five or six union women met in Chicago in the early seventies and decided they would try this thing that we had talked about five years previous. I was not amongst them. It seems it started for me here in Philadelphia. Gloria Johnson contacted me and said she was coming up from Washington, that she was on a planning committee for this meeting here in Philadelphia to see what we could do.

I went to the meeting. There were people that I had never met before. Young people, which made me very happy. I felt like a grandmother there, literally. We had the meeting down at the Amalgamated Clothing Workers' hall, and four hundred women came to that from all walks of life, all unions, all the way from the teachers down through the laundry workers, if you want to distinguish between people. All they wanted was that women get recognition in the union for their input. Over and above that, there were some people who thought, and probably rightfully so, that anytime they opened their mouths they got a put-down because they were women or because they were viewed as mouthy young women trying to upset the apple cart. So that's how CLUW started.

When we went into our first CLUW founding convention in 1974, there were 3,200 women there in Chicago. They couldn't even let them in; they closed the doors to the hotel because we were a fire hazard and they were afraid the floors would fall in. They came from all over the country! Thirty-two hundred women on their own! Gosh, I'll never get over it, I never saw so many women in my whole life. And still buses coming up with loads of women, who couldn't even get into the hotel where we were staying for the founding convention. So that was the start of it.

If you belong to any organization that can bargain a bona-fide contract, you're eligible to join CLUW. This is a step forward. This is something the men have never been able to do. The IUE left the UE; the UAW left the AFL-CIO; the Teamsters were thrown out of the AFL-CIO. Now women from all of these organizations got together as union people and hammered out some goals. The first is to organize the unorganized thirty-four million women workers. We're not going out on our own as CLUW, but we work through our own unions trying to do this. I think this may be a shot in the arm and may lead to some women taking more leadership in their international unions, because now their confidence has been built up. I think from here, it'll be a matter of just getting the votes of the people that you want to represent. Like anything else, it will take ten years, but I think this is the beginning. It will never go away. It won't disappear.

For a woman to be active—I can only talk for my own local—they're between the ages of nineteen and twenty-five. Then they either leave to get married and don't come back, or, if they have children, they just drop out because they want to be home at night with the kids. Somebody's taking care of them during the day. Then, at about thirty-five years old they come back out again and get active. But also, wives haven't taught their husbands that they also have something to do with raising these kids. I mean, if the man can go on a fishing trip from four o'clock Saturday morning and come home Saturday night and sleep all night Saturday and rest up on Sunday, then they should change places once in a while. I think younger women will make sure it is that kind of a household. They realize that it's a two-way street when you get married, and it's supposed to be a partnership. That's what it should be.

I have always had this. My second husband was a union official himself. He knew what it was to go to school on weekends for union classes. That's where he went. So did I. Then when the war came along, he was gone for thirty-three months. I just became independent. I could do it because I wanted to live this way. It so happened, I guess, that he figured that was the only way he was going to live if he was going to be happy with me. I wouldn't be where I am today if I didn't have the happy marriage I did. My husband always thought that if God gave you brains, use them. We laugh amongst ourselves in the IUE that he's the best personal relations man anybody could have.

On women presidents of locals, the IUE has a very high batting average, but not president of the international union. Not in my lifetime, no. I don't know of any woman that would step forward, and that includes me! There are a lot of qualified women around, but I think it's a matter of numbers. I don't think any woman thinks she has the backing at this time. But I'm sure it will come in the future.

Forever in Her Debt

Mary Callahan retired from the IUE in 1977 for health reasons. In 1981 she died of cancer at her home in Philadelphia. She left her husband, two sons, three grandchildren, and her brother and sister. On hearing of her death, the president of the IUE, David J. Fitzmaurice, said, "Mary Callahan was a hard-working, articulate and spirited leader who made a tremendous contribution to the building of IUE. IUE members, past and present, owe her a lot." In "Sing a Song of Unsung Heroes and Heroines," Alice Hoffman wrote, "Mary Callahan believed that women working together could make a better life for themselves and their families. She also believed that unions would benefit from the active leadership of their women members."[18]

Chapter 7

The Challenge Is Still There

Ah Quon McElrath, International Longshoremen's and Warehousemen's Union (1915–   )

Ah Quon McElrath, or "AQ," as she is known in Hawaii, was the first social worker and only woman hired on the staff of the predominantly male Local 142 of the International Longshoremen's and Warehousemen's Union (ILWU). She began her union work while still in college by volunteering in the 1938 strike of the Inland Boatmen's Union. In her first job, working for Hawaii's Territorial Welfare Department, she organized the social workers and clerical staff. She married a union activist, Bob McElrath, and with him raised two children. Together Ah Quon and Bob fought for their Marxist beliefs in the wave of anticommunist sentiment following World War II.

During the ILWU strikes of 1946 and 1949, Ah Quon designed and carried out relief programs for the families of the sugar and longshore workers and contacted social service agencies to gain supplementary assistance for the strikers. In 1954, Local 142 created the position of social worker. In that job until her retirement in 1981, she worked closely with the ILWU education department to develop social service and employee assistance programs for members as well as a community referral network of private and public agencies.

In 1988 Ah Quon was awarded an honorary doctorate from the University of Hawaii, where she had received her bachelor's degree fifty years earlier. Four years later, in 1992, she received the Pioneer Award from the Asian Pacific American Labor Alliance, AFL-CIO. Today, this eighty-year-old volunteer leads Hawaii's Committee on Welfare Concerns. The *Hawaii Herald* headlined a 1991 article "Ah Quon McElrath—Fire Still Burns in Veteran Labor Leader," describing her as "a devout unionist and a staunch feminist."[1]

A Picture Bride's Daughter

In 1837 sugar became a major commercial export in Hawaii and rapidly developed into the largest industry on the islands. Five large plantation owners, known as the "Big Five," took control of most of the economy and much of the political system. To supply additional labor, men, women, and children were brought from China, Portugal, Germany, Scandinavia, Japan, and the Philippines to work the sugar plantations. Their employment relationship was controlled by the Masters' and Servants' Act of 1850. Between 1879 and 1898, over forty-eight thousand people arrived in Hawaii from China. Ah Quon Leong's parents were part of this wave of immigration.[2]

My mother came here at the turn of the century. She came as a "picture bride." My grandparents remained in China. I remember her talking about how difficult life was in China, about the selling of girl children and even the committing of infanticide during periods of great drought and famine when it was impossible to raise a whole family. The attitude toward girls was that they couldn't work in the fields and do any other work, and it was useless to keep them around.

Mother had bound feet, which impeded her locomotion considerably. One of the things I remember was washing my mother's feet, especially during the period when she became older, and having her wince in pain because her toes were curled almost completely under her instep. While she may not have come from a rich family, still the custom of binding the feet filtered down to her particular village in Kwantung. She used to talk in aphorisms. She would have a moral saying for everything that we did wrong. This particularly indicated to me that Mother must have had some education. When her eyes were good, she did read the Chinese newspapers.

The usual way of greeting you in Chinese means "What is your surname?" and you tell them your surname. Then they ask, "What is your father's name?" I would tell them my father was Leong Chew. "Ohhhhhh! Rich man Chew. Your father get one store on Nuuanu Street." No, that is not my Leong Chew. My Leong Chew is a different Leong Chew. The Leong Chew who came to work on the plantations. Who landed in Oahu prison because he smoked opium or made moonshine or whatever. Who drove a hack, who was a carpenter, who did everything under the sun. Who also died when his youngest child was three and a half. You always had to explain when people asked you, "What was your father's name?" No, we are not of that Leong who has the Leong Chew dry goods store on Nuuanu Street. It wasn't ours.

My mother never expressed any regret at having come as a picture bride. Whatever regrets she might have had were probably engendered by the fact that our father worked only intermittently, and raising a family was really very hard on her. That might be the only regret; but I suspect, as with other immigrants who came to the United States, whatever they had here was much better than what they had at home.

Collecting Bones and Kiawe Beans

Ah Quon was born on December 15, 1915, the sixth of seven children, four boys and three girls. Her father died when she was about five. As many immigrants did all over the United States, family members pooled their resources and the older children dropped out of school to help support their younger brothers and sisters. Planting pineapple for commercial use began in 1899, and commercial canning followed in 1901. By 1915 pineapple canning was the second-largest industry in Hawaii, offering low-wage job alternatives to plantation work for immigrants' children, like the Leongs.

My brothers and sisters left school very early in order to work. I remember, even as a youngster, our going out to pick up dried bones and kiawe beans to sell to the fertilizer company. They paid us variously from 10 cents a bag to 25 cents a pound for bones. We would also go out and pick brass off the beach or any other place that we could get it and sell it to the scrapdealers—just as we went out and picked up wood in order to fire our stove to cook our meals. We worked in the pineapple canneries from the time we were fourteen or less—there were no child labor laws then in Hawaii—and earned money in order to pay for our books and tuition. Mother used to do a little bit of laundry, but she never went out and worked for wages. She did not speak English at all, and shortly after the birth of my younger brother she became blind.

After my father's death we were scattered among relatives, among friends, because we could not afford to find a house on which we could pay the rent. Then we lived in this camp that was built by the gas company, a company camp of about thirty homes. One of my older brothers had a job with the gas company while he was working his way through high school. They were benevolent capitalists. They never bothered us. They provided all of the water, all of the gas that lighted up the camp at night. We used to sit under the gaslight and read the newspapers to those indivi- duals who couldn't read. This was the first time, following my father's death, that we'd lived together more or less as a family. We lived our childhood among very mixed ethnic groups. There were Hawaiians, part-Hawaiians, Puerto Ricans, other Chinese, Japanese, Filipinos, and even a colony of Molokans, a group of Russians in an obscure religious sect. I know that everybody was poor and everybody worked. There were few so-called rich people living in the camp.

Schools and Unions

The Leongs were poor, but they worked together and the youngest children, as Ah Quon describes, received good educations. Early in her schooling Ah Quon began to learn about alternative economic and political systems, such as com- munism and socialism, and about labor unions. She also learned to speak and work with groups, valuable skills that would later help her in her union work. De- spite the extensive control of Hawaiian life by the Big Five sugar plantations, the immigrants' children were being educated as American citizens in the public schools. Social histories credit the Hawaiian schools and teachers in the 1920s and 1930s with being the "godparents of modern Hawaii" and undermining sugar plantation control.[3]

Mother wanted us to grow up and become productive members of soci- ety and honest individuals. Always the feeling that you need to get an edu- cation was foremost in her mind. I loved everything about school, because this was a whole new world to me. In seventh grade I remember one spe- cific section on economics where Harold Rugg wrote about the second five- year plan of the Soviet Union. What an impression that made on me! I said to myself, "How is it that a nation can plan its economy and give to and assure each one of its citizens a full consistent standard of living?"

At the time I went to McKinley High School, or Tokyo High School as it was then called, there was a great deal in the philosophy of education that students should learn by doing things. The period of student government became the order of the day. It did give some of us skills that we could use when we were outside: how to organize committees, conduct meetings, make reports. Things that occur in everyday life, certainly in any corporation, in any union, in any community organization, and in the legislature. I count myself fortunate to have had teachers who knew their subject well, who brought into the classroom other than what we were supposed to cover in a specific school year. Teachers who were imaginative, who spent a lot of time with the students, and who demanded excellence from the students. Teachers who were not satisfied with mediocre performance.

Now, mind you, we were just then rolling into the Depression of the late twenties and the early thirties. The concept of planning an economy was fascinating to me. I remember having had an everlasting interest in the economic system and what it meant to people. And hearing some of the stories about the early organizing efforts of unions on the mainland. At that time, I knew almost nothing about the organizing efforts of the various Filipino and Japanese groups in Hawaii.[4] Then, of course, during the time that President Franklin Roosevelt was first elected to office in 1932, some of the excitement of the early National Recovery Act and Federal Employment Recovery Act days made a great impression on me. There was a kind of glimmering at that time of unions.

College, Communism, and the ILWU

Harry Bridges, Pacific Coast director of the International Longshoremen's Association (ILA), wanted to include warehousemen in the union. In 1937 he established the ILWU, which joined the CIO. That October the first ILWU local was chartered in Hawaii. The next year the Inland Boatmen's Union struck the Inter-Island Steamship Company, which provided the only transportation between islands. The Boatmen were joined by the ILWU and the Metal Trades Council in the port of Hilo in what became known as the "Hilo Massacre." Women who were also on strike at the Hilo Star Laundry and at the Kress Store joined the longshoremen on the Hilo dock. Fifty-one people were injured, including two women, when the sheriff and his men began firing into the crowd. Ah Quon learned about this tragedy while attending the University of Hawaii. At this time she met Jack Hall, soon to become regional director of the newly developing ILWU, and Bob McElrath, her future husband. Both were seamen organizing for the CIO-affiliated United Cannery, Agricultural, Packing, and Allied Workers of America. She also met John and Aiko Reinecke, teachers and union activists.[5]

A number of courses in economics, sociology, political science, Oriental literature, and history more or less congealed into a kind of attitude toward the world that I have continued to keep since that time. I had classes

Ah Quon McElrath (*far right*), leading a membership services meeting to explain the dental plan in the Honokaa ILWU hall to a group of sugar workers from the Paauhau Plantation, Manakua Mill, 1963. *International Longshoremen's and Warehousemen's Union, Local 142.*

with John Reinecke, who was very interested in the labor movement. I used to give Jack Hall a hand when he did the "Voice of Labor," the union newspaper. There was the early strike of the Inland Boatmen's Union in 1938. There was a massacre in the port of Hilo, Hawaii, where the police shot children, women, and men, hit them with their bare fists, with gun butts. It seems that in periods of intensive crisis all people in the union—men, women, and children—are galvanized into action. They're welded into a solid group because they realize where their class interests lie. This is the kind of support that keeps the union going.

The Boatmen used to have their rallies in our park, Aala Park. There was a place called the Dewdrop Inn, right on the corner where these strike rallies were held. I was going through the magazine rack and picking up what was obviously left-wing literature and having this open my eyes even more to what was happening in the outside world on a national and international basis, reading articles about the Civil War in Spain. That's when the unions became extremely important to me.

I used to go to all of those rallies and got to meet some of the people in the union. I met Robert McElrath. Originally Bob was from Seattle. When he left high school, he became a seaman and ended up in San Francisco and worked with a lot of people in the left wing who were interested in Spain, just as I was interested in the Spanish Civil War. They all got into left-wing politics. Let's face it, they were members of the Communist Party. Nobody makes any secret of it now, but at this point nobody gives the members of the Communist Party any real credit for the magnificent job of organizing that they did.

I would have wanted to go to school to get an advanced degree, but there was the matter of money. I worked all through the time that I was getting my bachelor's, with the exception of one semester when I received a scholarship. But I worked as a maid. I worked in the school cafeteria. I taught English. I wrote for the school publicity bureau. I worked in a curio store. When I was a senior I had five jobs going.

There was also a professor whom I admired a great deal on campus with whom I talked about the possibility of going on for graduate work. I remember his telling me, "Well, there are two problems. First of all, you're a woman, and there aren't too many possibilities for graduate work, at least now, in the field of sociology for women. And secondly, you're an Oriental." He was white. If I had more gumption or if I were completely sold on an academic career, I might have told him to go to hell and gone on to graduate school. Might have been that I didn't have enough spunk. I don't know, but if I were to live those years over again, I probably would have made the same decisions. By that time, my youngest brother was going on to college and my older sister, through a great deal of sacrifice, was able to buy a piece of land and had a home built near the university. I had an obligation to contribute toward the payment of that home.

First Job, First Union

In 1938 jobs in Hawaii, especially for educated young women, were still scarce. A 1937 survey of young people aged sixteen to twenty-five found 43 percent of young Hawaiian women in the lowest categories of unskilled workers and servants. Ah Quon took a job with the Territorial Welfare Department as a volunteer. After passage of the Wagner Act in 1935, industrial unions grew dramatically, and the territory of Hawaii followed the national trend. By 1941 some 23 percent of nonagricultural workers were organized. Ten percent of the public sector was organized by then, and Ah Quon was part of this effort.[6]

Following my university graduation, I got my first job by volunteering with the Board of Public Welfare, in the research department. In the beginning I worked for nothing. In January 1939, I got a paid job, as only a part-time worker for $75 a month. Later they hired a number of us as full-time investigators at $105 a month. I got married, went through the war, and also tried to organize the first union of social workers on an industrial basis. With the CIO's broadening influence, the whole idea of organizing social workers on an industrial basis became an extremely fascinating thing to me. I had earlier become interested in unions, so it was a logical outcome of my work as a social worker with the Hawaii Board of Public Welfare.

We were very successful. We organized all of the professional social workers, plus the clerical staff, into what was called the Department of Social Security Employees' Association. About 80 to 90 percent were women. Very early in the game we learned that, as a practical matter, it was unwise to call it a union, simply because not everybody in the group was willing to countenance the organization of a union. We met on a number of topics with the administration: job classification, wage rates, discrimination against public welfare clients on housing, and all of those kinds of problems.

At the time there was no collective bargaining for public employees. We didn't have a contract. We had certain understandings with regard to the working conditions. We had a certain understanding about what would happen when there was a wage increase and why we felt it was important for the department head to talk with the state government as to why the job classifications should be changed. Being paid $125 for a forty-hour week and carrying case loads of 250, 300 cases isn't exactly a lark! Not getting paid overtime and sometimes getting only compensatory time off: those weren't good conditions under which to work.

We were also interested in a lot of things that affected the clients. For example, at that time they wanted to raise the rents on public housing, and we said that it was not correct. These people who were living in public housing received very small grants, and they should not raise the amounts of rent they were charging the women. There was a big fuss about it. We had meetings with the administrator of the public housing section, and she agreed with us and she didn't raise the rents.

Marrying a "Haole"

In 1940 there was a ten-month ILWU strike on the island of Kauai. The people at the port of Ahukini, mostly Filipinos, also worked the sugar fields and lived in company housing because they were employees of the Lihue plantation. The strikers, however, were evicted from their homes by the employers. The longshore-

Ah Quon McElrath (*left*) and William Amaral (*right*), business agent for ILWU Local 142, the Big Island, Hawaii Division, talking with union members about publicity and education activities, 1973. *International Longshoremen's and Warehousemen's Union, Local 142.*

men nearby in Port Allen, mostly Japanese, also struck in sympathy. The strike brought different ethnic and racial groups closer together as they survived these months. This strike also brought Bob McElrath back to Hawaii.

The strikers were living in a skating rink at Ahukini, and I remember visiting the people there and seeing all the bedding all over the place. Men and women of every ethnic group together cooked their meals, developing a camaraderie and feeling of community they probably never had before. Bob had come back to Hawaii in 1940 to help Jack Hall with this strike. Harry Bridges, president of the ILWU, sent someone from the mainland to clean up the mess because it had been going on now for ten months. They had just settled that strike at Ahukini. That was a temporary job for Bob, so when I married him he was unemployed. I was married in August 1941.

When I told my family I was going to get married to this "haole," a white, and a seaman to boot, "My God! Don't you ever come home. You are not welcome." I mean here was a Chinese woman marrying a white man and a white who at the time had no job. This was unheard of. Shame on the family.

This was my sister writing to me. The reason she was so incensed was that I was the first college graduate in the family. My sister, who went to normal school and became a damn good schoolteacher, was disturbed about the fact that here I was marrying a man who didn't have a job. Quite understandable in those days, given the very strong ethnic identification and the need to marry someone in your station.

War broke out December 7, 1941. Bob and I had a rapprochement with my family because on December 7, we were driving down Liliha Street going to breakfast with a friend of mine when the bombs fell. People said, "Get off the street. We're being attacked." I went up and talked to my mother to see if she was all right. A lot of the bombs fell in the area where my family lived. She allowed us to sleep there in my old bedroom in the family home.

Now my husband is a crackerjack machinist, so he got a job with the Inter-Island Steamship Company. They put him on one of these small ships that had been made a liberty ship. He used to take supplies to Christmas Island and dodge torpedoes, and he was gone for long periods. We had a hard time finding a home. At one time he lived at the YMCA and I lived with a friend who was one of the union organizers in the late 1930s of the Kress Store.

Organizing and Family

While working at the Territorial Welfare Department, Ah Quon continued doing volunteer union work, helping her husband organize for the Marine, Engineering, and Drydock Workers Union of Hawaii. They were both active politically, campaigning for candidates and working on legislation. They had two children during this period, and their lives were committed to the left-wing political movement and working with the ILWU.

Bob and I organized under the name Marine, Engineering and Drydock Workers Union of Hawaii. I helped him in all of the organizing of those units. During the war he left the marine section and went to work on the drydock section, and he helped to organize the union. I was a kind of helpmate in setting up the files, keeping the records, typing the minutes. All that kind of stuff. Then he also organized the workers at the Hawaiian Tuna Packers' Company, which canned tuna, and I helped to set up the records, writing the minutes and doing the financial reports. He also organized the American Can Company.

Jack Hall had organized pineapple workers on the island of Kauai in 1938, but we were instrumental in organizing the Hawaiian Pineapple Company, which was the largest pineapple company in the territory of Hawaii, and the way we did it was this. My sister and her husband worked at the company. They did not have a place to stay, so I said, "Look, we have an extra bedroom, come and stay with us until you can find an apartment." So they moved in with us for a short while. We talked about why it was important to have a union and all this kind of stuff, and they said, "Yeah, why don't we organize a union."

So my brother-in-law called in several of his friends. There were five pineapple workers, plus Bob, plus me. We sat in our kitchen and said, "Look, what are the best ways to organize the Hawaiian Pineapple Company?" They all agreed it was easiest to get the frozen food section. We showed them the sign-up cards, how you sign workers up, all this kind of thing. They took the cards with them and I would say within a month, we got the majority. The pineapple workers joined the Marine, Engineering, and Drydock Workers Union.

By that time my husband was interested in the ILWU. Obviously he still had connections with Jack Hall because of the 1940 strike on Kauai, and they kept up their contacts. By then Jack Hall was regional director for the ILWU Hawaii region. In 1944 we just turned over the Marine, Engineering, and Drydock Workers' units to the ILWU. No problem. We had only one local, which was ILWU Local 142, but we had over two hundred units under the local, each one of which was autonomous. We had sugar, pineapple, longshore, and miscellaneous, which was called general trades—anything from hospital to cemeteries. Hence the term "from the cradle to the grave," truly with the ILWU.

Then Jack hired Bob as a publicist for the ILWU regional office, and Bob put out the union newspaper, the original investigative reporter. He also had a fifteen-minute radio program that ran for several years. He used to do the ads during political campaigns, and everybody tried to pattern their radio programs after him. The pineapple company had a show. The right-wing group had a radio program.

When I had my children, I took leave. Gail was born in July 1943, and my son, Brett, was born in November 1945. My agency allowed you several months' leave, and I took the maximum leave when each of my children was born. When I went back to work full time in 1945 I had my daughter in the first Lanham day-care center, which was built on the grounds of McKinley High School. America felt it had to win the war, so what the hell did it do? It appropriated money for day-care centers. Why the hell can't we do the same thing now?[7]

Anyhow, then I had my son with a private family because there was an age below which they would not take a child in the day-care center. When he became old enough, I just switched him to the day-care center. My sister took care of my children during the summer. It was nice to have them with a family, because by that time Mother was completely blind and she had bound feet, so she obviously could not do a good deal of taking care of the children.

Work and Political Conflict

In 1939 Jack Hall drafted a labor relations act for Hawaii. Eventually, largely through the political action of the ILWU, the Hawaii Employment Relations Act, passed in 1945. The act enabled the organizing of the sugar workers, because unlike the Wagner Act, it included farm workers. In 1946, with sugar industry contracts for twenty-six of twenty-seven plantations, the ILWU sought to end the plantation system through which employers controlled housing and medical care and, instead, to develop a systematic job classification system. Ah Quon actively volunteered in these political and labor efforts, leading eventually to her resignation from the Welfare Department to work directly with the ILWU. Red-baiting in Hawaii, however, had begun as early as 1937, when government hearings pointed to "Moscow influences" on professional agitators and alien seditionists in the union.[8]

I think we were the first state in our union, because of political action on the part of the ILWU, which passed a "Little Wagner" act. It permitted the organization of agricultural workers into unions, not then permitted in the federal law and only recently enacted by the state of California to assist the organization of farm workers there. Then the sugar strike began in September 1946. I volunteered my services for the ILWU as a social worker, working out relief policies, discussing the kind of agencies in the territory that could be used to alleviate some of the workers' needs, and I did a lot of other volunteer work, such as passing out leaflets and talking to people in groups about the strike issues.

With the coming of the ILWU, we also had very strong political action committees. It was through the activities of the PAC that union people became elected to office as members of the Democratic Party. I took time off from my job. You couldn't stay off longer than a specific period. During one session of the legislature I was trying to get some signatures from people who would be interested in voting for a bill on the closed primary. I was talking to the head of the Hawaii Department of Public Welfare, and he said, "Oh my God, Ah Quon, you know that you'll never be hired back by the Department," because at that time the red-baiting had already begun. However, nothing happened during the war, for heaven's sake. We were all busy winning the war. It happened after the war, with all the U.S. Un-American Activities Committee hearings in the late 1940s and 1950s. We had gone through the sugar strike and there was all of that red-baiting and I was very politically active. I left the public welfare department in about 1948. I resigned.

One of the things that came out of the sugar strike of 1946 was to have a uniform classification system of the workers at the twenty-six plantations that we had struck. The union asked workers to send in information about their jobs. They brought in an economist to help. They hired me temporarily as a research assistant. I was able to do part of the calculations of what came in, the returns on job classifications, so that we could say that the people said they did this, this, and this. Then when you set up the classification system, you could weight the classifications according to the responses that came in. Then I had to work in the library as well when there weren't these classification things to work on: the filing, the assessing of which groups were where, the beginning things of setting up a union library. It was temporary work.

Fighting the Broom Brigade

In 1948 there was a successful longshore and maritime strike on the West Coast of the U.S. mainland. The next year Hawaii's seamen and dock workers wanted the same pay and benefits for doing the same work for the same companies. Demanding a wage increase of 32 cents an hour and arbitration if agreement was not reached, the ILWU struck for 177 days. Through the efforts of employers and union alike, the entire Hawaiian community, including families, became involved in the strike. The "Broom Brigade" was organized by the employers to show community opposition to the strike. Although as many as four hundred women and thirty children participated, an estimated nine out of ten were haoles.[9]

In the 1949 strike, I volunteered my time with the union as a social worker to draw up relief policies, to work out problems of nutritious meals for the soup kitchen, and in the event people could not come to the soup kitchen, what was absolutely needed as food rations for families to take home and meet the minimum requirements for so-called decency and health. This also involved the referral of individuals to social agencies for supplementary assistance, medical care, and the like.

Of course, during that particular period, as with the sugar strike in 1946, all of the resources of the conservative elements in the community were thrown against the strike. The newspapers, radio stations, community organizations, church groups, all of the employers, et cetera, mobilized to fight the union. The "Broom Brigade" was a group of women that was formed with the blessing of the employers to mobilize women in the community to form a counter-picket line against the longshoremen who were on strike. The employers let their secretaries, their nurses, their clerks take time off from work in order to march in this picket line. It was led by the more conservative elements of the community, and they held a lot of meetings, hoping that they could turn the sentiment of the community against the union.

I remember one meeting that was called at the McKinley High School, which was designed to mobilize the community and to pass resolutions against the Longshoremen's Union. There were only a very few of us from the union who went to the meeting, but through our superior parliamentary skills, we were able to maneuver the meeting so that they ended up not taking any action at all on some of the resolutions that they wanted passed. We had our own radio program and our own newspaper. We put out our own bulletins so that people could understand what the issues were. We also did a good deal of talking to community groups. We were successful, for example, in getting merchants and the community to contribute money and food to our soup kitchen and to our food ration program.

Those were very troublesome times. It required, for example, a great deal of building of the morale among the strikers, the identity of interest among all working people, the mobilization of the wives and children of strikers to realize that their husbands and fathers went out on strike for fair wages. The strike lasted for about six months and was a true testing of the ability of workers in longshore. That, along with the sugar workers, was a turning point in the lives of the community—to see the strength of the workers to overthrow the kind of exploitation and oppression that they had suffered. It solidified certainly my own thinking about the need to organize workers into unions and to bring their families into the whole process.

The Smith Act Trials

Harry Bridges, the controversial ILWU president, was charged with being a member of the Communist Party by the federal government, which wanted to deport him to his native Australia. In 1945 he was found innocent by the United States Supreme Court and granted U.S. citizenship. Always maintaining his innocence, Bridges was tried by the federal government five separate times over twenty years.[10] In 1950, as tension mounted between the communist and noncommunist factions within the labor movement, Bridges took the ILWU out of the CIO. (The ILWU did not return to the AFL-CIO until 1988.) Reports of these activities were front-page news in the *ILWU Reporter,* the Local 142 newspaper, along with the accusations of communism in Hawaii, mostly focused on the ILWU. Bob McElrath was subpoenaed, and Jack Hall went to trial with six others, including John Reinecke. They became known as the Hawaii Seven, charged under the Smith Act of 1940. The Reineckes had their teaching licenses revoked and were not reinstated by the Hawaii State Board of Education until 1976.[11]

Harry Bridges came to Hawaii often, and every time he came, it was an occasion for people to red-bait him or to feel that the world was coming to an end. People from the World Federation of Trade Unions came here. The WFTU was the left-wing organization of the international unions. We had dinner with them, and we talked about where the WFTU was going, et cetera. These were some of the things that set people's teeth on edge because they figured we were too left wing.

Then came the Izuka pamphlet, called "The Truth about Communism in Hawaii." It was all about the ILWU. Izuka was an early union leader on the island of Kauai. In early 1950, we were called to testify before the U.S. House Un-American Activities Committee. They quashed the subpoena on me, because they figured they didn't need that many people and one McElrath was probably enough. Bob was called, and all of them took the Fifth Amendment. They were called "the reluctant thirty-nine." They spent one day in jail. Then in August of 1951, there was the arrest of the Hawaii Seven, the Smith Act trial. Jack Hall was one of the Hawaii Seven.

After the arrests, Dave Thompson, the union educational director, was approached by two FBI agents, James Condon and Richard Burrus, to see whether or not they could talk with Jack Hall about the Smith Act trial. If Jack would cooperate with the FBI, if he would do things to weaken the union, they would get the charges against him dropped. How do we know that? My husband recorded the FBI propositioning Dave Thompson.

There were about three sessions, and all of them were two or three hours. That was a hell of a lot of tape. They were transcribed in our living room at 112B Elm Street for the simple reason that we didn't want anyone to know that we had taped the FBI. Bob played the tape over his radio station. It was also in the newspaper. They were so goddamned embarrassed, what could they do? The union attorney from San Francisco subpoenaed the two FBI agents. Obviously, they didn't talk. This was one big story and a real coup. But nobody would touch it, because the FBI was held in such sacred honor by so many people in the United States. To me, this is the fascination of that whole story.

The trial went on. We set up an office to provide support for the lawyers. I helped to run the office. We needed people to analyze the transcripts of the trial. The court reporters would give us the transcript and what you had to do was make a name index and an occurrence index. You had to analyze what went on in order that the attorneys would know what to do the following day. It was a really big job. "Could you do some research on Joe Doaks who was mentioned by such and such?"

Of all the people who were indicted, the only union person was Jack Hall. Eileen Fujimoto was a secretary in the ILWU, not in any position to effectuate union policy. There was a soil scientist (Eileen's husband), three newspaper people, and a former construction worker. It was so wrapped up in cloak and dagger. These were good people, for heaven's sake. We closed up the office following the guilty verdict, although the appeal was proceeding. When the Supreme Court issued the decision in another case in Los Angeles, it wiped out all of the cases. Jack Hall never went to jail. He stayed as ILWU regional director. Even during the trial, we had a number of job demonstrations, a number of plantations closed down, because we were negotiating for a new sugar agreement during that particular period.

I was a member of the Communist Party. It's no secret, I've been named, I can talk about it. I don't need to be afraid of anything. Bob was thrown out of the Communist Party because he questioned what was happening. I continue to be a Marxist because I think this is the one way of analyzing the world that makes sense. I don't mean just Karl Marx, without seeing the changes in the world. But to me this is the only way of making sense of our life. You have to have an ideology. Otherwise, forget it. You wander all over the bloody lot.

But it was a tough time for the children. They were called "commie rats" by schoolmates who refused to play with them. You can't do too much explaining if their experiential world and their intellectual world are at odds. There's no way you can intellectualize this thing. So it was always, "Daddy is doing good things for the people who pay his salary. It's not going to be easy, because not everybody thinks the same way that your daddy or Jack Hall think." You just try to give them a lot of love. But that's water under the bridge and that's all you can do. I'm sure the children of all left-wing parents who have gone through this kind of thing have the same problems. There's no easy way out.

Sugar Contracts, Social Work, and Education

Beginning in 1946, collective bargaining for the union-employer sugar contracts brought about a unique need for Ah Quon's training as a social worker. On the sugar plantations, in addition to wages, workers had received housing and medical care. But 1946 saw the first collective bargaining contract under which resources for housing and medical care were turned over to the union and the workers. In the years that followed the union began to negotiate medical and pension plans in longshore and pineapple contracts for its membership, which was racially and ethnically diverse. There was a union ban on discrimination by race, creed, color, or political activity. The 1934 ILWU constitution included as an objective, "First, to unite in one organization, regardless of religion, race, creed, color, political affiliation or nationality, all workers."[12]

I was hired by the ILWU in 1954 because the union had just begun to negotiate insured medical plans for longshore and pineapple, and all the other units followed suit because the model had been laid down for fringe benefits. Because these were insured plans, we insisted that all of the claims handled by a commercial insurance company come through the ILWU. You don't know what to look for unless you have someone who is trained along those lines, and since I was a social worker, I knew what were some of the kinds of things we should be looking for. For example, based on the nature of the claims and disease entities, what kind of educational programs should we be instituting? If you had medical plans, what effect did they have in sick leave policies? Our union membership services department administered a very fascinating repatriation program, because our pension plan now provided for the repatriation of permanent alien residents to the country of their origin with a lump-sum pension settlement. All of those kinds of things interwove. I had to work with the union education department to determine how the union could best use what it had in order to improve the health of our people—in order to make suggestions as to what should go into collective bargaining agreements, et cetera.

In the early days of the union we used to have explanations of all kinds of things in all the different languages. They would ask me to go to the unemployment compensation office and pick out the Chinese women workers and talk to them in Chinese and tell them why it was important to join the union and why they should listen if anybody came up to them and talked to them about signing up on the union card. I would have a union card with me, and I would tell them exactly what it provided.

As we moved further into the life of the union with the institutionalization of a number of programs, we did a lot of things such as role playing, using a woman teacher and a man teacher. Dave Thompson at that time wanted to do all of the educational work, and I said, "David, you're crazy in the head. You talk a half hour, I come on for a half hour, you get somebody else for a half hour, or you'll drive them completely mad. Also, you've got to do role playing, so that you involve the people and it's not just strictly lecture." We did video, we did all kinds of things. Part of our educational work was training people on the membership services committees and on the education committees to do the work of paraprofessionals. In other words, we trained a lot of "social workers" without advanced degrees to do this kind of work, because we felt they were the ones who knew the membership. We didn't.

It was one way of breaking the monotony of an educational process that was given to a group of individuals so disparate as far as education, interest, ethnicity, culture, and job classification are concerned. It took a hell of a lot out of an individual leading these education programs. We did a lot of sketching on the blackboard, used a lot of "pidgin English," did a lot of waiting for responses, and saying, "Do you understand what this means?" and then doing the role playing to be sure that, in fact, the lessons got learned. I think we were really quite effective. The job is not through. More members come in. You've got to constantly revise how you do things to make sure that everybody gets it. That's the challenge.

Our political action program was geared primarily to workers, and we made no bones about it. It wasn't only for workers who belonged to the union, but for workers who didn't belong to the union. As a matter of fact, one of our strong points is that, look, much of the social legislation we propose doesn't help our own union people. Through the collective bargaining agreement, we've covered all of these contingencies. A large section of the employer press, perhaps I should say employer-oriented press, has said that we have literally cut our own throats in organizing because we have been so successful on the legislative level in passing much of the social legislation that is unique to the state of Hawaii, such as the prepaid health plan, temporary disability insurance, wide improvements in the workers' compensation law, and a very liberal unemployment compensation law. It is a challenge.

Women in the ILWU

Longshore work and the ILWU are both predominantly male. In the early days, the union programs tried to include wives, but in 1935 the first Hilo ILWU local passed a motion to exclude women as "too much a restraining influence in union meetings."[13] In the 1940s the number of women workers began to increase, as Ah Quon describes, in the pineapple and sugar sections of the union, but this did not translate into leadership positions for women. Local 142 established a Women's Auxiliary in 1950, as the benefits of support from wives and family became more obvious, but the number of women union officers and staff is still small. In Ah Quon's experience, there was little encouragement for women from the union.

In the earlier years when our organizing was in longshore, which is traditionally a man's industry, we had a very, very small percentage of women workers. However, following our major thrust in sugar in 1944, we found that there were a number of women who joined our union. We won those elections by as high as 99 percent of the total work force in the bargaining unit. At every plantation there were women who worked in the fields, and their job was to pick up the stalks of cane that fell off either the trucks or the railroad cars. They did some of the weeding. Not too much. Perhaps out of a work force then of about twenty-six thousand, we have had about two thousand women who were in the ILWU.

In all of the union meetings I have gone to, and this goes back to about 1937, I have found that up to the middle 1940s, there weren't very many women, but even those who did come to meetings with their husbands were unwilling to get up and talk. I think that many of the women, again, suffer from the traditional attitudes that women should not get up and say anything. That was a man's role. As I look back to the early days of organizing, I can think of women who joined women's auxiliaries, for example, in the longshore section, and this was the only instance when women had the kind of courage to get up and speak.

I recall going to meetings of women's auxiliaries, where the Hawaiian and Portuguese women have been much more willing to get up and speak than a Filipino, Japanese, or Chinese woman, although we don't have very many Chinese women at the production level. Of course, our culture has been such that the Oriental woman is supposed to be seen but not heard. I think also that a lot of Hawaiian women, at least in my experience, have been single-parent women, and they really need to be very aggressive in order to get from some social agency that to which they have a right. I don't know whether it is ethnicity as much as experience and circumstances. These are all variables that enter into the situation. I'm not so sure that ethnicity has the strongest pull in this situation.

Because of the mechanization of sugar operations, we have found that with the retirement and the dying out of the earlier immigrant workers who came, let us say, in the 1890s and early 1900s, that there are fewer and fewer women workers in the fields. Later on, of course, as we went into organizing the pineapple workers, we had a large contingency of women workers, because almost all of the packers and trimmers of pineapple at that time were women. I suspect that our total women membership might have been about 50 percent of the total work force.

You pass either a sugar or a pineapple field and women are hardly distinguishable from men, for the simple reason that they must wear wide-brimmed hats to keep out the sun and a kind of netting over the hat because of the prickly things on the leaves and fronds of the sugar cane and the pineapple. They also wear very long-sleeved shirts to the end of their wrists so that their skin will not be pricked by the sharp leaves and the eyes on the fruit. Likewise, they need to wear boots, because they're working in fields that are muddy. They need to protect their legs from the prickling by the leaves and fruits.

So, although in sugar we don't have as many women in the fields, in pineapple, we still have them during the summer picking season, some of them supplementing their husband's income. After working so many hours, they acquire a different status, according to our collective bargaining agreement, and they are given the benefits of the contract, such as coverage under the medical plan, access to severance pay, temporary disability, sick leave, and those kinds of things that seasonal workers would generally not have because they would be working only during the season, which might be fourteen to sixteen weeks.

At the time I was hired, I was the only woman on the professional staff. At the moment, the highest office that is held by a woman in the ILWU is as a member of the international executive board, which is a policymaking board that carries on between union conventions. Here at the state level, we do have some women who act as chairs of their units. They are doing a very good job, but as of 1976, there has never been any kind of encouragement. If memory serves me correctly, I do not believe the ILWU has had any women business agents, nor any women who ran for the office of business agent. We don't have any permanent women organizers on the staff. When we organize areas where there is a preponderance of women, we will get a leave of absence for a particularly strong woman organizer from one of the plants that has already been organized.

While we are a very democratic union, prejudices die hard. Basically the men in the union can still not visualize a woman being a business agent or a high-level union officer. This is so much outside of their experience that getting them to change their attitudes involves a great deal of work. But as women begin to show that they are just as capable as men in running an organization, I think perforce the men's attitudes will be changed, whether or not they like it. They would have to doff their hats to women who can run an organization, perhaps even better than they can. Women themselves, however, are victims of the old attitudes about what a woman can do.

It's up to women now to take prominent positions in the union. They must assess their own feelings, their own capabilities, as to what kind of contribution they can make. They must put on top of the agenda the need to change attitudes on the part of husbands if they are married. In addition, it is extremely important for the officials of the union, at every level, to give encouragement to women to participate in the work of the union and not just feel that simply because someone is a woman, and can type or write in a neat hand, that all she should be elected to is secretary of the unit. It means that union officials must provide the kind of education so that the attitudes of men can be changed. The changing of attitudes would encompass wider participation of women in positions of leadership and not have men feel threatened by this kind of participation.

Women's Issues

Ah Quon's speaking engagements and newspaper articles reflect a wide range of concerns, including public health, jobs and the environment, consumer protection for seniors, and nuclear contamination in the Pacific. In 1965 she left Hawaii and did graduate work at the University of Michigan. She learned about poverty and racism on the mainland by spending three months in Alabama working on the Tuskegee Institute's community action program.[14] Over the years, Ah Quon became increasingly vocal on working women's and poor women's issues. In 1976 she was appointed second vice chairperson of the Hawaii State International Women's Year Coordinating Committee, part of the official observance of International Women's Year.

Obviously we should not discriminate against women. We should offer them choices, with the protective provisions in the contract, so that if a woman wants to apply for a job as an electrician and she is trained, she ought to have just as much chance at it as the others that apply. Quotas might help, but I don't think that this is the answer. Let's assume that you have a certain number of women who come to a union convention, and you freeze them out by hooting them down whenever they get up to make a speech or a motion. The quota isn't going to help. The problem is much more deep-rooted than that. But, if quotas will help, I'm all for them.

Part-time employment can be both a saint and a devil for women. The answer is not either/or, as in so many problems that we face. Women must be given the right to choose that which best meets their needs as a person, as a wage earner, as individuals for whom there must be opportunities to move back and forth between households and paid jobs. In my experience, because of the traditional roles to which a woman has been confined, whether or not the work is part-time or full-time, she is the one who is expected to pick up her child from school if the child is ill, to take the child to the doctor when the child is ill, and thereby sacrifice, for example, her vacation pay or her sick pay.

Employers must recognize that until there is a massive change in attitudes toward women workers, that they must expect and must make certain kinds of concessions to a work force that is composed largely of women. This should not be an excuse for them to continue to exploit women workers. This will take a long time in coming, but women themselves should not take a divisive attitude. Our job is to say, "What can we do to offer the best opportunities to women, regardless of what they choose, part-time work or full-time work," and therein, it seems to me, lies the solution to the problems of women workers. Trade unions are still, in our kind of society, the only social organization that can lift women immediately out of poverty and give them some measure of control over their lives.

Until Retirement

The ILWU grew and changed, reflecting the changes in Hawaii's economy. In the 1946 sugar strike, there were twenty-eight thousand workers from twenty-six plantations. In 1991, the number of sugar workers was down to six thousand on twelve plantations.[15] As agriculture declined, tourism became the dominant Hawaiian industry. Increases in ILWU membership were due to expanded boundaries of organizing, such as the cashiers in large supermarket chains, the predominantly female jobs in hotels, and workers in the food and beverage trades. In 1958 Ah Quon reduced her hours to part-time to spend more time with her children, but continued her union responsibilities as an educator and social worker. Bob became more involved in contract negotiations and in 1969 was named ILWU regional director. He retired in 1978.

Today the ILWU represents all of the longshoremen, all of the sugar workers, plus some of the clerical workers who work for plantation companies, all the pineapple workers, plus some of the clerical workers who are engaged in timekeeping, computerized operations, the large bakeries, large automotive firms, a few ranches, the largest chain of supermarkets, many of the large hotels that are on the outside islands; plus egg examiners, papaya packers, employees of credit unions, and a whole mishmash of workers. We operate on the principle that any unorganized workers should be organized into a union and should enjoy the benefits of union organization. Therefore the world is our oyster as far as workers are concerned.

Our union is considered one of the most democratic unions in the nation. Our constitution has been held up as a model of democracy. We have here, in the state of Hawaii, a local union that has three officers, and under the local union are four divisions made up of the four counties of the state of Hawaii. Under each division are scores of individual units. Local 142 has several departments: education, contract administration, and membership services. I happen to work for the membership services department. However, we work very closely with the education department, and one of the jobs that we have been doing over the years is a very heavy educational series for our elected, as well as appointed, officials at the local division and unit level.

For example, we completed a series of classes on all of the islands which took up such subjects as workers' compensation, unemployment compensation, social agencies in your community, and how you can use them to meet the problems of your membership. We also handle a lot of immigration cases. We represent our members at hearings before the administrative law judges of the Social Security Administration. I worked with an alcoholic whom the company wanted to fire. Because we have worked out an alcoholism program with some of the employers in the state of Hawaii, we were able to get the employer to rescind the firing of the worker on the basis that we would be working with the man and referring him to some of the agencies in the city and county of Honolulu, which offer services for a person with a drinking problem.

We refer a lot of our cases to private children's and family agencies that do long-term counseling with individuals who have marital and other problems. This is done especially if it looks as though the case requires more than a few office counseling sessions on my part. Obviously I'm unable to do this kind of long-term counseling, not only because we have so many other kinds of different problems to deal with, but because I work part-time. It would be unfair for me to devote many hours of the week to just one union family.

Those are some of the kinds of things we try to do in our union programs. We aren't always successful; this is the kind of thing that you have to work at for many, many years, and I've been at it for twenty or more long years. While I see certain changes in attitudes taking place, this is perhaps not as readily measurable as the kinds of things we include as union benefits in a medical plan. So the challenge is still there; it's still fascinating, and I wouldn't give it up for anything.

Retirement

Ah Quon retired in 1981 at the age of sixty-six, three years after her husband. She moved to Washington, D.C., for two years to work for the Villers Foundation, a "left-of-center advocacy group for seniors." She visited her family's village in China and took a trip to Russia with a group of trade unionists. Back in Hawaii, she formed the Committee on Welfare Concerns, a coalition of organizations seeking to help improve the welfare system. Her sister lives with her, and although Ah Quon is separated from her husband, she does "a lot of care giving for him as well." "I live on social security and a union pension. It's been very, very satisfying. I'm at the legislature every day of the week during the sixty-day session. I have the time and I love it."

Chapter 8

Sometimes You Have to Rock the Boat

Dorothy Haener, United Auto Workers (1918–)

In 1966 Dorothy Haener was among a dozen women who sat in a hotel room with Betty Friedan in Washington, D.C., and developed the concept of NOW, the National Organization for Women, because she knew that "nothing was going to happen unless you had a pressure group that was going to be pressuring." On the staff of the Women's Department of the United Auto Workers (UAW), she brought her twenty years of UAW experience to her participation in NOW, President Kennedy's Commission on the Status of Women, and the 1965 White House Conference on Equal Employment Opportunity.

During World War II, Dorothy worked as an inspector at Ford Willow Run, a large bomber plant. As an officer of UAW Local 142, she fought for herself and other women workers to regain their jobs after their layoffs in the auto plants in the postwar period. In the 1950s she crossed the country as an organizer for the UAW Department of Technical, Office, and Professional Workers and also became active in the Democratic Party. She was an early supporter of the Equal Rights Amendment, a position unpopular with many women in other unions. She was appointed to the 1975 International Women's Year Commission and was a delegate to the 1976 Democratic National Convention, where she spoke in support of a woman's right to choice being included in the party platform.

After her retirement in 1982, Dorothy was appointed to the Michigan Civil Rights Commission and the National Advisory Council of UAW Retired Workers. In 1983 she was one of the first women inducted into the Michigan Women's Hall of Fame along with Rosa Parks and Congresswoman Martha Griffiths. Dorothy is active in UAW Region 1A's Retired Workers Council and serves on the 1995 White House Conference on Aging. She lives outside of Detroit near several brothers and sisters and the family farm where they grew up.[1]

The Farm Years

Dorothy Haener was born in Detroit, Michigan, in 1918, the sixth of seven children. Her mother was German, and her father came from the German part of Switzerland. When Dorothy was three years old, the family moved to a farm thirty miles from the city because of her father's health. Her father, like many others in the twenties, overextended himself financially to maintain the farm. When the stock market crashed in 1929, farm prices plummeted and farm life became increasingly difficult.

When I was a very small child I worked for neighboring farmers, picking strawberries and beans when I wasn't occupied at home. If you got 2 cents a quart you were doing pretty good. We would work in the morning from the time the sun came up until sundown. When you first started to work, your muscles would ache terribly. My knees never quite reached the point where they didn't hurt. The work was tiresome and monotonous and difficult and hot. I used to keep looking up at the sun and the clouds and praying that it would rain so we could quit working.

I considered it very definitely work, because when we moved into the Depression we were extremely poor. People were starving in the city, and people on farms couldn't buy shoes. I wore shoes with cardboard shoved in the holes. We had potatoes and the pork that we raised and the chickens and the eggs. We didn't literally starve. I really can remember that, early on, I felt that there had to be an easier way to make a living.

Education was important. We walked a mile and a half to a country one-room school. I'm the only member of my family, a family of seven, that graduated from high school. The nearest high school was nine miles away and you had to pay tuition, because we didn't have a high school in our school district. I kept telling people that I wanted to go to high school. My parents separated during my second high school year, when I was fourteen. My mother ended up with twenty acres of land and the house. It was extremely difficult for my mother to hold the family together. At that time, I always felt that my mother was the really weak member of the family and my father was the strong one. But, in retrospect, I know that wasn't true. Essentially it was my mother that held that family together.

Later, I never really felt badly about bringing my money home and giving it to my family, because if the rest of my family had not been willing to do that when I was younger I never would have gone to high school. They all helped. In those years we all of us brought home whatever we earned, because it was the only way that we could survive. I graduated in 1936, but it was absolutely impossible to find a job.

Factory Work

Under the New Deal, union organizing activity and related labor-management conflict escalated, especially among unions emerging in the mass production industries. In the mid-thirties, as the economy began to recover, the United Automobile Workers organized women and men in the auto industry. Dorothy's brothers worked and organized at plants like Ford Motor Company's River Rouge, and her sister was at Ternstedt, a General Motors parts plant employing over six thousand women. Before the war, Dorothy followed their example at a small factory, but with less success.[2]

We had no identity with anyone who was a union member when we were growing up, but I was sympathetic to the whole concept. The UAW was being organized. I had a sister who worked at Ternstedt's when a sit-down strike took place in 1937. She was not working when they sat down, but she helped by bringing lunches to the people who were sitting down at work, and handed them through the windows. Then I had brothers who worked at Ford, where they were trying to organize.

When my brothers hired in at the Ford Motor Company, we lived far enough out in the country that it was a twenty-mile trip for them to go the Ford Rouge plant. They would get up around 12:30 at night and put on all the warmest clothes they had and then go down to the Ford Rouge plant. They would have to stand in line, out there in the cold. Day after day they did this. Then when the managers opened the doors in the morning to take the applicants, they would just stand there and say, "You ten can go in and put your application in. You ten just leave." It was very arbitrary and very inhuman. At the Rouge plant, the practice of giving bosses a bottle of whiskey at the end of the week was entrenched. How could you grow up in that time and not be sympathetic to unions?

In 1937 I went to work at Wayne Wire Cloth Company as a spot welder, and also I worked on the punch press part of the time. I had to go repeatedly to put my application in and to stand in line to get hired. There were a lot of people who were absolutely desperate for the work. I felt it was almost a miracle when I finally got hired and put on the day shift.

In 1960, more than five thousand signatures were on the petition that Phyllis Haver, an office worker laid off at the Chrysler Missile plant, was handing Congressman James O'Hara on the steps of the nation's capital. The petition sought more contracts for the plant to keep its employees at work. Looking on is Dorothy Haener (*center*), staff for the UAW Technical, Office, and Professional Department, along with UAW Region 1 and local union officials. *Archives of Labor and Urban Affairs, Wayne State University.*

The conditions were extremely difficult. Some days you'd stand around for two or three hours, and if there wasn't any work that day you were just sent home and you didn't get paid. You ate by the machines, and there weren't proper safety precautions. You didn't have automatic rest periods. Depending on the atmosphere with your supervisor, management would complain that you were taking too many breaks to go to the restroom, particularly with a woman and especially during the time of your period. The definition of what was a woman's job and what was a man's job at that point was very clear-cut. The jobs that the women did naturally received less money, even on the presses. Foremen wanted to go out with you. Coming from the background I come from, it was really very difficult for me. I was young and very close to my family at home; it just would have been an impossible situation. But that went on. It was just expected.

The jobs that were preferable or easy I never got, because I was not cooperative. I lost my job at that plant because I had been so foolish as to talk to people about the fact that I thought a union was a good thing. I instinctively knew that talking about a union would be dangerous there. I had not even mentioned it at work. I only mentioned a union to people outside of the workplace and to some who worked there. I was just absolutely fired without any warning or any reason at all. I had not done anything wrong. I hadn't got any reprimands. I had friends of mine check with Personnel to find out why I had lost my job, and there was no justifiable reason. I felt terrible about it, because I needed the work. I really believe it was only because of my talking about the union.

The War Years

In 1941, after the bombing of Pearl Harbor, employment increased dramatically as companies converted to defense production. As young male workers joined the military, women were hired to replace them. In the auto industry, women went from 30,000, or 6 percent of the workers, in 1940 to 185,000, or 25 percent of the workers, in 1944. Women represented 28 percent of the UAW's one million members. Dorothy was one of them. She worked for the Central Specialty Company, a foundry where she first joined the UAW in 1940, but then finally got hired at Willow Run, a new multimillion-dollar factory built by Henry Ford to mass produce airplanes for the war.[3]

In 1941, I went to work at Ford's bomber plant. The wages that were offered in a war production plant were much higher than anyplace else and,

The AFL-CIO Industrial Union Department called upon members of affiliated internationals to lobby for an "Equal Pay for Equal Work" law. There were about twenty participants from UAW locals in 1962. Shown are (*right to left*) Dorothy Haener, UAW Women's Department; Caroline Davis, Director, UAW Women's Department; and Martha Griffiths, congresswoman from Michigan and a leader in the fight to end sex discrimination. *Archives of Labor and Urban Affairs, Wayne State University.*

of course, the prospect that we would continue to have work was much better. All I considered was the fact that the job at the Ford bomber plant would pay so much more money. I convinced them I was qualified to do clerical work and they finally hired me as a department clerk, which was a union job. Then, hopefully, somewhere along the line, if they were training people to do other jobs, I would avail myself of some additional training.

I lived in an apartment all the while I worked at Central Specialty. Shortly after I got to work at the Ford bomber plant, I moved back home. My sister and younger brother were there with my mother. It was closer. There were people who had a round trip of a hundred miles to get to their jobs. Also, our home had burnt down in January of 1941, so we very quickly put up just four rooms. I didn't move back willingly. I had enjoyed living on my own. Frankly, I moved back home because the financial help that I could give my family was needed. At that point in time, with the conditions and culture I grew up with, I really expected to get married, have children, stay home with them.

"Rosie the Inspector"

As women flooded into the labor force, they were hired into the previously all-male jobs that paid much more than the ones they had before the war. "Rosie the Riveter" became a household term as the government encouraged employers and women to join the war effort. Magazines and newsreels pictured Rosie the Riveter as a "blue-eyed, rosy-cheeked woman with a kerchief on her head, a rivet gun across her lap, and a powder puff in her coverall pocket, the perfect combination of health, strength, and femininity."[4] Despite the pressure, change did not come easily. Unions played a positive role for women like Dorothy, who became a member of UAW Local 50.

I worked all three shifts at that plant. It was terrible. I never did adjust to working the midnight shift, I just couldn't. I worked as a clerk for only about five to six months, and I was not happy with the superintendent I worked for. He was extremely difficult to get along with. He went out of his way to make life difficult for me. I used to complain all the time with the people I rode with, my oldest brother and some others, myself and three men. They finally said to me one day, "You know, we have a union here now." As a department clerk I was part of the union. "We're getting awfully weary listening to you gripe all the time. You either should go do something about it or just quit griping."

So I finally worked up the courage to go and complain about it and to ask to be transferred to another job. The union won the grievance for me. I did get the new job and increased pay. The union really was fairly good to me. I would never have taken the initial step to move on to doing inspection work if the union hadn't been there. I would have been afraid to even question what the superintendent was doing if I had not known there was a union there to support me.

They sent me to the Ford Trade School for two weeks. Ford always had a very excellent trade school. They taught me how to be an inspector. I had to take math and geometry, and learn how to read all the various gauges and tools and how to read blueprints. As a result I worked as an inspector in what was called the small parts department, which was located in the corner of the "L," because the bomber plant is shaped like an "L." You did have a considerable amount of responsibility. It was the first time airplanes had ever been produced on a kind of assembly line. At the end of the war there was one plane coming off the line every fifty-five minutes. It's almost impossible to believe.

Some of the inspectors I worked with were men, some were women. Supervisors were all men. The only place where you had a woman in a supervisory capacity was maintaining the restrooms. They had a woman who used to do a kind of policing job: seeing what was going on in the women's restrooms, and criticizing if there were too many people loafing in there. There were so many restrooms that she couldn't watch them all. During those years you were still not allowed to smoke. That was when Henry Ford was still alive. Naturally the women would go in the restrooms and close the door and take a quick smoke and this supervisor would move around, policing.

Of course I remember when Franklin Roosevelt toured the plant. I was down toward the middle of the building, in the area that wasn't completed. They really covered up everything that wasn't finished to make it look like it was finished. They built walls where they really didn't need walls to cover the fact that part of the building wasn't done. None of us knew until the day he came. When he came down I had a very good view of him, because we were allowed to quit work and stand along the aisles as he went through.[5]

Because of the war, rationing for things like gas and tires made transportation difficult, and it was hard for people to get together socially. I was active in the church, and we would have card parties in people's homes. My mother had a large family and we got together frequently. There were the beer gardens, and I would think nothing of a group of four or five women getting together and sitting in a bar and people would ask you to dance. It was acceptable. I did form close friendships with a number of people during that period of time. There were occasions when some of us who had come from Central Specialty would make arrangements to get together. There was a bar we used to go to quite close to the plant, and they had a band. We would go there, but not real often, because the hours on the job were so long and it was extremely difficult to do that sort of thing. Unfortunately a lot of the fellows that I knew were drafted, and they were gone during that period.

After the War

In 1946, at the end of the war, the number of women in the automotive manufacturing industry dropped to 61,000, down from 185,000 in 1944. Their reduced numbers formed only 10 percent of the auto manufacturing work force.[6] Decreasing production and the large number of veterans returning from the war to their old jobs created conflict for the women and the union. Many employers failed to honor the union contracts and seniority rights and arbitrarily laid women off. The women had to fight within their unions to protect their job rights.[7] In Dorothy's case, the bomber plant was sold to the Kaiser-Fraser Company and converted to an automobile plant, where "all the jigs and fixtures that they had installed to produce airplanes had to be changed to produce cars." Dorothy and her women co-workers were laid off.

When the Ford bomber plant folded up I was laid off, arbitrary, just like all the other women workers. My feelings at being laid off at the end of the war were unhappiness because I was losing this good pay, but also, you know, we were very happy because the war was ending and the soldiers were coming home. Our friends and relatives and boyfriends were all coming home and we were happy about that. We hated to lose our jobs, but on the other hand, there wasn't that kind of sorrow that you would have nowadays with plants folding up. Most women didn't believe that we were going to get shafted the way we did. At least I didn't.

I still felt that I would be called back because Kaiser-Fraser bought the plant I had come from and they were going to use the plant, and some of the UAW Local 50 people were still employed in that plant doing maintenance and keeping up the plant. That assumption was incorrect. I had that assumption because I had a couple of brothers who were never laid off from the Ford bomber plant. Even when Kaiser-Fraser took jurisdiction, my brothers were never laid off at all.

Women were primarily hired to work on the sewing machines or on small assembly jobs that were traditionally considered women's work. They hired enough of the Local 50 women under the preferential hiring set-up to say, at least, "Well, we are hiring them." My problem was that I had no history of having been employed at the Ford bomber plant either as an assembler or as a sewing machine operator. My whole history was as a clerk or as an inspector in that plant. After the war, they were not about to hire a woman to do inspection.

In spite of the fact that Kaiser-Fraser was considered a more liberal corporation, and much easier to deal with, they weren't about to continue with all the changes Ford had made in the past. The excuse they used was that producing airplanes is different than producing automobiles. They said that the work on automobiles was much heavier; the women were not going to be able to do it, and they said that women really didn't want to work in shops with all the men. Of course, the other argument was that there were all these GI's coming back who had to have jobs. To a certain extent the company didn't really feel compelled to give any rationale. They could go ahead and do pretty much as they pleased.

I went to work in a toy factory on piecework. My wages were probably less than half what I made at the bomber plant. I knew when Kaiser-Fraser was hiring. I went and applied numerous times. I started trying to get a job by doing the clerical work again, because the work I was doing at the toy factory was difficult and so low-paying that almost anything would have been better. I was finally able to get hired at the Kaiser-Fraser plant as a department clerk, but it was not based on my preferential hiring rights, because the clerical workers were not organized in the union. As a result, they were very low-paid compared to workers in other auto jobs. But that's where I worked.

Union Activist

By this time the UAW had been enormously successful in organizing assembly line workers and skilled craftsmen in the auto factories. As in most industries, less attention was paid to the clerical workers, most of whom were women. Dorothy recalls, "We quickly figured out that the reason we were so low-paid was that we didn't have a union." She was part of a small group that organized eight hundred people in the clerical and engineering departments in the auto plant. At a UAW convention in 1946, Local 142 was given jurisdiction over Local 50, and Dorothy became an activist in Local 142. That same year Walter Reuther was elected president of the UAW. Like many union women activists at that time, Dorothy did not marry and have a family, as she had expected, and she continued to live at the family farm.[8]

All in all, the group of people who were really active in the local union was comparatively small, because people were afraid of management. In spite of the fact that the law said you could organize, people were afraid to really get active and the numbers that would come out for the meetings were very small. I attended many union meetings during that time and I was fearful. But I also had some strong feelings that unless we organized the union, conditions were never going to get better and we were never going to get a decent wage. I guess that overcame my fears. Even some of my family expressed fears about my activity and that I might end up getting in trouble.

I was elected to the union committee that negotiated our first office and engineering contract. There wasn't much animosity, because it was a small group and the fighting over the position was not as strong as in later elections. On the committee there was one other woman. Now once we were certified as a union, we voted to become part of Local 142, and I then became active in this total local. I ran for trustee, and it was in this local that I finally got elected to the top negotiating committee of the entire local.

The local union was divided into caucuses. I had to fight the men in my own local caucus to be put on the slate to run for the larger Local 142 bargaining committee. It was almost impossible to get elected without caucus support. The men felt it was just not a spot for a woman. A woman could run as a union trustee. She could run as recording secretary, but she just had no right to be sitting in when you were doing the top negotiating. Their rationale for how they justified this was ridiculous. First, they justified it on the basis that I was young and naive and that I really couldn't stand all that dirty language that took place. When that didn't work, they reversed the tactic and chopped me literally to pieces on the basis of how "immoral" I was. I was very unhappy.

I became very angry at some of the tactics my opposition was using. They were chopping my whole record and making me out to be a person that I was not. I asked a lawyer friend in the union for advice. He said that from a legal point of view, I had a good case. But he also said that I ought to really sit down and seriously think about what I wanted to do in the union. If I tried to fight all those who were slandering me, I would just waste my energy. If I really wanted to get involved in the union, I had to make up my mind right now to just ignore that and do my thing. It was not just women, but men too that this happened to, and you just have to figure out some way to deal with it and forget about it.

That was probably some of the best advice that I ever received, because a lot of women who get active, even today, unless they understand that ahead of time, they're really not going to get very far. It was part of what a woman had to accept to be active. Four years later, a fellow who had got religion and knew he had been wrong came out to our house to see me to tell me how viciously he had chopped me. Sometimes you say to yourself, as the years go by, "Well, you had a tendency to build things up, to elaborate." But when a fellow comes back four years later to personally apologize, you know it wasn't your imagination. This point needs to be made. The other point that needs to be made, too, is that the kind of fulfillment you get from what you accomplish in the union more than offsets all the kind of pain and trouble you had as you went through the problem times.

Restoring Jobs

The UAW established a women's bureau in 1944 as part of the UAW War Policy Division. The first national conference of UAW women, called to develop plans to protect women workers after the war, made strong recommendations, Dorothy recalls, in terms of "women maintaining seniority, not being shoved out of the shops, the need for full employment, equal pay, and all that sort of thing." Carrying out the program on a local union level was more difficult, however. Dorothy learned to use the union structure, often overcoming the opposition of union men, first to help the other women from her old Local 50 and then to regain a higher-paying job for herself, similar to the inspection job she had had during the war.

It took some time for me to get active enough to get elected to the top negotiating committee, and then I really put pressure on management to finally call back all of the laid-off Local 50 women when they were hiring for new job openings. They finally did do that. We really made an issue of this during one negotiation. Management had to go through the mechanics of at least sending notices out to all the Local 50 women who not been notified that a job was available and that they could apply for the job. Even while the company was doing that, you had to watch them very closely or else they would put the women on jobs that were deliberately too difficult, which they wouldn't have done with a group of men.

During that period, some of these women, personal friends of mine, would call me up at home or come to me and say how desperate they were for a job, which completely put to rest this concept that the women didn't want the jobs. They desperately wanted the jobs, and they knew that if they didn't get a job working at this kind of a plant where wages were good, that they were going to end up the rest of their life in a job like I had at the toy factory. I could not have existed on that job if I wasn't living at home, because I wasn't making enough to support myself.

Now I'm not saying that I did this all myself. What I'm really saying is that I did initiate the pressure to see that it was done. I couldn't have done it unless I had pressured some other people into helping me. I made a big ruckus about it and about the fact that it was a UAW Local 50 caucus that had pushed to get many of the committee members elected to the convention that finally got Walter Reuther in the leadership of the UAW international executive board. It was our group that had finally pulled the votes together to do that, and, therefore, we really had a responsibility to do something for those women.

The union men were very angry at me. I really had to pressure our own people. They didn't care. It was a terribly awakening experience for me. I was a member of Local 142's Fair Practices Committee. I really believed all this stuff we preached and believed that everybody was going to do it. It's a terrible disillusion to discover that, having got this far, now you really have to fight your own people.

Having got active in organizing, I started to learn a little better how the preferential hiring right functioned. I felt that I ought to have been hired back as an inspector because there were inspection jobs open that they would not give me. First, on my lunch hour for several days, I went out in the plant and had somebody teach me how to run the sewing machine. Then I insisted on getting preferential hiring rights as a sewing machine operator. If they really needed production workers, they would transfer us down on the line. I was making more money, but some people thought I was crazy. They felt it was below me.

I went back to Cass Technical High School in Detroit and took the necessary training in statistical quality control. I was weak in math and in knowing how you do the statistical work. Even today I get very angry when I think about the fact that men worked in statistical quality control and got those jobs without having the kind of math background the company insisted that I have. When I worked on that classification it became very clear to me that I didn't need to have it, but the company was not going to consider me unless I had it. Management strongly resisted giving me the statistical quality control job. It was very high-paying and a technical engineering classification. The point is that I did go back to school, and I did get the job, and that was a first. There was no other woman working in that classification. I never would have got the job, however, if I hadn't understood how a union functions. Our contract provided that they had to give me the job.

Organizing Office and Technical Workers

From 1952 to 1961 Dorothy was on the UAW organizing staff for the Technical, Office, and Professional Department (TOP), where she helped develop strategies for organizing women clerical workers who worked in the auto industry. Like Carmen Lucia and many other organizers, she had to learn the rules and regulations of the National Labor Relations Board, the organization that governed union elections under the 1935 National Labor Relations Act. Women were only 10 percent of the UAW membership, and they held few of the elected officer and staff positions. Although Dorothy enjoyed many organizing successes, she also faced difficulties and disappointments as the only woman staff member in her department. In those days, she said, "You didn't fight it." She did a great deal of traveling and for periods of time rented an apartment in Detroit to be closer to Solidarity House, the UAW headquarters. Her base, however, remained the family farm in New Boston, Michigan.

I was offered the staff position by Walter Reuther, president of the UAW. Doug Fraser, then his administrative assistant, set up my interview with Walter.[9] The TOP department staff were told that they had to completely train me to do everything in that department. There was a lot of technical work involved, especially when you go to a hearing before the National Labor Relations Board: who's acceptable to be in the unit; how you hold an NLRB election; when you go before the board; the information you need to know to comply with the law; what you could and couldn't do. The union staff was very good at doing that kind of training. No one thought of teaching us how to organize. They assumed that we would come with the skills. We learned from each other. When we worked together, especially on a big organizing drive, we would get together and compare notes on what we thought was a good approach and what we thought was not. We would keep a record.

I worked for nine years organizing office and technical workers for the UAW. The first big drive I worked on was in Bridgeport, Connecticut, where we picked up almost one thousand office and technical workers, about half men, half women. The technical group tend to be men. We made a few house calls and we did publicity, leafleting, and we put a newspaper together for the final day or so before the union election. It was in that newspaper that I started using some of my ideas on the comparison of the income of women who work in an office with the pay of what are supposedly the lower-paying

jobs in the plants and how clericals still make much less money. The workers were so fearful that you couldn't get them out to meetings. No one
thought we would win that election. But we won that election by better than
two to one.

The first drive that I did all by myself was with the Chrysler Trenton
plant. The first time 'round, we lost that election by a very close vote. The
following year I handled it by myself. I didn't do a lot of leafleting. I sat
with my workers' committee from the plant and listened to what they had
to say. It has taught me this: on any organizing drive that I handled by
myself, I paid very close attention to what the members of that organizing
committee told me, because they work in that office. They know the problems they have, and you shouldn't go contrary to what they suggest unless
you have some absolutely essential reasons why. The thing is that from
my own union department I did get flack on the way I was handling this
organizing drive, because the whole idea of not handing out a lot of leaflets, not holding a lot of meetings, was contrary to what they had planned
to do. But we did go ahead our way and won the election. I was really pleased
that I won that one, because it was my first union organizing campaign on
my own.

I'm probably being a heretic to my sex, but as the years went by, we
also started to accept the fact that it wasn't necessarily the best thing in
the world to always have a woman call on a woman, and a man call on a
man. Once in a while, in a family situation, you might have resentment or
someone thinking that there's something wrong with this approach, but often I could convince a man just as easily as I could convince a woman to
join the union. That was a sort of mutual decision that the staff arrived at.

But the one thing that we never changed, and I have not changed even
to this day, is if you call a meeting of the workers and organize a drive, at
some point you should make an effort to call a union meeting that is going
to be just for the women to get together and to meet. There's a tendency on
the part of women, especially the groups that we tend to be dealing with,
that they're reluctant to come out to a meeting where there's not going to
be anyone they know, where there may be only men, and they're going to
feel out of place, especially if they are young.

One issue, of course, that women were concerned about was promotion to higher-paying jobs. In the plants where they were organized, they
were covered by union contract language that provided that seniority should
prevail. I had to be careful of how I worked on this issue. If you impressed
upon the women in an organizing drive that if they were members of the
union, that they could move into higher-paying jobs, you had to watch the
number of women's votes you were going to get against how many men's

votes you were going to lose. At one time I had wanted to do up a leaflet addressing the promotion issue, but having considered all the pros and cons, I didn't follow through with it. You had to become more concerned about winning the union election than convincing people of these principles.

I was the only woman on the staff for a long time organizing white-collar and engineering workers. One area where I was not very happy with the union was that they were not really too anxious to have me ever get involved in the whole servicing end of it. I was not even being considered to go in and negotiate a contract, after winning an election.[10] My credentials were just as good as anyone else's in that department in terms of what I had done in my local union and having served on the local's negotiating committee. But the UAW office and technical department continued to have the kind of hang-up that it was all right for me to go out and organize, but I really wouldn't be able to help a plant solve a problem or negotiate a contract. It would be better for one of the union staff men to do it. That was a problem I was always aware of and resented, but I didn't fight it. In those days these kinds of decisions were accepted. There wasn't any need to explain why.

The Women's Department

In 1947 the UAW women's bureau became the separate UAW Women's Department. The UAW was one of the first unions to have such a department and to focus explicitly on women's employment issues. Although the department provided a visible platform to raise issues of concern to women auto workers, the staff did not have any direct influence over the local unions and had to rely primarily on the "power of moral persuasion."[11] As a union member and staff organizer for UAW-TOP, Dorothy was active with the Women's Department. Then, in 1961, she transferred to its staff. She also became very active in the Democratic Party.

I always had a relationship with the Women's Department. I was appointed to the women's committee for my region when it was first set up, about 1947. I was one of the original members of that committee. The purpose was to have women get together to discuss their mutual problems and to plan program activities that would encourage women to be active in the labor movement and to participate in the total program of the union, both in the union and in the community and on the national level.

Caroline Davis, who was the director of the UAW Women's Department, was a very good friend of mine, and we built up a close relationship working on the regional women's committee and during political campaigns. I had become very active in the Democratic Party. In the 1940s, somebody from the union asked me why I didn't run for precinct delegate and explained to me how to go about doing that. I served on the Democratic Party executive board for my fifteenth district for quite a long time. In the 1960 presidential election I was very involved in the whole effort to get participation in my district. For about five weeks before the election I was setting up and conducting meetings in people's homes and neighborhoods. I was listed as an available speaker, and I also was doing coordination in the district to try to get other women to become involved in the political process. Caroline was also involved in this.

After I moved into the Women's Department, I remember that the women workers in one of the Big Three auto plants (Ford, Chrysler, or General Motors) were having difficulty moving into the higher-level jobs in the auto plants although they were qualified. Now, that was when we were going through that period in the auto plants when the companies were using the excuse of overtime hours and the weight lifting and so forth to stop women from getting the better jobs. The union was able finally to get a few women moved into those better-paying jobs, but then what happened is the language on promotions and seniority was the same in all union contracts—engineering, office, and production—and it was not very strong language. This meant that whenever the company didn't want to promote by seniority in the unit, they could hire a new employee from outside the company.

Then what happened is the auto companies started this bit of, let's say that there were two men with less seniority than a woman available for a job and the company put the senior man on the job. The men then started saying to the women, "Well, look, if you start raising a fuss, you're just going to jeopardize our chance of getting it and the company will go outside." Well, the women listened to this for a while, but they were kind of getting sick and tired of it. So we had a meeting down here at UAW Solidarity House. The one basic problem involved was that the language in the labor-management contract should have been cleaned up at negotiations, but enough pressure had not been built up to do it.

But after we talked it over for a long time, we finally came to the conclusion that the women were going to start filing grievances. If the jobs were not going to be filled by women, then they'd be filled by somebody outside the collective bargaining unit or a new hire from outside the company. At the point that started to happen, we thought there'd be enough of an uproar that something would be changed. That strategy did work, and the women did start filing grievances and moving into higher-paying jobs. I was pleased about that.

The other problem they had was part of what you still run into with women who work in a situation where they have become conditioned to not ever rocking the boat. You have to take a look at how to rock the boat. You don't want to spill yourself out if you can avoid it, but sometimes you have to rock the boat. What happened is that when the women really got this action going and they filed their grievances, then women who had been sitting there saying, "You shouldn't be doing this to the men, you aren't going to want that job when you get it," they suddenly decided, because they had more seniority, that they wanted the job now.

I'm not sure it would be legal today under the laws, but the position was taken that the woman who filed a grievance, who put her name on it, who was willing to stick out her neck, was the one that got the job. I thought that was fair, because some of the women who were in that early part of the fight, they took an awful lot of guff from both sides, as well as some of their women friends working with them. That was one issue that I was involved in where I can look back and see there were a few victories.

The UAW leadership has never been terribly happy with having these equality concepts implemented, especially when it hits them personally. There was a reluctance on the part of regions in the union to have staff from the Women's Department come in and get involved in talking about what they called the "women's problem." They felt that we tended to incite people. They really did! That I don't think is completely changed. There is that resistance and always will be. I really think that's basically true of all society.

Developing Sex Discrimination Laws

In 1961 Caroline Davis joined Esther Peterson and Mary Callahan in their work on President Kennedy's Commission on the Status of Women. She was appointed to one of the four committees, the Committee on Private Employment. Dorothy worked with her, doing the staff work and going to meetings when Caroline was unable to attend. For years, the UAW Women's Department challenged protective labor laws that discriminated against women. They thought the laws that limited the number of hours a woman could work or the weight she could lift were used to bar women from high-paying skilled jobs rather than to protect them from onerous working conditions. The department supported sex-blind treatment in the workplace as the way to secure equal employment opportunity for women. Department members' support for sex-blind policies sometimes put them at odds with other women in the UAW and often at odds with women in other unions, like Mary Callahan, who thought the protective laws should be extended to men. On the committee Davis argued unsuccessfully to include sex discrimination in Executive Order 10925, prohibiting employment discrimination in federal contracting. She was the only committee member to issue a dissenting report. The UAW Women's Department disagreed with many in the labor movement and the civil rights movement who thought that including a clause prohibiting sex discrimination in the executive order, and later in Title VII of the Civil Rights Act, would weaken the fight against race discrimination.[12]

I came into the UAW Women's Department in 1961 after I had worked in the Kennedy presidential election campaign. I knew what was going on, and I wanted to be part of it. Kennedy's Commission on the Status of Women was the forerunner of the women's movement. It was an important stepping stone, bringing people together. Not just union people, but you met people you would not have met otherwise. You met Republicans who took excellent positions on important women's issues. This was a crucial thing about that commission. It gave us a chance to know each other.

I sat in on some of those meetings for Caroline Davis because she was a member of the commission's Committee on Private Employment. We would argue this whole question of the state protective laws and, of course, including the word "sex" in the presidential executive order. I would sit in a meeting with maybe eight, ten people and I would be the only one there raising these issues of the problems caused by protective legislation. The others would just kind of brush me off. I was so angry, but that's how it was.

We were very unhappy with the commission report. It didn't address the whole question of the state protective laws except to say that a larger study ought to maybe be done in this area. The 1963 Equal Pay Act really came about because of Kennedy's commission. It was the least undesirable thing they could give us, and that's what they did. The commission refused to take a position that the President should include the word "sex" in his executive order, which was the only federal regulation providing equal employment opportunity at that time. Caroline was the only member of that commission to issue a minority report. Considering how much we thought of Kennedy, that was not very easy for us to do. But she did it.

When the congressman from the South inserted the word "sex" in Title VII of the 1964 Civil Rights Act, he expected to destroy it. The argument in the beginning was that you had to get black people covered first. If you included women you would weaken the effort and destroy the bill, but the bill passed anyway. The Democratic Party hierarchy was absolutely opposed to having the prohibition on sex discrimination in the 1964 Civil Rights Law enforced. Mary Keyserling, who was then head of the U.S. Department of Labor's Women's Bureau (1964–1969), was just absolutely deaf to anyone who suggested that the state protective laws didn't protect, that they did discriminate sometimes. This was in spite of the documentation. You have to understand that or you don't understand any of what went on behind the scenes.

It's incredible when I look back on it now. In 1965, the White House Conference on Equal Employment Opportunity was commemorating the fact that the 1964 Civil Rights Law had been enacted and was going into effect. The government had this big meeting in Washington and invited Caroline Davis to speak. She was not terribly well at that time, but she accepted, and she made it clear that she was going to address the whole area of the so-called state protective laws and their relationship to Title VII. The last ten days before that conference there was enormous pressure on her not to show up. The last thing they did behind the scenes was to not let Caroline insert the entire text of her talk in the record. All we were doing was asking them, "Please take a position saying that you will let an investigation be made of what the state laws are doing. If they really are discriminating then the federal law ought to supersede it." Of course, nowadays, it is so accepted, but it was just terrible in those days.

Basically, the guidelines that the Equal Employment Opportunity Commission (EEOC) eventually adopted literally took the language we had prepared with the assistance of Steve Schlossberg, the head of our UAW Legal Department, for Caroline's speech on the protective laws and on the hours of work, the overtime, and the relationship that the laws should have. This would not have happened if the UAW Women's Department had not existed, if Walter Reuther had not been around, and if there had not been some other people in the UAW such as Irving Bluestone, Walter's administrative assistant. It was a very crucial time to live through.[13]

I don't mind saying that I had the opportunity to move out of the Women's Department on several occasions, but I stayed there because I thought that what we were doing needed to be done. Speaking out as I have on women's issues has not always helped me in the UAW. It's really made life difficult for me in many cases. But it's been worth it to me. I really feel very strongly that if there had not been a few people like me around doing the kinds of things that we have done, that much of what we have seen happen in the women's movement might not well have happened.

NOW and the ERA

In 1963 Betty Friedan's book *The Feminine Mystique* struck a nerve with many women around the country. The National Commission on the Status of Women issued a report on problems women confronted in the United States, state women's commissions were established, and Title VII of the 1964 Civil Rights Act prohibited sex discrimination in employment. Despite all this activity, there was considerable question about whether or not Title VII was being adequately enforced. The debate about state protective laws dragged on, as did the debate about the Equal Rights Amendment. In 1966, at a meeting in Washington of women from all of the state Commissions on the Status of Women, some women held that not enough was happening to make equality for women a reality. Dorothy Haener and Caroline Davis helped form the National Organization for Women. Although the UAW is given only brief mention in the histories of this movement, Caroline became secretary-treasurer and the UAW provided most of the administrative support during the first year. The UAW was the first union to officially support the ERA in 1970. Other unions followed, and the AFL-CIO changed its policy from opposition to support of ERA in 1973. Dorothy provides a perspective on the involvement of union women in the emerging women's movement. (See also Catherine Conroy's comments in Chapter 11.)[14]

Now, Dolly Lowther Robinson was a labor attorney from New York and former union activist, who worked for the U.S. Women's Bureau during part of this time, and we had her in to speak to a UAW Region 10 conference in Milwaukee, Wisconsin. After the conference was over, she and the staff of the UAW Women's Department got together and hashed over what was going on. She was a black woman and the one that first gave me the concept of what we needed. "What we need," she said, "is an NAACP for women." She talked of the U.S. Women's Bureau saying one thing and then instructing her to go up on Capitol Hill in Washington and talk to the congressmen about doing the other thing. That's the way it was behind the scenes all the time. You just knew that nothing was going to happen unless you had a pressure group that was going to be pressuring.[15]

I was among the ten or eleven people who sat in a hotel room with Betty Friedan and put together the concept of NOW. If you've read her book, you know that the night when that happened, Caroline and I had lunch with her that day. That evening when we met, we had pretty well put our concepts together when we were disrupted by a group that felt this was a party where we were just going to have fun and drinks. The dean from a college in Madison, Wisconsin, talked to us like we were a bunch of campus students, saying, "Do you think we really need another women's organization?" If some of us had not been around, that might have well been the end of it, at least for that point in time. I had very strong convictions for almost a year that we needed that kind of an organization.

The history of NOW shows that for the first year and a half, the UAW Women's Department, actually it was the UAW clerical center, produced almost everything that NOW used. We did letters and press releases and applications, reports, and those kind of things. But what happened at the second meeting of NOW was that they went on record supporting the Equal Rights Amendment and they also went on record supporting abortion. We didn't have a problem with abortion because the UAW didn't have a policy position on abortion, but in 1966 we did have a position opposed to the Equal Rights Amendment. We had asked NOW to try to postpone trying to make a decision on this issue until we could reason with our organization to change the UAW position. At this point in time we were convinced we should change it. We recognized that those laws that were really protecting people should stay on the books, but those laws that were discriminating against women should not.

We had to pull out of NOW. We couldn't support a group that was contrary to our UAW policy position. I continued my personal membership in NOW in spite of that fact. I paid my dues, but I couldn't be active. After the UAW policy on the ERA changed in 1970, we got involved in NOW again. I subsequently served on the NOW executive board for a number of years.

The 1970s

With the growing awareness of discrimination against women in many areas, women in the UAW began to challenge the lack of women in union leadership positions. A campaign was mounted to elect a woman to the UAW international executive board, and in 1966 Olga Madar became a member-at-large. In 1968 the UAW left the AFL-CIO, and contacts with women in other unions were limited to informal meetings—for example, those organized by Elizabeth (Libby) Koontz, director of the U.S. Women's Bureau from 1969 to 1973. In the early 1970s the UAW took a leading role in organizing the Coalition of Labor Union Women, and Olga Madar was elected president at the first CLUW convention in 1974.[16] The UAW also took a lead in filing sex discrimination complaints against the auto companies and helping locals meet their responsibilities under the laws. Dorothy's experience confirms the positive effects of affirmative action on women's employment. Although Dorothy joined the CLUW, she was not active and focused her efforts more on implementing the employment laws within the UAW and the auto industry.[17] She also increased her involvement in the Democratic Party and helped to found the National Women's Political Caucus and the Women's Equity Action League. In 1969 her mother died, and Dorothy moved away from the family farm and into Detroit. Her sister, however, still lives on the farm where she grew up, along with three brothers and their families who built homes there, "a quite close family."

One day we had a luncheon meeting to discuss how we could recruit women for the apprenticeship trades, the kinds of things we need to do, and the reasons why the women are not applying for those jobs. There were representatives from the Chrysler Skilled Trades Department and a number of officials from the Chrysler Corporation. After this meeting, there was quite a lengthy discussion in which the union members all aired their views. I have strong feelings that the reason women don't apply is that they've been turned off so completely and so conditioned to believe that they'll never be accepted and that things will be so rough for them if they do try, that they just aren't doing it. So we were given the assignment of meeting and drawing up a proposal on how to recruit women for apprenticeship trades.

Part of our discussion was, number one, to call a meeting of the representatives from the local unions involved. This is the greater Detroit metropolitan area, with a couple of union women representatives either from a local union women's committee or who were active in a local, and then the apprenticeship coordinator from the local union, the local union president, or chairman of the bargaining committee, and the apprenticeship coordinator from the company as well as the plant manager and someone from the company's personnel department. Talk to them about this recruiting drive for women in the apprenticeship trades and what needs to be done to make it successful. Convince the women there that, yes, these jobs really are going to open up and that they should carry the message back to the plant. Then plan to have a meeting also at each local union level with as many women as we can get together and some of the leadership of the plant from both the union and the company. We're hopeful that this is going to get results.

I've lived in this union for twenty-five years, and it's the first time I'm ever participating in this kind of effort. I feel that if it does happen, it's happening because of the pressure of the 1964 Civil Rights Law and the fact that "sex" was included in the Executive Order on government contracts.

These corporations have been told, "You've got to show us some affirmative action or else you're going to be in trouble." This has really helped. It is one of the reasons you need an outside enforcement agency like the EEOC. If it happens, that's why it happened.

Recently I've done a number of things that I've never done before. For instance, for the first time in my life I served on the Democratic Party Platform Committee. I was a delegate to the 1976 Democratic National Convention and was chosen to speak for keeping in the platform the right of choice, on the question of abortion. There was a great effort made to remove that from the party platform, and I was pleased by being able to be a part of that and by being asked to help do that. I got to go to the presidential inauguration and to visit the White House the next day and meet President Carter and Vice President Mondale. 1976 was really an exciting year for me. These are things that don't tie in so much I guess with the labor movement, but I think in the broader sense, they sure do tie in.

Reflections

In 1982 Dorothy retired from the UAW. She was appointed by Governor James Blanchard as a member of the Michigan Civil Rights Commission, where she served for eight years, three of them as commission chair. She was also appointed to the National Advisory Council of UAW Retired Workers and is very active in UAW Region 1A's council, where she has served as chair for six years. In 1994 she was in Washington, D.C., actively lobbying on health care reform, an issue of great concern to retirees. She currently serves on the Michigan State AFL-CIO executive council and was appointed by Congressman William Ford of Michigan to the 1995 White House Conference on Aging.

In 1983 Dorothy was one of the first women inducted into the Michigan Women's Hall of Fame. She was very proud to share this honor with Rosa Parks, who started the Montgomery bus boycott in 1955, and Martha Griffiths, the congresswoman from Michigan who led the effort to include sex discrimination in the 1964 Civil Rights Act.[18] In 1994 Dorothy was also awarded a medal of honor, along with Betty Friedan and several other prominent leaders in the women's movement, at a national meeting of the Veteran Feminists of America. Her reflections in 1976 remain pertinent today.

Over the years, the most frustrating part of union work is sometimes the inability to reach people in areas that you know are absolutely right. The other is having to deal with the employment problems in your own life. You know how things ought to be and what you ought to be dealing with, but you have to force yourself to deal with the reality of the situation, the way it is, and do the very best you can within that reality. That can be just terribly frustrating, sometimes, and very discouraging. I always felt like I was lucky to be working at something that I enjoyed doing. Of course I had my trials and tribulations like anything else, but basically I liked my work.

For example, I recognize very much the improvements the union made in my life at the point I had become a member of the union. I helped to organize the office and engineering group, and when we negotiated the increase in salary and better working conditions, I understood how much I had benefited by that. Later on I got very active in the union, and I really believed all the things the union leaders said to me about nondiscrimination and fair employment and so forth. When the reality hit me that what we say in the labor movement we don't really always practice, even at the local union level, it was very difficult for me, but I have come to accept that you have to work within the realities.

I do blow my stack once in a while, which I think maybe helps to relieve some of the tension. The other thing I do is to recognize the problems and learn from them. It's one of the things you need to teach women. At the point you convince them to get active, they need to know the difference between becoming angry about something and expressing their anger, and becoming so angry that they're angry all the time, which is very sad. I've seen this happen to women who are very qualified and who are very able and have great potential, but they reach that point where they've been made so angry that they're not reasonable about anything anymore.

In spite of some of my unhappiness even today, I can still look at what has been accomplished and it's to me a beautiful time to be alive. We have accomplished a great deal, although we've got a long way to go. The reason I've been able to keep on going is that I've had some success, and during the rough times I can sort of coast on that. Yeah. I have had success. And I am hopeful about women in the labor movement and in the UAW. So I can sit here and say, "Well, sure, I've taken a lot of guff and it's been rough at times, but I'm beginning to see results."

Chapter 9

The Vote Does Make a Difference

Fannie Allen Neal, Amalgamated Clothing Workers of America (1919–1990)

Fannie Allen Neal was the great-granddaughter of slaves. Born in 1919, she grew up during the Depression in Montgomery County, Alabama. The lessons she learned from her grandmother and her sharecropper parents provided the foundation for her workplace activism in a shirt factory and as a shop steward for the Amalgamated Clothing Workers of America. She applied her skills as a union leader to the civil rights movement, through voter registration drives, while also serving as recording secretary of ACWA Local 490 and as an officer of the Alabama State AFL-CIO and the Montgomery Central Labor Council.

Fannie was part of that critical grass-roots coalition of union members, civil rights advocates, and politicians that led to the passage of the nation's civil rights laws in the 1960s. She joined the NAACP in 1945, was a charter member of the Montgomery Improvement Association, and in 1955 helped with the Montgomery bus boycott under the leadership of Martin Luther King, Jr. In 1962, after she lost her job when the shirt factory closed, she became a staff member of the AFL-CIO Committee on Political Education and traveled across the country registering African-American voters. Always committed to the labor movement, she worked in local and state elections, congressional campaigns, and in every presidential election from 1960 through 1984.

Despite her travels, Fannie never left her home base in Montgomery, where she lived with her sisters, raised her daughter, and was active in many community groups. She was on the advisory board of the A. Philip Randolph Institute and taught in the Southern Summer School for Union Women. At her retirement in 1987, the Alabama State AFL-CIO called her "one of the most loved and respected members of our union." Fannie Allen Neal died in August 1990.[1]

The Great-Granddaughter of Slaves

At the end of the Civil War some four million African-American women and men were given their freedom. In the 1870s, about 6 percent of the freed families in the South owned their own farms, and by 1910, 14 percent of southern farm owners were African-Americans. Reconstruction was over, however, and white communities were developing new ways to control the children and grandchildren of former slaves. Between 1880 and World War I, racial violence was rampant in the South. At the same time, black farmers increasingly became sharecroppers, rather than farm owners. Fannie's family followed this pattern.[2]

I am the great-granddaughter of Washington McCloud, who was a slave and the father of seventeen children. He was a very strong man, and at the end of slavery the master, whose name was Mr. McCloud, gave my great-grandfather sixty acres of land. This land was to be our property, and we were told that it was never to be sold. My grandmother was born two years after the surrender, and her name was Mary McCloud. She only finished the second grade, but she was a schoolteacher because she went through the Bluebook Speller and was qualified to be a schoolteacher. I believe that she was a very excellent teacher, because she really helped us in our early childhood in learning to read and to spell. My grandmother was a very strong woman, except that she *was* a woman and regardless of how strong we are, sometimes we are taken advantage of.

When she was about seventeen, a very unfortunate thing happened to her. The black daughter of an ex-slave, you can imagine the work that she still had to do. One of my grandmother's responsibilities after she had worked in the field all day was that just before night she'd have to go into the woods to round up the cows to bring them in so that they could milk them. One afternoon, the master's son, who rode his horse through the woods, he took advantage of my grandmother under a Chinaberry tree, and this was where my mother was conceived. The same man did her the same way when my mother was two years old, and my Uncle George was born.

Now my grandmother made a marriage, to a man named Mr. Amos Huffman, and they didn't ever have any children. But my grandfather went to the master and told him that if his son bothered my grandmother again he would physically kill him. I don't think he bothered my grandmother anymore. But my grandmother was the leader. She did all the work in the fields. She plowed; she hoed; she planted; and she did everything. Grandpa

Fannie Allen Neal (*third from the left*) joins her nine brothers and sisters at a family reunion in Alabama, 1954. They are stading in order of age, from oldest to youngest (*right to left*). *Courtesy Alonzetta Ford.*

Amos stayed home and he cooked and washed and ironed. It was just a reverse role of what my concept of what a woman's role is versus a man's role.

My mother and my father were married in 1900, Jonas Allen and Lilla Huffman Allen. Then to this union, kids started coming. She had eleven children and ten of us lived. I was born in a log cabin in 1919. My father was a sharecropper. He migrated toward the city of Montgomery. Nobody, nobody knows the life of a sharecropper except the sharecropper himself and his wife and his kids, because they are worked to death. In the end, they are the ones who still have nothing. My father started us working in the garden as soon as we could walk good. By the time you were seven, you were going to the field and working in the field.

Unfortunately, between my seventh and eighth birthdays, my father died. This was in 1927, and times were lean, but they had been lean to us all of our lives! I never knew that Santa Claus brought anything to a child or anybody except one apple, one orange, some nuts and raisins, so help me! But my father fell with a stroke on a Sunday morning. On Tuesday he died. It was very emotional because there Mama was with ten children, nine of them still living in the house with her, and no father. It's very touching, even now, to think about the sacrifices that my brothers made for Mama and, as they refer to us, the "children." We are a very, very close-knit family. After Papa died, my brothers didn't farm; they went to work at this gravel pit.

I was a problem child. I was the only child that my mother had, out of all the children, that she said was "talking back" to her. I thought I was defending myself. I had to stand up for my rights! But all my life I've had confidence in myself, and I believe if anybody else can do it, I can do it. My grandma told me this as far back as I can remember. She said, "You are as good as anybody. Don't you ever let nobody make you think you're not as good or better than they are." So that's part of my grandma's philosophy. She also told me, "You can do anything, if you want to."

Life in the City

Although sharecropping offered some independence, black sharecroppers were trapped in a system of indebtedness to white landowners and merchants. When women were widowed, "survival on the farm became very difficult and many migrated to the cities."[3] After Fannie's father died, the white owner took everything but a few hogs, chickens, and a cow. Fannie and one of her brothers went to live with her mother's cousin for two years. In about 1929, the family moved to "town." Her grandmother was ill and had moved with them, and they all lived in three rooms with a kitchen and no water, no bath, no toilet, and no lights. Her brothers got up at 3:30 in the morning and walked back down to the country to work. Lilla Huffman Allen was a good mother and proud. They took no handouts; they all went to church, and Fannie went to school.

Back in 1935 in Montgomery County, when you finished the ninth grade as a black, you couldn't go to high school unless you could get $12.50 every three months to go to Alabama State, which was the State Normal School. There was no public high school for blacks in the whole county. So I finished junior high school in 1935, and then I went to Alabama State.

Before that year passed, I jumped up and I got married. We had a child. The marriage just wasn't working out because the man I married was many years my senior. I was sixteen and he was twenty-eight. I don't know why in the world we got together, but after my child was born, I wanted to go

Fannie Allen Neal with Hubert H. Humphrey, former Vice President of the United States and senator from Minnesota, at a Philadelphia AFL-CIO COPE dinner, February 28, 1976. *Courtesy Alonzetta Ford.*

back to school more than anything. We weren't really mad with one another. He just felt like if I went back to school, I wouldn't be his wife. I just smiled because I had "had it" with being married anyway. I knew nothing about taking care of a husband and all those kinds of things. I went back to school. I went to night school the first year, and then I found out that I could go to both night and day school. I finished behind my class, but not as far behind as I would had I not gone day and night. My daughter Alonzetta, my mama kept her.

In the meantime, we had a friend and she was white, but she was very, very kind to Mama and her children. Mama never allowed us to take advantage, and she said, "You're grown. You make your own way. You get a job." So I got a job, and I worked for Mrs. Hill as a maid. I did the washing and ironing and cleaning upstairs, and she had a butler that cleaned downstairs. That first year I'd get there around 7:00 A.M. and then I would leave around 2:30 to go to school. I walked from where we lived to her house, which was about five miles, and then I would walk from her house over to school, which was about two and a half miles, and many nights I didn't have bus fare and I would walk home. Of course, there were plenty of people who were walking.

When I finished high school Mrs. Hill got me a job immediately with her friends as a maid. I worked for 'em for two years, the McPherson family. They were very kind to me, but I just wanted something different. My mother had always preached to us that she wanted her kids to have a better opportunity and have a better way of life than she had. My father always said that he wanted his children to have a better life than he had. I wanted to do anything but domestic work.

The Shirt Factory

Between 1940 and 1950, four hundred thousand African-American women left domestic employment and their numbers in factory work doubled.[4] The movement led by A. Philip Randolph, which Maida Springer-Kemp talks about in Chapter 5, led President Roosevelt to sign Executive Order 8802 in 1941, prohibiting discrimination in the federal government and defense industries and establishing the Fair Employment Practices Committee. Fannie reports that the Reliance Manufacturing Company, based in New York with twenty-eight plants around the country, "had negotiated with Tuskegee Institute in the 1930s to get a plant in Montgomery specifically to hire black women."[5]

I went to this factory where I got employed. Reliance Manufacturing Company was commonly known in Montgomery as the "shirt factory." I went there in the afternoon after my work at Mrs. McPherson's. He started letting me come in the afternoon to learn to turn pockets. The first two weeks I worked for 15 cents an hour. Then the minimum wage went to 25 cents an hour. You had one week to learn the job. If you didn't learn within the week, the boss would send you home and hire somebody else. I caught on to my job pretty good. Learned to turn pockets and cuffs, and when they needed a printer to print labels, I got that job. The foreman of the cutting department started me learning to assemble the different parts of the shirt together.

All the ladies in the office were white and all the operators in the stitching room and in the shop was black, except the head woman who was in charge of the whole stitching room was white and the man in charge of the cutting department was white. Anybody in charge was white. Most of the males worked just in the cutting department and in the shipping department. Everybody would be pushing those machines, and they'd just have a song, almost, going . . . hummmmm . . . hummmmm . . . and it's just a continuous thing. There were some operators whose machines never stopped. They just could feed that material right on in and could hold it with one hand, pick up the garment with the other, and before it could get through the machine, they'd have another garment going. It's really fascinating to see them operate.

Well, the war came along and they had a guy named Joe who was the head "marker" who takes the patterns and assembles them on the paper. We would staple the paper to the material and we would cut just hundreds, depending on the weight of the materials. So Joe thought he was gonna be drafted—he was leaving. They tried a lot of white women in the job, but there was a lot of standing and the work wasn't that easy either. So they didn't work out, and then one day the foreman in the cutting room, Mr. Condon, said that he wanted to try me out to see if I could learn how to mark. Then he talked to Mr. Geising, the superintendent of the plant, and Mr. Geising said I couldn't learn it because I was "colored."

Well, I knew I had to learn it. People are funny. Mr. Condon had faith in me that I could, and he took time with me. In the evenings, I would work late for him to show me different things about the job. For about a week, I worked about two hours overtime every day 'cause I couldn't keep up, so he was helping me out and showing me different pointers, and I learned this job. I was this marker from about late 1942 until the plant closed in 1959.

Organizing in the South

In 1937 the clothing unions, the ACWA and the ILGWU, joined with the Textile Workers Organizing Committee for the first major CIO campaign in the southern textile industries. Shortly after this time, Carmen Lucia began her southern organizing effort for the hatters' union and the AFL (see Chapter 3). Although almost three-quarters of the nation's textile workers were employed in the South, only 15 to 20 percent were organized. Seventy-five percent of the organized textile workers were in the North. Interest in organizing African-American women also increased significantly with the rise of the CIO. A CIO organizer came to Montgomery and Fannie recalled, "We were the first shop with Reliance Manufacturing chain to get a contract anywhere in the country."[6]

***

Whatever happened to somebody else always affected me. People would come to work at seven o'clock in the morning, which meant that some of them had to leave home at six. They had to get up at 5:00 or 4:30 A.M. in order to get to work. They would get there at seven and they couldn't check in—couldn't hit the clock—until they could be given some work. The company wouldn't have work prepared for them, and people'd have to stand around, until sometimes it would be 9:00 or 9:30 A.M. Then the supervisor would come out and say, "I'm sorry. We just don't have anything for you to do." It wouldn't be just one person. There would be a lot of people. This would just burn me up so bad. When I get to thinking about it now, I just get furious!

There were just little things like, "If you don't like the way things are going, just hit the clock!" That attitude. We needed the jobs. That was the only job we had and the best job that you could get at that time with the type of education that we had. We were factory workers, that's all. I had mastered my job, and I didn't teach anybody else. But I wasn't happy with my pay. I was doing a job for 56 cents an hour that they had paid a white man a dollar, maybe a dollar and a quarter an hour, and I was aware of this. Then my supervisor, Mr. Babee, used to make little sly remarks about "You got a white man's job." Those things kind of burn you. So one day, he said this to me, and I said, "This ain't no white man's job. This is my job." All of us were frustrated. We were unhappy because the cost of living was going up, and times were hard. Our plight was a plight that all the people in the shop shared.

In the mid-forties, an organizer for the CIO came to Montgomery. The first meeting just five of us met at Frank Gregory's home. He was a cutter who ran the big machine that went into the material. He was the one the union person approached. We grew up in the community together, and nobody else could have come and talked to me and the other people and gotten us involved like Frank did. The organizer told us about all the things that the union could do for us. He really was an inspiring man, and he asked if we thought we could get a few union cards signed up and he left us some cards. I shall never forget those days. We got those cards signed up. Then the next meeting, we would bring even more people whom we could trust. The group continued to grow.

About the third week, the boss knew we were signing up union cards. In his anxiety to get those who showed leadership ability out of the union, he told me he would make me the supervisor of the stitching room. It was so comical. He knew that I didn't even know how to thread up a machine! I told him, "We aren't trying to organize against you, we're only trying to get a union because we feel that Reliance Manufacturing Company is mistreating us." You see, he had many things he could have straightened up, but as long as the top bosses tell a superintendent what to do, he's gonna do it. It might break his heart, but he'll do it anyway.

I'm from the old school. Thirty-three years ago we sang our way into the labor movement. We sang spirituals that we turned into union songs like, "We Shall Not Be Moved." Oh, we would sing the union songs. One that is still very dear to me is "We Gonna Roll the Union On." It says, "If the boss gets in the way, we gonna roll right over him, 'cause we're gonna roll the union on." That song still sticks in my mind, because "rolling the union on" is having full participation and cooperation from the members. You can't "roll" a dead union, and it'll die if you don't get participation. I think one of the reasons that we don't have stronger unions today is that we stopped singing and getting the spirit within our organizational campaigns and into the members. Not religiously "spiritual," but building up the union spirit. If people believe in it, then they can be more active.

We organized the plant in a short time, about three weeks' time. They sent a person from the National Labor Relations Board to conduct the election. It was on August the 14th, 1945. This was a great day because this was the same day that it was peace, "VJ Day." We were going home from work that afternoon and people were beating their tubs' cause the war was over and we had won the union that day too! We had won the right to bargain 'cause we had the election. We had 298 people who voted for the union and we only had 28 to vote against the union. We knew we had it sewed up.

Running the Local Union

The national union ran training programs for the new local union officers. Like hundreds of locals during this period, members of ACWA Local 490 had to learn to run for office, negotiate contracts, and then carry them out. Fannie was a shop steward and was elected recording secretary. Many of the union staff coming from New York, including the business agents that helped the locals, were white, and the membership of Local 490 was predominantly black. There were racial tensions with the national union, but that did not stop Fannie's active involvement while also raising her daughter.[7]

After we got the union, then we had trying times because we were real arrogant. For our first contract, we had the best organizers. They told us so many things that the union could do for us. I believed that the union could do everything that they told me it could do. But as you move into it, you find that there are certain things that just can't be done. The contract didn't say it. You must know your contract; what is written in your book. It's not how the company interprets it, or how you interpret it, but you have to go by how it is written. Sometimes it worked and sometimes it didn't.

Well, I got elected as the recording secretary. They sent people from the union educational department in New York, and we had shop steward training. I got elected as shop steward. As steward you have to listen to all the grievances, and when they take a worker to the office and management wants to give her a pink slip, you would have to go too. I always tried to be fair. Some of the workers didn't think I was fair, and a lot of times the company didn't think I was fair, but if a worker was really just guilty, I would plead for mercy and ask for her to be given another chance. But the chief shop steward got all the grievances from the departmental shop stewards and read them, and then we'd have to separate the gripes from the grievances. It's quite a problem to separate gripes from grievances. But there's two sides to everything, and we tried very hard to look at it from a broad spectrum. We got a lot of things straightened out.

The contract said that the union business agent or service person could never come into the shop and go into the office and talk to management unless they had somebody from the factory with them. We had some business agents who would come in and talk to management and go out and have dinner with them and then we would hear about it. So we'd run them off. They weren't concerned. They were white. They would stand off from us like we were nasty or something and want to talk from way off to us. We did get some good white business agents. One man was from a plant down in Mississippi, and he understood what we were talking about. These others were just hired people. We'd smoke 'em out real quick, and then we'd send them right on back to the Amalgamated.

Our national union vice president got mad at us and she wouldn't send us no business agents, and so we were mad at her. She always wanted to talk down to us and we were the kind that you didn't talk down to. She said we wrote "smart letters," but we were just stating the facts. She said that she wouldn't send us anybody from the national union office. By this time we were paying a service charge of $80 or $85 a month in excess of what we were paying as per capita dues. So we stopped sending the service charge, and this was a violation of the union. Then they decided that I was communist. They sent a black woman who was on their staff in New York down to see who was influencing me and any of the rest of them, what "communist group" we were tied up with.

This woman told us that perhaps we were right in taking the attitude that we took, but that we went about it in a bad way. She showed us how to write up things that we wanted the union to know. We should not stop paying, but we should document what bothered us and send them in and we would get action. But we never got any action as fast as when we would withhold our per capita tax. We were hard on business agents. We were tough! Really!

But the union took precedence over everything in my life. If fellows asked me out on a date, I'd say, "I'm sorry. I have to go to a union meeting." Nothing was more important than my union. Unfortunately, all the members weren't like that, but there were a few of us who were loyal to the end. We didn't put anything ahead of our union.

My sister started working at the plant, and she was in the union too. My daughter was so precious, and we called her "Sweet Pea." We used to take the kids to union meetings. My sister and I lived together and we were kind of a team. The youngest sister had two other kids and when they were born we hated so bad to take them out in the weather. Also Robert and Peggy, who were the older kids, had started to school and for them to come home to an empty house with a key wasn't what we liked, but it was all we could do. But then my oldest sister stopped work and stayed home and we paid her a small salary and gave her a home and everything. But she earned it, because she cooked, and she washed, and she ironed, and she's an excellent housekeeper. She enjoyed it and she loved the children very dearly. Even today all three of my sisters, we all live together.

The State AFL-CIO

In Alabama, the CIO state body had four seats designated for "vice presidents at-large." These were for African-Americans, who had representatives from the Mobile area, the Montgomery area, Birmingham, and North Alabama. In 1948 Fannie ran for one of the at-large seats, and won. At CIO meetings she met men like Barney Weeks, who later became president of the AFL-CIO Alabama Labor Council, and Earl Pippen, who became legislative director for the Committee on Political Education. In 1950 Fannie helped to organize the CIO Council in Montgomery. But segregation and racial violence continued to be problems.

The state did have a union organization, and we joined. I'm sure all of us are filled with prejudices, but that was an experience that I will never forget, because when we came into our state office down on 19th Street and we went upstairs, there was a rope coming down one side of the meeting room. All the white people were sitting over on the left and all the black people were sitting over on the right. The organizers had told us the union would make us free men and women and when I got up there and saw this, it really astounded me.

But this is the year I met many of the guys in the labor movement who were strong trade unionists. Some were from the steelworkers' union, and Emory Jackson had a newspaper. He was a fighter. He had a sister and I don't know what union she was representing, but she was there and she took the floor about that rope. Naturally this created a lot of dissension, but we argued it out. I say "we," but I didn't have a word to say 'cause I was frightened to death. Our white brothers and sisters wanted to get the benefits of the union, but they weren't willing for us to have part of it too. Some of them weren't. But anyway, I never came to another union convention where there was a rope in the building, but there seemed to have been a "gentlemen's agreement" that you whites sit over on this side and then we blacks sit over on this side.

In 1948, I ran for a seat on the state executive board and I won. It happened so fast. I never thought about it too much. I got out there and campaigned for myself. I said, "I'm a candidate to run for this seat at-large." I went around and I asked those white delegates. I said, "I'm Fannie, and I would like for you to cast your vote for me." And they said, "All right," and they did. I was about thirty years old. I got a lot of white votes. There was just a handful of us blacks there.

If somebody from a union came in to organize another shop within the area, as state vice president you were to assist them and help them make contact. If there was something going on in the community and if there was a shop that needed organizing, then you would write it up and send the information to the state organization. You looked out after the welfare of the unions in your district. Then you have your meetings on your local level and choose what side you go on. Eventually, I believe they started giving me three dollars a month to be recording secretary, for cab fare or bus fare, to get places and to do more things, but no pay, no.

In 1950 we organized the CIO Council in Montgomery. That was the Central Labor Council, and I ran in that to be the financial secretary. There was a white man from Prattville running, and there weren't but about seven or eight of us blacks who attended. Why, I beat him by thirty-something votes. I had friends. I made friends with my co-workers and the other labor people, and they supported me. We had board meetings and everything. We had a real good organization going. But nothing was more important to me than Local 490. I was still shop steward and still recording secretary.

But things were bad. I went to a labor council meeting one night over on Mt. Meigs Road. There were two guys there and when I walked by them, they were standing downstairs at the Coke machine, and I started up the steps and ohhhhh, look like a cold chill came on my back, and I was so scared. I went on up and I sat right next to Earl Pippen. He was a friend who was with the telephone company, who later became the executive vice president of the Alabama Labor Council. Oscar Junkis was there and he was with the union in Montgomery and he was black. I don't remember there being another black person. A woman who worked at the glass bottle blowers told Pip that those two guys, Brock and Welch, said that they were gonna "do me in" that night. I didn't know anything about it. After the meeting was over, I started out and Pip said, "Wait a minute, Fannie. I want to talk to you."

We started a conversation and I noticed that Barney was in front of me and then Pip and Harry was walking sort of behind me, but almost with me, and I came out between them. When we got downstairs, there was Jack Brock and Homer Welch, and they was talking about "nigger lovers!" Talking about, "We'll get her!" and all this, and it was at this time that I knew. I was afraid anyway, because I felt it when I was going up the steps. Barney drove his car maybe in front or behind, and Harry drove his car, and the car that I was in with Pip was in between the other two cars, and they carried me home. After that night, I didn't try to go to council meetings anymore for a long time because I was actually afraid for my own safety.

The Montgomery Bus Boycott

On December 1, 1955, Rosa Parks refused to give up her bus seat to a white man in Montgomery, Alabama. The Montgomery bus boycott began, led by Martin Luther King, Jr., and the Montgomery Improvement Association. On December 21, 1956, the city announced it would comply with the November Supreme Court ruling that declared segregation on buses illegal, a major victory for the civil rights movement. Local organizations were key in the emerging civil rights struggle and they worked with other groups, including the CIO.[8] Fannie spoke of the importance of their training in nonviolence, which was sometimes difficult for her.

She said, "I often felt that Dr. King sensed the fact that I have a tendency to strike back. Dr. King used to say to me, 'Now, Fannie, I want you to be sure to attend the classes on nonviolence.' "⁹ That same year, Sweet Pea graduated from high school.

I was a person who would get involved in whatever was going on. I was soooo tired of going to meetings so many evenings. We lived a long ways from work and we had no transportation. We'd be too tired to walk and so we'd ride the bus and the bus driver would want you to hand him the money at the front door and then you'd go around to the back door and get in. Oftentimes, he'd pull off and leave you! They were stealing from us. Then it was insulting that we would be on the bus and sitting down and all the seats were taken in the front and then you're white and you get on and I've got to get up and give you my seat and I paid my money. The way the drivers would treat us like animals. This was something that was *deep* in every black person in that city. They couldn't help but resent it. So when they did Mrs. Parks in that afternoon, at work that next day we heard about it, and we were mad.

They had this meeting down at the Dexter Avenue Church that night, and I went down there. This was the night that Martin Luther King was nominated as the temporary chairman, and somebody came up with name "Montgomery Improvement Association." I was late, so I wasn't inside the meeting, but they agreed that they would stay off the buses on Monday because Mrs. Parks's trial was going to be on Monday, and they were going to get somebody to run some notices off and we were going to put them in everybody's door throughout the community. So I helped get these leaflets out to the black community.

That morning nobody rode those buses. I won't say nobody, two or three got on, and they had the nerve to send the motorcycle cops out behind the bus. So we walked that day, and then that night we went on to the Holt Street Baptist Church. That was the night that Reverend King spoke to the group and he said all those magic things. He was a great speaker anyway, but then he was telling us how we had been treated and all those things. We decided that we were going to walk until Mrs. Parks was turned out, until the trial ended.

Then it just went on. Thursday night we had the meeting and things still hadn't been solved. The first thing we knew, we were nationwide. We opened up an office and everything. The first money that came into Montgomery for the bus protest was from the packinghouse workers' union, and the unions really rallied to the Montgomery bus protest. I worked at the factory every day, but when I would get off work every day I would go over to the bus boycott office, where a girlfriend was one of the secretaries, and I would hang around over there and do whatever I could do just as a volunteer.

In 1955 my daughter finished high school, and she wanted to go to Dillard University. My sister and me together was barely making enough to buy food and to pay the note and the utilities. But my child always believed that whatever she wanted, mother will do it. I couldn't see how I could let her down. There was a club called the Citizens' Club and you weren't supposed to be able to get in the club unless you had a membership card and your membership card would be that you had registered to vote. So I started working at the club. I worked Fridays, Saturdays, and Sundays at night and I made real good tips. If I didn't have to work at the plant on Saturdays, sometimes we'd stay up there until 6:00 in the morning 'cause of all the late owls.

It was a beautiful place at one time, with these pecan trees all out. I worked there for three and a half years and I never got tired. Well, occasionally, I'd just be so tired that I just couldn't make it. But I wouldn't touch my money. I had me a shoe box for my paper money, and I had me some jars that I put my change in. At the end of the month, my nephew and my niece, we would sit down on the floor and we would count the money and we'd roll it up and then I'd take it to the bank. Oftentimes, I had enough to pay my daughter's tuition, or her room and board. People would say that they admired me and would give me extra tips because so many people wouldn't make that sacrifice for their child. There are so many people that I will forever be grateful to because they were kind to me when I needed them so badly. My daughter finished Dillard University in 1959.

The Alabama Coordinating Committee for Registration

Sidney Hillman, president of the Amalgamated Clothing Workers and one of the co-founders of the CIO, was committed to the idea that the unions had to have a strong voice in the political process, as Esther Peterson discussed in Chapter 4. In 1943 the CIO Political Action Committee that he established developed an extensive economic, social, and political agenda, which included permanent status for the Fair Employment Practices Committee. Registering people to vote was an important part of this effort, especially overcoming the many barriers to the registration of African-Americans in the South. The unions worked with many other groups, like the YWCA, to involve black and white women.[10] Phil Weightman, an

African-American labor leader who worked for the CIO-PAC, helped establish the Alabama Coordinating Association for Registration and Voting. In 1959, when Fannie's plant closed down, he worked with her friends Earl Pippen and Barney Weeks, the ACWA, and other unions like the packinghouse workers and the steelworkers to raise $10,000 to hire Fannie as a special project worker on voter registration. He worked it out so "I could make seventy-five dollars a week, which was equivalent to what I was making in the shop."

In 1945, I registered to vote through the NAACP. I was in the NAACP and I worked with the YWCA and we did voter registration. We'd have clinics. I got eight or ten people in different areas and some afternoons I'd have two or three voter registration clinics in one afternoon with people filling out these forms, practicing how to register, how to fill them out. We used to have clinics on our lunch hours and at union meetings. People had been down to register and they still hadn't heard if they were registered and they were mad. So it was motivating. We could get people to register.

People who were working in the plant with me, we could motivate. We got a great majority of them to register. They just never had the confidence in themselves that they could fill out the form, and they didn't try. We would go to churches, to the schools, PTA meetings, anyplace where there was going to be a group of people, and we would always have a clinic because it only took a little while. My neighbors used to hate to see me coming. One lady told me, she said, "I just went on and got registered. I got tired of you worrying me." But now she never misses voting. I'm proud to say that everybody on my street is a registered voter.

When the plant closed, I became special project worker for the Alabama Coordinating Association for Registration and Voting, and my first trip was to Mobile. My friends from Mobile had always told me how easy it was and that they didn't have all the problems we had in Montgomery County. I got down there and to my amazement, people there had to have a voucher to register to vote. If you were to get registered, you had to carry someone with you to swear that they knew that you were who you said you were. It was so ridiculous and I was so disgusted.

We had ministers go from door to door in Montgomery to help get people to register to vote. We got their pictures made and got 'em to the black press and all this kind of stuff. When I got to Mobile, I tried it on the ministers down there. People said, "Aw, they won't do it." But I smiled at them and "conned" some of them and they came on out and we did it in the housing project and the ministers were just fascinated. They didn't realize. Going door to door, they found members of their churches that they hadn't seen in a looooong time. They said they didn't even know they were still alive. It was quite an experience.

I worked with the NAACP leadership there. I spoke at different churches about the importance of registering. We got people involved. Then we had transportation. People volunteered to take people and vouch for them. It's time-consuming to send ten people and ten vouchers down there. But this was just one of the ways they were trying to keep people from registering. We had a very good program that fall. We really got people registered during the fall of 1959 in Mobile, one of the best voter registration drives that we had before the civil rights bill was passed, the Voting Rights Act.

I left Mobile and went to Sheffield, Alabama, in Colbert County, and worked the whole county. The Laborers' Union had a black local, and we used their hall as our headquarters. All this was just blending together, so I knew people everywhere. It wasn't really just trade unions—it was black people. I was the coordinator, kinda' put it together, but I would work with the community leaders. You wrap it around that local group or leader. I've always said that it's irrelevant who I am or anything about me; it's the idea of the job that we're trying to get done. I worked in Alabama for six months. I had such successes with the little projects that I would put on that they decided that it "could be done" if you have somebody just working at it and can get the attention of people and get people involved. That's what I was able to do. It was such a good project that the AFL-CIO decided to underwrite the project for a year. It was not officially part of COPE until January of 1962.

Field Director for COPE

When the AFL and the CIO merged in 1955, the AFL Labor's League for Political Education (LLPE) and the CIO Political Action Committee merged to form the Committee on Political Education, AFL-CIO. There are state COPEs, congressional district COPEs, and each local is encouraged to have a Committee on Political Education.[11] Fannie's program was such a success that she asked the COPE director when she would become part of the official COPE staff with job benefits. She said, "It sort of caught him off guard and he said, 'Just give me 'till January' and come January, he did work it out and he put me on officially." In the 1960s the committee had a minority staff specifically focused on black voter registration. Phil Weightman became the minority field coordinator for COPE, working with Earl Davis and Fannie.

I was called a field director for COPE. I continued to do the same things that I had been doing all the time: bringing together groups, getting them interested in voter registration, getting them out to vote on issues and for a candidate endorsed by the labor movement. We worked all over the country with black people, getting them to register, because black people look to the labor movement for leadership. There are a few times that black people leave the labor movement's endorsements, but a long time ago black people realized that what's good for laboring people is also good for black people.

By this time, John Kennedy was getting ready to run for President. I was working in South Carolina, where I had one of the most intriguing experiences. At this time the only place you could live was to get a room in a black home someplace, because the hotels were not open to us. We had black hotels, but they were very undesirable and I couldn't live in them. So I was living with this lady whose name was Mrs. Wakefield, and she was a beautiful old lady in spirit and in courage. She must have been near eighty and she was carrying me around to her garden club meetings and to the civic club meetings.

I never shall forget Mrs. Nance, who was from a very prominent family there who was Republican. This was not unusual for a large number of blacks in South Carolina. They were still Abraham Lincoln Republicans. They still felt that the Republican Party should have them, regardless of what happened, because Abraham Lincoln freed the slaves. So Mrs. Nance was one of these kinds of people, and she was very nice to invite me to her garden club meeting at her home.

Naturally, me being a Democrat, I didn't know that she was Republican, and I started talking about the Democratic Party and what it had done for us, for the blacks, and how we were able to move forward, not only blacks, but working people. I reminded them that Roosevelt was the one who started us eating well again and having a little better housing. Then when I started talking about how we needed to register so we could elect John Kennedy, well!!! Mrs. Nance said, "Wait just a minute. I didn't know that's what you wanted to talk about." The other ladies said, "Let her finish, Mrs. Nance." She was a little reluctant, but she let me finish. Mrs. Nance got up and said that she could not be unkind to anyone who was a guest in her home, but she wanted me to know that she was Republican, and her father was, and her grandfather was.

Shortly thereafter, Reverend King was in Atlanta. For some little something, a parking ticket, they put him in jail. They had locked him up and sentenced him, and Bobby Kennedy phoned the attorney general and called and said to turn him loose now. It made the news right off. So Mrs. Nance called me later that night, and she said, "Darling, I am going to have to vote for your man," who was John Kennedy. That also changed a lot of other black people who thought they were Republicans. That was the very thing that changed them. We only carried South Carolina by between six and seven thousand votes for John Kennedy and more than ten thousand blacks voted for him just in Columbia itself. Ten thousand votes out of a black community was an awful lot of votes. That was one of the successes that I had in South Carolina.

In 1961 we went to New Jersey, and naturally Newark is the place where there is a large bloc of black and Puerto Rican people. In anything there is a little bit of fun and a little bit of anger. Black people are no different from white people when they get in power. This minister, Reverend Benton, was chairman of the district in the south ward, and we went in to do registration. We had cleared it with the registration commissioner. Well, when I got to the south ward, all the people were just standing up and looking crazy. I stopped the car and I went out and I said, "What's wrong?" "Reverend Benton won't let us work in this ward. He said he doesn't need any help."

Reverend Benton was a great big, fat guy, sort of like Santa Claus, and he was shaking. He came waddling to me, and he said, "Don't nobody come into my district unless . . . " So I just said, "Listen, preacher man, I'm not afraid of those white folks down in Alabama and you know good and well I'm not afraid of you preachers up here in New Jersey." I got the map and we just started and just walked all over him. We registered over six hundred people in "his" district that afternoon. The point was that they say that when a person gets in power, be he black or white, he doesn't want to change. They don't want to rock the boat if it's going to endanger their position in any way.

But if you could have seen the people and the joy that was on their faces when they came back from registering. They'd say, "Look what I got! Got my registration card!" They'd say, "We're first-class citizens!" You can consider yourself a citizen, but you really aren't a first-class citizen if you can't vote. They were so proud.

On the Road

Although always based in Montgomery, Fannie began to travel all around the country. The new civil rights laws enacted under Lyndon Johnson's presidency dramatically affected her day-to-day life. Important to her, however, was not only the Voting Rights Act of 1965, which directly involved her voter registration activities, but the provisions in the 1964 Civil Rights Act prohibiting discrimination in public accommodations. This law, because it successfully prohibited discrimination in restaurants, lunchrooms, gasoline stations, hotels, and motels as well as in sports and entertainment activities, dramatically affected where she could sleep and eat.[12]

When Kennedy was killed, Johnson got to be President. Johnson hit real fast and passed a whole lot of legislation. I have an argument with many blacks that Kennedy was the greatest thing that ever happened to us. If you look at the record, Kennedy talked good to us, said what we wanted to hear, but we were not making progress under Kennedy. He couldn't get any legislation passed. When Johnson got to be President, he made it real. There were laws on the books, but they were never made real until the Johnson days.

The biggest problem for me was rest rooms. Here I carried credit cards with any number of oil companies where I'm supposed to buy gas with a credit card, and I could buy the gas, but I couldn't use the ladies' room at the gas station. Any number of times I would drive up to restaurants where they have car-hop service. I knew not to get out and try to go in, but I would go up in the car and the person would come to get my order, only to come back and drop their head and say, "I'm sorry, but we can't serve you. I can't bring it to the car, but you can get out and go around there to that window." Well, I've always had so much pride that if I couldn't get it out of the front door, I didn't have to pay you and get it out of the back door. Oh, I'd just go on and almost ruin my kidneys drinking Coca-Cola and trying to squash my hunger. I oftentimes neglected myself physically because of eating problems and not eating properly because I didn't have a place to go.

The Civil Rights Act and the Voting Rights Act and all of these things that were brought about during the Johnson days, out of all of these, I think that the law that was most important to me was that of the Public Accommodations Act. To know that you could stop somewhere and sleep when you were tired. There were some nights we were afraid to sleep, but I did feel secure in having a place to sleep. Then to be able to go into a dining room and eat and to have a clean rest room to go into and relax my body. In my world, Johnson was the greatest president that black people will ever have in this country, because he made it real. But what a long way we have to go.

Cracks in the Coalition

The coalition of labor and civil rights groups helped win passage of the major civil rights legislation in the 1960s and also opposed legislation detrimental to unions. After the successes of the early 1960s, however, the coalition began to show strains. There were disagreements over which candidates to endorse and over issues such as seniority. Pushing the labor movement to do more for minorities while staying in the house of labor was a problem for leaders like A. Philip Randolph on the national level and for people like Fannie on the local and regional level.[13] Fannie was unequivocal in her support of labor, however: "As I look back, it was the labor movement that started the process of setting me free. There have been times in recent years when the civil rights movement and the union would disagree over politics, especially over what candidates we would support in statewide elections. I stood with the union in every instance."[14]

In January 1964, Earl Davis and I went straight from Atlanta to Oklahoma. We did research and broke down the state by where black people were in large numbers. So Earl took Oklahoma City and I took Tulsa. Through the NAACP, we had a meeting in Oklahoma City of black leadership from across the state, and then they had a meeting in Tulsa to talk about our registration drive. The NAACP and the unions ran a coordinated drive. They shared the expense and were in it together.

We opened a headquarters and got an old lady named Mrs. Clardy as sort of the receptionist to welcome people in. Then we recruited through the youth group of the NAACP, people to go out and knock on doors and talk about the importance of registering. I was not two-faced about it. I explained to them that the unions had an issue, the so-called right-to-work law, that was going to be on the ballot. It was going to be on as Issue 409 and we wanted to register our people so that we could vote against it.[15]

We registered over five thousand people in a short period of time and not just in North Tulsa. The newspapers started writing little nasty things. We had a black paper that really played it up good, but the white papers, the Tulsa paper, would either try to make fun or try to get white people to come in and register, to kill off what we were doing. But it motivated black people who lived in the black community to get registered. It was really an enriching experience for me. And we did defeat the right-to-work bill, Issue 409. Now we've got black representatives from Tulsa and from Oklahoma City, and blacks have been included in city government. It proves the vote does make a difference.

Hubert Humphrey was absolutely the greatest person that I have ever had a chance to know. My admiration for him went back to 1958, when he made the civil rights speech at the Democratic National Convention. In 1967, I was in Philadelphia working in a campaign for the governor's race. Humphrey came to Philadelphia to speak for the candidate and afterward the president of the central labor body had a room down at the Ben Franklin Hotel where the Vice President stayed. We went down there, eight or ten of us, and the Vice President started talking to me and he said, "Fannie, have you been in Pennsylvania?" I said, "I've been across the country, almost. I've been in Texas and Louisiana and I've been to any number of states." He said, "What do you find?" "Mr. Vice President, I'm sorry, but I don't know how to tell you this, but my people just aren't with you. I don't know what's wrong with them. They're saying that it ain't no use in all of this." So he looked at me, and he said, "I believe you, I believe you. But it's so hard for me to understand."[16]

We immediately started trying to build registration groups, hoping to motivate people so they would go forward and register in large numbers to try to keep the Democrats in the White House. But we had black people at that time who were saying that black people ought to "go fishing" because we were not getting our fair share. We had some black groups that were talking down voter registration. We're no different from anybody else. People will take the negative side before they will take the positive side.

In 1968 Richard Nixon got to be President and we figured it out; if just one more person had voted in every precinct in the United States for Vice President Humphrey, we would have had it. That's the sad story of losing one of the greatest heroes, I think, that this country has ever known. A person who was really for people having an opportunity and particularly the underprivileged, and my people, black folks.

I never realized how much I really believed in seniority until a few years ago, when the NAACP was attacking unions for the seniority clause, and I started looking back. Me getting old and everything, I had gotten a little seniority. What's wrong with some young bunch coming along and saying, "I don't believe in seniority" and acting like they may be able to move a little faster than we can and the company could move me out and give my job to somebody else because they were young and a little bit faster? It made me think. When black people started to say the seniority clause was wrong, I started to tell them that we were just getting to the place where black people within the unions were getting seniority, because those who were white were retiring. We're building up seniority and now we have it over some of the younger whites. It is a very dangerous thing not to support seniority. To me, seniority is one of the most sacred things that we have in our union contracts.

The 1970s

Fannie continued to travel the country, registering black voters for key candidates and issues central to both the labor movement and the black community and trying to reconcile differences when they arose. In 1977, the AFL-CIO Executive Council reorganized the Committee on Political Education. The minority program and the women's division of COPE became the Volunteers in Politics Program (VIP). Fannie became southern director for VIP, responsible for ten southern states. She described this as "a very challenging job, but I've enjoyed every minute of it." In 1976 she reflected on her years in the labor movement.

Organized labor has been very good to me. The labor movement has given me the opportunity that I would have never had otherwise. It has been an education that nobody could buy. I've had the opportunity to travel from coast to coast and work with people. There was a time when I was told that because I was new on the job and didn't have as much experience that I should not expect to be paid what the others were paid. But I didn't accept that. I was fighting to have the same rights that they had. It was a compromise that I refused to accept. I spoke up for myself. Now that's how I look at the labor movement as an individual and as a woman. I wish I could tell you that I felt that all the opportunities that were due women had been offered, or that doors had been opened for them so that they could come in, but I can't. I just cannot lie about it. Look at our COPE department of some seventeen or eighteen people. There are only three women. They have not gotten a fair share.

On the other hand, the union has insisted in bargaining for contracts that women be paid the same thing that men are paid for the same work. Unfortunately, more of our women don't know that they need to get involved in the union. I talk about the union and what the unions have not done, and then I look at management, at colleges, at the telephone company, at the power companies. I'll bet you wouldn't find five presidents of any kind of corporation in the country who are women. I think the union has done more because the union did fight for equal pay for equal work and also for seniority. The union gives us a whole lot of security, and this is what some of the companies want to take away from unions.

The AFL-CIO has done more for blacks than any other organization in the country, in the world. I'm sure I'm telling the truth because they have always fought for social legislation from which the black community was able to reap the benefits. They were willing to put funds in if they could get results and get blacks registered to vote. Unions realize that if they help get black people to register, they will be helping themselves, too, but they've always had compassion for the underdog and we were the underdogs.

A Very Special Lady

In 1987 Fannie retired from the AFL-CIO National Committee on Political Education. In retirement, as in her work life, she continued to live with her sisters in Montgomery and to be very involved in the community. She was a Life Member and Golden Heritage Member of the NAACP. She was active in her church, a member of the YWCA, the Capital City Boys Club, the Capital City Civitan Club, and the Montgomery Area Council on Aging. She continued as a volunteer for the Montgomery Central Labor Council and the Advisory Board of the A. Philip Randolph Institute and she taught in the Southern Summer School for Union Women. Fannie Allen Neal died on August 7, 1990. Her daughter, "Sweet Pea," who lives with her husband in California, paid tribute to her mother: "I appreciate you for serving as a role model for me. Before you were my mother, you were a woman who had set your own personal goals. You became a working woman who made contributions to many communities throughout the United States. . . . I will always remember your constant concern, wisdom, knowledge, thoughtfulness, tears, love, and your ability to share yourself and your time. . . . You are, and always will be, a very special lady in my heart."[17]

Rocking the Boat: Union Women's Voices 1915-75
ed by Brigid O'Farrell & Joyce Kornbluh
Rutgers U Press, 1996

Chapter 10

Just Sign a Contract and You Can Call Me Anything

Jessie De La Cruz, United Farm Workers of America (1919–)

Jessie Lopez De La Cruz is a farm worker who has spent most of her seventy-six years in the California fields: picking cotton, apricots, and peas; hoeing beets; planting, pruning, and picking grapes. In 1962, when she was forty-three, Cesar Chavez knocked on her door and asked her to join the group that developed into the United Farm Workers of America (UFW). With their six children mostly grown, she and her husband became union activists. In 1967 Jessie was the first woman farm worker to organize for the UFW in the Fresno area. Despite health problems, she ran a union hiring hall, was a shop steward, picketed farms, participated in UFW boycott activities, and always worked the fields. She testified in many public hearings and acted as a bridge between her community, the growers, and the government. She was appointed to the Fresno County Economic Opportunity Commission, the Central California Action Associates, and the California State Commission on the Status of Women. In 1972 she was a delegate to the Democratic National Convention. In the 1970s she, her husband, and five other families started an organic farm cooperative, where they worked until about 1984.

Jessie De La Cruz now lives in Fresno, a widow, near several of her six children and many of her twenty-two grandchildren and thirteen great-grandchildren. She continues to work as a volunteer for the UFW. In 1994, when union members marched from Delano to Sacramento on the first anniversary of Cesar Chavez's death to show the union's continued strength, she organized support for the marchers in Fresno, where she also joined the procession. In the fall of 1994 she worked hard to defeat Proposition 187, the referendum on the California ballot to eliminate public services to illegal immigrants and their children. The referendum passed and the court cases began. The battle for farm workers and their families is an ongoing one, and Jessie De La Cruz remains an active participant.[1]

Hardship

After the Mexican Revolution of 1910, thousands of Mexican peasants migrated north across the border into the United States. Fleeing revolution and extreme poverty, they provided the growers on large farms a new source of cheap labor. Among them were Jessie Lopez's grandparents. Her mother, Guadalupe Lopez, was born in California and married Bermin Fuentes. Jessie was the oldest of three girls. Her father left when she was only nine, and then "my little sister was burned to death in a fire, an accident. It was 1929, and then in 1930, my mother died: I think she had cancer."[2] The surviving sisters lived in Anaheim with their grandparents, but further tragedy, combined with the Depression, sent the family north into the fields as migrant workers following the crops.

As far back as I can remember as a child, I've done farm work. I went with my grandparents. Down in Orange County, Anaheim, that's where I was born in 1919. My grandfather used to work for a water company where he built cement pipes, and then he became injured. He crushed his finger with one of the pipes and he had to stay off of work, and when he went back, he had been replaced. He was out of a job, and that's when we started migrating. As soon as school was out or as soon as the crops would start, we left. We came up north, as far as around Sacramento, Brentwood, around there. Then we'd start going back, picking prunes and cotton. So in December or January, we ended back in Anaheim.

We were moving from town to town because there was no work. My grandfather was always looking for work and he couldn't find it, so we'd move. One of his friends told him, "Well, you might be able to pick some oranges out there," and we'd go out there. He might work three or four days, and then that was it. He'd start looking for some more work, so we went from town to town. But we were living in a house in the city.

My grandmother had seven children of her own and three grandchildren, who were three girls, my two sisters and myself. We traveled in an old car that we had. I would sleep in the trunk, or my grandmother would bring out blankets and spread them over the ground, and we would sleep there. Whenever they ask me, "Do your children ever go camping?" I say, "Are you kidding? We camped out everyday." It wasn't recreation or fun. It's been a hardship because we had to do everything out in the open.

We lost our home, and my grandfather died in 1930. Then we lived in Watts, in Fullerton, in Claremont, everywhere. A month here, two months there. In 1933 we came out here to the San Joaquin Valley. We had an old truck that was my grandfather's, and we piled all of our stuff on that truck. My two older uncles, I called them brothers, couldn't find work. I was ten, so they were between thirteen and eighteen then, and they were in charge of the whole family. They said, "Well, the only thing we can do is go up north where the younger kids can help us pick cotton."

We came north in this old truck—my grandmother, the younger kids, the whole family. I was in that cotton strike at Bakersfield in 1933. As young as I was, I was out there. We were coming from Los Angeles. We came through Bakersfield and we stopped at this ranch, hoping to pick some cotton. They'd been on strike, so we couldn't work. While we were in this old truck, we met all these people who were on this caravan. They was just blowing the horns, and yelling and all, so we joined them. We started yelling with them. I didn't know what it was all about, but I knew it was something to do with helping the people. So I started yelling and then we found out there was a strike; so since we didn't have any money and no food, we decided to come to Mendota.[3]

We spent a few days picking cotton until the rainy season set in and there was no more work. That left us stranded in Mendota in December. We stayed. We've gone back south to visit, but not to live. Some people told us, "Why live in a tent here when it's raining and freezing? You should go to Firebaugh. At least you'll find cabins there." We went to Firebaugh, and we found a cabin in this labor camp. We stayed there all winter, crying from hunger and half freezing because there was no work. We had to survive on mustard greens and mushrooms and fish from out of the canals. I say it's a miracle we survived and didn't poison ourselves eating all those things. My grandmother was old at that time and couldn't work. We did go to work, but she couldn't do anything. She felt helpless, and the only thing she could do was cry with us. It was a terrible life.

School

In the early part of the twentieth century employers regularly claimed that labor legislation to protect children would be a disaster for the country. It wasn't until the Fair Labor Standards Act was passed in 1938 that children working in industry were protected at the federal level, but child labor in agriculture was specifically excluded.[4] Children of Mexican-American families, legal and illegal, were far more often found in the fields than in school. The families needed the income to survive, and the children felt unwelcome in the schools. When Jessie was only thirteen her uncles taught her to carry twelve-foot sacks of cotton weighing as

Jessie De La Cruz has the microphone at a United Farm Workers rally in Parlier, California, 1970. *Courtesy Jessie De La Cruz.*

much as 112 pounds.[5] Jessie's own experiences led her to fight both for the end of child labor in the fields and for bilingual education in the schools.

When I'd start attending school, we'd move, and then I'd have to start a new school again. I was always the new kid in school. It wouldn't have been so bad if I had known how to speak English when I started school. What happened to me was quite an experience, and this is why I fought so hard for bilingual education in the schools. Not for the people that stay here all the time, but the people who come from Mexico each year. The parents don't speak English, and the children come out here and they can't speak English, and they are put into a public school. They sit there in the classroom and they don't know what anyone's talking about.

I remember the experience that I went through when I was a child when I started going to school in Anaheim. One day there was this nurse, this lady, that came in and she was dressed all in white and she sat on a chair. The teacher lined us up and all the kids came to that lady and she would tell them to open their mouths, because they opened their mouths and stuck out their tongues. I think they were checking for tonsils or something.

But when it came to my turn, I guess she told me to open my mouth because she went "Aah," and I did too. So she put her stick on my tongue, and at that time I vomited. I couldn't help it and I got her dress messed up and I started crying. I felt so bad about it. Then my teacher comes out and she starts shaking me, telling me something, and the harder I cried the more she yelled at me. Then she shook me and she was really red in the face, because I wasn't minding. I wasn't doing what she was telling me to. Not until years later, when I learned English, did I know that she was trying to tell me to say, "I'm sorry." But I didn't know. So she just kept shaking me.

I got to where I was scared of teachers at school. My grandmother who raised me didn't have money in the thirties. She had to rip open a pillow of red material which she had, a cushion, because I needed underwear. She made me a pair of pants. I was playing with some of the kids, and one of them happened to see my red pants. She started teasing me and trying to pull my dress up. Then the other girls did, too, and I didn't know how to tell them to stop it. They kept trying to pull my dress up and they pushed me and I fell. When I fell, one of the girls, I didn't know what she was saying because I didn't understand English, she started crying and the teacher came. She said, "What happened?" I couldn't tell her; I didn't know how, but this girl explains and the teacher turns around and slaps me. I skinned my knee and I was crying.

I was really scared of teachers. I really dreaded going to school, even one I had been in before. I felt something right here in the pit of my stomach every time I started a new school, because I knew what I was going to have to go through. But my oldest brother said, "You have to go to school." He wouldn't let me miss unless we were moving. Even on foggy days, if we missed the bus, we had to walk. I mean, he made us go whenever it was possible.

I hear a lot of people say, "Well, if you can't learn the language, go back to Mexico." People tell me this when I'm talking about bilingual education. Many of the green carders who have been here for ten or fifteen or almost twenty years, people say, "Why don't they go to school?" Have these people tried working ten and twelve hours out in the fields and then attend night school and then get up at four o'clock the next morning? They never have. The workers have a family to support and then if you miss work, you're out of work. That means food off of your table. They don't understand.

Work and Family

Jessie met Arnold De La Cruz when she was fourteen years old. He lived next door in the Firebaugh migrant labor camp, and she often helped his mother take

Jesse De La Cruz (*seated, center*) is part of the team negotiating contracts with Christian Brothers, 1971. Dolores Huerta, vice president of the UFW, is standing behind her. *Courtesy Jessie De La Cruz.*

care of her large family. They were married in 1938. They had both been raised in very traditional families where it was expected that the women would take care of all the housework and the children and, as Jessie said, "the woman just walked behind the husband and kept quiet, no matter what the husband does."[6] She and Arnold had six children of their own between 1939 and 1947, one of whom died. Later, they adopted a niece when Jessie's sister died.

After that terrible winter in 1933, since we didn't have any money and no food, we decided to come back to Mendota and we stayed. In 1938 I got married, and my first son was born in 1939. My youngest, my only girl, was born in 1947. Four boys and one girl. I've been a resident in Fresno County since 1933. As a child I had to go on from place to place. As a married woman I had to do the same. If we were lucky enough to have a tent, we'd use that tent. If not, we lived under a tree. Had to do our cooking. When we used to come to pick grapes, we'd get one of those big-sized boxes and just fill it with dirt, and then on top of this dirt we'd just put some rocks or bricks or a griddle or something or a wire to hold our pot and pans there for cooking. We were forced to do this, for there was nothing else.

Even up to 1949–1950, we had to live out in the open under a tree. The only thing between us and the cow and the horse that this farmer had was a wire fence. We had no tent; we had nothing. We were given some boxes just to sort of separate, to close ourselves in. So many flies, so many sick children. If there were laws, they weren't enforced. Just like every other law that goes into effect to help the farm worker, it's never enforced.

Doing the crops, my husband and I would go up north, like Sacramento, especially after our kids reached ages where they could help us pick prunes or apricots or whatever. It was cooler up there, and picking grapes is hard. Oh, it just hurt my heart to see my children, my babies, out there where it was so hot. We wanted to work under a tree picking fruit, not picking grapes under the hot sun. That's why we went north when the children were young. Now I have a younger girl, who was my sister's daughter; my sister died when Susan was four months old. I raised her and so I have another daughter. She's nineteen right now and she's working. So I raised four boys and two girls.

Women's Work in the Fields

Entire families, men, women, and children, worked in the fields. Pruning operations in the grape fields were limited to men, a practice the union eventually ended, but for most jobs, "women picked, pruned, and packed in the fields, canneries, and sheds, side-by-side with the men."[7] In work, Jessie says, "I've been equal to men since I was a child, working alongside men, doing the same hard work and earning the same wages."[8]

About half of the farm workers are women. If my husband had worked alone in the fields, he would not have earned enough to support us. That means I had to go out with him and help. I did the same type of work at the same speed and everything. Women would be tomato pickers, prune pickers, vine pruners, everything. I've done all types of heavy work out in the fields. You have to lift seventy to seventy-five pounds about five hundred times a day. I'm telling you, that's killing. It's hard work. You have to keep going fast, because if you go slow, you're not going to make any money; you're not going to make a living. I used to work at the hardest that there is, which is thinning beets with a short hoe. My back feels bad from doing that bent over double. The farmers said you can do a better job if you have a short handle, but we have proved it is not true, because some have gone along with a long handle and a good job is being done.

In 1970, I was working in Calexico, close to the Mexican border, picking tomatoes. We had to carry forty-pound lugs almost as far as two city blocks. They were empty, but they were heavy. We had to take as many as we could up to where we would be picking and then fill them and carry them to the end of the row, then stack them there for the checker to come out and check so many boxes for this name with this number. I had to carry some, and I slipped and fell. That made me angry and I took the boxes to where I was working, and I could only carry three boxes, and I filled those and I carried them to the end of the row. I asked the labor contractor why couldn't they bring those boxes in to where we were working. He said, "Well, we'll ruin a lot of these tomatoes. That's what you have to do. Everybody's doing it."

So my nephew went and got the next load of boxes. Then I wanted to go to the rest room and I asked him, "Where's the rest room?" He said, "You see that little spot way up there?" You couldn't even tell it was a rest room; you couldn't even see a white spot way out on the field. I said to him, "Why do you keep it out there?" He says, "Well, that's where it's been." I said, "Why don't you take a picture of it and give each of us a picture for all the good it's doing?" So he says, "Well, you can just leave right now if you don't like it." I said, "Fine, I'll leave."

The owner comes in, and he started arguing with the labor contractor about the tomato vines being turned over. So the labor contractor turns around and says that there's a whole bunch of cattle working here. When I come back, this lady tells me, "Oh, I wish you had been here a minute ago. This labor contractor came out here and said we were a bunch of cattle." Oh, I got so angry that I told him off and then I quit. I'm not going to work for him. But then I asked the lady, "Why don't you quit?" She said, "Lady, I live across the border and I had to pay somebody to bring me here to work. If I earn a dollar, that is bread for my children." So they couldn't complain.

I was offered a job with a tomato-picking machine and I said, "No, thank you." I refused. I would have to work from four o'clock in the afternoon until eight o'clock the next morning. Those tomato machines work day and night. They have a light and you work there all night. Then whenever anyone who works there wants to go to the rest room, they can't go until the machine stops and then they say, "All right, everybody go." The workers don't get any breaks; they don't get nothing. They have to work hard, sorting those tomatoes on this conveyor belt, jumping up and down all day, all night. I would rather pick where I could put the tomatoes in a bucket and take them out to a box and dump it and come back for some more.

Women and the UFW

Farm workers were excluded from coverage under the National Labor Relations Act, which facilitated the organizing of industrial workers in the 1930s. It wasn't until 1962 that Cesar Chavez formed the National Farm Workers' Association at Delano, California, a grass-roots organization made up largely of Mexican-American farm workers. It merged with the largely Filipino Agricultural Workers' Organizing Committee and in 1970 became the United Farm Workers, AFL-CIO.[9] Women had to overcome traditional cultural attitudes about the proper roles for women and men in the union, but Dolores Huerta, co-founder of the union and first woman vice president, said that the union "made a conscious effort to involve women, give them every chance for leadership, . . . [although] the men did not always want it."[10] Jessie became an organizer and a shop steward.

When I first heard about a farm workers' union, there were three men that came from house to house in Parlier. My husband had first been attending meetings in Fresno, where the union had an office. That's when I first heard about it, because he was attending the meetings, but I didn't know about it because he never talked about it. These men talked to us about the farm workers' union, that we had to unite, to work together to solve the problems we were facing each year. They talked about what we needed, about enforcing the law, that sort of thing. Well, we liked it, and later I heard that one of those men who came out was Cesar Chavez. At the time I didn't know him. I hadn't even heard his name.

So after that, I started reading everything I could find about the union. We were mailed pamphlets and leaflets. I kept up with everything that was happening. Then I started talking to other people about the union which we had discovered, and telling them about how by joining the union we could change all these things we had been suffering from. That's what it's been, suffering. I got a lot of people interested. When I first became a union member it was 1965. After that, on December 31 of 1967, I was made an organizer. This is one of the things I am very proud of. I was the first field woman organizer in the union in the Fresno area. Of course there were men organizers, but for a woman who works in the fields, I was the first one![11]

I would have meetings at my house, and sometimes I would meet a friend and say, Why don't you have a meeting at your house? Then I'll come and talk to them. My husband and I used to talk to them, and I'd bring my union book along with me. They wanted to know everything—what benefits, everything that we were going to do. The workers became interested and after learning about what we were doing, they became members. I signed them up; they paid their dues. We were right there and they became members. I got a lot of members that way. I organized a lot of people that were really hard to organize: the people that came in from Mexico every year and then go back.

Over in the Biola area there was a three-month-old baby run over by a tractor out in the field while the mother was picking grapes. With us that doesn't happen, because we see to it. We have stewards. I'm one of the stewards where we work. There was this lady who for the first time came to work with us. We were pruning vines, and she had two children in a station wagon. We told her she couldn't bring them out to the field. She either had to hire a baby-sitter or she would have to stay home and take care of them. She found a baby-sitter and the babies got left at home. She couldn't bring them out to the field. But the labor contractor and the grower, they don't see to it that these things are enforced.

The Braceros

In 1942 there was a shortage of farm labor to meet the increased need for produce resulting from World War II. Through a series of agreements with the Mexican government, known collectively as the "bracero program," large numbers of day laborers or "braceros" were brought into California and the Southwest at harvest time, paid extremely low wages, and trucked out again when the harvest was over. The bracero program was so popular with employers that it was kept after the war was over. In 1964, with enactment of the civil rights laws, Public Law 78, the last of the bracero programs, was allowed to lapse, providing some hope for the farm workers to improve their situation. By 1965, however, when the grape strike began, the growers began to use Public Law 414 (the Immigration and Nationality Act of 1952) to bring in large numbers of foreigners to work in the fields as "permanent resident aliens" with special green visa cards. They became known as "greencarders."[12]

The braceros, the Mexican people who work with their arms, are people who came from Mexico under government visa to work out here and then were taken back. We were very much opposed to the bracero program, because the growers were trying to do away with our union. It only caused a lot more fighting among Mexican people, fighting each other. This is what the growers have always done. They try to pay lower wages by getting cheaper labor from Mexico. We've been sending letters, and at our meetings this is one of the things we discuss. We were trying to get the Mexican representative who is here in Fresno to have a meeting with us, but he said he could not get involved with politics. We were going to ask him to draft a letter and send it to the President of Mexico on behalf of farm workers here. But he said he could not come to one of our meetings because he could not become involved here.

From what I saw when the braceros were coming out here, it was just terrible. They were mistreated, fed very poorly. They were given food they weren't accustomed to, and most of them were sick. We lived in a labor camp where they had these braceros. The cooks would fix breakfast for them and pack them up a sack lunch consisting of macaroni between two loaves of bread. That was their sandwich, and so they were sick. At noon they would sit outside the houses we were living in and throw the food up on the roof and say, "Who can eat this garbage?" Every day was the same. They were always complaining about the food and the way they were forced to work for lower wages.

When my husband used to go up to Stockton to pick tomatoes, he was getting 25 cents a box for picking tomatoes, those forty-pound boxes, and when the braceros came they were paid 12 cents, half of what we were getting. When the bracero programs ended, the growers had to find another way of keeping the wages down, so they recruited whole families from Mexico. There's always hundreds of them coming each year. This year there were seven hundred; next year it will be nine, ten hundred. This keeps the wages down, especially with the illegals coming from across the border. These people are really hard to organize because they keep saying, "What do I care what happens out here? As soon as the harvest is over, I'm going back to Mexico."

So I kept going into their homes and explaining to them that they were not only harming us but themselves because they were coming out here to work at lower wages and no benefits. I explained everything about the union to them. They became union members, and they're the best supporters we have. I mean, once they've joined the union, nobody's going to tell them what is good or bad for them, because they know that it's good for them.

Strikebreakers

The braceros were brought into the country legally to work on the farms, but thousands of workers also entered the country illegally. In the fall of 1968, according to the *Fresno Bee,* an "estimated twenty to thirty thousand 'wetbacks' (that is, illegal immigrants) were working in the Valley; though their presence is illegal, there is no penalty for hiring them and since they are both economical and defenseless, the growers replace their domestic force with 'alambristas' (fence jumpers) at every opportunity."[13] Employers used braceros and wetbacks as "scab" labor during farmworker strikes and other labor disputes.

The illegals are a threat to the union. They are used as strikebreakers. As a matter of fact, I have had to call the border patrol quite a few times on them. In the summer of 1972 we were on strike in Dinuba, and a grower was saying that there were no illegals working there, but we knew they were. We talked to some of them, and they told us they hadn't been told there was a strike. They just were told there were jobs out here. Transportation was provided. So they came and they started working. We told them to get out, and they said they couldn't because as soon as they left, they would be picked up. I said, "Well, you're going to be picked up anyway." We told them to go where there wasn't a strike, where we weren't picketing, and we wouldn't bother them.

I called the border patrol. They said they were so busy they couldn't do anything, because there were only seven men to work the Livingston, Fresno, and Merced areas. So I went through their office. All seven of them were there in that room; it was air-conditioned and they were playing cards with their feet up on the desk, all seven of them! I told them, "You will either have to go kick these illegals out or I'm going to do something." One said, "We have orders from Washington that we can't cross a picket line to get the illegals out."

I went home and called Bernie Sisk in Washington, a congressman from Fresno, and talked to his aide. He said it wasn't true. He said they are supposed to go out there whenever there's a report there are illegals out there, and they're supposed to go out and pick them up. So I gathered up some students and farm workers, and we took our flags and picketed the border patrol office. Right away, the man comes out and he says, "Mrs. De La Cruz, you surprise me this morning." I said, "Well, yesterday you surprised me when you told me you had orders from Washington not to go out to the fields."

Right away the border patrol got in their cars and a bus and they drove off to the field in Dinuba, but when we got there the patrol men were walking off the field. They said they couldn't find anybody. I asked our pickets out there what had happened. They said, "We saw these men running. They knew the border patrol was coming. They're hiding." That meant that the border patrol must have told the growers about the raid. That's what they usually do. We've known this for many years. We went back to the border patrol and told them we knew the grower was tipped off. I said, "I want you out there at certain street corners at six o'clock tomorrow morning, and you stop all the cars and buses going through there. I'm going to be there tomorrow morning to see that you do it."

I went the next morning. By the time I got there, all the jails in the towns of Reedley and Dinuba were full of illegals waiting for buses to take them to the border. This grower who the day before had over a hundred workers had this day about seventeen. And they claimed they were not illegal. I told some of them, "You see what happens? These growers are using you to fight us. Why do you allow yourselves?" They said they needed the money and weren't told there was a strike. "But you signed a paper," I said to one. "Lady," he said, "I don't even know how to read."

Now that the growers know we won't take it, that we'll fight back any way we can, they're trying to enact a law that will bring these Mexican workers back legally for the same purpose of breaking our strikes. The laws weren't enforced, like all the laws passed to help farm workers, like any law about sanitation out in the fields. The law existed, but it was never enforced until we made them enforce it. We had hearings and we pushed them, and we told them we wanted bathrooms and individual drinking cups and fresh water and a place to wash our hands. That's when we got it. Same with child labor. Yesterday, as we were going to work, there was this lady and she had two children with her, trimming vines. I think one of them was about ten years old and the other about twelve. What were they doing out in the field when they should have been in school? Because the law isn't enforced. The grower is not going to enforce it. The labor contractor isn't either.

The growers say we are communists and we're going to put them out of business, but it's not true. I keep telling them, "You small farmers should get together and fight the big corporations who are buying you out." When I was out on the picket lines I was called a communist and so many ugly names, and I said, "That's okay; just call me anything you want. Just sign a contract and you can call me anything you want." So that didn't hurt me.

Labor Contractors

Cesar Chavez felt that "the labor contractor who sells his own people in job lots to the growers is the worst evil in an evil system."[14] Growers would hire the "contratistas" to find the strongest and cheapest workers, including children. The contractors would then supply the migrant workers with food, shelter, and transportation to and from the fields and towns. They would take a percentage of the workers' wages and also make a profit from supplies that they sold to them, often keeping the migrants in constant debt.

The growers send buses to the border to pick up illegals. Labor contractors drive these buses. The majority of these labor contractors are former farm workers. They just had a station wagon. They'd get ten to twelve people to ride with them, and they'd go to a small farmer and say, "I can bring twelve people to work here. How much will you pay me to bring men in?" The farmer would say, "Well, I'll give you so much"—20 cents, 15 cents, or 10 cents, or whatever it was. Then the contractor would drive the people to work and back, and he got paid for each ride.

First, he'd start charging 50 cents; then he went up to 75 cents; and I think what they're charging right now is $1.50 to ride to work and back with the labor contractor. Then they got bigger and bigger, as they got to know other people. They'd get a bus; they'd get two or three vans. Out of each worker's wages, they kept 5 to 10 cents perhaps, and then the grower would give them 35 cents more for each worker that they bring in.

This is how they support themselves. This is how they can afford to have new cars, nice homes, and everything without working. They call it work, but it's not work. They just live off the farm workers' wages plus what the growers give them for each person they bring in. If there are any grievances, the labor contractor won't go out to the growers and tell them about it. They won't solve anything. When they say farm workers are against the union, it's not the farm workers who are; it's the labor contractors.

The Hiring Hall

The union immediately established hiring halls to replace the system of labor contractors and the growers hiring workers directly. The union hiring halls keep employment records to establish seniority for longtime workers and to help prevent abuses such as excessive charges for room and board or the arbitrary firing of workers. The union had to gain experience in running such operations, and the growers often failed to comply with the rules established in the collective bargaining agreement.[15]

I ran the first hiring hall in Fresno County. All the small farmers around there knew me, because at one time or another we had worked for them. We lived in Parlier for fifteen years and so they knew me. One farmer that I'd worked for the last five years, during the time that I was an organizer, he came to the house after calling me several times, and he came out there and he saw this great big banner and he says, "Well, I guess you're not working for me anymore." I said, "No, I'm not, not unless you sign a contract." He left and he never came back. It was hard, because we had the growers and the people that came in from Mexico to fight. We convinced the people that came in from Mexico, but the growers still haven't been convinced.

With the union hiring hall out where I worked at Christian Brothers, we had a seniority list of names and how many hours each person has put in since they first started working there. When work starts, we pick from the top of the list, the worker with the most seniority, and go down the list to assign people to go out there to work. The labor contractor would not do that. He would look around for the hardest workers, the youngest and strongest ones. I'm old; I'm fifty-four years old right now. If it was up to the grower he'd hire my daughter before he'd hire me, even though I could do a better job. I have more experience. I've worked out in fields all my life; but my daughter would be stronger and probably could work longer hours and harder than I could. This is why we need the hiring hall. When we go work for another grower, we work under a signed contract, and my hours would be adjusted so that they would contribute toward my medical benefits and vacation.

At the beginning of the hiring hall, we just had one contract, Christian Brothers ranch. Then we got more and more people started working under a union contract. The seniority system works on how long a person worked at the ranch under contract. The workers accumulate seniority and health benefits when they start paying their dues. Even if that person is seventy years old but is still able to work, he would be allowed to work under the union. Even now if I could find light work that I could do, I could work. But farm work is never light.

This means that if a person worked there for twenty years, or fifteen, or twelve, we go down the list until we come to the last people that were hired. We have the whole list, so if the company calls and they say, "We need twenty hands up, start calling the people," we can. The company is supposed to send a written letter seventy-two hours before we could send the people in. I would call people and I would tell them you have to be at work at this date, at this hour, and they were there.

The first time that we had a contract, something happened that we had to enforce the contract because the supervisor at Christian Brothers called on the telephone. It was Friday night, and he says, "I'm going to need twenty hands for Monday." "All right, I'll try to send them in that Monday." I couldn't find all of them. Saturday, since you're not going to work, you're going to be visiting somebody or you're going into town. And Sunday, you're not going to be home because you don't expect to work Saturday or Sunday. They can send you to work probably during the week, not over the weekend.

He made a point of calling Friday night, and then he said that we could not provide the workers. He calls Cesar Chavez and he told him that we couldn't provide the workers. So Dolores Huerta comes out there. That day I was out at the ranch 'cause they had a grievance out there, and the supervisor comes up and he told Dolores, "We have a signed contract and you're not obeying what you said you would. You couldn't send enough people."

I said, "You know there is a clause in the contract where seventy-two hours prior to sending the people out to work we have to have a written statement saying that you need so many people. I never got this. You call me on the telephone on Friday night. Saturday, I could find a few, but Sunday I couldn't find anyone. I couldn't send them on Monday, and I sent them Tuesday." That was our way of enforcing the contract. After that, every time they needed people, they sent in a letter.

There was a Labor Department office set up there too, in Parlier. The man that was going to run that office, it was a little trailer house, he called me and he said he wanted to work together with me, because it seems like I knew a lot of the workers. He says, "I would like to talk with you. Could you come to my office?" I went and he talked to me. He got calls from the farmers where they needed people to work and he could call me, and I could refer them to him and he would send them to work. I said, "Well, yes, I'm willing to do that. I'll send the people out there, but you'll have to show me a signed contract before I will do that." You know, he was trying to use me in order to say, "I'm doing a good job." So that didn't work out. He never called me again.

People know that you just can use so many people at one ranch. Say they'll need two hundred and they'll call their names and these two hundred people come and they're sent out to work. The rest of them know that they couldn't make it because it's just a small contract. Then we got more, and more people started working under a contract. This is when they pay their dues. We deduct their dues when they start working, their first paycheck under a contract.

Support for Families

Besides seeking to improve farm workers' wages and working conditions, the UFW addressed many family needs. These efforts were particularly important for farm workers who lived in the migrant labor camps and constantly moved around to follow the crops. The hiring hall became a meeting center where people could come and talk about off-the-job problems and socialize.[16] In addition to improving life on the job, Jessie, like Ah Quon McElrath in Hawaii (see Chapter 7), got very involved in opening up social service programs to help the farm workers with many other problems.

When many of these people came from Mexico, from Texas, they go into a migrant camp in Parlier. These camps open about two months before work starts. These people have to go to a financial company and borrow money to get them to California; then there's no work, no food, no money, no nothing. So they come out to the hiring hall. They heard that we had social services for farm workers, and they came. They talked to me; they had no food. I said, "Well, go to the welfare department. The farmers got you out here. Now you go to the welfare department and tell them that you don't have any food."

The social service people came out here with some staples: powdered milk, corn meal, food that Mexican people don't eat. You can't make tortillas out of cracked corn meal. We don't eat cracked oats or powdered milk or anything like that. The people used whatever they could, and the rest they buried, because they felt if they refused this stuff, they wouldn't get the butter and peanut butter and things that the children ate. The migrants couldn't speak English. I had the welfare department deliver the food around Parlier to these people that didn't have any food and they had no money. Some of them didn't have a car. They started delivering the food out there. Then we got food stamps for the people who needed meat and fresh vegetables and milk, and then we got bilingual education in the schools.

We had hearings here in Fresno, and I was one of the speakers. This is the sort of thing I just love to do. I am one of the persons that has gone with different groups to Sacramento to ask for unemployment benefits for the farm workers. We are not covered by this bill. It passed the California Assembly, but when it got to Governor Reagan, he vetoed it. No unemployment benefits for farm workers. So we are still pushing for it. How can packing shed workers in canneries have unemployment benefits and not the farm workers? It's because the growers give money to Reagan and Nixon. But we'll get it. We won't take anything less than we've got right now, even if we have to go without our contracts this year and next.

The Boycotts

Like other unions, the UFW used tactics such as home visits and strikes to organize workers and demand higher wages and better working conditions. But the union faced strong and often violent opposition from the growers without any of the protections of the National Labor Relations Board and with few resources to sustain long strikes. Because of their minority status, the farm workers shared many similarities with participants in the civil rights movement of the 1960s. Union organizers were concerned with issues of racial heritage and dignity and had a philosophy of nonviolence. They made use of Hispanic traditions, such as the pilgrimage and the consumer boycott. In 1966, for example, with support from the UAW and politicians like Robert F. Kennedy, the UFW organized a 230-mile "peregrinaciones," or pilgrimage, from Delano to Sacramento to support the Delano grape strike. The first grape boycott resulted in contracts with several grape growers, including the Gallo Company, in 1970. A lettuce boycott followed in 1973–74. Nonunion volunteers, such as students and clergy, were sent to supermarkets, church groups, and community meetings around the country to explain the boycotts. The farm workers themselves, including Jessie, took their message to the 1972 Democratic National Convention.[17]

The growers refuse to listen until they're losing money. That's the only way to hurt them, through the pocketbook. This we've learned from the first grape boycott that brought the growers to the bargaining table. We had the support of the Catholic bishops and from people in the cities—from everywhere. We had a lot of support and we still have it. People are more aware now of what's going on.

First, we went out and talked to the store managers about not handling any scab grapes, and they said, "We'll keep them here as long as people will buy them." After a lot of meetings in Delano, some people suggested we ask other people not to buy grapes, and that's how the boycott all got started—spreading the word around: "Don't buy grapes." It became an international thing. I still have my big banner from the international boycott demonstration of March 10, 1970.

Something funny happened when I was picketing the Safeway store during the Easter season, out near Palm Springs where most of the people who have money go for summer vacation, the well-to-do families from San Francisco and all over. There was this Safeway and I was out on the picket line talking to people and along comes this lady who says, "What do you think you're doing?" And I said, "Well, I don't *think* I'm doing; I *know* what I'm doing." Then she says, "Well, Cesar Chavez doesn't know how to go about it. You should do it the way we're doing it. We're boycotting meat. We don't picket. We don't make a—" how did she say it, like saying that they weren't crazy to be on a picket line. "What we do is go from store to store, and we tell them, You are either going to lower your prices or we won't buy here. We only shop at the stores where they have lower prices. This is how we go about it and this is how you should go about it," she said to me.

I said, "What do you mean, meat boycott? Didn't you learn to boycott through the grape boycott? Nobody ever heard of boycott until the grape boycott, so don't you come out here trying to tell us how to do it. Besides, what you are fighting for is not what we are fighting for. We're fighting for our lives; we're not fighting to have steak two times a day. We're fighting for a loaf of bread for our children working out in the fields." I said, "You don't know anything about it. We're not the lower rung; we're the grass-roots, the farm workers who put all the fruit and vegetables on your table. This is why we're asking you to help us." She said, "You're crazy. " And she just walked off. She just couldn't see what we were doing. I don't think she had ever talked to Chicanos before.

Then in 1972, at the Democratic Convention, there was a lot of support for the grape and lettuce boycotts. I was so happy to hear that some states were 100 percent in favor of the lettuce and the grape boycotts. The only people who were against this were the George Wallace people. They had lettuce all over the floor, in their hats. They had lettuce everywhere, and they were eating it, but we just ignored them. It made me feel great!

I was a delegate to the Democratic National Convention. It was a great experience. I felt so good about it, because for the first time we did have meetings and we would discuss or listen to what was being said, and then we would go out to the convention center. During these meetings I learned a lot. I got to vote on proposals at meetings, like with the Chicano Caucus. I told them the most important thing is to get education for our children.

We were asking for bilingual education and ethnic studies. Our children need to know their background. We need them to know how we were raised, so they won't have to go through the same things we had to.

The Teamsters

In addition to fighting the growers, the UFW faced severe challenges from the International Brotherhood of Teamsters (IBT). Growers were more willing to sign contacts with the Teamsters' union than with the UFW, and bitter fights broke out between the two unions. The IBT signed "sweetheart" contracts with growers without holding elections, which would be illegal under the NLRA. Teamster contracts were similar to the UFW in wages, but did not provide for hiring halls, protection from pesticides, or other benefits. The AFL-CIO supported the UFW. An agreement was finally reached between the two unions, but the toll was heavy on the UFW.[18]

My son was working for Gallo, and he's out on the boycott in Los Angeles. They're picketing all Gallo wines up and down the state because Mr. Gallo refused to renew the union contract. Workers that had been working fifteen to eighteen years there walked out on strike, and they were replaced by other workers who were brought in by the Teamsters' union. The Teamsters had been there talking with Mr. Gallo while the UFW was negotiating a new contract. Teamster union organizers were out in the field trying to sign up the old workers with the Teamsters' union. The Teamsters were chased out of the fields by the farm workers with clods or whatever they could find. They said, "We don't want anything to do with you." They knew what Gallo was doing, working both ends. Our union farm workers walked out and were on a picket line, and Gallo brings in the Teamsters with their crews, their labor contractors. With the Teamsters' union we could never have any benefits. Gallo has an announcement out in the newspaper and in Safeway stores saying that the people that are picketing against Gallo are not his workers; that his workers are still working out in the field. This just goes to show how much money Gallo can spend, millions of dollars to build a big image of himself in the news, the television, and the magazines, but he refuses to spend the money for his own workers who make all this money for him. He's not the only one. Most all of them are the same.

But he evicted his workers from their homes. I know a young man and his wife from Texas who had their first baby and she was expecting her second baby, and they were being evicted. He said, "I can't take my wife out on the street." The union had a meeting at their house, and other farm workers said, "If they try to evict you, they'll have to carry all of us out." There was about twenty persons in that house with them. They were evicted and on the way back to Texas, the baby died and his wife was very, very sick. So now his wife is in Texas, and he is back on the picket line.

Ranch El Bracero Co-op

While Jessie was working at Christian Brothers Company in the early 1970s, she and Arnold and several other families tried to buy some land on which to establish their own cooperative farm where everything could be grown organically. At first the growers refused to sell to them, and they had to use many of the UFW techniques, such as testifying at public hearings, to succeed in purchasing some acreage. Jessie and Arnold worked on the co-op farm until about 1984, when the commute from their home became too difficult and the work too hard.

I haven't been an organizer for about five years, but anytime they need me, I'll be there. At Christian Brothers, I had to lift about seventy-five pounds about five hundred times a day into a gondola of wine grapes and that's almost a killing job, especially at my age. Three years ago I didn't feel very good, and I went to the doctor. He told me I had to give up the hard work because my heart wasn't very good, and I had to take it easy. I've never been told what causes my illness, but I think that it is pesticides. My nails have black spots and break off. I have headaches all the time. First I thought it was my eyes, but then I got glasses and that didn't help very much. I think working with these pesticides, that's what caused it. We weren't aware of the danger of pesticides. We didn't know that we were being poisoned. I would read some of the labels on these cans that were left out in the fields, but I didn't know they were poison until Cesar Chavez set up the first clinic in Delano, and they found out that this was what was causing all this illness with the farm workers and the children.

Migrant work is the hardest life anyone can lead, and that's how we were forced to live. But we're farm workers. There's always in the back of your mind while you're working, "Oh, if only this land was mine." You put all your sweat and all your work on that land. You want to own the land that you work on. I hate to talk about myself, but several years ago my husband and I started visiting families in Del Ray and talking to them about getting together to buy a piece of land, because that's always been our dream, and even our fathers and grandfathers before us, owning a small farm where we could do our own farming, raise a few chickens, and be able to stay in one place. So we started with other families who invited others to our meetings, and when we organized a large group, we went to talk with one of the big growers in the Westlands district, and we knew that he was selling his land. He wouldn't sell to us.

One of the men who came out here and attended our meetings with the other families was Roger MacAffee. He's a small farmer, and he's always talking about helping people. He calls himself a communist, but I don't know what it takes to be a communist, so I couldn't say whether he's a communist or not. To me, he's just a man who's just helping people. He rented us six acres in 1973, and that's how our co-op got started.

Now I do work, but at my own pace. I mean, if I had to work for someone, nobody would hire me because they know that I could have a heart attack or anything out in the field. At our place, I go out there and I work and as soon as I feel tired, I go back and sit in the shade for about fifteen minutes or for whatever time I want, and I can do this. Like yesterday, we were out there, and between twelve and four it was hot: 98 degrees. We didn't work those hours. We stayed there under the shade and when it cooled off, we worked until it got dark. We can do this at our place. We can't do this any other place.

Retirement

Jessie now lives in a retirement community in Fresno. Arnold died in 1990, but others continue to farm the cooperative the De La Cruzes helped to start. Jessie continues to do volunteer work for the union. In the 1990s she helped to organize women farm workers in the Imperial Valley, where they were working on their hands and knees in 117-degree temperatures. In 1994 the UFW held a march from Delano to Sacramento on the first anniversary of Chavez's death, reminiscent of the march in 1966, to demonstrate the union's continued strength. Jessie was in charge of the committee to get food and housing ready for the marchers when they got to Fresno. She then joined them for the rest of the march.

Jessie believes that the UFW membership is growing. She, Dolores Huerta, and several other UFW members recently met with members of the California Agricultural Labor Relations Board to put pressure on the board to be more active. Jessie also worked unsuccessfully to defeat Proposition 187, the referendum on the California ballot in 1994 that prohibits illegal aliens and their children from receiving any government-subsidized services. While keeping involved in social issues, she is also busy with several of her six children who live nearby as well as with many of her twenty-two grandchildren and thirteen great-grandchildren. In 1976 she talked about the importance of family and the importance of the union.

We're a very close family. Like for next Sunday: my son said, "We better plan something big for my dad for Father's Day." Everything has been planned. I do most of the managing of the food and all on these days, the cooking and preparing of things, and they'll give me the money. My youngest boy, he's an organizer for the union in Stockton. He's the district manager and an organizer there in the Stockton area. My son who lives in Mountain View, he is a doctor. But they're all coming to get together here. They're bringing all the children, and they'll bring friends and other relatives.

Like on Mother's Day last year, I was supposed to speak at a rally in San Francisco. I wrote them a letter and said I refuse to go anyplace when my children, my family, are expecting me at home. I wish I could be two persons at once so I could be there and be here. My family comes first, so I didn't go to that rally, but no matter who I talk to I always talk about the union, because that's the best thing that ever happened to the farm workers. It gives me great pride to know that I had something to do with it— that I was involved, that I was organizing people.

Rocking the Boat: Union Women's Voices
ed. by Brigid O'Farrell & Joyce Kornbluh
Rutgers U. Press 1996

Chapter 11

Somebody Has to Have the Guts

Catherine Conroy, Communications Workers of America (1920–1989)

Catherine Conroy, trade unionist and feminist, helped to rock a very big boat— the American Telephone and Telegraph Company (AT&T). Raised in the Midwest during the Depression, she looked to the telephone company as a "good place" to work, but resented the rigid rules and "bullying" behavior of managers. When the National Federation of Telephone Workers (NFTW) went on strike, she be- came a picket captain, then a steward, business manager, and secretary-treasurer of the union's Wisconsin division.

In 1951 the union reorganized and became the Communications Workers of America (CWA), and Catherine was elected president of Local 5500. Known as a good organizer, skilled negotiator, and community activist, she fought for women's rights in a world of strictly sex-segregated jobs and rapid technological change. In 1960, she became one of the few women CWA staff representatives and in 1971, the first woman to run for CWA district vice president. She lost the vice presidential election, but four years later became the first woman elected to the Wisconsin State AFL-CIO executive board.

In the 1960s, Catherine was appointed to the Wisconsin Governor's Com- mission on the Status of Women, helped found the National Organization of Women, and was president of the first Chicago NOW chapter. She was presi- dent of the Milwaukee chapter of the Coalition of Labor Union Women and a vice president of Wisconsin CLUW. She sometimes felt she was "a token woman in the labor movement, and a token labor person in the women's movement." In 1976 Catherine was named Milwaukee Woman of the Year. After retiring from the CWA in 1982, she remained active in the community. Wisconsin NOW named her Feminist of the Year in 1986. When Catherine died of cancer in 1989, friends said: "She was able to inspire people"; "she was also able to teach others how to organize and how to empower themselves"; "she was a force to reckon with."[1]

A Child of the Depression

Catherine Conroy's father was born and raised in Milwaukee. Her mother, the daughter of a homesteader, was born in Fargo, North Dakota, but her family moved to Wisconsin after selling the farm. Married for ten years without children, Catherine's parents adopted her. Her mother was near eighty when she told Catherine about the adoption and asked how she felt at the news. Catherine said, "It doesn't matter. The only parents I know were wonderful to me, so what's the difference."

The Depression came along when I was probably seven. My parents never burdened me with any of these problems, I just knew there were problems; that we were very short of money. My father was a man who was badly affected by the Depression. He lost everything. He wasn't equipped for anything. He was a typical Irishman, although he wasn't all Irish, and they were Catholic. In his youth he aspired to be a doctor, but then he got involved with an art dealer in a store with antiques and Oriental rugs. He quit school and worked for a while for this man and then opened his own shop and sold paintings and vases and various things.

When the crash came and the Depression followed, that was the first thing everybody stopped buying—oil paintings and whatever. He was a very proud man; it was a terrible blow for him. He would not accept welfare. That was forbidden. He borrowed money until he owed, by the time the war came, an awful lot of money to a lot of people. We tried to have roomers to help pay the rent; it was really a very rough time. We stumbled around somehow, and then finally my mother was able to work for friends.

My mother took care of their child. We had just a little housekeeping room by this time. Our possessions had dwindled down to not much. She had to stay there, because this woman was a nurse and she worked strange hours and there was a two-year-old. I would go with my mother, and then we would come home one or two nights a week and Sunday to be with my dad. Then my mother had a chance at something that paid a little better— also caring for somebody's child, but that didn't require us to live there, so we rented a little larger tiny apartment. But I don't feel that my childhood was really deprived. I had a lot of fun. I enjoyed myself. My parents were not strict with me. They were pretty permissive, my mother particularly. Then, with the war, my father did get a job and he paid everyone back.

My mother was a rather remarkable lady. She was a very loving, gentle mother whom I remember most tenderly because she was so kind. Nobody could get her to gossip! That was not her nature. I think there was some feminism in my mother's heart. She wanted me to be free. She'd always treat me as if, somehow, I was quite special. She gave me, I'm sure, great confidence that I couldn't get from anything else. But I kind of baffled my parents because my interests were so varied. I just seemed to be always involved in something. My mother's idea of what my life ought to be like was a stereotype. You meet somebody; you marry; you have a family; and that's all anybody should ever do. I obviously didn't fit that, and I never met anyone that I wanted to marry.

The Telephone Company: A Good Place to Work?

American Telephone and Telegraph Company, more commonly known as "Ma Bell," had a well-established pattern of hiring women and men for specific jobs. By 1920 the company employed 190,000 telephone operators, mostly women, and 192,000 male electricians. From Boston to San Francisco AT&T hired many young Catholic women, often referred by other family members, who were single, well educated, bright, dependable, and, as in parochial school, very good at following the many company rules. The jobs within the telephone company were carefully segregated by sex. Women with high school degrees worked as telephone operators, and those with some college were commercial representatives. Men were hired in the "plant" department and held skilled craftsman jobs as telephone installers and repairmen in the central offices in each town.[2]

I finished high school in 1938, and I started working that fall for the county on a temporary job in the kitchen at Meridale Sanitarium. I was only about eighteen. I worked there a couple of years. My father had some family that worked for the telephone company, cousins. So that was the place to work, that's a secure job. My first salary that I clearly remember was from the Wisconsin Telephone Company, and that was eighteen dollars a week. That would be in 1942.

The operators, many of them, had just hung in during the Depression, had some seniority, and had been carefully disciplined by the company. Prior to the war it was hard to get a job with the telephone company. They owned you body and soul. They didn't keep married women for a long time. For the operator job, they wanted daughters right out of school to mold them to whatever it was they wanted from them. For commercial represen-

In 1961, Catherine Conroy (*left*) hands an arbitration award to Mary Karls (*center*), a telephone operator who had filed a grievance, while Galen Comeaux, president of CWA Local 5530, looks on. *Communications Workers of America, Wisconsin State Office.*

tative jobs, where the company dealt with the public on bills and whatever, they usually looked for some college students. Oh, they really ran your life. They told you when you were sick and when you weren't sick. At election time, the company would gently tell people what would be a wise way to vote, what would be good. The people they were pushing were usually Republicans.

Well, the war comes along and they have to double the work force, and triple. It was just crazy. Where it would take you ten years to get anywhere, now it only takes you six months. I was only an operator at the board for about six months. They needed people to train so badly that I went into the training department and became an instructor. Management had to tone down their discipline a little bit because people would quit. They could get better jobs.

But whatever miserable hours they had, as a new employee, I worked them all, and they were horrible. All of us who worked them hated them, but you worked with others who were suffering the same problem, and you pretty soon built up a little group of friends who worked till ten o'clock at night, and you amused yourself as best you can at ten o'clock at night by eating hot fudge sundaes and gossiping a lot. There was no contact with the men. That in those days was almost forbidden.

In the operating rooms we had what you could call "straw bosses." The company called them chief operators. They really made very few decisions, just make the operators do this, get them to do that. They were issuing the orders. The manager was always male and he'd walk through maybe once a day. Everywhere you turned, somebody was supervising. Some were just bullies. Nothing could get my dander up quicker than to see an operator who was defenseless being brow-beaten and in tears by somebody who had a little power. That bullying kind of thing infuriated me!

Now I used to personally argue with management people a lot about things that were happening. The operator's job dehumanized people. The whole company program was to almost make the operators into machines. You weren't supposed to talk to your neighbor, and you hold the pencil this way, and you hold the ticket that way. They had many little rules, like you must keep your feet flat on the floor. I never did. I'd sit on my foot and that would absolutely infuriate my boss. Then when they'd say, "You know you're not supposed to sit on your foot," I'd say, "Am I doing my job?" They'd say, "Well, yes," and I'd say, "Then don't bother me." I'm convinced we've got to stop crying in the corner about our troubles and fight. Women just suffer and endure. They cry in the washroom; tell each other at lunch. It's all great therapy, but it doesn't solve the problem.

The Bell system is great for regimentation and discipline. Production supposedly is going to be better if you discipline people. No matter what operator you talked to from wherever part of the telephone system anywhere in the nation, they all had the same rules. Every telephone man drove a green truck with bells on it. The pencils you used were green. Everybody had the same kind of pencils. I mean it was like being in the army. Those things used to annoy me a whole lot, and a lot of it we haven't even gotten rid of yet.

Forming a Union

From the early 1900s to the mid-1920s, the telephone company grew rapidly. The number of female operators went from 19,000 in 1900 to 190,000 in 1920. The number of male electricians grew from 51,000 to 192,000 during that same period. Following early efforts by the International Brotherhood of Electrical Workers to organize the telephone industry, including a very strong group of women activists, AT&T established Employee Representation Plans, or company unions, all around the country. In 1937 the Supreme Court found such unions illegal under the 1935 Wagner Act. These organizations, however, provided the basis for the independent National Federation of Telephone Workers formed in 1939. Catherine was a part of this newly emerging independent union in Wisconsin.[3]

I had trouble finding out about that union. I didn't know a lot about unions, except I gathered that they gave you certain rights. It wasn't too clear what they were. It was a little independent traffic operators' union. The men had a different union. The Bell system had decided to beat the labor movement to the punch with what they called their Employee Representation Plan. When the Wagner Act was passed, that wiped out the management control of that union, but the union that was left and represented the operators was very weak. I remember asking somebody how you could join this union, and nobody could tell me. The union was run pretty much by a lawyer from Chicago. Just a handful of women, they'd all meet him at the station, and whatever he said was right, and they never questioned anything. Unless you knew this handful of people, you just didn't know what was going on. They didn't work in my building. I never saw them.

In the early forties, the men started to get things together. About 1945 the plant union, the men's union, which was called the Guild, decided to organize the women, and they raided this independent union. I was watching this whole raid, and I noticed we had a couple of people that were really working on people to join and they were signing cards. They talked to me about it, and I said, "I don't know anything about that organization and I don't know anything about the one that's here, either. I just don't know what to say." So a couple of us decided, well, we'll go down and see the officers of this independent union and discuss this with them. We find our way to the headquarters; we'd never been there before. This woman who was the president, she didn't realize how strong that move was. They were signing people up right and left, and she didn't believe it when I told her.

They held an election and the Guild won. So there we were; we now had a different union. That wiped out the leadership of this old independent union. The union men had to quickly find people to provide some union work, signing people up and organizing and whatever. I had known a lot of people in the toll office, and several of them were after me to get involved. I said, "Well, I don't know what to do." And they said, "Come to a meeting."

I went to a meeting and I was elected steward and I hadn't even joined yet. The reason for that was our group in the training department. It was more relaxed work. We could talk as we worked, and, as a result, we were always organizing something. We'd built up quite a training department gang, and we used to rent cottages and go picnicking. We didn't do anything important, just had a good time. We didn't exclude anyone; everybody was always welcome, but the only people that really participated were the people from the training department. So we had bit of a reputation for organizing all the time. People thought we could do a lot with the union. I felt so dumb. Except I realized nobody knew anything. I suppose the beginning of my union career was kind of being in the right place at the right moment. I accepted this steward thing, but the union grew so fast. We were all sort of fumbling around, trying to put this organization together. Then the real turning point, when I really just sort of plunged right in, was the famous 1947 telephone strike.

The 1947 CWA Strike

The National Federation of Telephone Workers was made up of loosely affiliated independent unions. AT&T was strongly opposed to any kind of national agreement and negotiated separately with the affiliated unions. In 1946 the federation was disbanded and replaced with one union, the Communications Workers of America. On April 7, 1947, the CWA called a national strike for national recognition and over issues such as across-the-board wage increases, a union shop, improved schedules, and pensions. Of the 345,000 strikers, 230,000 were women, "the biggest walk-out in American history of women."[4] The six-week strike ended without national recognition, but with a stronger union movement. Catherine Conroy was a picket line captain and, from then on, a union activist.

I mean, what better way to cut your teeth in a union than a strike? A six-week strike—it was a nasty one! We had a big building, and we needed to cover about five doors with pickets because the company had lots of people going in. They were working hard on people to go in. I became a picket captain very fast. It was convenient for me. I only lived two blocks from the office and that was a golden opportunity. I could run home and get back and I was on that picket line about nine hours a day. It rained every day; I got soaked.

Oh, we had all kinds of problems. There was no one who was physically violent to people, but there was mischief. We were on strike over Easter. I don't know were the idea came from, but somebody got the notion that we'll form a double line and make the people scabbing walk between us, and we will have lipstick in our hand, rolled out of course, just walking peacefully along. We'll be so close they'll have to rub against this lipstick. I can't tell you how many people in their Easter coats, pink and pastel, went into the building with streaks of red on each side. That's the kind of stuff that we had troubles with.

Those of us who were picket captains tried to preserve the order. We knew the cops pretty well; there was always some there. They were nice. The management didn't give us too much trouble. Some management provoke a lot of trouble, but they were pretty sensible. There were more problems in other areas of the state. Somebody was getting married, and we had a big shower on the picket line. We had card tables and had gifts and cake. We always had somebody with a baby going around that picket line with a stroller or a buggy. It was relatively peaceful. The pickets were cheerful; they were singing and so on. We had fun.

When you are trying to build an organization and get people to participate, you do examine your own past to see what it is that happened that got you involved, when others seemed to escape that whole thing and are totally unconcerned. As I examine my past, I suppose I had reached a point in my life where just playing was not enough. It didn't appear that I was going to marry anyone. I wasn't eager to marry just to marry, and I hadn't met anyone that I could see myself tied down to and spending a lifetime with. I was easily caught up in anything that was interesting to me, and the union interested me because you spend a lot of your hours at a job, and there were a lot of things that I just didn't think were right and ought to be dealt with.

The strike really tuned me into the whole labor thing. Then I really became fascinated by it. Those were exciting years for CWA because we were really building a union, writing a constitution, changing its name, long debates. We would sit in convention and debate all night long two or three articles for the constitution. At five in the morning we were still arguing should it be this way or this way. I wouldn't have missed it for anything. It was such an exciting time.

Business Agent: Growth and Change

Union leaders had to address problems of internal organization and rapid technological change in the industry simultaneously. Joseph Bierne, president of the new union, and the union executive board regrouped after the less than successful 1947 strike and in 1949 took the new union into the CIO. In 1951, however, the first long-distance dial call was made, and the long-distance operator job began to disappear. Between 1953 and 1955, potential union membership went from 358,000 to 252,000. At the same time, workers and union members like Catherine were adjusting to these changes at the local level. Catherine began working on training programs somewhat similar to those Maida Springer-Kemp describes for the garment workers in the 1930s (see Chapter 5).[5]

At the next union state convention we had just created this new structure, and I became a business agent for the Milwaukee operators, about 1948. At that time, the potential membership was about three thousand. We didn't have them all signed up, and it was a great challenge. The Milwaukee operators were divided up into about eighteen locals. They had one in every department in every building. It was crazy, but it grew from the old independent set-up. The company never encouraged people to get together, and so these locals didn't do anything. That was a beautiful opportunity for me to learn by trial and error. I didn't know what to do. We just had to try to figure it out. We reduced those sixteen locals to four for the whole city. Then we decided, after we operated with four for a while and that worked much better, that we really needed only one, Local 5500.

This is, by the way, back when the system was changing to dial telephones, and dial telephones were wiping out whole offices of people. We did some good things. We worked out a plan together for absorbing a lot of these people in the toll office or the remaining dial offices. I spent long hours in meetings with management. They were offering to put operators in any clerical jobs they could do, but the operators were afraid. They would take them into the employment office and test them and one thing I discovered: the way they operated the discipline in those operator rooms, the operator usually didn't take long to decide she wasn't good for much. The expectations they had for themselves for doing anything else weren't too good.

So I met with a vocational school and set up a program of testing, and the local union agreed that we would pay half the cost and the employee would pay the other half, and go through some testing where the telephone company wouldn't be involved. Testing where you can really let your hair down and be yourself, and if you don't like the results of your test the company will never know that you had one. If it is good, then you can take the test to the company and say, here, I have an aptitude for mathematics, or I'd like to try a clerical job. That was very useful. A lot of women learned some good things about themselves in the process. Many of them did get out of telephone operating and into other kinds of jobs and did very well, turned out fine. We felt real good about the program. You see, in those days, before affirmative action, it was terribly hard to break out of the bind women were in.

When I was a business agent, we decided we had to have an education program to teach new people about the union. I didn't know anything about writing an education program, but when there is nothing else, anything you do is better than nothing. I put together a program. After we changed our structure again, we had a national education department, and we produced some programs for the whole union with material and outlines. Then I taught those. In the summer time, we'd hold a week at the University of Wisconsin for union leadership training. In addition to university faculty, there would be one or two instructors from the union, and I would participate in that. I was very interested in the development of people who knew nothing when they started, and I tried to share everything with them.

President, CWA Local 5500

The national union continued to struggle with questions about the best organizational structure in the ongoing fight to gain national union recognition by AT&T. In 1950, to increase strength at the national level, the union voted to move to a two-level system, the national executive board and the local unions. This change had a dramatic effect for officers at the divisional and local level. Although Catherine sometimes described her union activities as accidental, or "being in the right place at the right time," this time she demonstrated a conscious decision to develop a career in the union.[6]

We had restructured, and we had a state executive board and officers. In about 1950, we had a state election and I ran for secretary-treasurer of the Wisconsin CWA. It was kind of interesting, because even back then I realized that I probably can't win this because I'm a woman. I mean this whole operation was male-dominated and run. You weren't going to do anything without the approval of the guys. I ran against a young man from Madison, and I'm not too clear why he lost, but I became secretary-treasurer of the Wisconsin CWA.

Meanwhile, we restructured again and wiped out all this state level. One of the things we had to do to deal with AT&T was to centralize our collective bargaining. We could not have every group doing their own, because AT&T was really together. We put all the responsibility for bargaining a contract in the international executive board. We wanted locals to be more active, to eliminate this state level, and then the union would be run by the locals, the international executive board, and the convention, of course, which is made up of local people.

There was an agreement made among the leadership that we would set up a national staff. Well, I didn't want to be on a national staff, because I hadn't been a local officer and I thought I ought to have that experience. My local accepted me very well; I was very close to the people in this local. So I talked to them about it and said, "I could go on the national staff and I'd have job security and everything, but we need to build this local and I need to know all about that." I said, "If you elect me president, I won't take the staff spot." Everybody was for that, so I was local union president full-time for about nine years, from 1951 to 1960.

I was still working for the company, sort of, but I had a lot of union work so I was off a lot. I tried to hang on to the company job and keep my salary going, but it was tough doing it. I had the title of service assistant, and I trained operators. But the hours weren't good. I was getting evening work, and I had a lot of meetings to go to. This was interfering with my union career. I gave that title up. Now that cost me about eight dollars a week, but then I had the kind of seniority as an operator to pick the hours that fit my union activity. So I was at the telephone office at seven in the morning and I'd work for Mother Bell until four P.M. Then I went to the union office.

I learned to run all the machinery, because if we wanted to put a newsletter out we had to write it and run it and mail it and do whatever. So we learned how to do all that—broke every machine in the office. I had quite a bunch of active people who were just great. We painted the office, and we just did everything. The guys were intrigued by all of this. We were so busy! I had no personal household responsibility. I lived on Lloyd Street here in town with both my parents in a two-bedroom flat, and they were good to me. They charged me a little room and board, but it wasn't too bad. I wasn't involved in any emotional way with anyone, that I would want to make a different kind of life.

My father died around that time of cancer, so I decided I'd move the local union office to our house, and we'd save a little rent. I had a fair-size bedroom, and I'd wake up in the morning and there's that mimeo machine looking at me. The dining room table was always a mess, and my mother'd say, "I wish you would clean this table off." And I'd say, "Yes, I'm going to do that," but it never really got too clean. The phone rang all day. It was just wild. I have sort of a one-track mind, so I fell right into this. It was such an exciting time in the union. Every day—some new crisis! It was just very exciting, I just rushed at it.

Community Involvement

The National Community Services Committee, CIO, was established in 1945 and directed by Leo Perlis, who then directed the AFL-CIO Community Services

Committee when the two labor federations merged in 1955. The first chairman of the merged committee was Joseph Bierne, president of the CWA. All local unions and state and central bodies were encouraged to establish community services committees. Catherine became very involved representing the CWA on various social service boards, where she was often the only labor person and the only woman.[7]

Meanwhile, I also got involved in labor's community services program here in Milwaukee and ended up on the board of the labor council here. As a member of the board, the merger of the AFL and the CIO came up, and so I was part of the merger committee. We were on the CIO board. I wasn't the first woman on the CIO board, but after the merger, I was the first one the AFL had ever had. They didn't know quite what to do with that. I had some good support from other unions, because I was very active in the community services program. The new constitution for the Milwaukee Labor Council called for the board members to chair all the committees. We had no one else on the board who knew anything about the community services.

I became a member of the United Fund's board of directors as a labor person. I was on the Catholic Social Services board and Child Care Inc.'s board, and Cerebral Palsy's board. There weren't that many labor people available, for one thing, and a lot of these groups did want a woman and I was it. It was kind of a curious assignment, and I think that some labor people are very uncomfortable, but we had some labor people that were very effective. For example, we were anxious not to have fees for some services or to hold the fees down to something reasonable that working people could afford. We would often speak out and raise a little hell about things, but we could never seem to find enough labor people to do it.

CWA Staff Representative

CWA restructuring and technological change in the 1950s caused many union women to lose their union leadership positions. When locals that had been all-female or all-male merged, Patsy Fryman, assistant to the union president in the 1970s, recalled "Almost universally, women gave up their positions, usually to white males who were all ready to take over." Catherine agreed, saying, "Nobody really noticed this happening."[8] As the number of operators continued to

Catherine Conroy (*left*) was named Woman of the Year by the Milwaukee chapter of the National Organization for Women in 1976. With her are (*left to right*) Kathryn Clarenbach, Mary Jean Collins, and Gene Boyer. Conroy, Clarenbach, and Boyer were all founders of NOW. Milwaukee Journal, *July 9, 1978.*

decline, so did the number of women leaders. In Catherine's case, her local could no longer afford the salary of a full-time president, but she moved to a union staff position rather than go back to work for AT&T. Although the union membership was over 50 percent female, she was one of a very few women on the two-hundred-person staff.

The telephone industry was converting quickly to mechanized equipment. Unless we got some other members of some kind or another, CWA would shrink. I'd resolved when I became full-time local union president that I didn't want my salary, which was modest, to become a burden to the local. I knew and the local members knew that the end was in sight, and finally about 1958, I told the CWA state director that the next staff opening he had, I wanted to put a bid in for it. By now I had lost any chance of going back to the telephone company. At that time we were allowed a three-year leave for union business, and then you had to make a decision—go back to the company or you're through. I weighed that one for about a minute or two and thought, I can't go back to the company. I want to stay in the union. I can't tolerate that company job. Then an opening for staff developed. I applied and went on the union staff in 1960.

I'm a staff representative for the east side of Wisconsin, which is where most of the people are. At one time we had CWA locals in every town. However, mechanization's hit those, too, so now I have sixteen locals. I have contracts to negotiate, eighteen of them. I have all the public employees and we have some small towns to negotiate with. I don't bargain all of them myself, but I'm responsible for them. I meet once a month with the sixteen local union presidents. Fourteen of them are male, and they're craftsmen. They do work like maintaining all the electronic equipment and installing telephones. When we come to the time to discuss "good and welfare" in the local union meeting agenda, we talk about the problems of the telephone craftsmen.

Even with a slight majority, the women union members have a tendency to defer to the male who wants to talk about his problems. She's still waiting to see what the union's going to do about her problem. Now I say harsh things like, "Never mind what the union's going to do about your problem. What are you going to do about your problem? I'm just going to help you; I cannot do this for you. That's why you're in this mess for so long, because you keep waiting for somebody to do it for you. All the union does is make it possible for us to do something together." I think that's slowly going to get through.

The Women's Movement and NOW

As a result of President Kennedy's Commission on the Status of Women, the states developed commissions to carry on the work of fostering equity for women in the workplace. Catherine was appointed to the Wisconsin commission and became active, along with Dorothy Haener and other women from the UAW, in founding the National Organization of Women. The story is told that at the founding luncheon in Washington, Catherine tossed $5 on the table and said, "Well, if we're going to form an organization, we'd better put our money where our mouth is," and the NOW treasury was created. A friend said, "Catherine . . . is the builder, the person who makes the by-laws; she's the one who makes things go."[9] At these meetings, Catherine met Kathryn Clarenbach, a professor at the University of Wisconsin, and many other feminist women, who became close friends.

The report that was produced by the Kennedy Commission on the Status of Women, *The American Woman,* called on the various state governors to appoint commissions on the status of women. Talk about how much timing affects my life: I happened to be at the University of Wisconsin and Professor Jack Barbash was on campus and he came up and said, "Catherine, they're putting some kind of a committee together and they want you to serve." He didn't know much about it, but I found myself on this planning committee and we put this Governor's Commission on the Status of Women together. They had the president of the Wisconsin State AFL-CIO on it, and Kathryn Clarenbach is on it. She chaired this commission in Wisconsin for many years, and this one has been very vigorous. We put together a very successful conference. Then the U.S. Women's Bureau of the Department of Labor set up a Conference of Governor's Commissions, and there were twenty-some around the country. We went to Washington and each commission reported what they were doing.

The following year they had another gathering of commissions. By this time, there were about thirty-eight. The Women's Bureau set up workshops, and they asked me to chair the one on employment. Now in my workshop I had a woman sitting there whom I'd never heard of before. That was really a shame, because I should have heard of her. Somebody said, "Betty Friedan's in your workshop." I asked, "Who's Betty Friedan?" "Oh, she wrote a book." "What book?" *The Feminine Mystique.* Never heard of that either. Somehow that had escaped me, but anyway, Betty was there. We talked in that workshop about fighting for voluntary overtime, because we knew a lot of industries have workers who are forced to work overtime. This limits women's job opportunities. It isn't right for any person.

Anyway, that evening Kay Clarenbach and I talked to each other, and we had decided we wanted some resolutions passed at that conference. There were a lot of us involved. We had been on this for a couple of years, and we had decided it's about time these commissions are producing some action. Kay knew the Women's Bureau very well, including the director, Mary Keyserling. They were a pretty conservative gang. Kay discussed with them the possibility of passing resolutions. A number of workshops wanted to do that and Kay came back and reported, "There will be NO resolutions. It is not appropriate." We got mad!

There was a meeting that night in Betty's hotel room. The next morning at breakfast we decided to set up NOW, the National Organization for Women. The Women's Bureau had a luncheon, and they had a podium thing that had tiers of people at the head table. The luncheon was the biggie and they had some senators there and they had the head table and the head head table and the head head head table. You never saw so many people at the head table. Anyway, there were twenty-six of us, I think, at two different tables, passing notes around, creating NOW right there in this luncheon in front of these people. I know that Mary Keyserling wondered what in the hell's going on down there at these tables, 'cause we're running around.

Then Betty says, "This is a historical moment; we have to have a photographer take a picture of these founders. We're going to call it the National Organization for Women." She immediately comes up with a statement of purpose of sorts. We decided Kay Clarenbach will be the first temporary chairperson and the headquarters will be in Madison, Wisconsin, and Kay will put together some kind of a conference so we can really launch this thing officially. We will all tell everybody we can think of and we will get something started. From that moment on, NOW was born, with twenty-six people. Those of us who were that involved in it were on the first board. Kay became, after the first conference, the chairperson of the board. Betty was the first president of NOW.

I'm a real fan of Betty's. She has good vision; she has good sense. Writing, speaking, having visions of the future and analyzing problems is her thing. She does it very well. She's a terrible organization person. That's not her thing. NOW, from that day to this, seems to live with one crisis after another. A lot of good things are happening, and a lot of crazy things are happening. My first impression of the board was that here is a group of people that know very little about organization, and I was big on structure.

I thought I knew a lot about by-laws. Finally, we came up with a set of by-laws very quickly that we were pressed, as a board, to adopt. There was this great pressure to get this thing going. At the board meeting when we got the by-laws, I thought, "Oh my, we are going to have all kinds of problems with these by-laws." They have been plaguing us ever since. There is no delegate system. If you could afford to come, you were a participant.

That smelled like trouble to me already. To be truly representative of the rank-and-file members of NOW, we had to have a delegate system. I served on some by-laws committees but we couldn't get them off the ground then, 'cause nobody wanted to talk about them. We're too busy with saving women.

I was disturbed by the failure of the leadership of NOW to come to grips with these housekeeping problems, which I found very depressing, because I just had a feeling that unless we did something dramatic, we were going to be the victim of all kinds of problems. Of course, shaping up was what now I guess they call themselves the militant feminists. The argument was should we be the lead organization or should we have broad-based appeal. I think the majority of NOW people are more conservative than to want to be labeled as radical feminists. They want action; they want to get things done, but I doubt the majority of NOW members and the majority of women care about the off-the-wall crazy stuff. I don't either; I just don't see that. I think it may be fun for the kids, but it's no way for adults to act. So all these internal battles, of course, took place.[10]

I left the NOW board mainly because I hadn't the time to spend on the national level and I didn't have the money. My union was willing to help pay my expenses for a while, but I just couldn't get away to travel all over the country to these board meetings, so I told them I just couldn't serve. Of course, they wanted a union person on their board and that's to their credit. There was myself and Dorothy Haener from the UAW and a woman from the airline stewardesses. But I did promise, because Chicago's a major center, that I would start a chapter in the city of Chicago. I was the first president of the Chicago NOW chapter.

What intrigued me was that NOW grew by itself. It was an idea whose time had come. I couldn't believe it, because here I am trying to organize a union and I'm having a terrible time. But the *Daily News* had done a story on NOW and me as the president of the Chicago chapter. The only address we had was our office. I got more mail from women begging to join, and I didn't answer it. I didn't have time. A week later, I'd get another letter saying, "I wrote to you a week ago." I thought, we just have to knock people on the heads to join unions, but NOW—you can't keep them away. They bother you to death, call you up, call you back. I couldn't believe it.

Automation and Adjustment

Catherine continued to work with NOW in an advisory role both at the national and at the local level. Because of automation, the phone company was facing a continuing loss of jobs, and the union was developing new strategies to address a shrinking membership. The union was trying to organize in other industries as well as organize new independent communications companies that were developing in response to new equipment and attacks on the regulated monopoly status of AT&T. Catherine moved to Chicago as part of this effort. She remained there until 1972, commuting back and forth to Milwaukee to take care of her mother.[11]

As a union, in 1965, we knew we were going to shrink, and we felt we could not let the union shrink because the payroll is shrinking. We've got to still have a strong union to deal with Mother Bell, so we have to find members somewhere else. The telephone is kind of a limited industry. We decided to organize whatever telephone companies aren't organized, then reach out to other kinds of workers. Because what difference does it make? How many teamsters do you see in the Teamsters' union? So we have to expand. We're into everything. We have egg handlers and hat manufacturers and government workers and city workers and county workers. But we're taking the no-raid pact very seriously. We're all committed to that in the AFL-CIO, so we don't raid each other's unions. No, our interest is in people who have no union.

Growth is our number one priority. We're going to grow by publicizing our union's getting involved in communities, in organizing. Every CWA district was to produce what they called their best rep to go to Washington for a couple of weeks and learn about this program and then come back and implement it in their own districts. I went for CWA from this district. Then I had to move to Chicago, because that's where the district office is. I wasn't particularly eager to move out of Milwaukee. Now my father had died by this time. This was about 1966. I went to Chicago and got a little one-room apartment. My mother was still up in Milwaukee, not doing too well.

I worked on that program. It had to be set up and then you had to train union staff, and we had to train local officers. I did this in three states and traveled quite a lot; Indiana and Illinois and then went back and did some follow-up for around three years. Then, finally, it was decided administratively that it should be up to the staff to follow through. They needed a staff person in the Chicago office for the state of Illinois, so I stayed on and worked there another three years. I finally moved my mother down to Chicago. She was failing more and more, and she wanted to be in the same city with me. She felt very lonesome, although I came home every weekend. It was a crazy way to live.

I dealt with Illinois Bell, and I was given United Airlines. We had two hundred people in United Airlines which we negotiated for. Negotiating with United was my first experience bargaining with a company outside of telephone. Airlines? Especially United Airlines! But it all worked. Really, if you know anything about bargaining procedure, you can do something with any workers, if you have a contract. So we did all right there. That unit, by the way, was wiped out by computers, too. They've all had to be transferred to other jobs. United had a giant computer. They used to teletype all their freight orders and everything. Now they just push buttons on a computer and it all comes out somewhere.

Change in the 1970s

In 1973 Catherine moved back to Milwaukee, where she continued her work as a staff representative. In 1975 the CWA had 575,000 members, half of them women. They were considered the "prototype of the white collar, professional organization."[12] The majority of these members continued to work for AT&T, but there was increasing concern over AT&T's loss of status as a regulated monopoly and what that meant for workers. This development was the beginning of the break-up of the Bell system into several independent telephone companies under court order in the 1980s.

The problem today versus twenty years ago is that the management in those early days, they were crude. They just did such obviously bad things, it wasn't hard to build up some spirit to fight. But today, management is sophisticated and they're very subtle, and the battle is for the minds of people now, and their loyalties. The kind of management that would have a temper tantrum's gone. They're smoother, more skillful today. So people get manipulated into doing what management wants them to do without realizing it's happening to them.

In view of the size of the problem we have to deal with, 'cause Bell is a giant, there's no doubt it's unique in a lot of respects. It's guaranteed a profit. The managers work and don't do anything right during a strike, but the industry is now so highly mechanized that when we strike, management doesn't need us. I mean the machinery goes on; the customers still put their calls through, and they pay their bills faithfully. The money comes in. The last strike we had, somebody figured the company saved eleven million dollars a day by having us out on strike. The union has to design some different ways to deal with the problems, because Bell's an employer who can buy whatever kind of information, know-how, and wherewithal that is possible to buy, which is unlike other companies.

The Bell system is in trouble for the first time in its history, and admits it. AT&T was a regulated sort of monopoly, but a monopoly. This permitted it to provide what is reputed to be the best telephone service, and I think it's true that it is. The service is good and the price is not outrageous. Now, it's also a powerful monopoly, and power is a dangerous thing. I don't know that AT&T has used that power in a bad way for either the public or the employee. I mean, we do a lot of complaining, but as workers go, telephone workers are doing as well as any. I mean with pensions, fringes, salary benefits. Job security, until recently, was excellent, and that's a big item. But other countries are creating telephone equipment now, answering services and PBX boards, and all kinds of things. The Federal Communications Commission opened the door to this kind of competition.

It's becoming a very serious problem. First of all, from our standpoint, we have a lot of jobs at stake. A lot of new businesses will exploit the people they hire, nonunion. We call them inter-connect companies. We've been trying to organize them. They don't stay in business very long. Then you add to that, Wisconsin Bell is now installing what they call modules wherever they get into a home. This is the kind of equipment that you put on the wall in two or three rooms and plug in your telephone. Nobody will have to come out here and touch it. That wipes out a guy called the installer. What we're working out with the companies all over is to keep the workers we have.

Nothing would make American business happier than to wipe out the whole labor movement. Most of them—they think they know better than we do what's good for us. Employers love to say the door is always open. "If you're unhappy, come and see me anytime." God, that's old! But actually people, when they go through that and they find out the employer just humors them or fires them, one of the two, it still doesn't connect to them. Somehow, it doesn't all come together that there's some legal protection you've got to have before the employer really acts. There's no substitute for a union.

Affirmative Action and Ma Bell

In the early 1970s the Bell System, the largest private employer in the country, was charged with race and sex discrimination in employment under Title VII of the 1964 Civil Rights Act. After years of investigation by the Equal Employment Opportunity Commission, AT&T signed a court-ordered consent decree, which included an extensive affirmative action plan to integrate its jobs by race and sex. The unions, however, were not party to the agreement. Under this type of affirmative action program, seniority, especially for determining layoffs, came into direct conflict with equal opportunity goals. The seniority issue was a major point of disagreement among union and nonunion feminists. Mary Callahan and Dorothy Haener also discuss this problem (see Chapters 6 and 8).[13]

I think that we've got to work hard for some kind of affirmative action without violating seniority. Wherever union women have sat down and really examined this, you just cannot stomp on seniority. See, I don't believe that you can use seniority to solve the economic ills of this country. I think we have to have jobs for people, and it is not the fault of the union that the employers discriminate in hiring. The members of the union shouldn't have to pay the penalty; it should be the employer. And there's a lot of different ways to handle it, such as a money benefit of some sort where the employer pays the price, not a fellow worker.

There's been recognition of seniority in the AT&T program, but when a target comes along and the employer's not hiring and you're talking transfer, seniority gets zapped real bad. The Bell system, for example, has over half women and has kept them within the traditional female jobs. There are clear distinctions between male and female work. So they have a lot to do, and they're desperately trying to find female garage mechanics and female linesmen, or female whatever—also male telephone operators.

Male operators; they meet that quota just fine. But they're having a hard time finding women who are willing to work in construction, climbing telephone poles and splicing cables. Few are interested. So we've got to work on trying to get affirmative action to make sense and make sure that it's implemented. We have the doors open to improve the opportunities for women in better jobs between upgrading traditional female jobs and opening doors to traditional well-paid male jobs.

The Coalition of Labor Union Women

As divisions within NOW continued, union women like Mary Callahan and Catherine Conroy turned to each other and helped organize the nationwide Coalition of Labor Union Women (also discussed in Chapter 6). Catherine was very supportive of this development and served as president of the Milwaukee CLUW and vice president of the Wisconsin CLUW. Her involvement was limited, however, by lack of support from the CWA male union leaders in her district, her mother's deteriorating health, and her own battle with cancer. She was again frustrated by organizational problems and political struggles with more radical organizations, but remained very optimistic about the future for working women.[14]

In Chicago, several of us tried to get union women together. There was no CLUW, but we were trying to get union women talking to each other. I had felt as a member of NOW that somehow union women had to start worrying about themselves. With some help from Libby Koontz, who directed the U.S. Women's Bureau, finally, we did set up a meeting. We wanted to share our problems. We felt that the women's movement had something to say to union women, and we ought to get on board. We had a lot in common as union women, working women. There were a lot of things the women's movement was doing that would be valuable to union women. Not everything would concern them, but that whole economic thing—jobs—would be of concern to us. We didn't really produce a whole lot that evening.

The real origin of CLUW began with the UAW and Olga Madar talking with some other union women. They invited our participation. At the time they started, I wasn't available. CWA endorsed the idea of some kind of coalition, and we did have a representative at the meetings. They decided in those first meetings that they should set up regional meetings, and I helped with the regional meeting held in Chicago. Out of the regional meetings came a committee that got together to plan a national meeting. Of course, the famous big national meeting in Chicago, I was there for that. That was exciting. That particular convention made me think that I had been reborn and could see the beginnings of the CIO, because everybody was so full of idealism and enthusiasm, but I think probably everybody realized the rough road was still ahead. The real problem is to coordinate these things, translate them into union action.

I had trouble because my district vice president was not very interested in us. I was so annoyed with him by that time that I decided, okay, if you don't want to participate, I'm not going to give you any credit for participating. I will participate as an individual. This union district has done nothing to help. But when they met in the East or the West, I just couldn't get an okay to participate at the union's expense, and I couldn't afford to spend my own money at the time. My help was kind of sporadic.

CLUW has a lot of possibilities. Union women are slightly better off than nonunion women, but they, too, have only begun now to get the message that there are some things that ought to be changed and you're the only one that's going to change them. Unions like my own, where women are the majority but men have the majority of leadership, and I mean almost 100 percent with a little exception. The men, I think, are very nervous in this union. They don't know what it all means. Since we have the votes, they are holding their breath waiting for us to exercise it, and we haven't done that yet.

The men are practical, but any subtle way that they can avoid having to deal with the women question, they're going to. I know of some instances where it's happening. I see just little signs that are probably not too evident. For example, I think I am on the state AFL-CIO board because there are leaders in the labor movement that are a little uneasy about the fact that we had no women on the state board. Union women are not attacking anybody for that, but the women's movement is attacking. The president of the state AFL-CIO means well, but he is a male chauvinist. He does, however, see the advantage to having a woman on the state board. I mean, I'm the token woman. He can say, "Yes, of course, we have a woman!"

The change is not going to be dramatic and it's not going to be overnight. But pressures on a state AFL-CIO president or my international union president are just going to get stronger and stronger for women's issues. So there's an enormous job of consciousness raising that I think only CLUW is going to do. The unions are not going to do it. The male leadership isn't aware enough. CLUW has no staff; it has little or no help. Everybody is trying to do something for CLUW around the edges of all the other things they're in to. There's no history to look at. This is a whole different kind of movement. Be patient! Help, don't criticize. CLUW's going to be effective. Once union women have got a sense of unionism and the power of unions and the role of unions and the potential of unions for themselves, then they've got to examine all aspects of their contracts.

Sisterhood

Catherine Conroy practiced what she preached with compassion and good humor. She had a comfortable home, specifically chosen in a racially integrated neighborhood, that she shared with cousins, friends, and her dogs. She held frequent union committee meetings at her home and, for a number of years, weekly luncheons for her young women protégés in the union. She said that women "are great at handling strikes; we fight hard, stay out, picket. . . . So we're really a significant part of the union. But we never seek policymaking positions, and we don't seek them because we get no support to go out and get them."[15] She took care of her mother and underwent her own fight with cancer.

I keep saying to our gang, to people I talk to here, we have to develop a real active sense of sisterhood. Men achieve because they get a lot of support from the "old boy" system. We have to have that same sense of, even if I'm not ambitious to do anything more than I'm doing, I must make sure you are doing everything you can do. I think we have to develop a sense that this will succeed because we help each other do it. So, if there's an opening for something, find a sister to fill it. And help your sisters find their own potential. That's my advice.

I've missed very few union conventions, particularly in those very exciting years when I was an officer of the union local and a delegate who voted and could speak. I just got so totally wrapped up and absorbed in all this. I realize that not everybody can take that kind of interest in the union organization, the union constitution and structure. Well, to me that was just a very important subject. I was very thrilled with all that. I was totally absorbed with it. The years just flew by. As a matter of fact, 1977 is the anniversary of thirty years of just about 100 percent of my time.

At this time, in a period of two years, I was in the hospital five times. My health problems didn't slow me down a whole lot, but did cause me some concern because I was so scared and my mother was so poorly. She was already in a nursing home. She was not mentally able to deal with anything, because she suffered so severely with hardening of the arteries. So trying to take care of all these problems without letting her know was hard. Maybe it wouldn't have mattered. I kind of realized after a while that she didn't remember anything I told her anyway. I moved from Chicago back to Milwaukee during that time, so things were kind of wild. I thought, I've got to live longer than my mother, because I don't know what's going to happen—because I had no brothers and sisters. It was a great pressure. My mother died a year ago September.

I did run scared for a while, although it was interesting after the first surgery, after telling me that it was very successful, the doctor told me, "Even if you do develop another malignancy, don't be upset by it, and don't assume that every pain you have means you're dying of cancer, because you probably won't be," and he was very encouraging. Well, with all this assurance that I shouldn't live in fear, I'm learning to cooperate as much as I can, so I try not to worry. I don't think in terms of a long haul; my plans are made on a short-term basis, figuring ahead a year or so, thinking I will retire and live to a ripe old age possibly, but that on the other hand I might not. I'm kind of a fatalist. I always figure God has something in mind and whatever it is, it's all right with me.

You know if you're well organized, you can do anything. If you aren't organized, you can't get anything done. Some of the younger women I know are complaining about the idea that in order to achieve anything a woman is supposed to be superwoman, and yet maybe that's what we should encourage everybody to be—super people, men or women. But what it comes down to is somebody has to have the guts or nothing's ever going to change.

Divisions

In her interview, Catherine passed over a number of her important activities and involvements.[16] In 1971, when she returned to Milwaukee, she ran for the position of vice president in her CWA district. She was the first woman ever to run for the office and had she won the election, she would have become only the second woman ever to serve on the CWA national executive board. When she saw the incumbent, who was retiring, she asked for his support. He responded, "Catherine, I can't support you because I just don't think you're qualified. . . . I guess we all have our prejudices. But I can't see a woman on that board." Nevertheless, Catherine held to her belief that women had to compete or they wouldn't get anywhere. She lost the election overwhelmingly and was very disappointed, especially that the women didn't support her. She ran again and lost, but not as badly, and then she was elected the first woman to the Wisconsin State AFL-CIO executive board.

In 1974 the union appointed a man as Wisconsin state director of the CWA. Catherine had seventeen years of staff experience compared with his one, and they had similar experience in local union affairs. She filed a sex discrimination charge with the state. She was reluctant to talk about the charge, but she did say, "The charge is only to sensitize the leadership, not to hurt the union, but to make us better, because women just have to stand up for their rights." Edith Jones, then president of Catherine's old Local 5500, said, "Catherine has a way of making you believe in yourself. She encourages you by doing things that other people wouldn't have done. It took a lot of guts to file that charge, but that's Catherine. The only reason I can see for Catherine not getting it [the job] was because she was a woman. The situation doesn't reflect well on the union, but we have to put our money where our mouth is." Catherine didn't get the job, but she did reach a settlement with the union.

She continued her community involvement and was appointed by President Carter to his Advisory Commission on Women and to the Wisconsin Natural Resources Advisory Board. When she retired in 1982, the president of the CWA, Glenn Watts, spoke at the dinner honoring her.[17] After retirement, she was appointed by the governor to the Board of Regents of the University of Wisconsin, where she fought for issues such as collective bargaining rights for faculty.

Patsy Fryman reflected, "When Catherine was a feminist back in the early '60s, we all looked at her with a jaundiced eye. Many of us felt that she was sticking her neck out too far by being part of this radical group, the National Organization for Women, and vocally supporting women's rights, asking questions about why women weren't getting certain jobs, equal pay for equal work. Nobody was asking these questions but Catherine. She was way ahead of her time. It turned out that she was completely right and now we're all feminists."[18]

When Catherine died of cancer in 1989, Betty Friedan remembered her as a heroine. At her funeral mass, Sister Joel Reed, president of Alverno College, read the eulogy written by Kay Clarenbach: "Her enormous contribution, which has national implications, has been bringing together women and the labor movement and educating people that their goals are the same: a more humane, democratic society, one that's fair to everybody."

Chapter 12

People in the Plant Looked on Me as a Fighter

Alice Peurala, United Steelworkers of America (1928–1986)

Alice Peurala was a fighter and a persistent union and community activist. As a young woman in the early 1950s, she served as a union organizer while holding a series of low-paid jobs in clothing stores, small factories, and assembly plants. She joined the Congress on Racial Equality and participated in demonstrations to end segregation in lunch counters in downtown restaurants and department stores in St. Louis, where she was born and raised.

In her early twenties, she moved to Chicago despite her close-knit Armenian family's disapproval. When facing life with an alcoholic husband, she got a divorce and raised her daughter alone. Challenges continued after she was hired at the South Works plant of the U.S. Steel Corporation and joined Local 65 of the United Steelworkers of America (USWA), the union to which her father also belonged. She sued U.S. Steel for sex discrimination and won a promotion. An outspoken socialist, she worked closely with the Fight Back caucus in Local 65, challenging the local and the national leadership of the steelworkers' union and always pushing for more rank-and-file participation in union decision making. Her union activism increased, but she also continued to participate in civil rights, antiwar, and feminist movements.

In 1976 Alice was elected to the Local 65's grievance committee and became one of ten union grievers in South Works. In 1979, at age fifty-one, she was the first woman to be elected president of a USWA local union in the basic steel industry. She defeated two male candidates in the 7,500-member local. She served two terms as president and, though ill, was the first USWA woman to run for district director. In 1986 Alice died of cancer. She was described in the *Chicago Tribune* as a heroine to the plant's female workers. Some of the union men, the old timers, said, "That gal is the best griever we ever had."[1]

A Socialist Childhood

The second of four children, Alice was born on March 29, 1928, to Setrak Melikian and his wife Azniv, both Armenian immigrants. She grew up in a mixed working-class neighborhood in St. Louis, but spoke Armenian at home. She recalled that talk around the dinner table always concerned grievances and injustices at the plant where her father worked. "He gave a running commentary on whatever strikes might be in the news. No matter what, he always sided with the workers."[2]

My father was a tailor. He must have known tailoring before he was drafted into the Turkish army, because he made the officers' uniforms. There were a lot of Armenian fellows drafted into the Turkish army. During the Balkan Wars, the Turkish army was going to attack the Armenians. He escaped from the army and hid. He got a fake passport and all of that and came over here.

He went first to Worcester, Massachusetts, where he had a couple of half-brothers. Eventually he made his way to St. Louis. He met my mother there. He went to work in a foundry as a hand molder. He was there just a few years when he helped organize the steelworkers' union and was a shop steward. He worked there for forty-some years. Finally the place shut down, went bankrupt. But the workers never got pensions. This was years before workers had pensions. In the early days, there was no severance pay or anything like that. That was just the end of his paid work, so he went on social security.

My feelings about unions started with my father, who probably was a socialist. He had a great deal of dedication to working people and conscious-ness about the needs of the working people. He was also very sympathetic to the cause of the Soviet Union, because they gave the Armenians a home during the war with Turkey. I grew up in an atmosphere where I learned by being close socially and personally to people who were socialists of one kind or another, but not any particular group. Some of them were very anti–Communist Party. Some were anti–something else. But most of them were dedicated unionists who really believed that the working people's answer was in a strong labor movement.

We lived in a mixed working-class neighborhood—kind of German, En-glish, Irish—about two blocks from the Anheuser-Busch Brewery in St. Louis. My father owned a four-flat apartment building, and we lived in one of the apartments on the ground floor. We lived there until I got out of grade school, and then my father bought a house in a better residential neighborhood in South St. Louis, a $5,000 house.

At the end of eighth grade, when I was about fourteen, I started working as a cashier in a movie house. Then I worked summers in little two-by-four factories. One was a place where they made soles for shoes. It was a messy job. You did everything by hand. You cut out the soles and soaked them in different solutions. Your hands would get messy, and the solutions would smell terrible. It was probably dangerous to your health, but I didn't think it then, because we were making money. It was only young people working there. Then I worked in a venetian blind factory after school when I was in high school. I went at four and worked until ten every day and all day on Saturday. They made me an inspector on the afternoon shift and I got a little bit more money.

Early Activism

Alice's first job after high school was at a men's clothing store in the midst of an organizing campaign by the large amalgamated local of the Retail, Wholesale and Department Store Union (RWDSU). Under the leadership of Harold (Hal) Gibbons, a powerful and controversial St. Louis labor leader, Local 688 soon affiliated with the International Brotherhood of Teamsters. In the late 1940s, this local was considered a model of industrial and union democracy, studied by academics and visited by foreign observers on tour through the U.S. State Department.[3]

Local 688 was governed by a five-hundred-member stewards' council that approved all union expenditures and major programs. Members were offered free legal advice, a nonprofit grocery store, and unlimited medical care from fifty-seven part-time doctors affiliated with the union's Labor Health Institute (LHI). Attendance at union meetings was mandatory. All union officers and staff received the same salary and raises, set by a rank-and-file committee. The local was also active in desegregating St. Louis schools, restaurants, and other public accommodations. The union encouraged women's participation, and it was here that Alice honed her commitment to rank-and-file-based unionism while also developing her political activism.

After high school, I was working in this men's clothing store. I was a cashier and the hours were nine to five, with a half-hour for lunch. I was one of the few women there, because all the salesmen were men. The Retail, Wholesale and Department Store Union had just organized, and I joined the union.

Alice Peurala was first elected to the grievance committee of the United Steelworkers of America Local 65 in 1973. She was a strong advocate for change within the union, especially more rank-and-file participation. Chicago Sun-Times.

Shortly after I joined, that local split from the RWDSU international union and became an independent union. After about a year, they finally affiliated with the Teamsters' Local 688.

It was an amalgamated local. They had shoe factories organized and clothing stores, and others. There was a lot of attention given to women. I was encouraged by the officers and staff people of that union to become active. We were sent to labor schools and encouraged to come to classes at the union hall and to write articles for the paper. There were women officers, and women were part of the negotiating committees. I was on the negotiating committee. Every time there was a contract to be negotiated, there was always a negotiating committee elected in the plant that went with the staff man to negotiate with the company. He never went and negotiated alone. There was leadership by the staff guy, but there was not dominance.

They nominated me and I was on the board of the Labor Health Institute, which was a pretty good health-care kind of program that the union had negotiated with all the plants that they organized in St. Louis. They had doctors of every specialty who worked for various hospitals or had their own practices, and they came to the LHI one day a week. The employer paid about 5 percent of his payroll to the LHI board.

The leadership in that union was really concerned about building worker participation. They tried to develop people, and they practiced a great deal of democracy. They recognized the need to make the union strong and to have people know what was going on, and what their rights were. They really believed that the union was as strong as the people who were in it. They spent what money they had freely on the workers around them. They didn't live extravagantly. They were pretty regular people. I haven't had a lot of experience, but I think they were unusual leaders.

My friend, Bernice Fisher, was an organizer and also involved in the civil rights movement, in CORE, the Congress on Racial Equality, which was breaking down the barriers in public places. They had chosen a number of department store lunch counters for sit-ins. We would go every Saturday morning and every other seat at the lunch counter would have a black person, empty seat, white person, empty seat, black person, so that if you came in and sat down you would have to sit next to a black person. At the time, in the 1940s, these department store lunch counters would not serve black people.

At first people were startled, and there were some nasty comments by waitresses, and managers were kind of nasty. But we weren't hassled physically at all. Some pushing and bumping accidents and all, but customers did sit down and eat. The public reacted less negatively than the managements and waitresses. Eventually, we did succeed in desegregating Styx, Baer and Fuller, the Famous Barr lunch counters, and Pope's Cafeteria in downtown St. Louis.

I also belonged to the Armenian Youth of America, an Armenian youth organization that was part of the progressive wing of an Armenian group to which our parents belonged. This elder group was trying to get back the lands that Turkey had taken from Armenia during the wars. About this time, I attended the World Armenian Congress in New York. Being a progressive group, a bunch of us went to a Progressive Party convention in 1948 in Philadelphia, and Henry Wallace was nominated for President of the United States. While we were there, the *St. Louis Post-Dispatch* listed the names of

Alice Peurala arrives at union headquarters in 1979 after being elected president of United Steelworkers of America Local 65, the first woman to head a local unit in the basic steel industry. Chicago Sun-Times.

all the people from Missouri who had gone to the convention on the front page. When I got back, the guys in the union were a little upset, because it was supposedly such a left-wing group.

At this time, my friend Bernice had some conflicts with the Teamster union policies in our local. She thought they were doing some raiding of members in other unions. She resigned from the union staff and came to Chicago. After she found a place to live, I joined her. My parents didn't like it. They were very upset about my leaving St. Louis. I was just twenty-two years old. You know, Armenian girls stayed home until they got married, and you were looked at kind of funny if you left your family home before you got married. It just "wasn't right." But I left. I moved in with Bernice and went to work.

Chicago Organizing

For her first three years in Chicago, Alice continued her organizing activities by taking jobs at potential organizing sites. She was often fired when the company discovered her union activism. She clerked at a woman's apparel store in the Loop, where the RWDSU lost an election. She spent a short time working with other low-paid women in the hot, wet, back room of a South Side potato chip factory, and she bent over an assembly line in a candy factory boxing chocolates. Like Carmen Lucia, Dorothy Haener, and other organizers, she became familiar with employers' delaying tactics in union representation elections, the time-consuming process of filing unfair labor practice charges, and the resulting National Labor Relations Board hearings. Like Mary Callahan and Ah Quon McElrath, Alice felt the anti-union impact of the Taft-Hartley Act with its right-to-work provisions and requirements that union leaders sign anticommunist affidavits.[4]

My whole working experience involved the fact that workers need unions. I found everywhere I worked that conditions were bad, and the few places that I worked when I was younger, I knew that conditions were better where there were unions. I became very interested in organizing, getting workers into unions. I thought that was really the answer. Meeting staff people, or people who were active, in the union in St. Louis I learned a great deal about socialism. When I came to Chicago I met other people in CORE, who were doing work in the field of civil rights, who also seemed to have socialist tendencies. I don't think any of them belonged to any organization, but they had a socialist philosophy and I could buy a lot of their thinking. They seemed to be the kind of people I liked to be around and to work with, because they were doing something for working people.

The International Union of Electrical Workers (IUE) was an organization that came into being in 1949, after the parent CIO body had expelled a number of unions, including the United Electrical Workers (UE), because they were accused of being communist dominated. They were interested in organizing some of the plants that had been sort of disenfranchised. The Stewart Warner plant in Chicago had been organized by the UE but they lost an election to the IBEW, the International Brotherhood of Electrical Workers, a union for contractor electricians. The IBEW got pretty good conditions for electricians as craftsmen, but in the plant they were mostly thought of as a company union.

I met an IUE organizer who was in Chicago, and he asked me if I would help him by going to work in the Stewart Warner plant. It would be a big plum for the IUE; there were five or six thousand people working there. I went and got a job in the plant and was there for a couple of years during the whole organizing campaign. I was part of the rank-and-file organizing committee that we formed. We rented a storefront and had regular rank-and-file weekly meetings.

We got enough cards signed through the rank-and-file committee, and just before we petitioned the NLRB for the election, the company fired me for allegedly being a Communist Party organizer. I was working at my machine one day, and two security guards came up and said that W. W. Miller, the company's chief personnel guy, wanted to see me. So I went down to his office. He said they had information leading them to believe that I was a Communist Party organizer from St. Louis and they wanted to know if there was any truth to it. I said, "No, of course not." "Well, okay, we just wanted to know because that's what we have been told." So they let me go back to work.

Then about a week later they came again and took me to his office and said, "We would like to know if you would sign this affidavit or not." I remember what the affidavit said. "I'm not a member of the Communist Party and I don't believe in any of its programs and policies, etc." So I just scratched out everything else in the affidavit except the part that said, "I'm not a member of the Communist Party," and signed it and went back to work.

Three days later, they called me down again, and they said, "You know we really have to trust our information." I said, "Well, who's telling you this?" They said, "We can't divulge that, but we would like you to take a lie detector test to validate your affidavit." I talked it over with some of my friends and they said, you know, the company's just out to get you and there's just a limit to what you can compromise yourself about. So I refused to take the lie detector test. They fired me! They gave me a letter, which I still have, which says that it is the policy of the corporation to give lie detector tests and I had refused, so that was the end of my employment with the corporation. I went immediately down to the NLRB and filed an unfair labor practice charge. The official IUE organizer went down with me, and the charge was signed by the international union as well as myself.

I don't know what the hell it was. Probably my going to the 1948 Progressive Party convention in Philadelphia. I never found out. W. M. Miller was supposed to be the real communist fighter in Chicago, and he named me in newspaper articles as being a communist. The company tried to take advantage of this UE-IUE conflict and confused the whole thing. A new guy from the international IUE, who was in there as an organizer supposedly to help us, tried to get rid of me at that point. But I was secretary of the rank-and-file committee and the committee stood behind me.

We went on organizing during this time. We filed our petitions for the election; we leafleted the plant and had demonstrations there. We had all kinds of help from the other plants that were already organized. The footgear company guys used to come out at three or four o'clock in the morning and play poker until it was time to help us put out union leaflets. We got a lot of help from the UAW people. We had the election and it was between the International Association of Machinists (IAM), the IBEW, and the IUE. No one got a clear majority, so we had to have a second election between the IBEW and the IUE.

It was a month between elections and we really needed to put on a big organizing campaign. The company threw in another plant. We had organized the workers in one plant, and then the company threw in a television or radio plant. So between the time we got the date of the election, we had to go over and organize at this other plant too. It was pretty difficult because it was very, very hard in just a few weeks to try and organize another plant. We lost the second election. I was on unemployment compensation. The IUE assistant director used his expense money to give me carfare and buy me lunches and dinner. There were a couple of staff guys there who took care of my day-to-day expenses.

Then for three or four weeks I worked in a candy factory. All women workers. It was around Easter time because we were packing chocolate-covered Easter bunnies. Because I was a new employee, I was put on the end of the line. This was a belt. It came out of the room where the candy was made and the belt carried rows and rows of these little chocolate-covered bunnies.

It was piecework, and the older women who had the seniority were at the head of the line. They were first, second, third and fourth, and I was like about eighth, near the end of the line. They were standing on both sides of this belt, and you picked up the candy and threw it in boxes. I'll never forget how amazed I was at these women, the way they picked up the candy between the thumb and first finger, like a machine, and dropped them in the box. They never missed. Rolled their hands and then dropped the candies right in the box.

When it got to me, there was one bunny left, so it was very hard for me to make any money on piecework. The packing I did, it was all bending over, because you had to reach over for the last ones. After a couple of weeks, my back was absolutely breaking. During the five- and ten-minute breaks we'd have, I'd try to stretch and exercise a little, because my back was so sore. I remember looking up at the head of the line and those women that had been there like for fifteen years, every one of them were hunched over. They were permanently hunch-backed. It was a union shop, but I thought, God, it's a good thing for me to get out of here.

The South Works Plant

In 1953 Alice was hired at the South Works plant of the U.S. Steel Corporation, a large, hundred-year-old steel mill in South Chicago that employed nine thousand well-paid union workers and, in those years, made record profits for the parent company. Alice was a member of Local 65 of the United Steelworkers of America in one of the jobs that women had gained access to during World War II. Before the war, the only jobs women held in the basic steel industry were the sorting and inspecting of tinplate. By 1943 they were employed in almost every division in a wide range of jobs that included crane operators, inspectors, and pumpmen. As in the auto and electrical industries, after the war, the women were laid off to create openings for the returning veterans.[5] In 1954 Alice married a former merchant seaman of Finnish descent who worked in Chicago as a carpenter. They met through friends in the socialist movement and a year later, her daughter, Jami, was born. They soon divorced, however, and Alice said, "I was never one of those people who say you have to have a guy support you. I've supported my daughter and myself."[6]

I found the steel mill very interesting when I first went in, very unique. It was a challenge in a way. Women had been hired in the steel industry during the war and there were some left, but many of them had gone. I didn't think too much about my being in a plant that was mostly men, except that there were men on the job who still felt that women didn't belong in the steel mill and said so. But on the whole, most of the men were okay.

I was a metallurgical observer. When they hired me they told me they had hired women in that particular occupation during the war. There were two other women on that job. There were other women who were either pit recorders, ingot buggy operators, or oilers. A lot of them were oilers. They had stayed since the war.

When I was new there, it was strange. In the beginning, I really needed help to get along and to make it. I had the kind of job where I had to keep logs on the steel that came into the rolling mill. I worked in the beam mill, and you really had to get along with the men in order to do your job effectively. I was fortunate. I had some marvelous bosses. The metallurgical foremen that I had were very good, and the pit foremen who were not my direct bosses were pretty good guys on the whole.

I worked for five months during my pregnancy and had four months when I was off. I remember wanting to work, but the company rule then was that you couldn't work any longer than four months if you were pregnant. Of course I didn't tell them I was pregnant until I was pregnant already a month. I went back to work when the baby was about two months old. Layoff for pregnancy was not covered by state unemployment benefits.

I would attend union meetings sporadically. I was working a swing shift, and I had a daughter. That made it almost impossible for me to go to meetings. It was hard. My daughter was two months old and my husband happened to be alcoholic and I didn't trust to leave my baby at home alone with him. I mean, I had tried it and I would leave for work at eleven o'clock at night and he thought it was okay to go down to the corner bar. I would call home sometimes and there was no answer and I would be frantic, wondering if he was going to come home or if my baby was safe.

I finally hired a baby-sitter. I would just bundle Jami up in the car and take her over to the baby-sitter in the evening, then go to work and pick her up in the morning. She'd be wide awake after that. I'd have to wait for her nap until I could go to bed. My husband didn't care. I paid the woman $22.50 a week. Baby-sitter costs amounted to about a third of my pay. When Jami was small it wasn't too hard, because babies sleep a lot. When they're little and can't crawl around yet, you can sleep even when they're laying in their beds awake. Eventually I ran into a woman who had been a high school teacher, and she used to come to my house to baby-sit, which made it very nice. She would come before I went to work. We got to be pretty good friends. If I worked nights, she'd just keep Jami at her house until one or two o'clock in the afternoon and then I would wake up and go get her. She eventually thought of Jami as her granddaughter. They were very close. I was fortunate. Myra was a grand person.

My daughter was about a year and a half old when Myra had to be put in the hospital. Most of the other women I worked with were married and had husbands. They had parents and relatives around. My problem was that all my family was in St. Louis. So I took my daughter to St. Louis while this lady was hospitalized for three months. She stayed with my mother until Myra came out of the hospital, and then I brought her back to Chicago.

When Jami started school, she would stay with Myra on weekends. I started Jami into a sort of private school when she was about six. They had semi-boarding facilities for a few kids. There were three or four little kids Jami's age and a couple of older kids. It was in a house and cost about $600 a year, plus so much per night if she stayed over. I would pick her up after school and bring her home for dinner and then about eight o'clock take her back to school.

Sex Discrimination

In 1967 Alice sued the U.S. Steel Corporation on charges of sex discrimination in employment, under Title VII of the 1964 Civil Rights Act, after her repeated attempts for promotion had failed and she had been passed over by less experienced men for a daytime job in the metallurgical laboratory. Alice first filed a grievance with the union and then filed a charge of discrimination with the U.S. Equal Employment Opportunity Commission, the agency established to implement the law. Finally, she went to court.[7]

From the time my daughter got to be school age, I had been trying to get a steady day job. I had heard that in the metallurgical division in one of the labs there were steady day jobs. I had been asking my boss for consideration for one of those jobs. They kept telling me that there weren't any openings, or that they had other people in mind for them. They never posted any of these jobs. You could never bid on them. You just didn't know about them. All of a sudden, somebody you are working with is moved up. When you inquired, you just got pretty vague answers.

Then the Civil Rights Act was passed in 1964, and I thought, here's my chance. In the fall of 1967 near the end of the year, a guy that I had broke in, who had about four years of service, was going to move up into the main lab. I asked my boss, and he said he didn't know anything about it. He finally admitted yes, it was true, my co-worker was going to go up there. Before the guy went on the job, I called the man who was in charge of hiring people for that job and asked him if I could be considered. He said, "No, we don't want any women on these jobs." I said, "But it's against the law, you can't keep me from any job because I'm a woman. Would you put that in writing?" He said, "No, I don't think so; I'll have to think about that." A few days later, the boss came over and told me that officially the reason I was not selected for that job was that I did not have the educational background and that I couldn't work overtime, and that there was heavy lifting on the job that I couldn't handle.

In the beginning of working on my case, I went to the union, to the union griever. The local union's seniority agreement was written in such a way that my job of observer was the only job in the seniority unit. All of the other jobs in metallurgical work were separate seniority units, and you couldn't go from one seniority unit to another seniority unit. But management could handpick employees for these jobs.

My claim was that if they could handpick a male, they could handpick a female. I wanted the jobs posted, and the griever said, "Morally you have the right; you should have the job. But contractually there is nothing we can do, because management is not violating the contract." He did have a meeting with management and told them that I had a moral right to this job. The company representative said, "Do what you want, but we're not violating the contract."

In the beginning of the contract it says there shall be no discrimination because of race, et cetera. After the Civil Rights Act was passed, the union added the word "sex" in there. They could have filed my grievance as sex discrimination under the contract. They either didn't think about it or didn't care about it. Nor were they interested in going to court with me. The local union people were not in the least bit interested.

So then I went down to the Federal Building and filed sex discrimination charges under the federal law. They proceeded to go to U.S. Steel and investigate my charges, and about six months later they wrote out a thing that said they felt there had been discrimination. They called me later and told me their decision. They found that the amount of overtime worked for a two-year period for the product testers, which was the job that I wanted, was a total of about two hours overtime. The educational level of the seven or eight product testers was all the way from grade school to two years of college. The heaviest piece of test steel that product testers had to lift weighed five pounds. EEOC felt there was something to my charges and they asked U.S. Steel to have a conciliation meeting. U.S. Steel refused.

The people at EEOC called me and said, "Now it's up to you to sue them." I told them, "How am I going to get a lawyer?" There's something in the law that says EEOC will supply you with a lawyer if they support your case. They sent me to a court-appointed group of lawyers that are there to defend people who need them. These lawyers were really mixed up. They thought I needed a lawyer to defend myself; they couldn't understand that I needed a lawyer to file an action. I met lawyers for about a week. One said I had a terrific case and he really wanted to get into it. It would cost me like $25 an hour. I said no, I could not afford that.

Finally I went back to him. He called me in the mill on a Monday and just took my name and enough information and ran down to the federal court without even meeting me again and filed the suit. I had thirty days after U.S. Steel's refusal to conciliate to file the civil suit. Saturday the thirty days was up, and he filed it on the Monday after. U.S. Steel went through about six months of challenging technically because of the tardiness of the filing. We had to meet and file all kinds of motions to justify why it was late. The judge finally agreed that he would hear the case and overruled the rest of those technicalities. Then it took like another six months to get it on the docket for a hearing.

The first response from people in the mill was, "They're going to fire you for filing suit. You know you can't beat city hall. U.S. Steel's too big a corporation." For the first six months after I filed my suit, I did have a little harassment from my boss in the sense of him trying to find something wrong with my work. But when you're on the job for fifteen years, you can do it with your eyes shut. I finally told him to quit trying to find fault with my logs, because he just wasn't going to find anything. He kind of smiled and said okay, and I was left alone.

Finally, in March of 1969, we had two days of trial before the judge on whether or not I was actually discriminated against because of my sex. That was really great! One of the other women came down to watch. I won because the boss had told me they didn't want any women on the job. When the boss got on the witness stand, my lawyer asked him if he interviewed me for the job. He said no, he had nothing to do with it. "Well, then how did you know about her educational background? Did you know that she had taken courses at Roosevelt University?" No, he didn't know any of these things. "Well, who did you interview for that job? Were they women, were they black, were they white?"

"Yes, they were white, three white males." He made the point that that was what the company wanted, and they just deliberately didn't even consider me. Management tried to say that they wanted people who had a certain educational background. Then he questioned them about the people who were in that job.

The judge finally told them that he believed there was a case, but he didn't want to rule on it. He wished the parties would come to some kind of understanding. The company agreed that the next time the job of product tester was available, they'd put me on it. I didn't like that, because I just figured they'll never ever need another product tester if they have to put me up there. The judge agreed that if there was any fussing around with this agreement, we could come into court and reopen the case within a two-year period.

I went back to work a little saddened but a little glad that we had won some kind of a concession. Then one good thing happened. My boss had some research that he wanted to do on the logs that we were keeping in the mill on steel yield. I would work for a week up in the conference room, which was up in the metallurgical lab building. One of the women came and showed me where the coffee pot was and introduced herself. Every day that week we talked, and eventually we talked about my case. I kept in touch with her after I went back to my regular job. She called me one day, and she said, "Listen, the steel analysts are down there doing product tester work. They're supervisors or bosses doing the product tester's job."

I called my lawyer and he called U.S. Steel's lawyer, and my lawyer went back to the judge. The judge got very mad at my lawyer and acted like he was persecuting U.S. Steel, but finally U.S. Steel's lawyer was called into court and told by the judge that if you keep futzing around there's going to be an order issued here. May 5, 1969, the company called me up and told me to come to work Monday morning in the lab.

When I finally got the job, I didn't need to be on steady days anymore. My daughter was about fifteen. But I think it encouraged women to fight back. And it was my case that forced the metallurgical division to combine some of these seniority units. After I went to work in the lab, they combined the seniority units and they began posting the job of product tester so that other women were able to come in after I did.

USWA Local 65

By 1972 the USWA was the second-largest union in America, with 1.4 million members and industrywide bargaining in four industries, including basic steel. A major problem for steelworkers, however, was the boom-bust cycle of employment and then layoff as steel companies stockpiled their products in anticipation of strikes. In 1973 the USWA president, I. W. Abel, signed the pioneering No-Strike Agreement with eleven large steel companies. The union agreed that there would be no national strikes if the company agreed to guaranteed wage increases and more stable employment. Insurgent rank-and-file initiatives challenging the national union leadership were spearheaded by Ed Sadlowski, the militant president of Local 65. He was elected director of Chicago's District 31, the largest in the union, overcoming strong opposition by the international union leadership headquartered in Pittsburgh. A coalition called Steelworkers Fight Back was formed and Alice, being well grounded in rank-and-file participation, joined the insurgents.[8]

There was a division in our local union between those members who supported the official candidate of the international union and the others who supported Eddie Sadlowski when he ran for district director. The local union executive board was split. Eddie was elected a director of USWA District 31. He was from our local, and it was an opportunity to get more democracy. Eddie was talking about union democracy and the rank and file running the union. There had been very little of that kind of activity in the district. I got involved because I thought that was an answer, to have more democracy: the right to vote on contracts; the right to vote on dues increases; more voice for the membership. That's what Eddie's movement represented.

It was important that the members have the right to nominate and select their candidates for the district office, rather than have the international union tell us who it was going to be, which is how it had been done in the past. The No-Strike Agreement was signed right after Ed fought and won his election as district director. We were organizing a districtwide organization to see what we could do about the No-Strike Agreement. There were union representatives from most of the big steel mills. It was the District 31 Committee. We put out a newsletter, and we tried to make contact with other steelworkers around the country. We had contact with RAFT—the Rank and File Team—a national organization of unions. There were a few people from the West Coast and a few people from the South. We had a conference once in Ohio and some meetings here in Chicago. We had a couple of lawyers who took an interest in the legality of the No-Strike Agreement. We went to court.

About fifteen of us signed the lawsuit against our international union officers for signing the No-Strike Agreement without the consent of the membership. The trial lasted three days. A bunch of us went to Pittsburgh to federal court. USWA president I. W. Abel had to explain how they negotiated this agreement, how it came about, how it was top secret, and how they were afraid it wouldn't pass if members knew about it. There were a lot of steelworkers in the courtroom from all around, and we had lawyers who donated a lot of time taking depositions. It was kind of exciting. But the judge ruled that the No-Strike Agreement was not against our constitution.

Alice In Wonderland

In 1970 women represented less than 7 percent of the steel industry work force, and the steelworkers' union reflected the industry employment pattern. With few women members, there were no women local union presidents, few women in other local union offices, and no women in national union leadership positions. Alice had received little help from the union for her sex discrimination suit against the company, and despite her support for the rank-and-file movement, there was no encouragement for her to win a leadership position in the local. She responded by becoming more active and developing a reputation as a tough advocate for members involved in workplace disputes. By this time her daughter was out of high school, sharing an apartment with another young woman and teaching modern dance. Alice reflected that they got along "pretty good," but commented that raising a child without a husband or family nearby had not been easy. "When Jami was a little girl, I used to take her with me to a lot of these meetings. I'm still trying to make up for the things she missed as a child. The guilt is always there."9

I began getting involved in our local, and I was going to union meetings. After my sex discrimination case was decided, I made a report to the local union membership meeting about my case and had written an article for our local union paper. In 1970, after I went to work up there in the lab, I first ran for recording secretary. I lost. I ran for griever with a small group, and we lost. In 1973, I ran for president of the local. I didn't win. Then in 1976 I ran for grievance committee. That's when I won. I'm a griever for division five. There's ten divisions and my division is the mason department, the metallurgical department, and a large portion of the yards and transportation area. They're mostly men. There's only 9 percent women in the basic steel industry. There's about 350 women and 7,000 to 8,000 men in my local.

Being a griever is very time consuming and it's very exhausting. When you're not working, you're fighting grievances for workers that are getting suspended and fired. You become very much involved in those human beings who are being fired and who need their jobs. You rack your brain to do your best in representing them, and it takes a lot out of you. You're also working within your union, trying to make your grievance committee more effective. I really felt strongly that I would win that election, but you don't know till you do. A lot of what I'd done and stood for and fought for in the union throughout the years had a lot to do with my ability to win that election. I have spent a lot of years in that union fighting for certain things. For example, we passed a lot of resolutions against the war in Vietnam, probably one of the few steelworkers' local unions that did. I felt pretty good about that. So many people that I personally like, and thought a lot of, really didn't believe it could be done.

In all the years that I was running for office, I don't believe there was ever any encouragement from union men. In fact, there was deliberate discouragement. I was constantly being told I couldn't possibly win an election in a plant with so many men. They said, "Quit trying. You're dreaming. You're being Alice in Wonderland. It's just not possible that men are going to vote for a woman. You got to go to a plant where there are a lot of women." When I won, they said it was an accident. Well, I ran against the male incumbent plus another man, three of us running for the job. I beat them both two to one so I guess there was something going.

Women in the Plant

By 1974 the USWA was actively involved in the complex process of ending job discrimination. The union signed a steel industry consent decree with nine major steel companies and the EEOC. Based in part on cases like Alice's, the agreement involved major revisions in the seniority system and setting goals for hiring and promoting women and minorities in higher-paying traditionally male jobs in the steel mills. The union negotiated and vigorously defended an affirmative action agreement with Kaiser Aluminum that Brian Weber, a white male, challenged as being reverse discrimination. The USWA and District 31 came out strongly for ratification of the Equal Rights Amendment. Between 1977 and 1979, the number of women in the steel industry increased by 20 percent. By the late 1970s, there were over five hundred women steelworkers in the South Works plant, and Alice was busy working with them.[10]

We began to develop a women's caucus shortly after I was elected to the grievance committee in 1973. Roberta Wood, the first woman on the Local 65 executive board, and I began talking about the need to get more women involved in the union, and we began working with some of the women in the mill. We'd been working with women anyway, and we were both at the founding conference of CLUW in Chicago. I was somewhat active around the abortion rights movement and some of the women's rights movement in Chicago.

We did form a Local 65 women's committee. Through pressure on the executive board our president did appoint a women's committee. We had hoped to have the women who were meeting select a chairman, but he appointed three women. One of them had been active in the group. The other two had not been, but they're good women. There was some resentment on the part of some of the women who had been meeting for months and hoping they could elect the committee members. We were talking about democracy and there they were appointed, but the tradition is that the president of our local union appoints the committees. But we have been able to work to a degree with the women.

The women wanted to try to improve the sanitary facilities in the mill. The locker rooms and toilets for women in the plant are really in pretty bad shape. There hadn't been any women there for so many years. Then after the consent decree, there was an influx of women because they had to hire a certain quota of women, a certain quota of blacks in certain areas, and in the apprenticeship program. A lot of young women came in and many of them are militant, young women, which is good. We made a list of conditions in the washrooms and gave it to the president of the local union and the chairman of the safety committee, and it was turned over to the grievance committee. We had asked as a local issue to have plant management recognize the women's committee as an official committee of the union, and to have management meet with the women's committee to discuss women's problems in the steel mill. Management turned that down.

Finally the assistant superintendent of the plant agreed to meet with three of the women. There were four of us, and it went very well. They had the company safety committee there and the head of personnel services. They hadn't really heard what some of the conditions were. I had a feeling they were going to seriously begin doing something. They agreed to tour all the women's washroom facilities. The company and union agreed that a woman could be part of the tour. He agreed that if we had an agenda beforehand he would meet with the women when they had particular problems.

That's real progress. It takes women being part of these committees, the grievance committee and the executive board, to make the union move on these issues. I'm the only woman on the grievance committee and Roberta's a trustee on the executive board. For the first time, they've appointed a woman to the union civil rights committee, a young black woman.

I believe it is necessary to pass the ERA. There was a time when I was not for it, when I believed it would take away some rights the women had, that the so-called protective legislation would be wiped out. But in my own case, the provisions of the so-called protective laws were used against me, the lifting and the overtime. None of it was true, but the company did use it to try to deny me the job of product tester.

I guess equality of opportunity on the job is the main issue women should work for: equality of opportunity and the union being effective and stopping the harassment of women by male bosses in the mill. You hear stories from some of the men who tell you how some of the women are being harassed. New women are being harassed by bosses so they'll quit. But many women are becoming more aggressive and militant and speaking up.

Her Last Years

In 1979 Alice was elected president of Local 65, the first woman in the United States to head a local union in basic steel. Running against two men, she polled a plurality of 1,205 votes to their 1,168 and 1,077. Some observers believe her victory was in part because women turned out in large numbers to vote for her. Others stress her reputation as a fighter, challenging the company on her own and other workers' behalf. Men in the local who supported her knew her reputation as a battling griever to whom they could turn if they had a complaint.

In an interview following her victory, she announced that she looked forward to improving the union as a fighting organization, declaring that the grievance committees had to battle the company to get decent working conditions in the plants. Then she added: "I did not win as a woman. I campaigned as a candidate who would do something about the conditions in the plant that affect 7,500 people— men and women. . . . People in the plant looked on me as a fighter. I think it demonstrates that the men in the plant will vote for someone who is going to fight for them, make the union work for them."[11]

She ran for reelection in 1982 and won a higher percentage of the votes than in 1979, but lost the election. She opposed the 1983 concessions in wages and working conditions that the international union had agreed to in the nationwide bargaining agreement with basic steel, and she long advocated changes in the union constitution to allow workers to vote on their collective bargaining contracts, rather than have them only approved by the international officers. She remained critical of union officers who discouraged rank-and-file participation in union affairs. On concessions she said, "They're telling workers that they've got to step back and do with less. What does that mean? Not having a car? Not being able to make payments on their house? Not being able to send their kids to college? Not having recreation? I thought that's what it was all about, to make the life of the worker decent and with the dignity and the ability to enjoy the things of society. . . . Now they're saying we've taken too much from the corporations. To me, that's reversing the goddamn ball of wax."[12]

Three years later, Alice ran again for the local's presidency and won by a large margin. Her victory, however, was short-lived. Despite the growth in wages and labor stability in the 1970s, the 1980s saw massive layoffs as mills shut down throughout the country and steel corporations demanded union wage and work-rule concessions. Production workers in basic steel declined from almost 900,000 in 1980 to less than 600,000 in 1990. USWA national membership dropped from almost one million in 1979 to fewer than 500,000 in 1989. Most of the recently hired women lost their jobs, along with thousands of men. In the greater Chicago area, 25,000 steelworkers lost their jobs between 1976 and 1986. Faced with foreign competition, changing technology, a deteriorating set of buildings, and the sending of steelwork functions and jobs to other countries, the number of workers at South Works dropped from 9,000 in 1953, when Alice was hired, to 772 by 1986. Politicians and consultants predicted that the South Works plant would be closed and razed. They proposed using the site as a casino, an airport, a sports stadium, or a golf course with condominiums.[13]

In the summer of 1985, Alice ran for director of USWA District 31, a district of 60,000 members, down from 90,000 in 1981. She was the first woman in the union to get on the ballot for regional director of the USWA and, if she won, would have been the first woman on the international union executive board. Despite her long record of militant activism and two terms as Local 65 president, she lost that election in a three-way race. Observers attribute this loss to the possibility that many male steelworkers would not vote for a woman to head their district, as well as to her relative lack of contract negotiating experience and her opposition to the USWA leaders in Pittsburgh.

In addition, at age fifty-eight, Alice was battling cancer. Undergoing chemotherapy with a portable catheter, she told the union men who wanted her to run for district director, "Look, I'm in treatment. I'm stable at the moment but I never know when it is going to go the other way. . . . I don't have to go to the hospital. It doesn't stop me. I'm out at the plant gates. I'm at meetings. It kind of tires me out, weakens me a little, but I've managed."[14]

Alice Peurala died in June 1986. In her obituary in the *Chicago Tribune*, she was described as "one of the most dynamic and controversial leaders in the national union . . . a heroine to the plant's female workers . . . and a forceful advocate of rank-and-file rights." To James Balanoff, former director of District 31, "she was a grand person to whom the working man and woman always came first."[15]

Postscript

Union Update

In the 1970s, the Amalgamated Clothing Workers of America merged with the Textile Workers Union of America to form the Amalgamated Clothing and Textile Workers' Union (ACTWU). In 1981, the United Hatters, Cap, and Millinery Workers International Union merged with the ACTWU. According to national staff, there are approximately 4,000 ACTWU members in the headwear industry today. ACTWU membership declined from 331,000 members in 1978 to 223,000 members in the 1990s. Women were 66 percent of the membership and held five of twenty-three seats on the national executive board.

By the 1990s membership in the International Ladies' Garment Workers' Union had declined to 175,000 members from 279,000 in 1978. Women represented 83 percent of the membership and held four of the eighteen seats on the executive board. On July 1, 1995, the ILGWU and the ACTWU merged to form the Union of Needletrades, Industrial and Textile Employees (UNITE), with 355,000 members. Women are an estimated 60 percent of the membership and hold ten of the forty-two seats on the executive board.

In 1995 the American Federation of Teachers has grown to over 900,000 members. Sixty-five percent of the members are women, and there are eleven women on the thirty-four-member national executive board.

The Communications Workers of America has grown from 443,000 members in 1973 to 600,000 members today. Half of the members are women, and they hold three of seventeen seats on the national executive council. The second-highest-ranking officer is Barbara Easterling, and she became the first woman to serve as secretary-treasurer of the AFL-CIO in 1995.

In the International Longshoremen's and Warehousemen's Union, membership has declined from 58,000 in 1973 to 44,000 current members. According to the national office in San Francisco, no statistics are kept regarding the number of women members, but there are two women serving on the eighteen-member executive board.

Membership in the IUE, the International Union of Electronic, Electrical, Salaried, Machine and Furniture Workers, has declined to 140,000, of whom 40 percent are women. There are three women on the thirty-member executive board.

The UAW, the United Automobile, Aerospace and Agricultural Implement

Workers of America, currently has 800,000 members. Twenty-two percent are women, and there is one woman on the eighteen-member executive board. The United Steelworkers of America (USWA) has about 560,000 members, and it is estimated that 15 percent are women. The number of women in basic steel is much smaller, however, because the number of production workers there declined from almost 400,000 in 1980 to fewer than 200,000 in 1992. There are no women on the national executive board. In 1995 the UAW, USWA, and the International Association of Machinists and Aerospace Workers (IAM) announced that they would merge over the next five years.

The United Farm Workers of America has approximately 20,000 members, according to national office staff. The union does not maintain information on women members, but three of the seven national executive board members are women.[1]

Notes

Chapter 2   *Lillian Herstein, AFT*

---

1. Lillian Herstein was interviewed in 1970–1971 by Elizabeth Balanoff, a labor historian at Roosevelt University in Chicago, for the Roosevelt University Oral History Project in Labor History in cooperation with the oral history project "The Twentieth Century Trade Union Woman." At the time of the last interview Lillian was eighty-five years old and had been retired from the Chicago school system for twenty years. Her papers, along with the archives of the Chicago Teachers Union, are held by the Chicago Historical Society. Additional information about Lillian can be found in two articles: Engelbrecht, "Lillian Herstein: Teacher and Activist," and Carol Kleiman, "Labor Is Lillian's Love," *Chicago Tribune*, September 5, 1971. The quote from *Life* magazine was included in Lillian Herstein's obituary in the *Federation News*, April 1983.

2. In its first four years, the AFT claimed 174 locals and approximately 9,000 members, according to Fink, *Historical Sketches*. Information about teacher unionism in Chicago and the United States can be found in the following selected sources: Murphy, *Blackboard Unions;* Johnson, *Teacher Unions in Schools;* Wrigley, *Class Politics and Public Schools;* and Eaton, *The American Federation of Teachers.* See also "171 Years of Teaching in Chicago: A Concise History of the Chicago Teachers Union and Public Education in the City of Chicago from 1816 to 1987" (Chicago: Chicago Teachers Union, AFT, 1987); and "AFT Bibliography," compiled by the Archives of Labor and Urban Affairs (Detroit: Wayne State University Press, 1980).

3. The WTUL brought together women from the leisure class and working class to address the concerns for women workers. The three-part program consisted of organizing women workers into trade unions, lobbying for legislation to regulate wages and hours, and developing education programs to educate women and men about the problems of working women. The national headquarters was founded in Chicago, with branches in cities such as Boston and New York, and in 1923 moved to New York City. WTUL received some financial support from unions and the AFL. For additional information on the WTUL, see the following selected sources: Orleck, *Common Sense and a Little Fire;* Kessler-Harris, "Rose Schneiderman"; Dye, *As Equals and as Sisters;* and Foner, *Women and the American Labor Movement.* The WTUL's educational activities and its training school for women organizers are detailed in Jacoby, "The Women's Trade Union League School for Women Organizers."

4. John Fitzpatrick was the charismatic and progressive president of the Chicago Federation of Labor from 1901 until 1946. He was also a leader of the Farmer Labor Party and a candidate for mayor of Chicago. His personal papers are in the Chicago Historical Society Archives. See Fink, *The Biographical Dictionary*, and Newell, *Chicago and the Labor Movement.* Additional information on the 1919 steel strike can be found in Brody, *Labor in Crisis.*

5. The Bryn Mawr Summer School for Women Workers, directed by Hilda Smith, was an eight-week summer program that included a variety of topics: composition, social history, public speaking, science, economics, and labor philosophy. The program followed no theory or dogma and was committed to freedom of discussion and teaching. Young women with at least two years of industrial experience who had completed six years of schooling plus some supplemental study, such as YWCA evening classes, were accepted each summer from 1921 to 1936, when the program ended. Additional information can be found in

Heller, "Blue Collars and Bluestockings." The film by Suzanne Bauman and Rita Heller, *The Women of Summer,* was named Outstanding Documentary by the Academy of Motion Picture Arts and Sciences, 1987, and is available from the Filmmakers Library, 133 East 58th Street, New York, N.Y. 10022, or can be rented from the AFL-CIO Film Department, 815 16th Street, NW, Washington, D.C. 20006.

6. A. Philip Randolph, born in 1898, was a co-founder of *The Messenger,* a magazine of black radical and social thought, and in 1925 became the general organizer for the newly formed Brotherhood of Sleeping Car Porters. Railroads were the single largest employers of black workers at the time. He became a leading spokesperson for black workers in the AFL and then the AFL-CIO until his death in 1979. For a summary of Randolph's life, see Harris, "A. Philip Randolph," and for a full-length study, see Anderson, *A. Philip Randolph.*

7. The Farmer Labor Party originated in Chicago in 1920 and was active until the late 1920s. In the 1930s, instead of a third party, the unions formed Labor's Non-Partisan League to unite progressive workers in support of Roosevelt. The political involvement of the unions in the league is chronicled in Fraser, *Labor Will Rule,* and information about the Farmer Labor Party is found in Weinstein, *The Decline of Socialism in America.*

8. Lillian also helped organize WPA adult education program teachers into a new local union, Adult Education Teachers of Chicago, Local 346 of the AFT, which elected Harold Gibbons as its first president in 1934. Additional information about WPA workers' education programs can be found in Kornbluh, *A New Deal for Workers' Education.* On activities of women, including Eleanor Roosevelt, in the New Deal years, see Orleck, *Common Sense and a Little Fire,* and Ware, *Beyond Suffrage.* Eleanor Roosevelt's membership and activism in the WTUL is mentioned in a number of her biographies, most recently by Cook, *Eleanor Roosevelt,* vol. 1.

9. Eula McGill from the Amalgamated Clothing Workers of America was one of the young women from the South who stayed at the White House. She was thrilled, but when she returned home, she found that the event had been written up in the local paper. She was fired and remained out of work for a year because of this union activity. See her interview in "Twentieth Century Trade Union Woman."

10. According to Eaton, *The American Federation of Teachers,* AFT members "who favored action against radicalism" supported Lillian's candidacy for AFT president. She lost the election by a vote of 336 to 274. See also Murphy, *Blackboard Unions,* chaps. 8–10.

11. AFT membership declined during the Depression, but 1973 the AFT reported 248,521 members in 1,032 locals, according to Fink, *Historical Sketches.* The difficulties of the public schools systems during the Depression are detailed in Tyack, Lowe, and Hansot, *Public Schools in Hard Times.* The Chicago public schools faced a severe financial crisis that continued until the federal government made massive loans to the city. Eaton highlights Lillian's role in soliciting "federal interest in the educational plight of Chicago" by using her longtime friendship with Secretary of the Interior Harold Ickes to make these contacts (Eaton, *The American Federation of Teachers,* 53).

12. Several Chicago AFT leaders were called to Washington to serve in federal government agencies during the war years. Analysis of the labor movement during World War II is found in Fraser, *Labor Will Rule,* and Goodwin, *No Ordinary Time.* Under the Community Facilities Act, known as the Lanham Act, signed by Roosevelt in 1942, nearly fifty million dollars was spent on child care for over a million and a half children by 1945 (Goodwin, 416–418).

13. The Jewish Labor Committee (JLC) was founded in New York City in 1934 to represent Jewish labor within the labor movement and the larger Jewish community. A major goal was to mobilize Jewish unions and progressive organizations to fight Hitler and fascism. The JLC joined forces with the Negro Labor Committee and other groups to develop the AFL and the CIO's human rights agenda both abroad and at home. See Malmgreen, "Labor and the Holocaust."

14. Kleiman, "Labor Is Lillian's Love." A second interview appeared in the *Topeka Daily Capital*, November 7, 1971.

Chapter 3   *Carmen Lucia, UHCMW*

1. Carmen Lucia was interviewed in 1976 by Seth Wigderson, a graduate student in labor history, and in 1978 by Bette Craig, co-director of the Labor Theater in New York City, for the oral history project "The Twentieth Century Trade Union Woman." At the time of the last interview Carmen was seventy-six years old and had retired from the UHCMW four years earlier. A third interview was done in 1976 by Howard Lackman and George Green and deposited at the Texas Labor Archives, University of Texas, Arlington. A fourth interview was done in 1978 by Faye Gamel, for her Georgia State University master's thesis, "The Hat Lady." The Carmen Lucia Papers are deposited at the Southern Labor Archives, Georgia State University. For additional information, see Bauman and Heller, *The Women of Summer*. A transcript and related papers from that film are held by Rita Heller, County College of Morris, Randolph, New Jersey. Carmen Lucia's daughter, Marge Whipple, was interviewed by Brigid O'Farrell for this book. Quotation: *Atlanta Journal*, July 30, 1947.

2. Sidney Hillman led the ACWA until his death in 1946. He pioneered innovative programs such as union-sponsored insurance programs, low-cost housing cooperatives, clinics, and recreational facilities for members, and co-founded Labor's Non-Partisan League. He also established the first political action committee for the CIO and took a leadership role in that organization. See Fraser, "Sidney Hillman," and Fraser, *Labor Will Rule*.

3. In the 1920s the YWCA recruited over thirty thousand participants in its programs in eight hundred YWCA industrial girls' clubs around the United States. Mary Frederickson concludes that the YWCA's experiments in workers' education reached more working women and affected more women's lives than did the educational efforts of any other contemporary organization. She also notes that by the late 1920s all the workers' education schools, including Bryn Mawr, looked to the YWCA as a "recruiting agency." See Frederickson, "Citizens for Democracy."

4. Heller, *Women of Summer*, transcript, 27. Several articles about the school appeared in the Rochester papers and are found in the Rita Heller material. For more information about the Bryn Mawr Summer School for Working Women, see Heller, "Blue Collars and Bluestockings."

5. The Neckwear Workers' Union was a federated local union, Local 11016, directly affiliated with the AFL. Affiliation with the Amalgamated Clothing Workers of America in 1935, with about 2,800 members, was reported to Brigid O'Farrell in a telephone conversation with Mike Donovan, librarian for the Amalgamated Clothing and Textile Workers Union, 1995.

6. Rose Sullivan was a vice president of the Telephone Operators' Department of the International Brotherhood of Electrical Workers (IBEW) in the 1920s and served as a business agent of the Boston Neckwear Workers' Union local during the 1930s. She was also a general organizer for the AFL. See Norwood, *Labor's Flaming Youth*.

7. Max Zaritsky was president of the Cloth Hat and Cap Makers of North America when they merged with the United Hatters of North America in 1934, and became the United Hatters, Cap and Millinery Workers' International Union. He became secretary-treasurer of the new union, but also retained the title as president of CHCM. He adopted Carmen as a protégé, and when he became president of the UHCMW in 1946, he urged that Carmen be elected vice president. See Gamel, "The Hat Lady," 33–34.

8. Gamel, "The Hat Lady," 39.

9. *Hat Worker*, September 15, 1960, in Gamel, "The Hat Lady," 95. Carmen was familiar with aggressive and often violent organizing experiences. She was beaten and jailed

by police and vigilantes. She herself taunted scabs, police, and employers, and in San Francisco, she encouraged the salesgirls to use their high heels on warehousemen crossing the picket line. She also had many experiences with company lawyers, unfair labor practice complaints, injunctions, court appearances, and all the more sophisticated antilabor activities that unions are faced with today. In response to the labor unrest following World War II, the Taft-Hartley Act was passed in 1947, as an amendment to the Wagner Act, to regulate unions more closely and allow states to adopt more restrictive laws against unions, the "right-to-work" laws. In 1959 the Landrum-Griffen Act also amended the Wagner Act, enabling the government to regulate union and management affairs more directly in an attempt to eliminate improper activities and provide some protection for union members. For summaries of these laws, see Gold, *An Introduction to Labor Law.*

10. In 1946 the CIO launched Operation Dixie to organize other southern industries, sending two hundred organizers to twelve southern states. The AFL also began to focus more on organizing in the South. For more on women and southern organizing, see Frederickson, "I Know Which Side I'm On," and for information about the union and the industry, see Fink, *Historical Sketches,* and Gamel, "The Hat Lady."

11. Gamel, "The Hat Lady," 70–71. This was considerably before the AFL-CIO and most other unions endorsed the ERA in the 1970s.

12. Under this State Department program, U.S. labor leaders went to other countries to talk to union people there about the trade union movement in the United States and to assess the effectiveness of the U.S. aid to those countries. Carmen went to France with J. William Belanger, president of the Massachusetts CIO Council and vice president of the Textile Workers Union, and Harold Gibbons, secretary-treasurer of the AFL Teamsters Local 688 of St. Louis. They concluded that the French program was not very effective in reaching the French trade unionists. For more information, see the Lucia interviews and Gamel, "The Hat Lady," 73–86.

13. Mark Temple, "Labor Circles Give Nod to Miss Lucia's Hats," *Atlanta Journal,* July 30, 1947, Rita Heller materials.

14. Andy Smith, D & C staff writer, St. Anne's Nursing Home, 1980, Rita Heller materials.

15. Hats and fashions, and especially the seven hats Carmen brought to the national AFL convention, one for each convention day, are discussed in Earl Almquist, "Delegate Brings Seven Hats to AFL Convention," *St. Paul Dispatch,* October 5, 1949, Georgia State University Special Collections, Carmen Lucia Papers, 683/15.

16. "Carmen Lucia Acclaimed at G.E.B. Dallas Meeting," *Hat Worker,* n.d., Rita Heller materials.

17. Bauman and Heller, *Women of Summer.*

18. Information about Carmen's love of hats comes from Almquist, "Delegate Brings Seven Hats to AFL Convention," but the idea of the literal and figurative hats that Carmen wore is presented in Gamel, "The Hat Lady," 6.

Chapter 4   *Esther Peterson, ACWA*

---

1. The first interview documenting Esther Peterson's labor career was conducted in 1978, by Martha Ross, an oral historian at the University of Maryland, for the oral history project "The Twentieth Century Trade Union Woman." Esther was then seventy-two years old and serving in the administration of President Jimmy Carter as head of the Office of Consumer Affairs. In 1992 and 1993, four more interviews with Esther Peterson were conducted at her home in Washington, D.C., by Joyce L. Kornbluh, Brigid O'Farrell, and Suzanne Moore, for this book. An earlier revised version of this chapter appeared in Kornbluh and O'Farrell, "You Can't Giddyup by Saying Whoa." For additional information, see the

U.S. Department of Labor, *Milestones*, and Halamandaris, "A Tribute to Esther Peterson." The Esther Peterson papers are available at the Schlesinger Library, Radcliffe College, Cambridge, Massachusetts. Other members of the Amalgamated Clothing Workers interviewed for "The Twentieth Century Trade Union Woman" project include Fannie Allen Neal (Chapter 9) as well as Sara Barron, Mary Lawrence Elkuss, Sara Fredgant, Eula McGill, Julia Maietta, Barbara Merrill, Dolly Lowther Robinson, Frieda Schwenkmeyer, and Barbara Wertheimer.

2. For more information on Käthe Kollwitz, a German artist, see Renate Hinz, *Käthe Kollwitz: Graphics, Posters, Drawings* (New York: Pantheon, 1981).

3. The Federal Emergency Relief Act was signed by President Roosevelt in 1933. According to Foner, *Women and the American Labor Movement* (292), direct relief for the unemployed was supplemented by several work-relief projects, including the Civilian Conservation Corps (CCC) and the Works Project Administration (WPA).

4. Homework provided a very cheap source of labor, mostly women and children who were paid on a piecework basis and were very difficult to organize into unions. From New York to Texas, families were engaged in work such as hand sewing, making artificial flowers and jewelry, and shelling pecans. Homework has been a controversial form of employment for most of this century. For a discussion of historical and contemporary issues, see Boris and Daniels, *Homework*.

5. An in-depth analysis of Fannia Cohen, a vice president of ILGWU, and Rose Schneiderman, president for many years of the New York WTUL, and their work as union organizers and worker educators is found in Orleck, *Common Sense and a Little Fire*. For more information on the BMSSWW, see Chapters 2 and 3; Heller, "Blue Collars and Bluestockings"; and Bauman and Heller, *The Women of Summer*.

6. Foner, *Women and the American Labor Movement*, 199.

7. J.B.S. Hardman emigrated from Russia and in 1911 began his lifelong career as editor, writer, and labor intellectual. He was the ACWA's first educational director and ran an ambitious program in the 1920s. When education failed to transform study into social action, the program dwindled. The ACWA education department was revitalized in the 1940s to train the new, more diverse union members in the functional aspects of trade unionism. For discussion of the changes in workers' education, particularly in the ACWA and the ILGWU, see Wong, "From Soul to Strawberries," and Orleck, *Common Sense and a Little Fire*.

8. In 1944 Rose Pesotta resigned as vice president of the ILGWU and went back to the garment factories, protesting the fact that women, who made up the majority of the union membership, were limited to one seat on the ILGWU executive board. Her union career and the Mode O'Day campaign in both California and Utah are described in her autobiography, *Bread Upon the Waters*.

9. Sidney Hillman's extensive involvement with the Roosevelt administration and Democratic politics are the focus of Steven Fraser's book, *Labor Will Rule*. See also Chapter 3, note 2, above. There is no comprehensive biography of Bessie Abromowitz Hillman, who helped found the ACWA with her husband and later served as a vice president, and her complicated relationships with both her husband and the union. She is barely mentioned in the Fraser book.

10. In 1938 the first minimum wage rate was 25 cents an hour and covered 43 percent of workers. During Esther Peterson's lobbying years, the minimum rate increased four times, from 45 cents and 55 percent of workers in 1945 to $1.15 and 62 percent of workers in 1961. See Ehrenberg and Smith, *Modern Labor Economics*, 69. For an interesting account of the early lobbying days, see John W. Edelman's autobiography, *Labor Lobbyist*.

11. Senator Joseph McCarthy was chairman of the Senate Government Operations Subcommittee on Investigations. At the height of the anticommunism hysteria and the

development of the Cold War in 1950s, he used his broad mandate to subpoena government employees, including members of the Foreign Service as well as members of the labor movement and many other citizens across the country. Esther relates a little more about this period in Fenzi, *Married to the Foreign Service*, but her family's experiences with McCarthyism were clearly difficult for her to discuss even in 1994.

12. At the outbreak of World War I, Women-In-Industry Services (WIS) was established as a temporary agency in the War Department to "insure the effective employment of women while conserving their health and welfare." WIS was transferred to the U.S. Department of Labor and in 1920 became a permanent agency called the Women's Bureau. See the U.S. Department of Labor, *Milestones.*

13. The Kennedy Commission is described by Flora Davis in her analysis of the women's movement since 1960, *Moving the Mountain*, as a window of opportunity opening up for feminists. The commission, with seven working committees involving hundreds of people, debated a wide range of issues affecting women at home and at work. An equal rights amendment, protective legislation, and equal pay were discussed at length. The final report made twenty-four recommendations, listed in the U.S. Department of Labor, *The American Woman.* The commission supported equal pay for comparable worth, not the more limited equal pay for equal work concept, but recommended that a constitutional amendment for equal rights not be pursued at that time. Based on the report, Kennedy established an ongoing organization to continue its work, the Citizens' Advisory Council on the Status of Women, and a network of state commissions developed.

14. On March 15, 1963, the Eighty-Eighth Congress began hearings on the Kennedy administration's Equal Pay Act, H.R. 4269, introduced by Congressman Adam Clayton Powell (Democrat, New York), and H.R. 3861, introduced by Congresswoman Edith Green (Democrat, Oregon). These were companion bills "to prohibit discrimination on account of sex in the payment of wages by employers engaged in commerce or in the production of goods for commerce and to provide for the restitution of wages lost by employees by reason of any such discrimination." The first two witnesses were the Honorable Willard Wirtz, secretary, and the Honorable Esther Peterson, assistant secretary, U.S. Department of Labor.

Congresswoman Green had been introducing her legislation since 1945. Esther Peterson noted that the principle was first written into law in 1870 for federal employees, but not fully implemented until the Classification Act of 1923; her testimony that day was accompanied by forty pages of charts and tables documenting the economic indicators, state court cases, and collective bargaining agreements related to the Equal Pay Act. See the *Equal Pay Act, 1963, Hearings.*

15. In this section, the interviews with Esther Peterson were supplemented with the draft text of two unpublished speeches, one in the early 1980s and the other for a Women's Bureau conference held in Washington, D.C., October 22, 1990. These were provided by Ruth Shinn, Women's Bureau, U.S. Department of Labor, 1993.

Chapter 5   *Maida Springer-Kemp, ILGWU*

1. The first interview documenting Maida Springer-Kemp's labor career was conducted in 1977 by Elizabeth Balanoff, a labor historian at Roosevelt University in Chicago, Illinois, for the oral history project "The Twentieth Century Trade Union Woman." Maida was sixty-seven years old at the time and working with the African-American Labor Center. Excerpts from the Balanoff interview are found in the "Black Women's Oral History Project," published by K. G. Saur, Schlesinger Library, Radcliffe College, Cambridge, Massachusetts. In 1994 an additional interview with Maida Springer-Kemp at her home in Pittsburgh, Pennsylvania, was conducted by Brigid O'Farrell for this book. Related articles include the African-American Labor Center, *AALC Reporter*, vol. 27, no. 4, 1992, and vol. 28, no. 1, 1993; and ILGWU, *Justice*, February 1986. Maida Springer-Kemp's papers are available at the

Schlesinger Library and the Amistad Center, Tulane University. The interview quotations in this chapter are edited from these oral history interviews and articles. An earlier version of this chapter appeared in O'Farrell and Kornbluh, "We Did Change Some Attitudes." Other members of the International Ladies' Garment Workers' Union interviewed for "The Twentieth Century Trade Woman" project include Evelyn DuBrow, Elizabeth Kimmel, Pauline Newman, and Bonnie Segal.

A very important resource has been Yevette Richards, *"My Passionate Feeling about Africa,"* vols. 1 and 2. This doctoral dissertation provides over nine hundred pages on Maida Springer-Kemp's life, with seven chapters of background and analyses alternating with seven chapters of Dr. Richards's in-depth interviews with Maida. Richards concludes, "This biography enriches the scholarship on pan-African, labor, and women's histories and demonstrates the ways in which international labor relations, pan-Africanism, African independence movements, the United States Civil Rights movement, and Cold War politics are intertwined" (Richards, 22). She concludes, "This collaborative work demonstrates the power of her oral testimony to reshape our understanding of the past" (Richards, 891).

2. The garment industry in New York, the growth of the ILGWU, and their relationship to the Communist Party is described by Foner in *Women and the American Labor Movement.* The ILGWU's education program to train these new workers changed from "workers' education," focused on the broad concept of changing society and exemplified by the WTUL and Bryn Mawr Summer School for Women Workers, to the more narrowly focused "labor education," training workers in how to run a union. See Wong, "From Soul to Strawberries," and Orleck, *Common Sense and a Little Fire.*

3. Charles "Sasha" Zimmerman emigrated to the United States in 1913. A member of the Communist Party, he was expelled from the ILGWU in 1925. He was reinstated in the union in 1931, and served as a vice president of the union and general manager of the New York Dress Joint Board from 1934 until he retired in 1972. Luigi Antonini was general secretary of ILGWU Local 89 and vice president of the union from 1934 to 1967. See Fink, *The Biographical Dictionary.*

4. The American Labor Party (ALP) and Labor's Non-Partisan League (LNPL) were formed in the 1930s by the leaders of the ILGWU, the ACWA and several other unions to help unite progressive people in support of Franklin D. Roosevelt. Although Maida did not seriously want to run for office, she became the first trade union member nominated from a Harlem district and won the primary on the ALP ticket. See Richards, "My Passionate Feeling," chap. 3, and "Maida Springer Represents New Type Leader Harlem Could Use," *New York Amsterdam News,* 1942, Maida Springer-Kemp Papers, box 1, folder 8, Schlesinger Library.

5. Richards provides a detailed history of the African-American labor movement in Harlem. Chapter 2 deals with "the strong connections between the ILGWU leadership and the anticommunist black civil rights and trade union leadership" (173). In 1935, 110 black and white AFL delegates organized the Negro Labor Committee, which offered organizing and education programs for the African-American community at its headquarters, the Harlem Labor Center. Competing programs were offered by the Garveyite Harlem Labor Union, the Father Divine Movement, and the communist-run Negro Labor Victory Assembly. The Hudson Shore Labor School was an interracial workers' education institution established in 1935 by Hilda Worthington Smith as a continuation of her work as director of the Bryn Mawr Summer School for Women Workers.

6. Richards, "My Passionate Feeling," 247.

7. For additional information on A. Philip Randolph and the rally, though not Maida's role, see Chapter 2, note 6; Anderson, *A. Philip Randolph;* and Harris, "A. Philip Randolph." The complicated fight by Randolph and the African-American community to end discrimination and achieve equality in employment in government, the military, and the private sector during World War II is also described by Goodwin in *No Ordinary Time.*

8. Richards, "My Passionate Feeling," 259. Edith Ransome was the first black business agent and the first African-American staff member of Local 22. She settled prices for finishers, but was not responsible for a district.

9. Richards, "My Passionate Feeling," 1.

10. Esther Peterson worked with Maida in New York and in 1951, when Maida went to Scandinavia, she stayed with Esther and Oliver Peterson in Sweden. Dolly Lowther Robinson was an activist laundry worker with the ACWA, who later worked with Esther at the U.S. Women's Bureau, was active with Maida at the National Council of Negro Women, and went on to receive a law degree and teach. Pauline Newman was one of twenty thousand shirtwaist workers in New York City who went on strike in the winter of 1909–1910, an event referred to as the Uprising of the Twenty Thousand. She witnessed the Triangle Shirtwaist Company fire in 1911, in which 146 workers, mostly women, were killed. She worked for the ILGWU until the 1980s. Fannia Cohn was the first female vice president of an international union and spent her long career in the education department of the ILGWU. Rose Schneiderman was an organizer for the ILGWU and then served as president of the WTUL from 1926 until it disbanded in 1950. Orleck's *Common Sense and a Little Fire* is a collective biography of these three women and Clara Lemlich Shavelson, who turned from the unions to the Communist Party and organizing neighborhood coalitions of housewives. The "Twentieth Century Trade Union Woman" project includes interviews with Dollie Lowther Robinson and Pauline Newman as well as Esther Peterson (see Chapter 4).

11. The importance of this event, and the luncheon honoring Maida, are described in "Women Labor Leaders Are Going to England in Good-Will Exchange with Four from There," *New York Times*, January 10, 1945, as well as the *New York Amsterdam News*, February 1945, Maida Springer-Kemp Papers, box 1, folder 8, Schlesinger Library. Julia Parker's early involvement with the telephone workers is discussed in Norwood, *Labor's Flaming Youth*.

12. The International Confederation of Free Trade Unions was established in 1949 in London, when many democratic unions left the communist-dominated World Federation of Trade Unions.

13. A review of the labor movement's long, complicated, and sometimes controversial history in the international arena is beyond the scope of this chapter. It is clear, however, that unions considered dominated by the Communist Party were forced out of the AFL and CIO federations after World War II and that during the Cold War, the AFL-CIO's international initiatives were guided by a strong anticommunist policy that coincided with the foreign policy of the U.S. government. Maida had rejected the communists organizing in Harlem during the 1930s, worked closely with the leadership of the ILGWU, and supported the AFL-CIO policies during the Cold War.

14. Richards, "My Passionate Feeling," 14.

15. Tom Mboya became the general secretary of the Kenya Federation of Labor in 1953. He was assassinated on July 5, 1969, leaving Jomo Kenyatta, whom Maida had met in 1945, the undisputed leader of Kenya. See Goldsworthy, *Tom Mboya*, and "Tom Mboya: In Memoriam," by Maida Springer-Kemp, *AFL-CIO Free Trade Union News*, August 1969 (in Richards, "My Passionate Feeling," 682).

16. During a 1958 strike, for example, she was described as a "militant Black woman" who told the strikers, "Our union will tolerate no gunka-munka business in the enforcement of future contracts!" Gunka-munka, described by President Dubinsky as a blend of dilly-dallying and monkey business by chiselers on the employer side, became the strike slogan of the 105,000 striking dressmakers. See Sugarman, "Echoes on Papers."

17. The United Nations declared 1975 International Women's Year (IWY) and convened a major conference in Mexico City. Six thousand women attended the meetings organized by the nongovernmental organizations to give women more access to the formal UN pro-

ceedings. In conjunction with IWY, the United States held a series of state meetings and a conference in Houston, Texas in 1977. See Davis, *Moving the Mountain.*

18. Richards, "My Passionate Feeling," 850, letter from Springer-Kemp to Dubinsky, November 23, 1965.

19. Formation of the National Organization of Women and the Coalition of Labor Union Women is discussed in Chapters 6, 8, and 11.

20. Richards also traveled to Africa with Maida and interviewed several people familiar with Maida's life and work. For an analyses of union policy and South Africa, see "My Passionate Feeling," chap. 6.

21. Richards, "My Passionate Feeling," 518.

Chapter 6   *Mary Callahan, IUE*

1. Mary Callahan was interviewed in 1976, first by Alice Hoffman and Karen Budd, labor educators at the Pennsylvania State University, for the oral history project "The Twentieth Century Trade Union Woman." Karen Budd then did two additional interviews. This was the year before Mary retired from the IUE, when she was sixty-two years old. Articles about Mary's union work are found in the *IUE News*, IUE, Washington, D.C. Also see the booklet for young students by Alice Hoffman, "Sing a Song of Unsung Heroes and Heroines," Department of Urban Studies, Pennsylvania State University, 1986.

2. To place Mary Callahan's story in the larger context of women in the electrical industry, see Milkman, *Gender at Work.* For general background and analysis of the electrical industry, the United Electrical, Radio and Machine Workers of America (UE), the International Union of Electronic, Electrical, Salaried, Machine and Furniture Workers (IUE), and the issue of communism, which dominated much of the early days of both unions, see Schatz, *The Electrical Workers.*

3. James B. Carey, only twenty-five when elected president of the UE, became secretary-treasurer of the newly formed Congress of Industrial Organizations two years later. He was described as the new unionist, young, personable, and not linked to the left or communism. He was defeated as UE president in 1941. See Schatz, *The Electrical Workers,* 97.

4. Milkman, *Gender at Work* (89), concludes that the UE was the most progressive union at that time in developing women in leadership roles and in fighting for equal pay for equal work clauses in its contracts.

5. Both Milkman, *Gender at Work,* (102), and Schatz, *The Electrical Workers,* (121), document studies finding that after the war, women overwhelmingly wanted to stay at work and in nontraditional jobs and that the unions were ambivalent about helping them.

6. For more information on demobilization and the 1946 strike, see Schatz, *The Electrical Workers,* chap. 7.

7. Fink, in *Historical Sketches,* reports that passage of the Taft-Hartley Act in 1947 further exacerbated the communist issue in the UE. Initially, both the CIO and the UE boycotted the section of the act requiring union officers to sign affidavits disavowing that they were members of the Communist Party. By the 1950s both the CIO and the UE had acceded to the requirements.

8. Elections were held all around the country at UE locals, and the IUE emerged as the dominant union in the electrical industry. A very active minority, however, voted for the UE, which continues to represent workers in some plants throughout the United States. In 1955, during the McCarthy era, the Justice Department charged the UE with communist infiltration, but four years later a federal court dismissed the charges. UE headquarters are in New York City.

9. *IUE NEWS,* May 23, 1955.

10. As of 1979 Evelyn McGarr was the second most senior member of the IUE executive board, having served as District of Canada secretary-treasurer for twenty-five years. She was also former president of Local 513. *IUE NEWS*, October 1979.

11. See Chapter 4 and also Davis, *Moving the Mountain*, and the U.S. Dept. of Labor, *The American Woman*.

12. Title VII of the Civil Rights Act of 1964, as amended, is the basic law against employment discrimination, prohibiting discrimination on the basis of race, color, religion, sex, or national origin, and now age. Affirmative action is permitted by Title VII, but never required, to enable employers to take specific actions to increase the number of women and people of color in a work force. The Equal Employment Opportunity Commission is the federal agency established to investigate and resolve claims of discrimination. For an overview of this now very complex set of laws, see Gold, *An Introduction to the Law of Employment Discrimination*. Flora Davis provides more information on the inclusion of sex in the law and the invalidation of the protective laws. She concludes, "It is impossible to overemphasize the significance Title VII had for women." *Moving the Mountain*, 39.

13. *IUE NEWS*, December 3, 1970.

14. For a description of the IUE's efforts on behalf of women workers, including the Title VII Compliance Program, see G. Johnson, "Unions and the Gender Wage Gap—Comments." A very useful review of the early union litigation in Title VII cases is found in Newman and Wilson, "The Union Role in Affirmative Action." During this period Winn Newman was general counsel for the IUE and Carol Wilson and Ruth Weyand were staff attorneys very involved in these cases.

15. General Electric Company v. Gilbert (429 U.S. 125. 1976) was decided by the U.S. Supreme Court in 1976; see Ross, "Legal Aspects of Parental Leave." In this class-action suit brought by seven women, it was argued that GE's disability plan discriminated on the basis of sex because it didn't cover pregnancy or childbirth. The Supreme Court supported GE, arguing that the disability plan didn't treat women and men differently, but distinguished between pregnant women and nonpregnant persons. The IUE helped form a coalition of feminists, civil rights groups, church groups, and unions to lobby Congress for legislation to reverse the decision. In 1978 Congress passed the Pregnancy Discrimination Act, as an amendment to Title VII, which defines pregnancy discrimination as a form of sex discrimination and requires employers to treat pregnancy as they do any other disability. See Davis, *Moving the Mountain*.

16. According to the *IUE NEWS*, October 1974 (3), six women received $3,218 in this case.

17. The Coalition of Labor Union Women was founded in 1974 and was the first interunion organization with an agenda for women that included organizing the unorganized, affirmative action in the workplace, political action and legislation, and increased participation of women in their unions. Diane Balser, in *Sisterhood and Solidarity*, writes: "CLUW was born as a result of the women's liberation movement, the increase in activities among union women and working women (such as the formation of women's committees in unions), and the increasing interaction between these two trends. This newly forming relationship between women's liberation and union women was marked most dramatically by a change in union attitudes towards the ERA" (151). In 1993 Gloria Johnson, now director of the IUE Department of Social Action, was elected president of CLUW and in this role was also elected to the executive council of the AFL-CIO.

18. Fitzmaurice: "Mary Callahan Dies at 66; IUE Is Forever in Her Debt," *IUE News*, June 1981, 9. Alice Hoffman: "Sing a Song of Unsung Heroes and Heroines," 61.

Chapter 7   *Ah Quon McElrath, ILWU*

1. Ah Quon McElrath was interviewed in 1976 by Marian Roffman for the oral history project "The Twentieth Century Trade Union Woman." This was five years before her retirement from the ILWU, when she was sixty-one years old. A follow-up interview was done with Ah Quon in 1994, at the University of Hawaii, by Brigid O'Farrell for this book. Additional information about Ah Quon is found in Chinen, "Ah Quon McElrath," and Smyser, "Lifetime of Laboring to Make Hawaii Better." Several articles written about Ah Quon and several written by her are on file at the ILWU Library, Local 142, Honolulu, Hawaii.

2. Unless otherwise referenced, data on workers, unions, and industries in Hawaii come from Beechert, *Working in Hawaii,* and until 1945, Wills, "History of Labor Relations in Hawaii." Ah Quon's mother came to Hawaii as the wife of a man who died shortly after she arrived. She then married Leong Chew.

3. See Theon Wright, *The Disenchanted Isle* (New York: Dial Press, 1972), 87–88, in Beechert, *Working in Hawaii,* 274.

4. Before 1900, workers in Hawaii were not allowed to organize. Between 1900 and 1937, there were many strikes by workers, but along racial lines. First the Japanese became active and then the Filipinos, but they never worked together and there was little financial or organizational support. The United States formally annexed Hawaii in 1898. See Wills, "History of Labor Relations in Hawaii," 10.

5. This is the same Harry Bridges that Carmen Lucia had difficulty with (see Chapter 3). Harry Bridges emigrated from Australia and was president of the ILWU from its founding in 1937 until he retired in 1977. For additional information about Jack Hall, the Communist Party, and the ILWU in Hawaii, including the Reineckes and Robert McElrath, see Zalburg, *A Spark Is Struck!* Ah Quon is mentioned only briefly in this volume, mainly in her role as McElrath's wife.

6. Beechert, *Working in Hawaii,* 254, 268. After martial law was lifted in 1943, Wills refers to the "almost overnight unionization of Hawaiian labor." "History of Labor Relations in Hawaii," 2.

7. This was the kind of program Lillian Herstein was helping to establish on the West Coast (see Chapter 2). The Community Facilities Act, known as the Lanham Act, was signed by President Roosevelt in 1942 to provide local aid to war affected communities for schools, hospitals, water and sewers, and recreational facilities. To help meet the needs of women war workers by 1945, $3 million had been spent for the construction of new day-care centers and $47 million for operating expenses, with more than a million and a half children in day care. Goodwin, *No Ordinary Time,* 416–417.

8. Beechert, *Working in Hawaii,* 269.

9. Zalburg, *A Spark Is Struck,* 250.

10. During the last two decades, excessive red-baiting actions by the government during the McCarthy era have been well documented by historians and political activists. With the collapse of the Soviet Union, the Communist Party files have now been opened to scholars. Preliminary reports indicate that Harry Bridges was not only a member but sat on the ruling central committee of the Communist Party USA. See Klehr and Haynes, "Communists and the CIO."

11. The teaching or advocacy of the violent overthrow of the U.S. government is prohibited by the Alien Registration Act of 1940, amended in 1948. It was introduced by Representative Howard Smith of Virginia and became known as the Smith Act. The Los Angeles Smith Act convictions were reversed in 1957 by the Supreme Court, which ruled that the law did not prohibit teaching overthrow of the government as long as no action was taken. On January 20, 1958, the Ninth Circuit acquitted the Hawaii Seven. See Zalburg, *A Spark Is Struck,* 323, 399.

12. The nondiscrimination and interracial policies of the ILWU are described in Thompson, "The ILWU as a Force for Interracial Unity in Hawaii."

13. Beechert, *Working in Hawaii,* 256.

14. Ah Quon's work in Alabama was reported in the *Honolulu Advertiser,* November 18, 1966, in the ILWU Library, Local 142, Hawaii.

15. Chinen, "Ah Quon McElrath," A-8.

Chapter 8   *Dorothy Haener, UAW*

---

1. Dorothy Haener was first interviewed in 1976 by Lyn Goldfarb, Lydia Kleiner, and Christine Miller, all of whom were on the staff of the oral history project "The Twentieth Century Trade Union Woman." Dorothy was fifty-eight at the time and working on the staff of the Women's Department of the United Automobile, Aerospace and Agricultural Implement Workers of America (UAW). In 1994 Brigid O'Farrell conducted a second interview with Dorothy Haener in Washington, D.C., for this book. Other interviews with UAW women completed for "The Twentieth Century Trade Union Women" include Mildred Jeffrey and Florence Peterson. A third interview with Dorothy Haener was completed by Marie Laberge as part of the project "Documenting the Midwestern Origins of the Twentieth Century Women's Movement." Nine interview tapes are housed at the State Historical Society of Wisconsin, Madison; one of them is closed to the public until February 1, 2003. Several articles and books have been written about women and the UAW. Two extensive analyses include Gabin, *Feminism in the Labor Movement,* and Milkman, *Gender at Work.*

2. River Rouge, located in Dearborn, Michigan, was the largest auto plant in the world. "An entirely self-contained twelve-hundred-acre unit, the plant generated enough power to light all the homes in Chicago, used enough water to supply all the families of Detroit, Cincinnati, and Washington combined, and wore out seven thousand mops a month to keep itself clean." Goodwin, *No Ordinary Time,* 226. Ternstedt was the largest General Motors parts factory in Detroit. Between twelve and sixteen thousand men and women were employed in five buildings on Detroit's West Side. Organized in April 1937, they pioneered in using the slowdown. Workers stayed at their machines and continued to produce, but at lower and lower rates. In June, afternoon shiftworkers initiated a spontaneous sit-down strike to gain further concessions. See Meyerowitz, "Organizing the United Automobile Workers."

3. For a full analysis of female employment in the automotive industry and the UAW during World War II, see Milkman, *Gender at Work,* and Gabin, *Feminism in the Labor Movement,* chap. 2. Willow Run is described in Goodwin, *No Ordinary Time,* chap. 14.

4. Goodwin, *No Ordinary Time,* 365. Nancy Baker Wise and Christy Wise interviewed over one hundred women to produce a volume of oral histories, *A Mouthful of Rivets,* concerning women who had worked in wartime jobs. Some women were successfully integrated into the men's jobs in the auto industry, but with "women holding 'male' jobs only for the duration." Gabin, *Feminism in the Labor Movement,* 261. The majority of jobs, however, remained sex-segregated. For example, at the Ford River Rouge plant, "62 percent of the women workers were clustered in just 20 of the 416 job categories. And nearly two-thirds of the occupational groups were at least 90 percent male." Milkman, *Gender at Work,* 58.

5. Franklin and Eleanor Roosevelt toured the Willow Run plant in September 1942. The plant had taken longer to complete than planned and had produced only one bomber by the time of the Roosevelts' visit. By 1944, however, it was producing six hundred a month. According to Goodwin, *No Ordinary Time,* "As Eleanor cast her eyes about the huge L-shaped room, she took great pleasure in the sight of hundreds of women standing side by side with the men. For the first time in the history of the company, women were working on the assembly line as riveters, welders, blueprint readers, and inspectors." (364).

6. Milkman, *Gender at Work*, 13.

7. The UAW introduced seniority as a criterion for layoffs in its first contracts in the late 1930s. Workers would be laid off when there was a shortage of work. When work picked up, they were recalled according to their length of time on the job or in the plant. This meant that those who had worked for the company the longest would be the last to be laid off and the first to be called back. Preferential hiring rights meant that employees who were laid off would be hired back before new employees were hired. Women's seniority and recall rights were often ignored, and they were laid off and not recalled or hired. Separate seniority lists by sex, or by job when the jobs were segregated by sex, also meant that women with more seniority than men might be laid off or not recalled. If rights were enforced for women, however, it would leave men without jobs. Thus union men were not always willing to fight for the union women. For a full discussion of the conflicts within the union, see Gabin, *Feminism in the Labor Movement*, and Milkman, *Gender at Work*.

8. The UAW had a long history of factional fighting within the union. In 1946 Walter Reuther, a political moderate and director of the UAW General Motors department, formed what became known as the "Reuther caucus" and defeated then UAW president R. J. Thomas. Reuther remained president of the UAW until his death in a plane crash in 1970. See Lichtenstein, "Walter Reuther and the Rise of Labor Liberalism."

9. Douglas Fraser was elected president of the UAW in 1977 and served until his retirement in 1983.

10. Unions have staff representatives who are employed by the union and usually come from local unions. These representatives provide guidance and assistance to local unions in negotiating contracts, filing grievances, and generally resolving day-to-day local union problems. This is generally known as "servicing" a local, in contrast to "organizing" new members.

11. Gabin, *Feminism in the Labor Movement*, 274.

12. The Committee on Private Employment recommended establishing a presidential Commission on Merit Employment for Women to consider methods of persuasion and voluntary compliance to end sex discrimination in employment. Caroline Davis dissented from this recommendation and recommended that sex discrimination be included in Executive Order 10925 prohibiting discrimination by federal contractors with legal enforcement powers, in U.S. Women's Bureau, "Report of the Committee on Private Employment," 15–18. This would have substantially weakened, if not overturned, the protective laws. Officially she did not support the Equal Rights Amendment, because at that time the UAW had not yet voted to support the ERA. See chapters 4 and 6 for discussion of the position in support of the protective legislation.

13. Steven Schlossberg served as general counsel for the UAW from 1963 to 1981. Irving Bluestone, a rank-and-file member, became a UAW vice president from 1972 until he retired in 1980.

14. Betty Friedan, *It Changed My Life*, similarly describes the involvement of Dorothy Haener and Caroline Davis in the forming of NOW and their need to withdraw by the second national convention. Both Friedan and Davis, *Moving the Mountain*, acknowledge the UAW's support in the early days of NOW and later support for the ERA, but they make no further mention of the UAW or the formation of the Coalition of Labor Union Women. Scholars have only recently discovered union women's activities in the postwar era and particularly in the women's movement. See, for example, Gabin, *Feminism in the Labor Movement*, and Cobble, "Recapturing Working-Class Feminism." Cobble concludes, "Yet by the late 1960s the postwar generation of working-class feminists felt the sting of rejection by the younger equal rights feminists who came to dominate the movement" (75).

15. Dolly Lowther Robinson was an African-American union activist with the ACWA before joining the staff of the U.S. Women's Bureau and receiving her law degree. She was

also interviewed as part of the oral history project "The Twentieth Century Trade Union Woman."

16. For more discussion of the formation of CLUW, see Chapter 6 and Balser, *Sisterhood and Solidarity.*

17. Unions, like employers, are prohibited from discriminating under Title VII of the 1964 Civil Rights Act. While primary enforcement efforts focus on employers, complaints and law suits are brought against unions on the basis of race and sex discrimination. See O'Farrell and Moore, "Unions, Hard Hats, and Women Workers."

18. Rosa Parks and the bus boycott are also discussed in Chapter 9. For more information on Martha Griffiths, see Davis, *Moving the Mountain.*

Chapter 9   *Fannie Allen Neal, ACWA*

1. Fannie Allen Neal was interviewed in 1977, by Marlene Rikard, a historian at Samford University in Birmingham, Alabama, for the oral history project "The Twentieth Century Trade Union Woman." Fannie was fifty-eight years old, working on the staff of the AFL-CIO Committee on Political Education, and based in Montgomery, Alabama. For the names of other interviewees in this collection from members of the Amalgamated Clothing Workers of America, see Chapter 4, note 1. Fannie told her story at a 1988 conference on race relations at the University of Alabama, which can be found in Neal, "Confronting Prejudice and Discrimination." Quotation: "Alabama AFL-CIO Newsletter," vol. 14, no. 7, May 6, 1987.

2. Sources on African-American workers in the South include Litwack, "Hellhound on My Trail," and specifically on African-American women, Amott and Matthaei, *Race, Gender, and Work,* chap. 6. See also Jones, *Labor of Love, Labor of Sorrow.*

3. Amott and Matthaei, *Race, Gender, and Work,* 60.

4. Ibid., 172. On A. Philip Randolph, see Chapter 2, note 6, and Chapter 5.

5. Neal, "Confronting Prejudice and Discrimination," 29.

6. For more specific data on African-American women, unions, and the South, see Terbor-Penn, "Survival Strategies," and Frederickson, "I Know Which Side I'm On."

7. Other African-American women trade unionists discuss the problems of racism within the labor movement, as well as the overall benefits of union membership, particularly in the South, in Lerner, ed., *Black Women in White America,* chap. 11.

8. New local groups like the Montgomery Improvement Association were an important base of the civil rights movement emerging in the 1950s. The movement also formed coalitions with existing groups like the CIO and the American Jewish Congress. See Jaynes and Williams, eds., *A Common Destiny,* chap. 4.

9. Neal, "Confronting Prejudice and Discrimination," 38.

10. Hillman's major involvement in politics, especially in the Roosevelt administration, is detailed in Fraser, *Labor Will Rule.* See also Chapter 4 in this volume. Mary Frederickson finds that the YWCA reached more working women in the South, black and white, than any other organization; see "I Know Which Side I'm On," 169.

11. "The AFL-CIO and COPE," COPE Publication no. 65C, Washington, D.C., n.d.

12. Although there was little systematic evidence, the conventional wisdom in the 1970s was that "through lawsuits, consent decrees, permanent injunctions, and voluntary compliance, the Civil Rights Act of 1964 had led to a broad-scale elimination of discrimination against blacks in public accommodations." Jaynes and Williams, *A Common Destiny,* 84.

13. In the 1950s Randolph directly confronted George Meany and the AFL-CIO on the issue of racial discrimination in unions. In 1960 Randolph formed and became president

of the Negro American Labor Council (NALC) to promote equality on the job and the full participation of blacks in unions. In 1963 he succeeded in pushing the AFL-CIO to create a Special Task Force on Civil Rights to focus on both "discriminating unions and civil rights issues beyond unions as well." Harris, "A. Philip Randolph," 275–276.

14. Neal, "Confronting Prejudice and Discrimination," 33.

15. Under the Taft-Hartley Act of 1947, Section 14(b), states are allowed to pass laws that prohibit union security clauses, in effect, requiring an "open shop," under which a union must represent all the workers in a bargaining unit, but the workers are not required to join the union or pay dues. About twenty states have what have become known as "right-to-work" laws. See Gold, *An Introduction to Labor Law.*

16. Hubert Humphrey served as Vice President of the United States under Lyndon Johnson, 1965 to 1969. In 1968, when Johnson decided not to seek reelection, Humphrey ran for President, but was defeated by Richard Nixon.

17. Mrs. Fannie Allen Neal, "Memorial Service," Saturday, August 11, 1990.

Chapter 10 *Jessie De La Cruz, UFW*

---

1. Anne Loftis conducted two interviews with Jessie De La Cruz, one in 1973 and a second in 1976, for the oral history project "The Twentieth Century Trade Union Woman." Jessie was fifty-seven years old at the time of the last interview and working on the cooperative farm that she and her husband helped establish. A telephone interview with Jessie at her home in Fesno, California, was done by Brigid O'Farrell in 1995 for this book. Additional information about Jessie De La Cruz is referenced from a longer interview by Ellen Cantarow, "Jessie Lopez De La Cruz." A great deal has been written about the farm workers in the last twenty years, but for the first extensive analysis of women in the union, see Margaret E. Rose, "Women in the United Farm Workers." Her articles include "Traditional and Nontraditional Patterns" and "From the Fields to the Picket Line." Selected history and analysis of farm workers and the UFW also include Mathiessen, *Sal Si Puedes;* Majka and Majka, *Farm Workers, Agribusiness, and the State;* and most recently, Mooney and Majka, *Farmers' and Farm Workers' Movements.*

2. Cantarow, "Jessie Lopez De La Cruz," 106.

3. There were several labor organizations active during the Depression, but grower resistance was often violent, there were no legal protections, and none of these unions survived. In this Bakersfield strike, after a decline in wages of 50 percent, the Cannery and Agricultural Workers Industrial Union led a strike involving eighteen thousand workers in cotton. Mobile groups of picketers covered a 114-mile stretch from Bakersfield to Merced. Thousands of strikers were arrested, and vigilantes fired into a union meeting, killing two members. The strike lasted twenty-four days and was the largest agricultural labor strike to that point in U.S. history. See Mooney and Majka, *Farmers' and Farm Workers' Movements,* 128–129.

4. Legislation to limit child labor was an issue fought at the state level for much of the early twentieth century and championed by women like Lillian Herstein (see Chapter 2) and groups such as Jane Addams's Hull House, the Women's Trade Union League, and the National Consumers' League. Federal legislation prohibiting children thirteen years and younger from working and regulating the employment of children between ages fourteen and seventeen in certain occupations was incorporated in the Fair Labor Standards Act of 1938, but the act specifically excluded agricultural workers. In 1950 the FLSA prohibited the employment of children under sixteen in agriculture during school hours. See the U.S. Department of Labor, "Child Labor Laws Historical Development."

5. Cantarow, "Jessie Lopez De La Cruz," 104–105.

6. Ibid., 118. Jessie describes her first daughter, who was only five months old when

she fell ill and died. Jessie commented that many migrant babies died from hunger, malnutrition, and the lack of money to see a doctor.

7. Women's farm work is described by Foner, *Women and the American Labor Movement*, 456–477.

8. Cantarow, "Jessie Lopez De La Cruz," 118.

9. Cesar Chavez was the charismatic president of the United Farm Workers of America from 1962 until his death in 1993. The new president is Arturo Rodriguez, Chavez's son-in-law. By 1970 the union had contracts covering 150 agricultural operations, representing twenty thousand jobs and more than ten thousand members. In 1975 the UFW succeeded in getting a California state labor law, the Agricultural Labor Relations Act, administered under a sympathetic governor. By the 1980s, however, there were serious disagreements within the UFW, and many union staff people left. A conservative governor took office, and the growers successfully moved their anti-union strategies into the courts. Even where the union won elections, the leaders had trouble negotiating contracts. In 1993 the UFW held only a handful of contracts covering about five thousand workers out of the 769 operations where they were certified. See Majka and Majka, *Farm Workers, Agribusiness, and the State*, for analyses of this decline. More about Chavez is also found in Daniels, "Cesar Chavez."

10. Dolores Huerta was also chief negotiator and in charge of much of the boycott activity. Marie Sabadado directed the medical plan; Helen Chavez, Cesar's wife, headed the credit union; and Jessica Govea was elected to the executive board. See Foner, *Women in the American Labor Movment*, 462–463. Unlike Chavez and De La Cruz, Huerta came from a more middle-class background. For more information about her family and union leadership, see "Dolores Huerta," in Bonilla-Santiago, *Breaking Ground and Barriers*, 97, and Rose, "Dolores Huerta: Labor Leader, Social Activist."

11. Margaret Rose documents the activism of many women in the UFW, some of whom were also organizers. She contrasts the experiences of nontraditional women, such as Dolores Huerta, who fit a "male" model of labor organizing and were rare, with Helen Chavez, whose activism fits a much more common, behind-the-scenes, supportive "female" model. See Rose, "Traditional and Nontraditional Patterns." Jessie De La Cruz took on the more nontraditional male activities of organizer, shop steward, and hiring hall director, but the union hiring hall was next door to her home so she could also watch her children. Her children were older when she became active, but she states in her interview that her family always came first. She also describes, in Cantarow, "Jessie Lopez De La Cruz" (134–139), some of the difficulties and strengths of being a woman activist.

12. Mathiessen, "Sal Si Puedes," 17–19.

13. Ibid., 19.

14. Ibid., 20.

15. The hiring halls and some of the problems with them are described by Mooney and Majka, *Farmers' and Farm Workers' Movements*, 169. Jessie, in Cantarow, "Jessie Lopez De La Cruz" (134–145), describes not only the hiring hall but also efforts to get women on the ranch committees, their activities on the picket lines, and contract negotiations. She comments, "It was very hard being a woman organizer. . . . Men gave us the most trouble. . . . They were for the union, but they were not taking orders from women."

16. Cantarow, "Jessie Lopez De La Cruz," 128.

17. In 1965, according to Mooney and Majka, *Farmers' and Farm Workers' Movements* (160), boycott organizations were active in forty or fifty cities, boycott committees were operating in hundreds of other communities, and two hundred strikers and their families joined the boycott efforts full time. Rose describes these families and the critical roles played by the women in "From the Fields to the Picket Lines." The "peregrinaciones" are described by Fink, *Biographical Dictionary*.

18. Mooney and Majka, *Farmers' and Farm Workers' Movements* (165), suggest that although the Teamster union activity was in part initiated by the growers, it also played into the internal politics of the union. The authors write that the Teamsters' union pursued legal battles with the UFW but was also as intimidating and violent as the grower vigilante groups.

Chapter 11   *Catherine Conroy, CWA*

1. Catherine Conroy was interviewed twice in 1976 by Elizabeth Balanoff, a labor historian at Roosevelt University in Chicago, Illinois, for the oral history project "The Twentieth Century Trade Union Woman." Catherine was fifty-six years old at the time of the interview and a staff respresentative for the CWA in Wisconsin. Additional background information about Catherine comes from an article about her written by Tony Carideo, "Catherine Conroy Points the Way," and from the statement at Catherine's funeral, "Catherine Conroy." Ruth Wiencek, interviewed for the oral history project, also describes working in the telephone company in the 1940s, and the development of the Communications Workers of America. Quotations: Dorothy Austin, "Conroy Fought for Causes of Labor, Women," *Milwaukee Sentinel,* March 1, 1989, and David Horst, "Conroy: A Leader, Role Model," *Post-Crescent,* n.d. (c. March 1989).

2. The development of the telephone industry and the unions is found in Barbash, *Unions and Telephones;* Brooks, *The Communications Workers of America;* and Schacht, *The Making of Telephone Unionism.* 1902 figures: Brooks, 11. For a detailed history and analysis of early women workers in the telephone industry, particularly the segregation of the jobs, company hiring policies, and women's union activity, see Norwood, *Labor's Flaming Youth.* He comments, "The policy in the Bell System was to hire only unmarried women as operators, and operators who married were expected to leave the telephone service" (40).

3. The Telephone Operators' Department of the International Brotherhood of Electrical Workers held its first convention in 1919 with Julia O'Connor (later Parker) as president. They had twenty thousand members across the country. A disastrous New England strike in 1923, however, led to the replacement of most of the strikers and the introduction of the company unions. Norwood, *Labor's Flaming Youth,* (7), found that the most critical source of support for the telephone operators was the women's movement in the early 1900s.

4. Brooks, *The Communications Workers of America,* 114.

5. Joseph A. Bierne was president of the CWA from its founding until his death in 1974. The specific effects of dial technology are found in Brooks, *The Communications Workers of America,* 191.

6. The importance of this change to two levels for increasing the CWA's strength is discussed in detail in Barbash, *Unions and Telephones.*

7. The modern-day concept of community services was an outgrowth of the National CIO War Relief Program. One of its ten principles included the "responsibility of organized labor to cooperate with community groups in improving the quantity and quality of social services, while at the same time educating union members about available health and welfare services and how to use them." See AFL-CIO Department of Community Services, "Community Services, Our Roots," Washington, D.C., n.d.

8. In Carideo, "Catherine Conroy Points the Way," Catherine went on to say, "We were all so preoccupied with dealing with this national utility and getting some overall unity that we didn't realize that these old-time women were dying, retiring or whatever and then being replaced by men."

9. This comment about Catherine was made in 1978 by the then president of the Chicago NOW chapter and appears in Carideo, "Catherine Conroy Points the Way." This article also identifies Catherine's friendships with Kay Clarenbach, distinguished scholar, president

of the Interstate Association of Commissions on the Status of Women, founder and first chairperson of NOW, and chairman of the Board of Trustees of Alverno College, as well as Sister Joel Reed, now president of Alverno College, and Sister Austin Doherty, vice president for academic affairs at Alverno. Friedan, *It Changed My Life* (76–119), describes the Women's Bureau conference where she first distrusts Kay Clarenbach as a "darling of the Women's Bureau" and later learns to rely on her. Sister Reed and Sister Doherty also become strong allies. Catherine is mentioned only as one of several people signing the Statement of Purpose and skeletal by-laws in 1966.

10. In the interview Catherine discusses more fully the problems NOW faced with the left organizations. See also Davis, *Moving the Mountain*, and Friedan, *It Changed My Life*.

11. By the 1970s there was enough information available to predict the automation and job loss. Operators made up only 26 percent of the employees, down from 43 percent in 1950. Almost 100 percent of local calls and 90 percent of long-distance calls were by direct dial. See Brooks in Norwood, *Labor's Flaming Youth*, 309. Yet the union grew from 260,000 in 1960 to 420,000 by 1970; see Fink, *Historical Sketches*.

12. Brooks, *The Communications Workers of America*, x.

13. The extent of discrimination in the Bell System and the court-ordered consent decree to change it are documented in Wallace, ed., *Equal Employment Opportunity and the AT&T Case*. African-Americans made no significant gains in employment with AT&T until the 1960s. AT&T agreed to pay $80 million in back wages and other pay adjustments. It was considered the largest and most comprehensive civil rights settlement ever agreed to in the United States. The difficult issue of seniority for union women is discussed further in Balser, *Sisterhood and Solidarity*, 178–183.

14. Catherine discussed the problems with the more politically left-wing feminists and the CLUW leadership in more detail in her interview. These issues are also addressed by Balser, *Sisterhood and Solidarity*, chap. 7.

15. Her three protégés were Annie Crump, Patty Yunk, and Joanne Ricca. Annie Crump is current president of Local 5500 and was very helpful in providing background material for this chapter, along with Colleen Davis on the CWA District 4 staff. Quotation: Carideo, "Catherine Conroy Points the Way."

16. Catherine's campaign for union vice president and her discrimination suit are discussed in Paul Anderson, "Catherine Conroy," unpublished paper, n.d., and in Carideo, "Catherine Conroy Points the Way."

17. The retirement dinner is described in "Maverick Catherine Conroy Honored by CWA and Friends," *AFL-CIO Milwaukee Labor Press*, May 13, 1982.

18. In Carideo, "Catherine Conroy Points the Way."

Chapter 12   *Alice Peurala, USWA*

---

1. Elizabeth Balanoff, a labor historian at Roosevelt University in Chicago, Illinois, interviewed Alice Peurala in 1977 for the oral history project "The Twentieth Century Trade Union Woman." Alice was forty-nine years old, was working for the U.S. Steel Corporation, and had been elected to the grievance committee of Local 65 of the USWA. Additional information about her life and work can be found in Flannery, "Alice and the Steelworkers," and Conroy, "The Silence in Steel City." Ola Kennedy from the USWA was also interviewed for the oral history project. Selected references on the more recent labor-managment issues and the USWA include: Bensman and Lynch, *Rusted Dreams*; Clark, Gottlieb, and Kennedy, eds., *Forging a Union of Steel*; Hoerr, *And the Wolf Finally Came;* and Nyden, *Steelworkers Rank-and-File*. Quotation: Flannery, "Alice and the Steelworkers."

2. Flannery, "Alice and the Steelworkers," 11

3. For more information about Harold (Hal) Gibbons and Local 688 of the Interna-

tional Brotherhood of Teamsters, see Smith, "An Experiment in Trade Union Democracy." Hal Gibbons was a trade union student of Lillian Herstein's in Chicago, organizer and president of a local union of Chicago teachers employed by the New Deal's Workers' Service Program, and one of the union leaders who went with Carmen Lucia to France as part of the Marshall Plan in 1950.

4. Labor unions and anticommunism after World War II are discussed in Chapters 6 and 7. For recent selected references on the relationship of the Taft-Hartley Act to changes in the NLRB procedures and the decline of organized labor, also discussed in earlier chapters, see Sexton, *The War on Labor and the Left;* Goldfield, *The Decline of Organized Labor;* Fried, *Nightmare in Red;* and Freeman, "Why Are Unions Fairing Poorly."

5. For more information about layoffs of women workers after World War II, see Chapter 8 and the following selected sources: Gabin, *Feminism in the Labor Movement;* Milkman, *Gender at Work;* Kessler-Harris, *Out to Work;* and Foner, *Women and the American Labor Movement.* More information about the South Works plant can be found in Bensman and Lynch, *Rusted Dreams;* Hoerr, *And the Wolf Finally Came;* and Nyden, *Steelworkers Rank-and-File.*

6. Flannery, "Alice and the Steelworkers," 12.

7. For more information on the steel industry, sex discrimination in employment, and affirmative action programs, see Deaux and Ullman, *Women of Steel.* For more information on Title VII and unions, see Chapters 6, 8, and 11; Newman and Wilson, "The Union Role in Affirmative Action"; O'Farrell and Moore, "Unions, Hard Hats, and Women Workers"; and Freeman and Leonard, "Union Maids."

8. I. W. Abel was president of the USWA from 1965 until 1977. In 1973 he signed the pioneering Experimental Negotiating Agreement (ENA), also known as the No-Strike Agreement. The insurgents were concerned about the lack of rank-and-file involvement in developing and negotiating national union collective bargaining agreements, in general, and about the lack of discussion or vote by the union members on the ENA, in particular. See Nyden, *Steelworkers Rank-and File.* Ed Sadlowski, a third-generation steelworker at the South Works plant, was elected president of Local 65 in 1963 and director of District 31 in 1973. The district election was contested by the USWA national officers and was resolved by the NLRB in Sadlowski's favor. In 1977 he ran, unsuccessfully, for president of the USWA against Lloyd McBride, who succeeded I. W. Abel. See Bensman and Lynch, *Rusted Dreams;* Hoerr, *And the Wolf Finally Came;* Nyden, *Steelworkers Rank-and-File;* and Flannery, "Alice and the Steelworkers."

9. Flannery, "Alice and the Steelworkers," 12.

10. See Deaux and Ullman, *Women of Steel,* and Foner, *Women in the American Labor Movement.* In 1979, the U.S. Supreme Court rejected the "reverse discrimination" charges of Brian Weber and upheld the voluntary affirmative action program of the Kaiser Company and the USWA. See Foner, *Women and the American Labor Movement,* 543–544.

11. Foner, *American Women and the Labor Movement,* 545.

12. Bensman and Lynch, *Rusted Dreams,* 118.

13. Conroy, "The Silence in Steel City" 19. For more information on plant closings of the U.S. Steel Company, see Hoerr, *And the Wolf Finally Came,* 426–443, and Bensman and Lynch, *Rusted Dreams,* 89–90, 136–146. Hoerr details the 1982–1984 conflict over a company-proposed rail mill at South Works in exchange for additional wage and hour concessions from the union. He writes: "The company cancelled the project and attacked the union in newspaper advertisements. . . . But another factor was involved. In the two years since USS first approached Local 65, the market for rails had shriveled and could not not have supported a third large mill at South Works, even with concessions. U.S. Steel used Local 65's refusal to meet the new demands as an excuse to cancel a decision that it believed no longer made economic sense" (425–426).

14. Conroy, "The Silence in Steel City," 22.

15. James Warren, "Alice Peurala, 58, Steel Union Leader," *Chicago Tribune,* June 21, 1986.

Postscript

1. Compiled from Pullman and Szymanski, "The Union Response to Sexual Harassment in the Workplace"; the U.S. Department of Labor; and telephone conversations with national union staffs.

Bibliography

Amott, Teresa L., and Julie A. Mathaei. *Race, Gender, and Work: A Multicultural Economic History of Women in the United States.* Boston: South End Press, 1991.

Anderson, Jervis. *A. Philip Randolph: A Biographical Portrait.* New York: Harcourt Brace Jovanovich, 1972.

Balser, Diane. *Sisterhood and Solidarity, Feminism and Labor in Modern Times.* Boston: South End Press, 1987.

Barbash, Jack. *Unions and Telephones.* New York: Harper and Brothers, 1952.

Bauman, Suzanne, and Rita Heller. *The Women of Summer: The Bryn Mawr Summer School for Women Workers, 1921–1938.* 1986. NEH film distributed by Filmakers Library, New York, N.Y.

Beechert, Edward D. *Working in Hawaii: A Labor History.* Honolulu: University of Hawaii Press, 1985.

Bensman, David, and Roberta Lynch. *Rusted Dreams: Hard Times in a Steel Community.* Berkeley: University of California Press, 1987.

Bonilla-Santiago, Gloria. *Breaking Ground and Barriers: Hispanic Women Developing Effective Leadership.* San Diego: Marin Publications, 1992.

Boris, Eileen, and Cynthia R. Daniels, eds., *Homework: Historical and Contemporary Perspectives on Paid Labor at Home.* Urbana: University of Illinois Press, 1989.

Brody, David. *Labor in Crisis: The Steel Strike of 1919.* Philadelphia: J. B. Lippincott, 1965.

Brooks, Thomas. *The Communications Workers of America.* New York: Mason/Charter, 1977.

Cantarow, Ellen. "Jessie Lopez De La Cruz: The Battle for Farm Workers' Rights." In Ellen Cantarow with Susan Gushee O'Malley and Sharon Hartman Strom, *Moving the Mountain: Women Working for Social Change.* New York: Feminist Press, 1980.

Carideo, Tony. "Catherine Conroy Points the Way." *Milwaukee Journal,* July 9, 1978.

"Catherine Conroy." *The Stateswoman,* 9, no. 5 (March 1989).

Chinen, Karleen. "Ah Quon McElrath: Fire Still Burns in Veteran Labor Leader." *Hawaii Herald,* March 1, 1991, A8.

Clark, Paul F., Peter Gottlieb, and Donald Kennedy, eds., *Forging a Union of Steel.* Ithaca: ILR Press, Cornell University, 1987.

Cobble, Dorothy Sue. "Recapturing Working-Class Feminism: Union Women in the Postwar Era." In Joanne Meyerowitz, ed., *Not June Cleaver: Women and Gender in Postwar America, 1945–1960.* Philadelphia: Temple University Press, 1994.

Conroy, John. "The Silence in Steel City." *The Reader: Chicago's Free Weekly,* February 21, 1986.

Cook, Blanche W. *Eleanor Roosevelt, vol. 1, 1884–1933.* New York: Penguin Books, 1992.

Daniels, Cletus E. "Cesar Chavez and the Unionization of California Farm Workers." In Melvyn Dubofsky and Warren Van Tine, eds., *Labor Leaders in America.* Urbana: University of Illinois Press, 1987.

Davis, Flora. *Moving the Mountain: The Women's Movement in America since 1960.* New York: Simon and Schuster, 1991.

Deaux, Kay, and Joseph C. Ullman. *Women of Steel: Female Blue-Collar Workers in the Basic Steel Industry.* New York: Praeger Publishers, 1983.

Dye, Nancy S. *As Equals and as Sisters: Feminism, Unionism, and the Women's Trade Union League of New York.* Columbia: University of Missouri Press, 1980.

Eaton, William E. *The American Federation of Teachers, 1916–1961.* Carbondale: Southern Illinois University Press, 1975.

Edelman, John W., and Joseph Carter, eds. *Labor Lobbyist: The Autobiography of John W. Edelman.* New York: Bobbs-Merrill Company, 1974.

Ehrenberg, Ronald G., and Robert S. Smith. *Modern Labor Economics: Theory and Public Policy.* Glenview, Ill.: Scott, Foresman and Company, 1982.

Engelbrecht, Lester E. "Lillian Herstein: Teacher and Activist." *Labor's Heritage* (April 1989): 66–75.

Equal Pay Act, 1963, Hearings. Washington, D.C.: U.S. Government Printing Office, 1963.

Fenzi, Jewell, with Carl L. Nelson. *Married to the Foreign Service: An Oral History of the American Diplomatic Spouse.* New York: Twayne Publishers, 1994.

Fink, Gary M., ed. *The Biographical Dictionary of American Labor Leaders.* Westport, Conn.: Greenwood Press, 1974.

———, ed. *Labor Union Historical Sketches.* Westport, Conn.: Greenwood Press, 1977.

Flannery, Michael. "Alice and the Steelworkers." *Chicago Sun Times,* July 6, 1979.

Foner, Philip. *Women and the American Labor Movement from World War I to the Present.* New York: Free Press, 1980.

Fraser, Steven. *Labor Will Rule: Sidney Hillman and the Rise of American Labor.* New York: Free Press, 1991.

———. "Sidney Hillman: Labor's Machiavelli." In Melvyn Dubofsky and Warren Van Tine, eds., *Labor Leaders in America.* Urbana: University of Illinois Press, 1987.

Frederickson, Mary. "Citizens for Democracy." In Joyce L. Kornbluh and Mary Frederickson, eds., *Sisterhood and Solidarity: Workers' Education for Women, 1914–1984.* Philadelphia: Temple University Press, 1984.

———. "I Know Which Side I'm On: Southern Women in the Labor Movement in the Twentieth Century." In Ruth Milkman, ed., *Women, Work, and Protest: A Century of U.S. Women's Labor History.* Boston: Routledge & Kegan Paul, 1985.

Freeman, Richard B. "Why Are Unions Fairing Poorly in NLRB Representation Elections?" In Thomas A. Kochan, ed., *Challenges and Choices Facing American Labor.* Cambridge: MIT Press, 1985.

Freeman, Richard B., and Jonathan S. Leonard. "Union Maids: Unions and the Female Work Force." In C. Brown and J. A. Pechman, eds., *Gender in the Workplace.* Washington, D.C.: Brookings Institution, 1984.

Fried, Richard M. *Nightmare in Red: The McCarthy Era in Perspective.* New York: Oxford University Press, 1990.

Friedan, Betty. *The Feminine Mystique,* with new introduction and epilogue. New York: Dell, 1974.

———. *It Changed My Life.* New York: Random House, 1976.

Gabin, Nancy. *Feminism in the Labor Movement: Women and the United Auto Workers, 1935–1975.* Ithaca: Cornell University Press, 1990.

Gamel, Faye P. "The Hat Lady: A Career Biography of Carmen Lucia." M.A. thesis, Georgia State University, 1979.

Gold, Michael Evan. *An Introduction to Labor Law.* ILR Bulletin 66. Ithaca: ILR Press, Cornell University, 1989.

———. *An Introduction to the Law of Employment Discrimination.* ILR Bulletin 68. Ithaca: ILR Press, Cornell University, 1993.

Goldfield, Michael. *The Decline of Organized Labor in the United States.* Chicago: University of Chicago Press, 1987.

Goldsworthy, David. *Tom Mboya: The Man Kenya Wanted to Forget.* New York: Africana Publishing Company, 1982.

Goodwin, Doris Kearns. *No Ordinary Time: Franklin and Eleanor Roosevelt—The Home Front in World War II.* New York: Simon and Schuster, 1994.

Halamandaris, Val J. "A Tribute to Esther Peterson, Champion of the Underprivileged." *Caring People,* June/July 1990, 30–42.

Harris, William H. "A. Philip Randolph, Black Workers, and the Labor Movement." In Melvyn Dubofsky and Warren Van Tine, eds., *Labor Leaders in America.* Urbana: University of Illinois Press, 1987.

Heilbrun, Carolyn. *Writing a Woman's Life.* New York: Ballatine Books, 1988.

Heller, Rita. "Blue Collars and Bluestockings: The Bryn Mawr Summer School for Women Workers, 1921–1938." In Joyce L. Kornbluh and Mary Frederickson, eds., *Sisterhood and Solidarity: Workers' Education for Women, 1914–1984.* Philadelphia: Temple University Press, 1984.

Hoerr, John. *And the Wolf Finally Came: The Decline of the American Steel Industry.* Pittsburgh: University of Pittsburgh Press, 1988.

Huerta, Dolores. "A Life of Sacrifice for Farmworkers." In Gloria Bonilla-Santiago, ed., *Breaking Ground and Barriers: Hispanic Women Developing Effective Leadership.* San Diego: Marin Publications, 1992.

Jacoby, Robin M. "The Women's Trade Union League School for Women Organizers, 1914–1926." In Joyce L. Kornbluh and Mary Frederickson, eds. *Sisterhood and Solidarity: Workers' Education for Women, 1914–1984.* Philadelphia: Temple University Press, 1984.

Jaynes, Gerald D., and Robin M. Williams, Jr. *A Common Destiny: Blacks and American Society.* Washington, D.C.: National Academy Press, 1989.

Johnson, Gloria. "Unions and the Gender Wage Gap: Comments." In Dorothy Sue Cobble, ed., *Women and Unions: Forging a Partnership.* Ithaca: ILR Press, Cornell University, 1993.

Johnson, Susan M. *Teacher Unions in Schools.* Philadelphia: Temple University Press, 1984.

Jones, Jacqueline. *Labor of Love, Labor of Sorrow: Black Women, Work, and the Family from Slavery to the Present.* New York: Basic Books, 1985.

Kessler-Harris, Alice. "Rose Schneiderman and the Limits of Women's Trade Unionism." In Melvyn Dubofsky and Warren Van Tine, eds., *Labor Leaders in America.* Urbana: University of Illinois Press, 1987.

———. *Out to Work: A History of Wage-Earning Women in the United States.* New York: Oxford University Press, 1982.

Klehr, Harvey, and John E. Haynes. "Communists and the CIO: From the Soviet Archives." *Labor History* 35, no. 3 (Summer 1994): 442–446.

Kornbluh, Joyce L. *A New Deal for Workers' Education: The Workers' Service Program, 1934–1943.* Urbana: University of Illinois Press, 1987.

Kornbluh, Joyce L., and Mary Frederickson, eds. *Sisterhood and Solidarity: Workers' Education for Women, 1914–1984.* Philadelphia: Temple University Press, 1984.

Kornbluh, Joyce L., and Brigid O'Farrell. "You Can't Giddyup by Saying Whoa: Esther Peterson Remembers Her Organized Labor Years, 1930–1960." *Labor's Heritage* 5, no.4, (Spring 1994): 38–59.

Lerner, Gerda, ed. *Black Women in White America: A Documentary History.* New York: Vintage Books, 1973.

Lichtenstein, Nelson. "Walter Reuther and the Rise of Labor Liberalism." In Melvyn Dubofsky and Warren Van Tine, eds., *Labor Leaders in America.* Urbana: University of Illinois Press, 1987.

Litwack, Leon F. "Hellhound on My Trail: Race Relations in the South from Reconstruction to the Civil Rights Movement." In Harry J. Knopke, Robert J. Norrell, and Ronald W. Rogers, eds., *Opening Doors: Perspectives on Race Relations in Contemporary America.* Tuscaloosa: University of Alabama Press, 1991.

Majka, Theo J., and Linda C. Majka. *Farm Workers, Agribusiness, and the State.* Philadelphia: Temple University Press, 1982.

Malmgreen, Gail. "Labor and the Holocaust." *Labor's Heritage* 3, no. 4, (October 1991): 20–35.

Matthiessen, Peter. *Sal Si Puedes: Cesar Chavez and the New American Revolution.* New York: Dell Publishing, 1973.

Meyerowitz, Joanne. "Organizing the United Automobile Workers: Women Workers at the Ternstedt General Motors Parts Plant." In Ruth Milkman, ed., *Women, Work, and Protest: A Century of U.S. Women's Labor History.* Boston: Routledge and Kegan Paul, 1985.

Milkman, Ruth. *Gender at Work: The Dynamics of Job Segregation by Sex during World War II.* Urbana: University of Illinois Press, 1987.

Mooney, Patrick H., and Theo J. Majka. *Farmers' and Farm Workers' Movements: Social Protest in American Agriculture.* New York: Twayne Publishers, 1995.

Murphy, Marjorie. *Blackboard Unions: The AFT and the NEA, 1900–1980.* Ithaca: Cornell University Press, 1990.

Neal, Fannie Allen. "Confronting Prejudice and Discrimination: Personal Recollections and Observations." In Harry J. Knopke, Robert J. Norrell, and Ronald W. Rogers, eds., *Opening Doors: Perspectives on Race Relations in Contemporary America.* Tuscaloosa: University of Alabama Press, 1991.

Newell, Barbara W. *Chicago and the Labor Movement: Metropolitan Unionism in the 1930s.* Urbana: University of Illinois Press, 1961.

Newman, Wynn, and Carole Wilson. "The Union Role in Affirmative Action." *Labor Law Journal* (June 1981): 323–342.

Norwood, Stephen H. *Labor's Flaming Youth: Telephone Operators and Workers' Militancy, 1887–1923.* Urbana: University of Illinois Press, 1990.

Nyden, Philip W. *Steelworkers Rank-and-File: The Political Economy of a Union Reform Movement.* New York: Praeger, 1984.

O'Farrell, Brigid, and Joyce L. Kornbluh. "We Did Change Some Attitudes: Maida Springer-Kemp and the ILGWU." *Women's Studies Quarterly* (Spring 1995).

O'Farrell, Brigid, and Suzanne Moore. "Unions, Hard Hats, and Women Workers." In Dorothy Sue Cobble, ed., *Women and Unions: Forging a Partnership.* Ithaca: ILR Press, Cornell University, 1993.

Orleck, Annelise. *Common Sense and a Little Fire: Women and Working-Class Politics in the United States, 1900–1965.* Chapel Hill: University of North Carolina Press, 1995.

Pesotta, Rose. *Bread Upon the Waters,* new release and introduction. Ithaca: ILR Press, Cornell University, 1987.

Pullman, Cydney, and Sharon Szymanski. "The Union Response to Sexual Harassment in the Workplace." Labor Institute, New York, 1995.

Richards, Yevette. "My Passionate Feeling about Africa: Maida Springer-Kemp and the American Labor Movement." 2 vols. Ph.D. dissertation, Yale University, 1994.

Rose, Margaret. "Dolores Huerta: Labor Leader, Social Activist." In Diane Telgen and Jim Kemp, eds., *Notable Hispanic Women*. Detroit: Gale Research, 1993.

——. "From the Fields to the Picket Line: Huelga Women and the Boycott, 1965–1975." *Labor History* 31, no. 3 (Summer 1990): 271–293.

——. "Traditional and Nontraditional Patterns of Female Activism in the United Farm Workers of America, 1962–1980." *Frontiers* 11, no. 1 (1990): 26–32.

——. "Women in the United Farm Workers: A Study of Chicana and Mexicana Participation in a Labor Union, 1950–1980." Ph.D. dissertation, University of California, Los Angeles, 1988.

Ross, Susan Deller. "Legal Aspects of Parental Leave: At the Crossroads." In Janet S. Hyde and Marily J. Essex, eds., *Parental Leave and Child Care: Setting a Research and Policy Agenda*. Philadelphia: Temple University Press, 1991.

Schacht, John. *The Making of Telephone Unionism, 1920–1947*. New Brunswick, N.J.: Rutgers University Press, 1985.

Schatz, Ronald W. *The Electrical Workers: A History of Labor at General Electric and Westinghouse, 1923–1960*. Urbana: University of Illinois Press, 1983.

Sexton, Patricia Cayo. *The War on Labor and the Left: Understanding America's Unique Conservatism*. Boulder: Westview Press, 1991.

Smith, Lon W. "An Experiment in Trade Union Democracy: Harold Gibbons and the Formation of Teamsters Local 688, 1937–1957." Ph.D. Dissertation, Illinois State University, 1993.

Smyser, A. A. "A Lifetime of Laboring to Make Hawaii Better." *Honolulu Star Bulletin*, August 31, 1989.

Sugarman, Tracy. "Echoes on Papers: Reflections on My Garment Workers Sketchbook, 1958." *Labor's Heritage* (Winter 1993).

Terbor-Penn, Rosalyn. "Survival Strategies among African-American Women Workers: A Continuing Process." In Ruth Milkman, ed., *Women, Work, and Protest: A Century of U.S. Women's Labor History*. Boston: Routledge & Kegan Paul, 1985.

Thompson, David E. "The ILWU as a Force for Interracial Unity in Hawaii." In Harold S. Roberts, ed., *Labor-Management Relations in Hawaii, part 3*. Honolulu: Industrial Relations Center, University of Hawaii, 1956.

Tyack, David, Robert Lowe, and Elisabeth Hansot. *Public Schools in Hard Times: The Great Depression and Recent Years*. Cambridge: Harvard University Press, 1984.

U.S. Department of Labor. *The American Woman*. Report of the President's Commission on the Status of Women. Washington, D.C.: Women's Bureau, 1963.

——. "Child Labor Laws: Historical Development." Washington, D.C.: Wage and Hour and Public Contracts Division, n.d.

——. *Milestones: The Women's Bureau Celebrates 70 Years of Women's Labor History*. Washington, D.C.: Women's Bureau, 1990.

——. "Report of the Committee on Private Employment." President's Commission on the Status of Women. Washington, D.C.: Women's Bureau, 1963.

Wallace, Phyllis A., ed. *Equal Employment Opportunity and the AT&T Case*. Cambridge: MIT Press, 1976.

Ware, Susan. *Beyond Suffrage: Women in the New Deal*. Cambridge: Harvard University Press, 1981.

Weinstein, James. *The Decline of Socialism in America, 1912–1925*. New York: Monthly Review Press, 1967.

Wills, Arnold L. "History of Labor Relations in Hawaii." In Harold S. Roberts, ed., *Labor-*

Management Relations in Hawaii. Honolulu: Industrial Relations Center, University of Hawaii, 1955.

Wise, Nancy Baker, and Christy Wise. *A Mouthful of Rivets: Women at Work in World War II.* New York: Jossey-Bass, 1994.

Wong, Susan Stone. "From Soul to Strawberries." In Joyce L. Kornbluh and Mary Frederickson, eds., *Sisterhood and Solidarity: Workers' Education for Women, 1914–1984.* Philadelphia: Temple University Press, 1984.

Wrigley, Julia. *Class Politics and Public Schools: Chicago, 1900–1950.* New Brunswick, N.J.: Rutgers University Press, 1982.

Zalburg, Sanford. *A Spark Is Struck: Jack Hall and the ILWU in Hawaii.* Honolulu: University Press of Hawaii, 1979.

Index

AALC. *See* African-American Labor Center

Abbott, Grace, 29

Abel, I. W., 272–273, 299n8

abortion, 180, 182, 275

ACTWU. *See* Amalgamated Clothing and Textile Workers' Union

ACWA. *See* Amalgamated Clothing Workers of America

Addams, Jane, 17, 295n4

Adult Education Teachers of Chicago, 282n8

Affiliated Schools for Workers, 54

affirmative action programs, 7, 9, 180, 182, 239, 251, 290n12, 290n17, 299n10

AFL. *See* American Federation of Labor

AFL-CIO. *See* American Federation of Labor and Congress of Industrial Organizations

African-American Labor Center (AALC), 84, 109

AFT. *See* American Federation of Teachers

Agricultural Labor Relations Act, 296n9

Alabama Labor Council, 196

Alabama State AFL-CIO, 184

Alien Registration Act, 291n11

ALP. *See* American Labor Party

Amalgamated Clothing and Textile Workers' Union (ACTWU), 279

Amalgamated Clothing Workers of America (ACWA), 8, 21, 24, 37, 38, 91, 133, 279, 283n2, 293–294n15; and the ACTWU, 279; and the CIO, 190; and communism, 194; and discrimination issues, 71–72; Lucia in, 34, 38, 42, 46; and minimum wage, 72, 74; and Neal, 184, 192–194, 196, 199; and Peterson, 58, 67, 68, 69, 70–72, 76, 78–79, 83, 98; racial tensions within, 192; and Robinson, 98; and Roosevelt, 287n4; and the Textile Workers Organizing Committee, 190; and the Textile Workers Union of America, 279; and workers' education, 63, 67–68, 285n7

American Civil Liberties Union, 33

American Federation of Labor (AFL), 31, 99,

282n6, 282n11, 288n13; and the AFT, 14, 27, 28; and the Brotherhood of Sleeping Car Porters, 24; and the CIO, 24–25, 73, 100, 103, 200, 242; and Herstein, 14, 24–25, 28; and the ICFTU, 101, 102; Lucia in, 34, 52, 190; Southern Policy Committee of, 34, 52, 284n10; and Springer-Kemp, 84, 101, 102; and the Taft-Hartley Act, 124; women and Negroes ignored by, 17, 33; and the WTUL, 281n3

American Federation of Labor and Congress of Industrial Organizations, 103, 128, 164, 248, 279, 288n13; Callahan in, 125; Committee on Political Education of (COPE), 125, 184, 194, 200–201, 206; Community Services Committee of, 241–242, 297n7; and the ERA, 131, 179; and the ILWU, 149; Industrial Union Department (IUD) of, 78, 79, 164; international work of, 103, 288n13; and Neal, 184, 200–202, 206, 207; and Peterson, 58, 78, 79, 80; and racial discrimination in unions, 294–295n13; and Randolph, 89, 282n6, 294–295n13; and Springer-Kemp, 84, 95, 107; and the UAW, 133, 180; and the UFW, 216, 227; and voter registration, 200–201, 207; and women, 253

American Federation of Teachers (AFT), 16, 279; and the AFL, 14, 27, 28; and the CIO, 27, 28, 283n2; and Herstein, 5, 27, 28, 29, 31; and Peterson, 58, 66

American Jewish Congress, 294n8

American Labor Party (ALP), 91, 287n4

American Red Cross, 70, 71, 94

American Telephone and Telegraph Company (AT&T), 247–248, 249–250, 298n11; company unions established by, 235, 236, 297n3; race and sex discrimination by, 233, 234, 250–251, 297n2, 298n13

American Woman, 245, 286n13

Antonini, Luigi, 89, 287n3

About the Authors

Brigid O'Farrell is a senior associate at the Center for Women Policy Studies in Washington, D.C. She has over twenty years of experience working with unions, employers, women's organizations, and governmental agencies on issues related to employment equity for women in blue collar jobs and labor unions, and related issues of child care and combining work and family. Recent publications include "Women in Blue-Collar Jobs: Traditional and Non-traditional," *Women: A Feminist Perspective* (Mountain View, Calif.: Mayfield Publishing Company, 1995); and coauthorship with Joyce L. Kornbluh, "We Did Change Some Attitudes: Maida Springer-Kemp and the International Ladies' Garment Workers' Union," *Women's Studies Quarterly,* Spring/Summer 1995 (vol. 23, no. 1 & 2): with Suzanne Moore, "Unions, Hard Hats, and Women Workers," *Women and Unions: Forging a Partnership* (Ithaca, N.Y.: ILR Press, 1993); and with Marianne Ferber, *Work and Families: Policies for a Changing Work Force* (Washington, D.C.: National Academy Press, 1991). She holds an ED.M. in social policy from Harvard University.

Joyce L. Kornbluh founded and directed the Program on Women and Work at the University of Michigan Labor Studies Center from 1972 until her retirement in 1990. She currently teaches for Goddard College and for the Antioch College Degree Program in Labor Studies at the George Meany Center for Labor Studies, AFL-CIO. She has over forty-five years of experience as a teacher, a labor historian, and an active leader for the development of adults in the areas of work life, education, and community involvement. Recent publications include *A New Deal For Workers' Education: The Workers Service Program 1934-1943* (Urbana: University of Illinois Press, 1989); with Mary Frederickson, *Sisterhood and Solidarity: Workers' Education for Women, 1914–1984* (Philadelphia: Temple University Press, (1984); *Rebel Voices: An IWW Anthology* (Ann Arbor: University of Michigan Press, 1963); and with Brigid O'Farrell "You Can't Giddyup By Saying Whoa! Esther Peterson Remembers Her Labor Years." *Labor's Heritage,* Spring 1994 (vol. 5, no. 4). She holds a Ph.D. in Adult and Continuing Education from the University of Michigan.